The Wyoming Guide

The Wyoming Guide

Sierra Adare

Fulcrum Publishing
Golden, Colorado

In memory of Dr. Fred Guynn.
His friendship, sense of humor, knowledge of Wyoming,
and wonderful meals will be missed.

The information in *The Wyoming Guide* is accurate as of March 1999. However, prices, hours of operation, phone numbers, and other items change rapidly. If something in the book is incorrect or if you have ideas for the next edition, please write to the author at Fulcrum Publishing, 350 Indiana Street, Suite 350, Golden, Colorado 80401-5093.

iv

The Wyoming Guide provides many safety tips about weather and travel, but good decision making and sound judgment are the responsibilty of the individual. Neither the publisher nor the author assumes any liability for injury that may arise from the use of this book.

Library of Congress Cataloging-in-Publication Data

Adare, Sierra.
        The Wyoming guide / Sierra Adare.
            p.   cm.
        Includes index.
        ISBN 1-55591-381-4 (pbk.)
            1. Wyoming—Guidebooks.   I. Title.
     F759.3.A33   1999
     917.8704'33—dc21   99–19889
                                                                                            CIP

Printed in the United States of America
0 9 8 7 6 5 4 3 2 1

Book design: Deborah Rich
Front cover image of the Grand Tetons: David Townsend
Maps: William L. Nelson

Fulcrum Publishing
350 Indiana Street, Suite 350
Golden, Colorado 80401-5093
(800) 992-2908 • (303) 277-1623
www.fulcrum-books.com

Contents

Acknowledgments

When I hear somebody speak the name "Wyoming," wide-open spaces, crusty, frigid nights, and centuries of time come instantly to mind. So do long hours spent on the road, traveling the state top to bottom, left to right, and lots of places in between. This book wouldn't have come into existence without the help and support of many super people. In particular, Carmel Huestis, my editor at the time I agreed to take on this project, deserves special recognition. Everybody at the Wyoming Division of Tourism, and especially Chuck Coon, the public information manager, gets a huge THANK YOU! Brian Olsen of Wyoming Game & Fish was also a tremendous help. Jeff Corney also deserves thanks for his help with the Casper, Dubois, Riverton, and South Pass City and Atlantic City chapters.

I received a nominal response or no response from a few of the chambers of commerce in my quest for information, phone numbers, and so on; however, some chambers went out of their way to be helpful. Cody, Gillette, Glenrock, Greybull, and Sundance really stick out in my mind, and I appreciate all they did for me.

Thanks also to fellow travel writers Candy Moulton and Sharon Niederman, and to Chrissy and Jr. Bendlin. Then there is C. W., my biggest supporter!

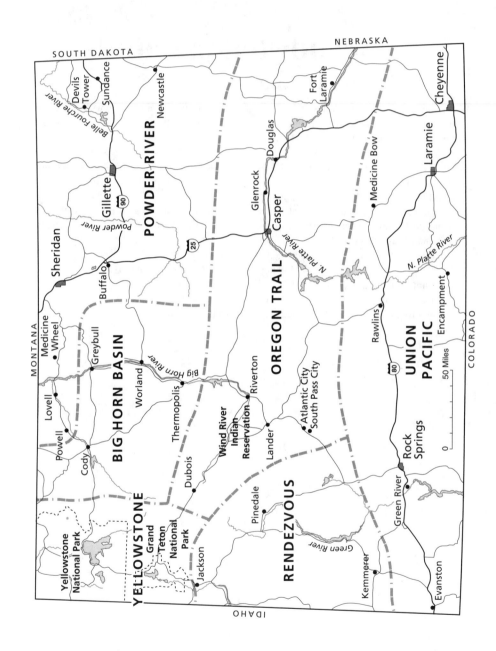

Wyoming State Map

Introduction

Background Information

What image pops into your mind when someone mentions Wyoming? The jagged peaks of the Tetons? The awesome spine of the Rocky Mountains? Deep mountain snowpack that supports incredible downhill skiing? True, the state has all these, but there's much more.

"Wyoming" actually means "on the great plains" or "at the big plains" in the Delaware Indian language, and this is what surprises tourists most about the state. Two-thirds of Wyoming is a high plains desert filled with sagebrush, tumbleweed, and cactus—a source of endless complaint from people expecting the entire state to look like Yellowstone or the Tetons. This diversity of terrain, however, allows for a divergence of history and activities to delve into. In 1889 Rudyard Kipling summed Wyoming up when he wrote, "Neither pen nor brush could ever portray its splendours adequately." This holds true for the desert, as well as the mountains. Each has its own charm, character, and role in forming a land that has something to offer every visitor, regardless of individual interests.

To make *The Wyoming Guide* a comprehensive travel guide, I would need at least triple the space allotted me for this book. Therefore, on my travels around the state, I looked for the more uniquely Wyoming places, events, lodging, and outdoor pursuits to include in the book. Many of the locales are old favorites, which I loved having the excuse to revisit yet again. Others I discovered quite by accident and am excited to share with you.

Suggested Reading

Wyoming: A Source Book (University Press of Colorado, 1996) by Roy A. Jordan and S. Brett DeBoer and the *Wyoming Almanac* (Skyline West Press, 1994) by Phil Roberts, David L. Roberts, and Steven L. Roberts provide lots of great facts, information, and quotes about the state. *Wyoming Place Names* (Mountain Press, 1988) by Mae Urbanek explains where some of the state's more unique names came from. *Wyoming: Land of Echoing Canyons* (Flying Diamond Books, 1986) by Beverley E. Brink and *Wyoming: A Guide to Its History, Highways, & People* (University of Nebraska Press, 1981) by the Federal Writers' Project offer great glimpses into the state.

History

Wyoming's human history predates recorded time. Ancestors of the Indian nations dwelling in the region at the time of first white contact left petroglyphs, cave drawings, and stone artifacts. Historians have put forth a variety of interpretations, but the true meaning of these works remains a mystery today. Historians have also debated the dates of first white contact. Some speculated Spanish conquistadors penetrated the Rocky Mountains in the 1500s and crossed paths with the indigenous population in what would become Wyoming. So far, no journals of the missionaries who accompanied the conquistadors definitively confirm this. Nevertheless, descendants of the horses the Spaniards brought to the New World did make it here. Visitors can see their progeny running wild and free on the Pryor Mountain Wild Horse Range and in the Red Desert.

Before the horse, native tribes drove small groups of buffalo over cliffs. The best remaining site discovered to date is the Vore Buffalo Jump near modern-day Sundance. After the advent of the horse, the tribes spread out. Their mobility allowed more access to a wider

The Wyoming Guide

Horsepacking on Eagle Creek Trail.

variety of foods and made hunting easier. The Indians who historically roamed the region—the Shoshone, Arapaho, Crow, Cheyenne, and Comanche—prospered, as did the Ute, Sioux, and Blackfeet who occasionally passed through.

The first documented contact with whites came when John Colter left the Lewis and Clark Expedition in 1806 and wandered alone along the Stinking Water River (later called the Shoshone), crossed the Wind River Mountains (commonly called the Winds), and made his way through the valley that would become Jackson Hole, before heading back to civilization. After that, a flood of fur trappers rushed up the river drainages of the Snake and Green in search of beaver pelts.

By the time the beaver felt hat went out of fashion, the mountain men and fur traders had made the West, with its breathtakingly beautiful and rich lands, known around the world. In the 1840s people seeking a better life hired veterans of the fur trade era to guide them across the vast stretches of land inhabited by Indians and wild game to a place of "milk and honey" called Oregon. Fort Laramie, originally a fur trading post, became a military fort, charged with protecting the estimated 350,000 emigrants who crossed the trail, leaving their mark on such landmarks as Register Cliff; the Oregon Trail National Historical Landmark, known locally as the Guernsey Ruts; and Independence Rock—all in current

Wyoming. Fort Laramie also became the focal point for treaty negotiations with various Indian nations to obtain permission for emigrants to cross Indian lands. Later, the Oregon Trail was used by the Mormons on their way to a new Zion in Salt Lake City, people touched with gold fever who headed for California, the Pony Express, and the Overland Stage Company.

Gold was discovered at the South Pass, and a city sprang up, forcing a renegotiation of a government treaty that recognized the lands as belonging to the Shoshones—just one of many treaties the government would break, ignore, or renegotiate.

As more white people moved in, the Indians were shoved off their ancestral lands. After the close of the War Between the States (also known as the Civil War), Americans wanted a fresh start, and the West offered it. Settlers poured in. The government beefed up its military presence to protect them. Unrelenting pressure was put on the Indians. Then gold strikes occurred in Montana and the Bozeman Trail showed gold-greedy whites the way to riches. Indians, however, had had their fill of trespassers, and the trail became known as the Bloody Bozeman. The military retaliated, then the Indians. The Fetterman Fight and the Box Wagon Fight took place near Fort Phil Kearny (out from present-day Sheridan and Buffalo).

The railroad arrived in 1867, cutting an iron path across the lower portion of what was not yet Wyoming. "Hell-on-wheels" towns sprang up. Some like Cheyenne, Rock Springs, and Evanston survive today. Others didn't fare as well and became ghost towns.

Wyoming became a territory a year later and established a territorial government the year after that, giving women the unheard-of rights to vote, hold office, and serve on juries.

Exploration then became the thing, with Major John Wesley Powell's two expeditions down the Green and Colorado Rivers in 1869 and 1871, followed by the government survey of Yellowstone in 1872, led by Ferdinand V. Hayden. Congress created Yellowstone National Park that same year.

Cattlemen eyed the lush grasslands and mountain meadows and brought huge herds of longhorns up from Texas, establishing enormous ranches beginning in the late 1870s. In 1886–1887 terrible blizzards killed thousands of head of cattle in what people called the "Great Die-Up."

Wyoming became a state in 1890, but that didn't tame things down. The Johnson County War pitted cattlemen against homesteaders in 1892. Butch Cassidy created the Wild Bunch and went on an outlaw spree, holing up near Kaycee at Hole-in-the-Wall.

The last battle with the Indians in Wyoming took place at Lightning Creek in 1903. That same year Congress formed the Shoshone National Forest, the nation's first. Throughout the 1900s, Wyoming has experienced a series of booms and busts in the oil, coal, iron, and uranium industries. Since the 1970s, more towns have emphasized tourism, offering visitors a wide variety of uniquely western activities and adventures.

Wyoming Firsts

- First of the 11 fur trapper rendezvous held, near Burnfork.
- First territory and then state to grant women's suffrage.
- First American woman to cast a ballot, Louisa A. Swain.
- First jury in the United States to include women, Albany County.
- First woman justice of the peace, Esther Hobart Morris.
- First woman governor in the United States, Nellie Tayloe Ross.
- First woman director of the National Mint, Nellie Tayloe Ross.
- First major national park in the United States, Yellowstone.
- First national forest in the United States, the Shoshone, which was originally part of the Yellowstone Timberland Reserve.
- First J.C. Penney store in the United States, Kemmerer.
- First dude ranch in the United States, Eaton Ranch at Wolf.
- First ranger station in the United States, Wapiti.
- First national monument, Devils Tower.
- First elk refuge in the United States, Jackson.
- First all-woman town council elected, Jackson.
- First underground missile silo in the United States, Fort F. E. Warren.

Suggested Reading

History of Wyoming (University of Nebraska Press, 1978) by T. A. Larson is considered the state's history book and is still used in some schools. *Roadside History of Wyoming* (Mountain Press, 1995) by Candy Moulton makes the state's history live. *Wyoming: A Pictorial History* (The Donning Co., 1989) by Mark Junge contains many moving photos. *Ghosts on the Range: Eerie True Tales of Wyoming* (Pruett Publishing, 1989) by Debra DiMumm might make the hair on your neck stand on end while visiting a few of the ghostly sights. *Lady's Choice: Ethel Waxham's Journals and Letters 1905–1910* (University of New Mexico Press, 1993), edited by Barbara Love and Frances Love Froidevaux, supplies a stirring insight into a woman homesteader's life in early statehood days.

xi

Top Ten Historic Sites in Wyoming

1. Yellowstone National Park—the nation's first.
2. Fort Laramie—the first permanent white settlement, established in 1830, and the site that played a huge role in shaping the modern West.
3. Oregon Trail—350,000 people traveled over it, leaving their names carved in stone and graves along every step of the way, a silent testament to the courage and endurance of the pioneer spirit.
4. South Pass City—built on gold and dreams, it's the ghost town that lives today.
5. Fort Fetterman—not much of the actual fort is left, but it has a feel of history that is inescapable.
6. Buffalo Bill Historic Center—considered one of the best museums of western history and culture in the West.
7. Outlaw Trail—used by the infamous Butch Cassidy, Sundance Kid, Kid Curry, the Wild Bunch, and the James-Younger gang—to name a few.

8. Castle Gardens—petroglyphs that remind us of a history and a way of life that far predate the history we know.
9. Wyoming Dinosaur Center—home of some of Wyoming's rarest and earliest citizens.
10. Wind River Indian Reservation—a living legacy of broken treaties, forced assimilation, and the struggle of the Shoshones and Arapahos to retain their tribal identities.

Suggested Reading

The Hog Ranches of Wyoming: Liquor, Lust, and Lies Under Sagebrush Skies (High Plains Press, 1995) by Larry K. Brown shows a highly entertaining aspect of Wyoming's history—which has nothing to do with the agriculture business. *Devils Tower: Stories in Stone* (High Plains Press, 1988) by Mary Alice Gunderson tells the stories of the people, the cultures, and the history of the nation's first national monument. Catch the gold fever and the flavor of boom and bust economics in *South Pass, 1868: James Chisholm's Journal of the Wyoming Gold Rush* (University of Nebraska Press, 1960), edited by Lola M. Homsher. *Fort Laramie and the Sioux Indians* (Prentice-Hall, 1967) by Remi Nadeau illustrates why this fort has so much to do with the West, Manifest Destiny, and Indian relations. *The Shoshonis: Sentinels of the Rockies* (University of Oklahoma Press, 1964) by Virginia Cole Trenholm and Maurine Carley; *The Arapahoes, Our People* (University of Oklahoma Press, 1970) by Virginia Cole Trenholm; and *Teepee Neighbors* (University of Oklahoma Press, 1984) by Grace Collidge depict the life and history of the tribes of the Wind River Indian Reservation. To gain real insight into army life, politics, and the military's role in Indian affairs, read *Frontiersmen in Blue: The United States Army and the Indian, 1848–1865* (University of Nebraska Press, 1967) by Robert M. Utley. *Wyoming: A Guide to Historic Sites* (Big Horn Publishers, 1988) by the Wyoming Recreation Commission is a dandy collection of over 300 sites. *Steamboat: Legendary Bucking Horse* (High Plains Press, 1992) by Candy Vyvey Moulton and Flossie Moulton tells the tale of Wyoming's unrideable horse that became the symbol on the state's license plate.

Geography and Geology

The ninth largest state in the United States, Wyoming contains more surface area than half the nations on earth. The average elevation ranges from the lowest point of 3,125 feet in the northeast to the highest of 6,700 feet in the west central portion. Gannett Peak at 13,804 feet stands as the highest mountain. Located in the Wind River Mountains, it is one of forty-three peaks in the range that rise higher than 12,500 feet, and one of nine over 13,000 feet. The highest point on Interstate 80 is located at the summit of the Laramie Mountains between Cheyenne and Laramie.

Fremont County (Lander, Riverton, Dubois) in west central Wyoming contains 1,000 square miles more than the state of Massachusetts. Crossing the state from Torrington to Cody, you'll cover more terrain than if you were to travel from Warsaw, Poland, to Berlin, Germany. A journey from Cheyenne to Powell covers more ground than a trip from Norfolk, Virginia, to New York City.

When plate tectonics shifted the continents 200 million years ago, what would become Wyoming lay in the tropics. Several times it sat at or near sea level. About the time the dinosaurs became extinct, between 144 and 66 million years ago, the major mountain building began in the West. During the height of the Laramide Orogeny, 66 to 58 million years ago, coal beds were created in the Powder River Basin, as were Wyoming's mountains and basins. Serious volcanic action occurred between 58 and 37 million years ago. Basins filled with volcanic ash, eruptions continued, and river drainages were established. The Teton Range uplift and erosion took place between five and two million years ago. Glacier periods occurred three separate times between two million and 500,000 years ago, when Wyoming finally began looking more or less as it does now—minus the human intervention.

Granite forms the core of Wyoming's mountain ranges. At 3.4 to 2.8 billion years old, it is the oldest rock in the state and the West. Travertine, created daily at Mammoth Hot Springs, is the newest rock. The two tons of dissolved lime that flow out of the spring every day make eight inches of new rock each year.

Congress has set aside 15 wilderness areas within Wyoming, totaling 3,081,047 acres. The state ranks fifth in the nation in the percentage of state-designated wilderness, with three million acres.

Suggested Reading
Roadside Geology of Wyoming (Mountain Press, 1988) by David R. Lageson and Darwin R. Spering and *Roadside Geology of the Yellowstone Country* (Mountain Press, 1985) by William J. Fritz can't be beat for an informative and entertaining look at the state's geology as you actually pass by it. *Wyoming: A Geography* (Westview Press, 1980) by Robert Harold Brown supplies interesting tidbits. *Rising from the Plains* (The Noonday Press, 1986) by John McPhee offers geology, geography, history, and humor all in one.

Flora and Fauna

Wyoming's ecosystems range from sagebrush deserts to aspen or lodgepole pine forests to subalpine and alpine meadows. In summer expect to see an abundance of wildflowers just about anywhere you travel!

Suggested Reading
I have been photographing Wyoming's wildflowers for years for later identification, and I have yet to find a definitive wildflower guide. However, *Wildflowers of Western America* (Chanticleer Press, 1974) by Robert T. Orr and Margaret C. Orr and the *Field Guide to Edible Wild Plants* (Stackpole Books, 1974) by Bradford Angier are adequate for limited, general Wyoming plant information. *Plants of Yellowstone and Grand Teton National Parks* (Wheelwright Press, 1981) by Richard J. Shaw gives good details for the region.

Climate

The turn-of-the-century western humorist Bill Nye offered a perfect picture of Wyoming's short summer season when he wrote, "The climate is erratic, eccentric and peculiar ... the early frosts make close connections with the

---

Ten Uniquely Wyoming Shopping Experiences

1. A hand-tooled, custom-made saddle from King's Saddle Shop in Sheridan.
2. A custom, handmade knife from Wind River Knives in Dubois.
3. Authentic period clothing from CNL Clothier in South Pass City.
4. Chugwater Chili from Chugwater.
5. A silk cowboy scarf from Cattle Kate's in Wilson.
6. Handmade beadwork from the Shoshone tribe on the Wind River Indian Reservation.
7. Custom, handmade lodgepole furniture from the Peg Leg in Saratoga.
8. Antler art, furniture, fixtures, and jewelry from just about every business located around the Town Square in Jackson.
9. A handmade, authentic cowboy hat from the Jackson Hole Hat Company.
10. A jackalope from Douglas.

---

late spring blizzards so that there is only time for a hurried lunch between."

Besides the cold and snow, there is the wind. Although everyone calls Chicago the "Windy City," Cheyenne, Wyoming, actually holds the record of being the windiest city in the nation with wind speeds averaging 12.9 miles per hour. The state, too, can claim the honor of being the windiest in the country with an average wind speed of 13 miles per hour.

Wyoming's weather should never be taken lightly. I was horsepacking in Elkhart Park near Pinedale one July, generally the hottest month of summer. The day started out quite warm (T-shirt and jeans) and very sunny. By midmorning a storm front had blown in over the mountains (as frequently happens during the summer), and I found myself in the midst of a raging thunderstorm. This turned into a hail storm, then sleet, then a heavy, wet snow. All this took place in a five-hour span—and it is not that uncommon. It can snow any month of the year in Wyoming.

I've known snowmobilers who went out riding for a couple hours in late April on an absolutely gorgeous day and got caught in a blizzard that came out of nowhere. They weren't rescued until the next afternoon. If they hadn't taken emergency supplies with them, there might have been an unhappy ending to the story.

Traveling comfortably through Wyoming means coming prepared. It could make the difference between a fantastic vacation and a miserable one. Therefore, I've included some basic, trip-related preparation tips that I hope will help ensure full enjoyment for whatever type of vacation and destination you choose in Wyoming. The highway department operates a several-times-daily updated road condition report between October 1 and April 30. Wyomingites call it before making any travel plans during these months. For more information, call Road and Travel Information at **(307) 772-0824.**

Visitor Information

General Information

The best way to obtain general information about Wyoming is to contact the **Wyoming Division of Tourism, I-25 at College Drive, Cheyenne, 82002; (307) 777-7777.** This agency offers packets of information designed for either a summer or winter vacation to the state. Check out the agency's website for even more details: **www.wyomingtourism.org.**

Each chapter has the address and phone number of the area's chamber of commerce and/or visitors bureau. As travelers enter the state, Wyoming offers seven locations where information and brochures are available—in Cheyenne at the **Frank Norris Jr. Travel Center, I-25 at College Drive,** open daily; in Evanston at the **Bear River Travel Information Center, I-80 East at Exit 6,** open daily; in Jackson at the **Jackson Information Center, 532 North Cache,** open daily; in Laramie at the **Summit Information Center, I-80, 9 miles east of the Happy Jack Exit,** open

daily; in Pine Bluffs at the **Pine Bluffs Information Center, I-80 at the Pine Bluffs Exit,** open late May to September; in Sheridan at the **Sheridan Information Center, I-90 at the 5th Street Exit,** open daily; and in Sundance at the **Sundance Information Center, I-90 at the Port-of-Entry Exit,** open late May to mid-October.

Tips for Visitors

Driving
Renting a car in Wyoming requires a driver's license from somewhere in the United States or an International Driver's Permit and a major credit card. It's the law that you must wear a seatbelt while on the road. Driving in Wyoming is quite different from most other states. There is not a service station on every corner, and the next town down the road might be 50 miles away with no businesses in between. It's a good idea to fuel up once the gauge hits the half-tank mark, especially in winter.

Another thing to remember about driving in Wyoming is the wildlife. Deer, antelope, elk, and moose can dart in front of your vehicle in an instant and without any warning. Wildlife is most active during the early daylight hours and late afternoon through the night—especially when the moon is bright. Wild animals are usually close to the roads in fall, winter, and spring, but don't be surprised to see them during any season, at any time of day. The stretch of highway between Casper and Shoshoni has lots of antelope on it, but they are hard to spot because nature designed them to blend with their surroundings. All the roads that go over passes can be thick with all sorts of wildlife. The highway between Cody and Yellowstone gets clogged with wild bison and herds of bighorn sheep in spring and fall. The best advice I can offer is for you to scan the sides of the roads constantly while you drive. If you hit an animal, it's the law that you must immediately report it to **Wyoming Game & Fish, 5400 Bishop Boulevard, Cheyenne, 82006; (307) 777-4600. Website: www.gf.state.wy.us.**

In winter bald eagles and golden eagles frequent the highways while they feed off roadkill rabbits and other small rodents. They cannot fly off to get out of the way of vehicles as quickly as other birds. When you see a bird in the road, slow down to give it time to get safely out of your path.

The Wyoming Transportation Department puts out a cold-weather driving guide and map, as well as a map of Wyoming's roadside rest areas and information centers. The publications are available through the **Wyoming Division of Tourism, I-25 at College Drive, Cheyenne, 82002; (307) 777-7777.** Wyoming rest areas are unique: All of the newer ones are solar heated.

Money

Credit Cards—Major credit cards such as Visa, MasterCard, and American Express are generally accepted at most businesses. Some smaller restaurants will take only cash, but they usually post a sign saying so. Automated teller machines (ATMs) are located throughout the state.

Traveler's Checks—Visitors from abroad should get traveler's checks in U.S.-dollar denominations because banks aren't set up to exchange foreign currencies.

Tipping—Fifteen percent of the overall bill (excluding taxes) is standard tipping in Wyoming. Porters expect at least fifty cents per bag. If you are with a large group, most restaurants will automatically add the tip to the bill.

Student and Senior Discounts—Many businesses, museums, restaurants, and motels offer senior discounts. Students can qualify for discounts at some museums with a valid student identification card.

Telephones

Any phone number beginning with either 800 or 888 is a toll-free call. The area code for all of Wyoming is 307. For every business that has a toll-free number, the local number is listed in this guide as well, because not all toll-free numbers are available outside the state or region. When dialing long distance, dial 1 before the area code and the number. Directory assistance is available by calling **(307) 555-**

Chuckwagon supper.

1212. For operator assistance, dial **0**. For emergencies, dial **911.**

Time

Mountain Standard Time (Wyoming) is two hours earlier than Eastern Standard Time (New York) and one hour later than Pacific Standard Time (California).

Getting There

Wyoming lies in the heart of the Rocky Mountain region of the United States. Casper, in the center of the state, and Cheyenne, the capital, located in the southeast corner, vie with each other for the most population. Both represent the major hubs for commercial air flights into the state. Nevertheless, air service and flights are quite limited and may only arrive once or twice a day at any airport that offers commercial service. Many locations in Wyoming have only an air field suitable for small private planes. **Powder River Transportation (800-442-3682)** offers bus service between many Wyoming destinations. The Jackson Hole Airport offers a shuttle service to lodging and ski resorts.

Getting Around

The ideal way to see Wyoming is by car. Drive your own vehicle or rent one. All airports that offer commercial air service have rental cars available. If you plan to rent a vehicle during the summer, however, reserve it well in advance. Rentals are in high demand between Memorial Day and Labor Day, the peak vacation season. You can request one with ski racks, a four-wheel-drive vehicle, or even a pickup.

Information for the Handicapped

Due to the historic nature of many of the buildings in Wyoming, handicapped access is rather limited. The national parks, monuments, and many of the historic sites can accommodate wheelchairs. I've listed the accessibility whenever possible.

Suggested Reading
For more detailed information, obtain a copy of *National Park Guide for the Handicapped* from the **U.S. Government Printing Office, Washington, D.C. 20402.**

How the Book Is Organized

The Wyoming Guide divides the wide-open spaces of Wyoming into six regions, based on a combination of physical location and settlement. The Union Pacific Region crosses the southern tier of counties between Nebraska and Utah, highlighting the rowdy "hell-on-wheels" towns that sprang up at the end of the rails. The Oregon Trail Region follows the overland migration route near the North Platte and Sweetwater Rivers. The Rendezvous Region travels through the state's earliest historical area and along the mountainous zone of its western edge. The Yellowstone Region explores the nation's first national park and controversial Grand Teton National Park. The Big Horn Basin Region moves from the domain of healing waters of *Bah-gue-wana*, Smoking Waters, of modern Hot Springs State Park to the Wild West town of Buffalo Bill's Cody. The Powder River Region, a longtime stronghold of

Indians in the northeast corner of the state, details battles that helped to bring about the end of a centuries-old way of life for the Cheyenne, Sioux, and other Plains Indian nations. By the same token, the region provided a safe haven along the Outlaw Trail that led to the famed Hole-in-the-Wall.

Each chapter for these regions begins with a general introduction, the region's history, and directions for getting there, much like the format of this introduction. Following this is specific information about the festivals and events, outdoor activities, sightseeing musts, lodging, camping, restaurants, and services. A few places also list area nightlife. There's a bar in every town in Wyoming (in some places that's about all there is in town), but only the really uncommon ones found their way into this book.

Many locations listed are open between Memorial Day weekend and Labor Day. This is the height of what Wyomingites refer to as the summer. By the calendar, this generally means the last full, three-day weekend (Saturday, Sunday, and Monday) in May and the first Monday in September.

Festivals and Events

Every location offers a wide range of festivals and events with something going on every month of the year. This guide highlights events that are unique to the area, such as the Pack Horse Races at Dubois, and major historic events, such as the Frontier Days Rodeo in Cheyenne, the "Daddy of 'em All!" The chambers of commerce throughout the state carry full listings of the events in their areas.

Outdoor Activities

The Bureau of Land Management (BLM) carries a dandy Wyoming Recreation Guide map that details developed recreation sites, trails, and points of interest. Obtain one from the **Wyoming State Office of the BLM, 5353 Yellowstone Road, P.O. Box 1828, Cheyenne, 82003; (307) 775-6256, fax (307) 775-6129. Website: www.wy.blm.gov.**

Ballooning

Without exception, the best ballooning experience in the state is to drift along the Snake River Valley, as it has the most awesome view of the Teton Range you could ever hope to see. If you prefer to watch balloons rather than ride in them, catch the hot air balloon rally in Riverton.

Biking

Mountain Biking

Old logging roads crisscross Wyoming's national forest lands, making ideal mountain-biking opportunities. Fat-tire riding is especially popular in the Jackson Hole area; rentals and lots of trail advice are available from several bike shops in the town.

A word of warning, however: Grizzlies live in many of the prime mountain-biking areas. To avoid potentially disastrous encounters, ask for the Wyoming Game & Fish brochure on mountain biking in grizzly country. **Wyoming Game & Fish, 5400 Bishop Boulevard, Cheyenne, 82006; (307) 777-4600. Website: www.gf.state.wy.us.**

Bicycle Touring

Touring the country via bicycle has gained in popularity in recent years. One of the main touring routes through Wyoming follows the highway along the Oregon Trail. Routes cover a wide variety of altitudes, and distances between towns with food and lodging can make for some extremely long days. There are few facilities between towns, as well, and there is absolutely no camping allowed along the roadside on the Wind River Indian Reservation. To avoid potential problems, check with the chamber of commerce of every town along your route when you plan your trip.

The Wyoming Transportation Department (WYDOT) put together a fabulous biking map, which shows significant grades, the average daily traffic volume on roads around the state, camping information, mountain-biking areas, miles between points, and points of interest. Get one from **WYDOT Planning, P.O. Box 1708, Cheyenne, 82003; (307) 777-4719.**

Suggested Reading

The Bicyclist's Guide to Yellowstone National Park (Falcon Press, 1984) by Gene Colling might give you a few ideas, as well as tips for biking in Yellowstone.

Climbing

Mountain climbing in Wyoming ranges from walk-ups that require no technical gear to very strenuous, highly technical climbs, such as some of the routes on Grand Teton, to rock, glacier, and ice climbing. Before you attempt any climb, climbing schools recommend that you get into shape first. Build stamina through participating in sports and aerobic exercise. Popular climbing spots besides Grand Teton in Grand Teton National Park are Split Rock on the Oregon Trail between Casper and Rawlins, Vedauwoo near Laramie, and the limestone buttresses in Sinks Canyon near Lander. If you aren't very experienced but want to be, contact a guiding service such as **Jackson Hole Mountain Guides & Climbing School, P.O. Box 7477, Jackson, 83001; (307) 733-4979,** or **Exum Mountain Guides, P.O. Box 56, Moose, 83012; (307) 733-2297.**

Suggested Reading

The Climbs of Greater Vedauwoo (Heel and Toe Publishers, 1994) by Skip Harper and Rob Kelman supplies detailed information about climbs in Vedauwoo. *Climbing and Hiking in the Wind River Mountains* (Chockstone Press, 1994) by Joe Kelsey and *Climber's Guide to the Teton Range* (Sierra Club, 1965) by Leigh Ortenburger provide great climbing wisdom.

Dog Sledding

Mushers the world over come to Wyoming for the International Rocky Mountain Stage Stop Sled Dog Race. In recent years, it has become a major training race for the Alaskan Iditarod. The 11-day race begins in Jackson, traveling through Moran, Dubois, Lander, Kemmerer, Pinedale, Evanston, Alpine, and back to Jackson's Teton Village, covering 420 miles. You can watch the race anywhere along the route or in one of the towns. **Jackson Hole Iditarod Sled Dog Tours (800-554-7388)** has the details.

The Wyoming Guide

*Curt Gowdy, Wyoming's most famous fishing son.
Photo courtesy of the Wyoming Division of Tourism.*

Great guided tours are available in Jackson and Dubois.

Fishing

The Red Desert is about the only place in Wyoming with lousy fishing! The only things that bite there are the mosquitoes. Otherwise, you can throw a dart at the Wyoming map and pinpoint a blue-ribbon trout river or a lake or creek filled with rainbows, browns, or cutthroats. It's difficult to go wrong with 15,846 miles of fishing streams and 3,400 lakes, reservoirs, and ponds. I'd be hard-pressed, however, to recommend one spot over the rest. There is excellent wading, boat, and bank fishing everywhere. Anywhere there is water, you'll find a guiding service and tackle shops. Enjoy, all you spinners and casters!

As I've already noted, much of Wyoming is grizzly country. Wyoming Game & Fish carries several brochures that are free and contain information about fishing in bear country that may save your life. In addition, their yearly updated Wyoming fishing-regulations booklet carries detailed information about fishing locations, as well as the types and times fishing is best. **Wyoming Game & Fish, 5400 Bishop Boulevard, Cheyenne, 82006; (307) 777-4600. Website: www.gf.state.wy.us.** The Wyoming Travel Commission puts out a family water-sports brochure that outlines public fishing areas, boating and floating information, and other water activities and facilities. It's available through the **Wyoming Division of Tourism, I-25 at College Drive, Cheyenne, 82002; (307) 777-7777. Website: www.wyomingtourism.org.**

Suggested Reading

Walking the Winds: A Hiking & Fishing Guide to Wyoming's Wind River Range (White Willow Publishing, 1994) by Rebecca Woods gives a good picture of the hiking and fishing conditions in the Winds.

Four-Wheel-Drive Trips

Of the state's 62 million acres, 18 million are overseen by the Bureau of Land Management (BLM). Although this land is open to the public, some vehicle restrictions may apply, and portions of the lands have not been developed (roads, camping sites, or other facilities). The BLM has a backcountry byways brochure that summarizes the state's scenic, four-wheel-drive treks. **Wyoming State Office of the BLM, 5353 Yellowstone Road, P.O. Box 1828, Cheyenne, 82003; (307) 775-6256, fax (307) 775-6129. Website: www.wy.blm.gov.** The U.S.D.A. Forest Service also assigns some dirt roads for four-wheel-drive use. Check with the agency before heading into the backcountry. (See Camping/In the National Forests below, for the address and phone number of each forest service district office.)

For a fun trip, be sure to fill the fuel tank before you head out. Check the air in the spare tire. Take plenty of water, snack foods, a map, and an extra layer of clothing. Carry your trash out. Don't chase or otherwise harass wildlife. Stay on the two-tracks. Don't cut new roads. (Tip: Generally there is no cellular phone service available in the backcountry or in the national parks.)

Suggested Reading

8,000 Miles of Dirt: A Backroad Travel Guide to Wyoming (Wyoming Naturalist, 1992) by

Dan Lewis offers practical guidance and routes for backroad adventures.

Goatpacking

Western goatpacking originated in Wyoming. It started in the 1970s and really caught on as an alternative for people who love to hike through the backcountry and over glacier fields but don't enjoy carrying the heavy weight of backpacks. Of all the pack animals available today, including llamas, goats impact fragile environments the least. And they love to be with people—sort of like traveling with the family dog. If you get the chance, give it a try. Set up trips through **Wind River Pack Goats, 6668 Hwy. 26, Dubois, 82513; (307) 455-2410.**

Suggested Reading

The Pack Goat (Pruett Publishing, 1992) by John Mionczynski, the creator of goatpacking, is a comprehensive guide.

Golf

Most Wyoming golf courses double as places to cross-country ski in the winter—provided you're willing to share them with the moose and deer. Playing at high altitudes will put a new spin on your drive. President Clinton's trips to Jackson Hole showcased the valley's golfing facilities. Other top-notch courses include Saratoga, Buffalo, and Sheridan.

Hiking and Backpacking

Wyoming contains 9.7 million acres of national forest land. Most of this is available for backcountry experiences. Each forest service district office stocks extensive trail information and maps for day hikes and backpacking trips of all lengths and challenges. (See Camping/In the National Forests below for the address and phone number of each forest service district office.) The most important thing to remember is to go into the backcountry well-prepared.

Spend several days allowing your body to become accustomed to the higher elevation and thinner atmosphere. Use sunblock even on cloudy days. Carry plenty of water and snack foods, even on short hikes. Weather changes can come quickly and drastically (see Climate,

above). On day hikes, bring a windbreaker and rain gear, light wool gloves, and a sweater or jacket. If you're hiking in shorts, include a pair of pants. Carry maps of the region, a flashlight, sunglasses, sunblock, waterproof matches, a knife, first-aid kit, some sort of fire starter (toilet paper works well), and an emergency Mylar-type blanket.

Places such as the tops of buttes are prone to lightning strikes (particularly during the summer months). If a storm blows in, leave the butte and seek shelter in a lower area. Stay there until the storm passes.

In bear country, try to avoid surprising bears: Talk while on the trail to make them aware of your presence, or wear a bear bell that tinkles while you hike.

Hike on established trails to prevent erosion. Remember to respect wildlife by maintaining a safe distance when observing or photographing. Don't approach animals or try to feed them.

Horses have the right-of-way on the trail. Step off the trail when you encounter them, and remain quiet until the horses have passed. If you have a pet with you, please keep it quiet as well.

Pack out what you pack in. It's illegal to remove, collect, or excavate any archaeological artifacts. Leave all gates the way you found them. Keep out of restricted areas. Respect private property adjacent to public lands. Let someone know where you are going and when you expect to return. No vehicles are allowed in wilderness areas.

Suggested Reading

The Hiker's Guide to Wyoming (Falcon Press, 1992) by Bill Hunger details 75 hikes around the state. *Guide to the Wyoming Mountains and Wilderness Areas* (Sage Books, 1965) by Orrin H. Bonney and Lorraine Bonney offers a wealth of information and background about the forest lands. *Backcountry Cooking: Feasts for Hikers, Hoofers, and Floaters* (Tamarack Books, 1996) by Sierra Adare includes wilderness travel narratives on backpacking, horsepacking, goatpacking, and canoeing trips in Wyoming's backcountry.

Wildlife rules of etiquette from the Great Plains Wildlife Institute in Jackson and the National Park Service

Don't point at wildlife. They see it as a threat or a challenge that they must escape from, meaning they must expend energy (in the form of stored calories needed for survival over winter) to move away from you. Wyoming winters are harsh enough without humans adding to the problem. Anything that disturbs wildlife from their primary function of consuming calories in the short summer months in order to put on enough weight to see them through winter contributes to the animals' mortality rate.

Stay in your vehicle while observing wildlife so you won't disturb them. Use spotting scopes, binoculars, or your camera lens. Avoid direct eye contact with animals you encounter, and don't stare at one animal for long periods of time. Many animals such as antelope and deer see as well as humans using binoculars! They will know if you're staring, and they see it as threatening.

Since the fires of 1988, the bison (buffalo) population in Yellowstone has skyrocketed. Bison may appear to be as lumbering as cattle, but this couldn't be further from the truth. Don't walk up to them to try to get that perfect picture. They perceive it as an invasion of their space and will retaliate by kicking and goring—which they do incredibly fast.

Yellowstone and Grand Teton National Parks are not petting zoos. The animals are wild. Give them a wide berth. Don't try to feed them.

Never approach bears while trying to get their picture. Given a choice, bears prefer to evade people. Generally, they only attack when people startle them at close range. Travel in a group rather than alone. Don't hike at night. In bear areas, it's wiser to not camp with pets along.

If you cross paths with a bear on the trail, try not to panic. Back away slowly. Avoid direct eye contact. Talk in a soft monotone. Whatever you do, don't turn your back on a bear, and never run from it. Although this is incredibly hard to do, stand your ground if a bear charges. Often this is a "mock charge" to test the adversary. If you can't stay still, play dead. Drop to the ground, tucking yourself into a ball and using your arms and hands to cover your head and neck. Stay in this position until you are completely certain the bear has left the vicinity. Also, don't jog in bear country. The scent of sweat may attract bears. Joggers usually aren't making any noise, they are alone, and they are running—all the wrong behaviors that invite attack.

Horseback Riding

The tradition of horsepacking through Wyoming dates back to not long after the Plains Indian nations captured the first wild horses. Explorers, mountain men, and miners, like these tribes, adopted horsepacking as a way of life. Nowadays, outfitters continue the practice of this custom. Horsepacking vacations are a relatively easy way to get deep into the heart of Wyoming's wilderness. They generally last three to seven nights, or the outfitter may offer a drop camp service where they will pack you and your gear in to a designated location and come back for you on a date of your choosing.

For a less intense horseback riding experience, try something different. Instead of a ride-around-the-stables kind of trail ride, head out over ranch- or rangeland, in the wilderness or over the prairies. **The Wyoming Outfitters & Guides Association** is a good starting point for these types of horse adventures. **P.O. Box 2284, Cody, 82414; (307) 527-7453, fax (307) 587-8633**.

Suggested Reading
Horses, Hitches & Rocky Trails: "The Packers Bible" (Johnson Books, 1987) by Joe Back is the best horsepacking book I've read. It is filled with humor and solid, practical advice. Back was one of the early packers who brought "dudes" into Yellowstone National Park.

Llama Trekking

Llamas offer another unique packing experience in Wyoming. Like goats, they can pack in the high country and have low impact on the environment. They aren't as friendly to pack with as goats, but they are fun. They will stick right with you and will enjoy looking over your shoulder.

Suggested Reading
Llamas on the Trail: A Packer's Guide (Mountain Press, 1992) by David Harmon and Amy S. Rubin is an informative guide.

River Floating

For those seeking the adrenaline rush of whitewater, look no farther than the Snake River in Grand Teton National Park and the Jackson Hole valley. They don't call it the "Mad River" for nothing! Cody also has its share of whitewater thrills in Shoshone Canyon and on the North Fork of the Shoshone River. Check out the action in Wind River Canyon on the Wind River Indian Reservation. Unless you are a very experienced river runner, don't attempt whitewater expeditions on your own. The Snake and the Shoshone Rivers also offer scenic floats filled with glimpses of wildlife. Outfitters in the regions will show you a great time on hourly, half-day, full-day, and overnight whitewater and scenic-float combination excursions.

Suggested Reading
Battle Drums and Geysers (The Swallow Press, 1970) by Lorraine G. Bonney tells of Lieutenant Gustavus Cheney Doane's insane winter trip down the Mad River, plus lots more

Excellent powder for downhill skiing. Photo courtesy of the Wyoming Division of Tourism.

history and river information. *Run, River, Run: A Naturalist's Journey Down One of the Great Rivers of the West* (Harper & Row, 1975) by Ann Zwinger is a travel narrative of her trip down the Green River through Wyoming and Utah and into its confluence with the Colorado River.

Skiing

Get into condition before coming to ski Wyoming's high elevations. Start with a good aerobics program combined with stretching exercises and some weight training. This will limber up muscles and strengthen the cardiovascular system, thus increasing your stamina. Warm up your muscles with a few light stretches before each workout and before you start to ski. Flexible muscles are less prone to injury, especially in cold weather. Eat a well-balanced diet to give muscles lots of energy. Most important, take time to acclimatize to the higher altitude before overexerting yourself. High-altitude sickness is not fun.

Downhill Skiing
Snow King in Jackson became Wyoming's first ski resort in 1939. It's the only resort located in a town. It makes for a unique skiing experience. Teton Village, out from Jackson, offers some of the most extreme double black dia-

Winter necessities for skiing, snowshoeing, or snowmobiling

Take plenty of water, high-energy snack foods, layered clothing made of wool or synthetics (no cotton, as it holds moisture), a hat that covers your ears, mittens or gloves, sunblock, sunglasses, maps and a compass, extra clothing (jacket, socks, and a sweater), extra food, extra ski pole tip and basket, a flashlight or headlamp with good batteries, a watch for keeping track of how long your trip will take for the return, fire-starting materials, a whistle, additional ski wax and scraper, a knife, duct tape for general repairs, snowmobile tools if you travel that way, and an emergency Mylar-type space blanket.

mond skiing in the West. Then there's superextreme heli-skiing. Due to the large volume of snow, mostly excellent dry powder, the ski season lasts from late November through the first part of April. If you're looking for fun skiing with fewer people, try Antelope Butte near Greybull, Hogadon near Casper, or the Snowy Range near Laramie. All the downhill areas offer rentals and lessons.

Cross-Country Skiing

Wyoming offers endless possibilities for cross-country and backcountry skiing; however, usually you must supply your own skis, as few of the areas groomed for cross-country skiing rent skis. The season varies, depending on the elevation. Generally it lasts from mid-November through April. However, I've gone backcountry skiing on Togwotee Pass in June.

Whether you go cross-country or backcountry skiing, the main thing to remember is to be prepared. Wear a day pack that contains extra layers of clothing, ample food, matches, water, toilet paper, sunblock, lip balm, sunglasses, an emergency Mylar-type blanket, first-aid kit, and an emergency flare. Always let

someone know your travel plans and expected return time. You might leave this information in your vehicle, as well. If you plan to ski in the backcountry, talk with staff at the regional forest service district office first (addresses and phone numbers are listed in Camping, below.) They will be aware of which areas are prone to avalanches and other hazards.

Suggested Reading

50 Ski Tours in Jackson Hole and Yellowstone (High Peak Books, 1990) by Richard DuMais and *Cross-Country Skiing in Yellowstone Country* (Abacus Enterprises, 1992) by Ken Olsen, Dena Olsen, Steve Scharosch, and Hazel Scharosch are both excellent cross-country skiing guides.

Snowshoeing

Snowshoe hikes are quite popular in Wyoming. Tours often provide the snowshoes or they can be rented at most ski shops. If you plan to snowshoe, you'll need to dress for it (see above). For footwear, choose a pair of warm boots with a removeable wool lining, cross-country ski boots, or waterproof hiking boots. "Moonboots" or boots with heels aren't appropriate.

Snowmobiling

Snowmobiling is bigger than big in Wyoming because of the Continental Divide Trail System. More or less following the Continental Divide through the state, the system covers 365 miles of groomed, marked trails, beginning at Lander and ending at West Yellowstone. Along the way the various areas offer additional trails that connect into the Continental Divide system. The wide variety of terrain and scenery are unequaled. Food, fuel, lodging, and repair locations are available along the trail; however, don't forget that as little as half an hour of travel on a snowmobile will take you farther into the wilderness than you can walk out in several days. (For what to bring see Skiing, above.)

Wyoming charges a users fee for snowmobiles brought in from another state. The funds collected go toward maintaining the state's truly awesome groomed trail system. For further information and maps, contact either the **Wyoming State Snowmobile Program (307-777-7550)** or the **Wyoming State Snowmobile Trail Coordinator (307-332-2637)**. Check out the state's snowmobile website link: **www.commerce.state.wy.us/sphs/snow/**. For avalanche conditions in northwestern Wyoming, call the **Avalanche Center (307-733-2664)**. License permits are available from the **Wyoming State Parks & Historic Sites** headquarters in Cheyenne **(307-777-6323)**. Send for permits from the **Wyoming Snowmobile Permit Agency, One Unicover Center, Cheyenne, 82008-0001; (307) 777-3680,** which also can supply full-color trail maps.

Seeing and Doing

The Oregon, Overland, Mormon, Pony Express, and California trails followed nearly the exact same route through Wyoming. Ninety percent of all the swales and ruts still visible along the entire Oregon Trail are found in Wyoming. Sixty percent of those are on public land. Modern-day highways conform to much of the actual trails through Wyoming, allowing for easy viewing. Great landmarks of the trail can also be seen—Independence Rock, Devil's Gate, and Split Rock. Get Oregon Trail or Mormon Trail maps loaded with information about the historic treks across Wyoming from the **Wyoming Division of Tourism, I-25 at College Drive, Cheyenne, 82002; (307) 777-7777. Website: www.wyomingtourism.org.**

Wyoming's abundant wildlife affords many viewing opportunities to travelers. Wyoming Game & Fish publishes a wide and very interesting variety of booklets on Wyoming wildlife, including a bird checklist, a mammal checklist, wildlife loop tours, and game-bird facts. Request copies from **Wyoming Game & Fish, 5400 Bishop Boulevard, Cheyenne, 82006; (307) 777-4600. Website: www.gf.state.-wy.us.**

Suggested Reading
Wagon Wheels: A Contemporary Journey on the Oregon Trail (High Plains Press, 1996) by Candy Moulton and Ben Kern covers the 150th anniversary crossing of the Oregon Trail, mixed with journal entries from original treks and showing both the historic and contemporary epic of this amazing trail. *Wyoming Wildlife Viewing Tour Guide* (Wyoming Game & Fish Department, 1995) by Wyoming Game & Fish staff shows the more interesting viewing areas and specifies what you can see there.

Dinosaurs

While Wyoming has the usual state tree, bird, flower, etcetera, it also has a state dinosaur, the triceratops. The state offers dinosaur lovers a cornucopia of fossilized remains. Digs have unearthed at least 21 genera of dinosaurs. Most of the quarry excavations have taken place in the Big Horn Basin region of the state with excellent sites near Shell, Ten Sleep, and Thermopolis. The importance of these paleontological discoveries prompted the Wyoming government to proclaim October as Wyoming Dinosaur Month. Special events and school outings to dig sites make up a significant part of the annual celebration. Excellent dig sites include Fossil Butte near Kemmerer and the latest discoveries in Glenrock.

Remember, because of the Antiquities Act of 1906, collecting fossils, bones, or artifacts from any of the paleontological sites or archaeological ruins around the state is a violation of federal law.

Hot Springs

There's nothing like soaking in a natural hot spring after a day of vigorous skiing or snowmobiling. Winter is the perfect time to visit "the world's largest, natural mineral hot springs" in Thermopolis, Granite Hot Springs in Jackson Hole, or the hot springs in Saratoga.

Museums

Quite a few museums in Wyoming rely on volunteers to keep them operating; therefore, museums may not be open all the hours listed in this book. It's a good idea to call ahead and make certain someone will be there when you plan to visit the museum. I've noted which

Rodeo! Photo courtesy of the Wyoming Division of Tourism.

roads make hauling a trailer tricky. It's advisable to leave them at the campground before heading out on these drives.

Many of the scenic drives also afford the best wildlife viewing, so be sure to take along a pair of binoculars. The best season for observing wildlife is generally between April 1 and October 31. Animals generally bed down during the day and become active early in the morning and the evening. Wildlife have become used to vehicles; however, they will run if you get out of your car. Scenic routes in this book travel through private property as well as public lands. Please respect landowners' property rights and don't trespass.

Where to Stay

Accommodations

I've tried to steer clear of listing chain motels in this book whenever possible. Their very nature subscribes to a "when you've stayed in one, you've stayed in them all" sort of feeling. Therefore, I have sought to suggest alternative lodgings that offer a more unique, one-of-a-kind experience. Many of the places I list are deeply rooted in history, such as the Hotel Higgins in Glenrock, or the essence of the Wyoming outdoors, such as A Teton Tree House B&B in Wilson. Then there are some mom-and-pop places that offer little or nothing more than the basics in motel accommodations because that's all that is available in the area.

You can obtain a nice listing of places to stay from the **Wyoming Lodging & Restaurant Association, P.O. Box 1003, Cheyenne, 82003; (307) 634-8816, fax (307) 632-0249. E-mail: lynn@wlra.org. Website: www.wlra.org.** The **Wyoming Homestay and Outdoor Adventures** (WHOA) publishes a guide about its member businesses that is well worth getting if you seek the bed-and-breakfast or guest ranch experience. **WHOA, P.O. Box 40048, Casper, 82604; (307) 237-3526, fax (307) 237-1290. E-mail: whoa@coffey.com. Website: www.wyoming-bnb-ranchrec.com.**

The price of accommodations varies depending on the number in your party, the sea-

museums are free. Those that charge admission usually cost from $1 to $5 per person, with places such as the Buffalo Bill Historical Center charging quite a bit more. Small museums exhibit some of the most unusual and uncommon artifacts, making them well worth your time, and they also offer great insights into local history.

Brochures outlining state parks, historic sites, and museums can be obtained from the **Wyoming State Museum Office, Division of Parks & Historic Sites, Herschler Building, 1st Floor East, 125 West 25th Street, Cheyenne, 82002; (307) 777-6323, fax (307) 777-6472. E-mail: msperl@missc.-state.wy.us.** In addition, a "Wyoming Museum and Gallery Guide" is put out by the **Wyoming Arts Council, 2320 Capitol Avenue, Cheyenne, 82002; (307) 777-7742. Website: www.commerce.state.wy.us/cr/arts.**

Scenic Drives

With rare exceptions, the scenic byways described in this book furnish no facilities such as gas stations or restaurants. Start with a full tank of gas and carry water and food. For the most part the drives listed are on unpaved roads but will accommodate passenger cars with no trouble. However, the winding nature and steep mountain passes of many of these son, and the type of services provided, and they can increase. The following price guideline will give you an idea of the per night/per person cost:

$	under $25
$$	$25 to $50
$$$	$50 to $100
$$$$	over $100

Suggested Reading
In *Tastes & Tours of Wyoming* (Wyoming Homestay and Outdoor Adventures, 1997) by Karla Steinle Pellatz and David W. Pellatz, member businesses have contributed not only details about their operations but also recipes they prepare for their guests.

Guest Ranches

The idea of guest "dude" ranches in Wyoming dates back to 1890 when John Sargent and Robert Hamilton constructed a 10-room log ranch house in the Jackson Hole valley to accommodate eastern dudes seeking a western experience. Sargent and Hamilton called it "Merry Mere," but the partnership dissolved before they opened it. The first to open was the Eaton Ranch in Wolf, in 1904. Since then, guest ranches have promoted every type of ranching vacation from the totally planned "keep the guests entertained every second" to the real working ranch "punch cows and ride drag and eat dust on a roundup." You'll find the full spectrum within the listings. The price of guest ranches runs over $100 per person/per night but includes all meals, lodging, and activities.

Learn more about guest ranches from a brochure put out by the **Wyoming Dude Ranchers Association, P.O. Box 618, Dubois, 82513; (307) 455-2084, fax (307) 455-2634. E-mail: motivations@wyoming.com. Website: www.wilderness-west.com/wyoming/wdrassoc/duderanch.** Or contact the regional office of the **Dude Ranchers Association, P.O. Box 471, LaPorte, CO 80535; (970) 223-8440. E-mail: duderanches@compuserve.com. Website: www.duderanch.org.** There is a small charge for the directory.

Suggested Reading
Historic Ranches of Wyoming (Mountain States Lithographing, 1986) by Judith Hancock Sandoval gives insights into ranching history in Wyoming, not all of it involving guest ranches.

Camping

Much of the national forest and BLM lands are open to primitive camping—no facilities, no water, no restrooms, nothing but scenic vistas and howling coyotes at night. However, much of Wyoming now falls under bear camping regulations, so if you don't want the hassle of rigging camp for bear camping, stay in one of the designated campgrounds.

Suggested Reading
Rocky Mountain Camping (Foghorn Press, 1989) by Tom Stienstra lists over 1,200 sites, both public and private, around Wyoming, Montana, and Colorado.

In the National Forests
Most of the designated campgrounds in the national forests have hosts on-site during the summer. Many offer restrooms, drinking water, picnic tables, fire grates, and trash removal. Depending on weather, the majority of campgrounds remain closed before early May and after October. Higher-altitude campgrounds are open shorter seasons. Check with the district office of the national forest you plan to camp in for rules, restrictions, and, of course, the necessity of bear camping. **Bighorn National Forest, 1969 South Sheridan Avenue, Sheridan, 82801; (307) 672-0751. Website: www.fs.fed.us/bhnf. Black Hills National Forest, Ranger Station, P.O. Box 680, Sundance, 82729; (307) 283-1361. Website: www.fs.fed.us/bhnf. Bridger-Teton National Forest, Box 1888, Jackson, 83001; (307) 739-5500. E-mail: btnf-info@sisna.com. Website: www.fs.fed.us/btnf/welcome. Medicine Bow-Routt National Forest, 2468 Jackson Street, Laramie, 82070; (307) 745-2300. Website: www.fs.fed.us/mrnf.**

The Wyoming Guide

In the National Parks, Monuments, and Recreation Areas

Wyoming boasts the first national park, Yellowstone, and the first national monument, Devils Tower. Many established campgrounds are in the parks, at the monuments, and at the recreation areas. Generally camping is only allowed in designated sites. Entrance fees as well as camping fees apply. Contact the individual areas for all the details:

Bighorn Canyon National Recreation Area, P.O. Box 487, Lovell, 82431; (307) 548-2251.
Devils Tower National Monument, P.O. Box 10, Devils Tower, 82714; (307) 467-5283.
Flaming Gorge National Recreation Area, 1450 Uinta Drive, Green River, 82935; (307) 875-2871.
Fossil Butte National Monument, P.O. Box 592, Kemmerer, 83101; (307) 877-4455.
Grand Teton National Park, P.O. Box 170, Moose, 83012; (307) 739-3300. Website: www.nps.gov/GTNP.
Yellowstone National Park, P.O. Box 168, Yellowstone, 82190; (307) 334-7381. Website: www.nps.gov/yell.

In Wyoming State Parks and Recreation Areas

As with national parks, the state parks and recreation areas offer designated campgrounds with entrance and camping fees. Annual passes (good at all Wyoming state parks) cost $25. For complete information, contact the **Division of Parks & Historic Sites, 125 West 25th Street, Cheyenne, 82002; (307) 777-6323, fax (307) 777-6472. E-mail: msperl@missc.state.wy.us.**

On Bureau of Land Management (BLM) Land

In addition to established campgrounds with all the facilities, the BLM offers a variety of primitive campgrounds that are more off the beaten path. Get the details from the **Wyoming State Office of the BLM, 5353 Yellowstone Road, P.O. Box 1828, Cheyenne, 82003; (307) 775-6256, fax (307) 775-6129. Website: www.wy.blm.gov.**

In Private Campgrounds and Cabins

These generally provide all the amenities, including some luxuries such as swimming pools, hot tubs, cabins for rent, playgrounds, and all sorts of other extras. The **Wyoming Campground Association** has a good listing of private campgrounds around the state. **1618 East Park Avenue, Riverton, 82501; (800) 528-3913 or (307) 857-3000, fax (307) 856-9559. Website: www.campwyoming.com.**

Where to Eat

The listings also show the spectrum of foods available in Wyoming. Why settle for a Golden Arches burger when you can have an incredible Wolf burger from the Wolf Hotel Restaurant or a buffalo burger (made from real bison meat) from Brooks Lake Lodge? You can generally get a great breakfast for under $5, a good lunch for about $6 to $8, a dynamite dinner between $14 and $20, and a five-course, gourmet treasure for about $25. I've included handicapped-accessible restaurants and ones that have children's menus and senior discounts. The dollar signs beside the restaurant listings reflect the price of a lunch or dinner entrée per person and are subject to change:

$	under $25
$$	$25 to $50
$$$	$50 to $100
$$$$	over $100

I hope you enjoy your trip to Wyoming!

The Wyoming Guide

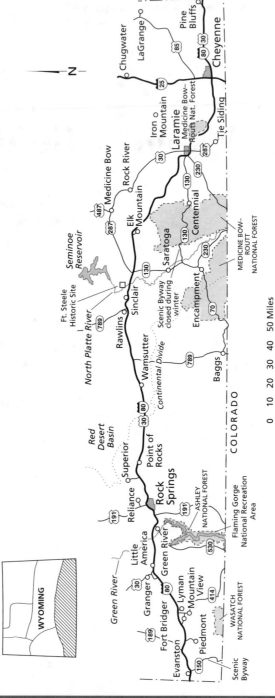

Union Pacific Region

Union Pacific Region

Boar's Tusk. Photo courtesy of the Wyoming Division of Tourism.

Cheyenne

History generally credits Major General Grenville M. Dodge, a railroad surveyor, with choosing the townsite and naming it "Cheyenne" after one of the main Indian nations that resided in the vicinity. Due to the incredible rapidity with which Cheyenne experienced its early growth, Cheyenne quickly earned the nickname the "Magic City of the Plains." As a Union Pacific Railroad (UP) "end of the track" tent town, it sprang up almost overnight. Writer Robert Strahorn asked one of Cheyenne's first settlers who erected the first house in the city and received this answer: "Well, one fine day, early in July 1867, four or five hundred of us pitched our tents here, where there wasn't a sign of civilization, and about half of us woke up at daylight the next morning to find that the other half was living in board shanties!"

Within four months of the creation of this makeshift camp, 4,000 people claimed residence of the town that boasted two daily newspapers, a town government, and a brass band to welcome the first train into town. Soon businessmen poured in and created a thriving community.

The Cheyenne Downtown Development Authority has put together a great brochure for a **Historic Downtown Walking Tour,** complete with walking directions. It's well worth the time to wander through the streets that show off an incredible array of period architecture and the feel of a *real* Old West city. You can pick up the brochure at any of the visitor information sites or send for one. **Cheyenne Downtown Development Authority, 2101 O'Neil Avenue, Room 207, Cheyenne, 82001; (307) 637-6281**.

History

Although trappers and other explorers began wandering into this region of Indian territory in the early 1800s, permanent settlement came with the railroad. Strategically located halfway between Omaha, Nebraska, and Ogden, Utah, the UP decided Cheyenne made the perfect place for maintenance and engine repair facilities. From there, the trains could be serviced and running at top performance before they had to tackle the highest point found on the entire transcontinental line.

Thus the presence of railroad workers ensured a certain amount of economic stability in the new town. The discovery of gold in the Black Hills turned Cheyenne into a financial center. In the 1880s, beef reigned supreme. In fact, during the peak days of the "cattle barons" and entrepreneurs, Cheyenne ranked as the wealthiest per capita city in the world. Mansions lined 17th Street, dubbed Cattlemen's Row, and the Wyoming Stock Growers Association met at the exclusive Cheyenne Club. The association held vast power well into the twentieth century, and it was from the Cheyenne Club that members planned the military-style invasion of Johnson County.

Cheyenne became the seat of the newly formed territorial government in 1869. When the First Territorial Assembly met in a modest wooden building on the corner of 17th Street, representatives made a gutsy motion and granted women equal rights to vote and hold political office, setting an international precedent—one that the U.S. Congress tried unsuccessfully to force Wyoming to rescind when it applied for statehood. The assembly stood firm and thus Wyoming became the 44th state on July 10, 1890, with Cheyenne as the capital.

Festivals and Events

Cheyenne Frontier Days
late July
Called the "Daddy of 'em All," this annual event began in 1897. The largest professional outdoor rodeo in the country, it takes place the final full week of July and lasts 10 days. Reminiscent of Buffalo Bill's Wild West Show, which entertained here in 1898, you'll see parades, top-notch country-and-western performers, a

carnival, chuckwagon races, Native American dance competitions, and, of course, daily rodeos where over a thousand cowboys and cowgirls compete for close to half a million dollars in prize money. Definitely check out the free pancake breakfast, a tradition since 1952. You've never seen anything like it! (They mix the batter in a cement truck and feed approximately 10,000 folks in a blink of an eye.) There is also square dancing in the city center parking lot, a chili cookoff in Lions Park, and Fort D. A. Russell Days with tours of the historic houses at F. E. Warren Air Force Base. Get your tickets well in advance from **4610 North Carey Avenue, P.O. Box 2477, Cheyenne, 82003-2477; (800) 227-6336** or **(307) 778-7222, fax (307) 778-7229. E-mail: info@cfdrodeo.com. Website: www.cfdrodeo.com.**

Outdoor Activities

Fishing

Named after the famous broadcaster and fisherman, **Curt Gowdy State Park (307-632-7946)** is located 26 miles west of the city on Hwy. 210, locally know as Happy Jack Road. The park sports legendary fishing, as well as camping, boating, and hiking in the vicinity of Granite and Crystal Reservoirs. Enjoy the archery range, playgrounds, picnic areas, recreational vehicle (RV) campgrounds, and a great view from the Crystal Dam Overlook. Handicapped access at Granite. Camping permits available at the park headquarters. No swimming allowed, as the reservoirs supply Cheyenne with drinking water.

Golf

Tee off for 18 holes at the **Cheyenne Municipal Golf Course, 4801 Central Avenue; (307) 637-6418.** Or play 9 holes at either **Prairie View (3601 Windmill Road, (307) 637-6420)** or **Little America (junction of I-80 and I-25, 307-775-8400).**

Wyoming Transportation Museum in Cheyenne.

Seeing and Doing

Wyoming State Capitol

The gleaming (lighted at night) 24-carat gold-leaf dome of the state capitol building has dominated the skyline since 1888. Constructed in the French Renaissance style, the capitol houses paintings, statues, historical displays, and a huge stuffed bison (the state's mammal and symbol on the state flag) that give visitors a quick profile of the state's past and present. Standing in front is a statue of Ester Hobart Morris, proponent of equal rights (which is the state's motto), a citizen of South Pass City, Wyoming, and the nation's first woman justice of the peace—a tribute to the

"Equality State." Free guided tours are available with a week's notice, or you can wander around on your own. Open weekdays year-round from 8 A.M. to 5 P.M. Handicapped accessible. **200 West 24th Street, Cheyenne, 82001; (307) 777-7220.**

Cheyenne Street Railway Trolley

Between mid-May and the end of September, you can hear the once familiar clang of the trolley bell. Climb aboard for a spectacular tour of Cheyenne's five primary historic districts—historic downtown, the state capitol building, the Rainsford District, F. E. Warren Air Force Base, and the Cheyenne Frontier Days/Old West Museum area, with a few surprises thrown in! The tour lasts two hours and is well worth the small fee. **309 West Lincolnway, Cheyenne, 82001; (800) 426-5009** or **(307) 778-3133. E-mail: info@cheyenne.org. Website: www.cheyenne.org.**

Wyoming Transportation Museum

Once the headquarters for the Denver-Cheyenne-Ogden Division of the Union Pacific Railroad, this depot ranks as the oldest UP property in the city. The building, started in 1886, covers more than a city block and is currently under extensive restoration. However, portions are open to the public and contain relics from the transcontinental railroad

Cheyenne Street railway trolley.

era. On September 6, 1887, the *Cheyenne Daily Sun* described the 128-foot clock tower as "the most conspicuous feature of the kind in the city, and with the exception of the capitol dome can be seen at a greater distance from Cheyenne than any other object of the kind in the city." The entire structure cost the UP "in round figures the princely sum of $100,000." In winter open Monday through Friday, 10 A.M. to 2 P.M. In summer, open 10 A.M. to 3 P.M., depending on volunteers. **15th Street and Capitol Avenue, P.O. Box 704, Cheyenne, 82003; (307) 637-DEPO (3376). Website: www.wtmk.org.**

Cheyenne Botanic Gardens

M. Fukuoka once said, "Gardening is not just the cultivation of plants. It is also the cultivation of human beings." Here's the place to get thoroughly cultivated! This is the only botanical garden in the state, and the solar-heated greenhouse conservatory displays an interesting mix of exotic tropical plants and food crops. The gardens also function as a municipal nursery, providing flowers, shrubs, and trees for city beautification. Handicapped accessible. Open Monday through Friday 8 A.M. to 4:30 P.M. and Saturday and Sunday 11 A.M. to 3:30 P.M. **710 South Lions Park Drive, Cheyenne, 82001; (307) 637-6458.**

Atlas Theatre

Boo the villain and cheer the hero at the Cheyenne Little Theatre Players' Western Melodrama, July through mid-August. Located in a National Register of Historic Places building constructed in 1887 in what was originally offices, a penny arcade complete with a nickelodeon, and a soda shop. Other productions scheduled throughout the year. Ten shows per year include a wide range of musicals, comedies, kids' shows, and heavy drama. Student and senior discounts. **211 West 16th Street, Cheyenne, 82001; (307) 635-0199** or **(307) 638-6543.**

Terry Bison Ranch

The ranch's slogan reads, "The West the way you want it." Located nine miles south of Cheyenne near the Wyoming-Colorado border; take

I-25 to Exit 2, then go south on Terry Ranch Road. Over a hundred years ago, the ranch belonged to Francis E. Warren, Wyoming's first governor, who ran cattle. Nowadays, the ranch herds almost 3,000 head of bison. Take in the Tumbleweed Buckle Series rodeo Tuesday and Saturday nights between June and September. Tour the ranch and watch the bison. See the range from horseback or relax with some trophy trout fishing. Open year-round. Old-style bunkhouse, RV campground, covered-wagon tours, chuckwagon dinners, boat rentals, and horse boarding. The Senator's Steakhouse serves bison—some grown on the ranch. For a real kick, tour Wyoming's only winery, built in 1881 by Charles Terry, the ranch's original owner; sample all 15 varieties of wine. **51 I-25 Service Road, Cheyenne, 82001; (307) 634-4171.**

Wyoming Hereford Ranch

This historic ranch dates back to 1883 and is part of one of the West's oldest cattle operations. Offers tours of the grounds to groups of 25 or more. Open year-round. **1114 Hereford Ranch Road, Cheyenne, 82001; (307) 634-1905.**

Cheyenne Gunslingers

You can witness a shoot-out in downtown Cheyenne weekdays from early June through July at about 6 P.M. and year-round on Saturday at high noon. **16th and Carey; (307) 635-1028.**

Museums

Historic Governor's Mansion

The first thing you'll notice (besides the exquisite sandstone columns) is that the mansion is located in a residential neighborhood and always has been. Constructed in 1904, the structure served as the Wyoming governor's home from 1905 until 1977, when the new ranch-style mansion was built near Frontier Park. No on-site security or other activities associated with governors' living quarters have ever detracted from this historic home. Today the mansion houses artifacts from the turn of the century through the 1930s and not

only offers a look into how the state's governors lived but also into the gracious yet modest tendency of the state itself. Open year-round Tuesday through Saturday 9 A.M. to 12 P.M. and 1 P.M. to 5 P.M.; free admission. **300 E. 21st Street, Cheyenne, 82001; (307) 777-7878. Website: www.commerce.state.-wy.us/sphs/govern.**

Wyoming State Historical Museum

This museum houses the natural history of Wyoming. It reopened in 1999 after extensive renovations. **Barrett Building, 2301 Central Avenue, Cheyenne, 82002; (307) 777-7022. Website: www.commerce.state.-wy.us/cr/wsm.**

Old West Museum

Not only is this museum housed on the spectacular Frontier Days rodeo grounds, it's the place to learn about "Dust and Glory," the 100-plus years of the "Daddy of 'Em All." In addition, wander through the carriage collection, featuring rides from a more elegant era, the overland stage, and chuckwagons. Kids can experience the fun of western life in the Hole-in-the-Wall room. Open Monday through Friday, 9 A.M. to 5 P.M., and Saturday and Sunday, 10 A.M. to 5 P.M., year-round. **4501 North Carey Avenue, Frontier Park, 8th and Carey Avenue, Cheyenne, 82001; (307) 778-7290.**

F. E. Warren Air Force Base Military Museum

At the same time as Cheyenne's founding (1867), to protect the railroad General Christopher C. Augur established Fort D. A. Russell (which would become Francis E. Warren Air Force Base) three miles west of town. The fort played a role in the Sioux War of 1876 and the Ute campaign of 1879. In 1871, when other army frontier posts were being abandoned, Fort D. A. Russell gained permanent installation status, due to its crucial position on the transcontinental railroad. It served as a major field artillery and cavalry training post during World War I and as an officer and quartermaster training facility during World War II. The air force acquired the installation in 1947 and ceded it to the Strategic Air Command in 1958. Today, the base serves as one of the nation's six Minuteman Intercontinental Ballistic Missile centers and is home to the Peacekeeper missile.

An excellent display of artifacts in the museum retells military and base history from 1867 to the present, as well as the transition from an army fort to an air base. The missile museum runs the gamut from the earliest versions to the latest technology. The oldest active installation in the system, Warren also offers a peek into the lives of nonmilitary personnel through its displays of period rooms. The kids' room is quite entertaining. Two hundred and twenty of the base's officers' quarters and other structures are listed in the National Register of Historic Places. Although the base itself is not open to the public, tours may be scheduled for groups of 10 people or more by calling ahead. You can call ahead for a pass to the museum or fill out paperwork at the main gate to get permission to enter the base. Admission is free. Open year-round, Monday through Friday, 8 A.M. to 4 P.M. **Randall Avenue and I-25, Cheyenne, 82005; (307) 773-3381. Website: www.warren.af.mil.**

Where to Stay

Accommodations

A. Drummond's Ranch B&B—$$$–$$$$

Bask in luxury here with privacy and personalized service—terry robes, fresh flowers, homemade goodies, and 120 acres of pure Wyoming landscape nestled between the Medicine Bow–Routt National Forest and Curt Gowdy State Park. Climb amid granite outcrops. Mountain bike through the countryside. Kick back in a hammock. Custom packages include lunch and dinner. They also offer guided mountain bike treks, "take a llama to lunch," overnight camp-outs, guided backcountry trips, and a tour into historic Laramie (these cost extra). In winter you can cross-country ski at the ranch or ski the slopes at Centennial. You can also board your horses and dogs. While you are there, pick up a copy of their cookbook, loaded with favorites from the B&B's menus. **399 Happy Jack Road, Cheyenne, 82001; phone and fax (307) 634-6042. E-mail: adrummond@juno.com.**

Adventurers' Country B&B—$$$–$$$$

The 150-foot front porch beckons you to relax at this B&B, as does 102 acres that spread out before the mountains. Fresh flowers decorate the cozy rooms—three bedrooms and one suite, all with private baths—at this modern getaway. Partake of five-course meals, all homemade. In the Bison Room, curl up in front of the fireplace, read a book from the library, or watch some TV or videos. Western dinners also available for an additional fee. Make prior arrangements. Kids can enjoy playing with the ranch animals—chickens, geese, and horses. Pets allowed only if you keep them in kennel boxes. Backcountry trips up to a week long can be arranged. No minimum stay. Not handicapped accessible. They'll even teach you how to ride a horse. Local tours, horseback riding lessons, and campfire sing-alongs available for an extra fee. Be sure to make reservations early. **3803 I-80 South Service Road, Cheyenne, 82009; phone and fax (307) 632-4087. E-mail: fwhite1@juno.com. Website: www.cruising-america.com/country.**

8

Rainsford Inn B&B—$$$–$$$$

A beautiful Victorian mansion amid the historic downtown district. Five suites, one handicapped accessible. Round 'em up in the Cattle Baron room or stay in "courtly" fashion in the Judge's Chamber in honor of Justice Van DeVanter, Wyoming's only judge to sit on the U.S. Supreme Court. Two rooms have a shared bath with shower only. Other rooms have private baths and whirlpool tubs—perfect after a long day of travel. Phones in the rooms, as well as cable TV. Choice of breakfast menu with delightful conversation and a home-cooked meal. Senior and other discounts are available. **219 East 18th Street, Cheyenne, 82001; (307) 638-BEDS (2337), fax (307) 634-4506.**

Howdy Pardner B&B—$$$

Convenient to activities in Frontier Park, as well as near the airport. Only 10 minutes from downtown. Gourmet breakfasts. Children and pets welcome. **1920 Tranquillity Road, Cheyenne, 82009; (307) 634-6493, fax (307) 634-2822. E-mail: janp9999@aol.com. Website: www.cruising-america.com/howdy.**

Nagle Warren Mansion B&B—$$$

An elegant residence built in 1888 by Erasmus Nagle that in 1910 became the home of Francis E. Warren, a Wyoming governor and U.S. senator. Located close to downtown, this B&B is decorated in comfortable luxury with period wallpaper and antique furniture. Central air conditioning, a private bath, telephone, and television in each of the 14 guest rooms. Exercise room, outdoor hot tub. Breakfast served from 7:30 A.M. to 9:30 A.M. (extended hours on the weekends). Choose from homemade breads and muffins, yogurt, fruit, and the daily special from Jacquie's "gourmet" kitchen. **222 E. 17th Street, Cheyenne, 82001; (800) 811-2610 or (307) 637-3333, fax (307) 638-6835.**

Porch Swing B&B—$$$

This 1907 restored historic home offers a great gourmet breakfast and homemade snacks served during the afternoon. Try the Rosemary Potatoes, or opt for traditional fare,

Downtown Cheyenne.

such as biscuits and gravy. Sit down at mealtime and talk with Tom and Carole about places to go and things to do in the area. They really cater to guests' needs. Rooms with either private or shared bath. Hike around the place on an informal basis. Another option is to reserve their cabin in the mountains. Mountain day hikes available as well. Pets allowed with prior approval. **712 East 20th Street, Cheyenne, 82001; (307) 778-7182. E-mail: porchswing@juno.com. Website: www.-cruising-america.com/porch.**

The Storyteller Pueblo B&B—$$–$$$

Relax amid the collection of pottery, baskets, rugs, weaving, and beadwork from over 40 Native American tribes, plus interesting antiques that give guests an idea of the contemporary and historic West. Wake up to a complete breakfast with coffee, juice, fruit, and plenty of hearty dishes. Four rooms, two with shared baths. Close to shopping and restaurants, and five minutes from art galleries and museums. Children welcome. You can arrange for kennel care for your pets. **5201 Odgen Road, Cheyenne, 82009; (307) 634-7036, fax (307) 635-9117. E-mail: HARTcntr@-wyoming.com.**

Camping

Private Campgrounds and Cabins

AB Camping offers full hookups, some with 50 amps, tent sites, a fenced dog run, laundry, game room, shower house, playground, and a

9

covered patio for group functions. Open summers. **1503 W. College Drive, Cheyenne, 82001; (307) 634-7035.**

The **Cheyenne KOA** provides cabins, long pull-through sites, private showers, tent sites with fire rings and grates, a convenience store that carries RV supplies, laundry, playground, and propane sales. Open April 1 through October 31. Pets allowed on leases. **8800 Archer Frontage Road, Cheyenne, 82001; (307) 638-8840.**

Where to Eat

The Albany Restaurant—$$–$$$$

Located across the street from the historic UP depot, the Albany has treated customers to some excellent western-flavor dining since 1949. Start with some Bull Fries, breaded and deep fried and served with red sauce. Homemade soups accompany dinner. Prime rib is the "specialty of the house." Open for lunch and dinner, 11 A.M. to 9 P.M. Closed Sundays. **1506 Capitol Avenue, Cheyenne, 82001; (307) 638-3507.**

Lexies—$$–$$$$

You'll find Lexies in the circa 1880 home of Erasmus Nagle, an outfitter and supplier nicknamed the "Merchant King of Wyoming." Nagle became the chairman of the Wyoming State Capitol building commission. He and a partner built the Cheyenne Black Hills Telegraph Company in 1875. The house breathes elegance from a bygone era. When the weather permits, sitting outside in the heart of the historic district makes for a special dining experience. Try the very popular filet Steak au Poivre, tenderloin with green peppercorns, cognac, and brandy in a demi-glaze sauce. For breakfast there's the hungry man's omelette, or "create your own omelette" on Saturdays. Senior specials available. Open 7 A.M. to 8 P.M. Monday through Friday, 7 A.M. to 9 P.M. Saturday. Closed Sundays. **216 E. 17th, Cheyenne, 82001; (307) 638-8712.**

Han River Cafe—$–$$$

A wide variety of authentic Chinese foods, fast, filling, and good. Delicious hot and sour soup. Family dinners available. Open Monday through Saturday from 11:15 A.M. to 9:30 P.M. **5225 Yellowstone Road, Cheyenne, 82001; (307) 632-2449.**

Services

Visitor Information

Cheyenne Chamber of Commerce, 301 West 16th, P.O. Box 1147, Cheyenne, 82001; (307) 638-3388. Cheyenne Convention & Visitors Bureau, 309 W. Lincolnway, P.O. Box 765, Cheyenne, 82003; (800) 426-5009 or (307) 778-3133, fax (307) 778-3190. E-mail: info@cheyenne.org. Website: www.-cheyenne.org.

Evanston

Named after Union Pacific (UP) surveyor James A. Evans, Evanston is referred to by locals as either the "Queen City of the Mountains" or the "Queen City of the Rockies." Historic Depot Square is a great starting point for a walking tour through the turn-of-the-century downtown. Pick up a booklet about the historic buildings you'll see. It's available at the **Evanston Chamber of Commerce** office, in Depot Square on the corner of **10th and Front Streets.**

BEAR Project.

History

Evanston exemplifies the power the railroad commanded over the formation of towns along its tracks. Arriving in what would become Evanston on November 23, 1868, a man named Harvey Booth pitched a tent with a wood floor near where the Union Pacific (UP) planned to lay track. The railroad reached him on December 1. In that short period, a community had sprung up. In addition to Booth and his restaurant, saloon, and hotel, approximately 600 people had moved into the area, throwing together other "raghouses" made of canvas and wood. Then news came that the railroad chose Wasatch, Utah, 12 miles farther west for its division headquarters. Within a single day everyone deserted the place—except for Booth and his saloon keeper, Frank More. However, the following June, UP executives decided to move the headquarters back to the one-time tent town, and Evanston was back in business—to stay, this time.

The economy continued to experience boom-and-bust cycles. Discovery of a rich vein of coal brought in a sizable Chinese population to work in the mines in the 1870s. The Chinese built shanties across the tracks in Chinatown—so named because of the 2,000 Chinese railroaders living in the area—and worshipped at the Joss House. In 1900, a search for water led to the UP Coal Company's drilling a well that struck oil instead. Wildcatting ran rampant, and Evanston's population blossomed into 4,000. Things leveled off from there until the Arab oil embargo in the early 1970s. Renewed interest in domestic oil exploration of the region, called the "Overthurst Belt," brought more speculators and all the associated businesses to Evanston.

Festivals and Events

Chinese New Year
late January or early February
The actual date of this celebration depends on the lunar calendar. (Check with the **Evanston**

Union Pacific Region

Chamber of Commerce (800-328-9708 or **307-789-2757)** for the current date.) Evanston began celebrating the Chinese New Year in the late 1800s. Over the course of two weeks, the Chinese population gave their homes a thorough cleaning. They bought new clothes, displayed orange trees around their houses to bring good luck, and brought out the 150-foot-long Gum Lung dragon. After a parade and fireworks, they shot a wooden ball into the air, and the people raced around to catch it. The person who succeeded would receive the keys and become the keeper of the Joss House for the next year. The New Year's celebration died out in the 1920s when the Chinese population dwindled. It was started up again as part of the 1990 Wyoming Centennial Celebration. It's held over a Friday and Saturday, with fireworks displays, noisemakers to ward off evil spirits, special tours of the Joss House, a tea house, ricksha races, and the traditional ball drop on Friday before fireworks. The catcher doesn't receive the keys anymore but gets the honorary title of "Keeper of Joss House." The ball drops twice, once for adults and once for kids, with each receiving the title. These days a 50-foot-long Chinese dragon appears in Saturday's parade.

Outdoor Activities

BEAR Project

In addition to some excellent fishing along the river and in the ice pond, the BEAR (Better Environment and River) Project and Bear River State Park extend opportunities for you to enjoy a variety of recreation. Hike or bike along the path that skirts the river and links the state park with Hamblin Park and points beyond, totaling three miles' worth of foot trails. Just over a mile has been paved with asphalt for handicapped access to some excellent scenery and wildlife viewing. You can also observe the bison herd maintained by the state park, open daily from early May to October. Tube in the river, or watch the wildlife in the

wetlands. Once snow starts, explore the area on cross-country skis. The park closes and the roads serve as ski trails. The walking paths are groomed for skiing, with ice-skating on the pond. No overnight camping is allowed. **601 Bear River Drive, Evanston, 82930; (307) 789-6547, (307) 789-6540** for camping reservations.

Golf

Tee off for 9 or 18 holes at the **Purple Sage Golf Course**. Located on **Uinta and Country Club Streets** just off **19th Street; (307) 789-2383.**

Hiking and Backpacking

The eastern edge of the **Wasatch-Cache National Forest** dips into western Wyoming. The Wasatch Range is the largest east-west mountain range in North America, and this national forest receives the most visitor use in the United States—6,155,500 people a year. Over 1,000 miles of trails exist in the forest, making hiking the most popular utilization of the woodlands. For more detail about the Wyoming section of the Wasatch-Cache National Forest, contact the summer visitor facilities, from Memorial Day through the end of October, at the **Bear River Ranger Station (435-642-6662)** or the **Mountain View Ranger Station, Lone Tree Road (Hwy. 44), Mountain View, 82939; (307) 782-6555.**

Horse Racing

Thoroughbred and quarterhorse racing kicks off the summer months at **Wyoming Downs Racetrack.** Gates open at 11:30 A.M. from June 27 through August on Saturday and Sunday, plus Friday on 4th of July weekend. Post time starts at 1 P.M. Located 10 miles north of Evanston on Hwy. 89, the Downs offers parimutuel betting and some great racing action. **P.O. Box 1607, Evanston, 82931; (800) 842-TRAC (8722)** or **(307) 789-0511.**

Cross-Country Skiing

In town take advantage of the **BEAR Project**'s 3.5 miles of groomed trails between downtown and **Bear River State Park** on the east end of town. (See BEAR Project on page 12.)

Lily Lake Ski Area offers several miles of groomed trails for exclusive nordic use in the Uinta Mountain Range. Trails are groomed weekly throughout the winter and provide a great getaway. Contact the **Evanston Ranger District** at **(307) 789-3194.**

Seeing and Doing

Historic Depot Square

This square contains what was originally the Carnegie Library, constructed in 1906, and is now the **Unita County Museum** and the chamber of commerce office. The Union Pacific depot, built in 1900, and the Chinese **Joss House**, a sacred temple, are also located here. **36 10th Street, Evanston, 82930; (307) 789-9690.**

Piedmont

Although hauntings don't seem to plague this ghost town, Piedmont maintains an air of intrigue. Three 30-foot-high and 30-feet-around-the-base beehive structures stand as silent guards to the town, the remains of five original charcoal kilns. Back in 1868, a man named Moses Byrne built the kilns in order to supply Utah with charcoal to fire the iron industry. The town itself started as a logging camp and was called "Byrne." Then the Union Pacific Railroad arrived. With it came a name change to "Piedmont," which means "at the foot of the mountains."

The town's one claim to fame came in 1869 when 300 railroad workers stacked piles of railroad ties across the tracks to prohibit dignitaries from traveling to Promontory Point, Utah, where they were to place the golden spike, signifying the completion of the transcontinental railroad. It seems the railroad had neglected to pay the workers somewhere in the neighborhood of $200,000 to $500,000 in back wages. The ploy worked. Not only did the

Getting There

Located 85 miles northeast of Salt Lake City, Utah, on I-80. No commercial air service is available; however, you can travel in via **Star West Aviation Charter Service (307-789-2256).**

workers successfully delay the ceremony, they forced the UP's vice president, Dr. Thomas C. Durrant, into wiring the funds needed to cover the back pay. The workers then cleared the track, and the golden spike connected the sections on May 10.

A legend also persists about Piedmont. Butch Cassidy supposedly buried stolen loot in the vicinity of the town. It hasn't been found yet!

Piedmont thrived as a town until the Aspen tunnel effectively diverted the tracks around it. The area's last known resident, a sheepherder named William Taylor, supposedly froze to death in a blizzard in 1949. Take I-80 east 20 miles to Leroy Road and follow the gravel road south.

Museums

Uinta County Museum

Housed with the chamber of commerce office, this small, free museum offers some unique pieces of Wyoming history. Rare stone fishhooks in the Walter L. and Ruth K. Jones Indian Artifact Collection will catch your eye, as will the Gum Lung dragon head, part of a 150-foot dragon used from 1880 to 1922 for the Chinese New Year parade. There's also Chinese money from the year 1127 B.C. during the Chou Dynasty and the Ming Dynasty of A.D. 1368 to 1644 and exquisite clothing, such as a black Chinese robe with gold embroidery, a beaded shawl, and a delicate 1800s christening gown. Well worth taking the time to wander through. Open during the week year-round, 9 A.M. to 5 P.M., and in summer 10 A.M. to 4 P.M. on weekends. **36 10th Street, Evanston, 82930; (307) 789-2757.**

Chinese Joss House Museum

Railroad and mining work brought many to the Chinese community in Evanston. A sacred temple and the cornerstone of Evanston's

13

Pine Gables Inn B&B.

Chinatown, the Joss House, constructed in 1894, was one of only three temples built in the United States (the other two are in San Francisco and New York). Unfortunately, the beautifully ornate structure burned to the ground in 1922. As part of the Wyoming Centennial Celebration during 1990, this replica was erected. The museum houses artifacts from the original Joss House, grabbed out of the burning building by brave people. Among the items saved from the fire were two large wooden panels from the exterior, embossed with Chinese characters. Others items were donated from the collections of local residents and things acquired in China through various people's travels. Archaeological digs in Chinatown have turned up bits and pieces of ordinary everyday life—buttons, pipes, dice, and so on. There are also hand-painted cups and plates from the Ranch Cafe, an early Chinese restaurant in town. Open daily during the summer. (If the door is locked, inquire at the chamber of commerce office next door.) Closed weekends in winter. Call to arrange a tour. **920 Front Street, Evanston, 82930; (307) 789-2757.**

Nightlife

Michael's Bar & Grill

This is a great place for those who enjoy visiting rather than yelling at each other over music that is too loud. Relax and settle into one of the couches arranged around coffee tables in a cozy living room. Artistic decor with old pictures; mood-setting lights in purple, pink, and blue. Pub-type food, good appetizers and sandwich menu. Open Monday through Thursday from 11 A.M. to 11 P.M., Friday and Saturday from 11 A.M. until midnight. **1011 Front Street, Evanston, 82930; (307) 789-1088.**

Scenic Drives

Mirror Lake Scenic Byway

From Hwy. 150 in Evanston, this 65-mile drive dips into the western end of the Uinta Mountains, named after the Uinta Indians. The road, open only from sometime in June to late October (maybe), winds through the High Uintas Wilderness. The section between Evanston and the Soapstone Guard Station in Utah is paved. From there it's gravel and dirt. A four-wheel-drive vehicle is *highly* recommended. However, you can take a paved alternate route from the guard station on Utah Hwy. 150 to Kamas, Utah. The scenery is spectacular, regardless of which route you take. For details about road closure call the **Evanston Ranger District** of the **Wasatch-Cache National Forest (307-789-3194).**

Where to Stay

Accommodations

Pine Gables Inn B&B—$$–$$$

Built in 1883, this B&B sports four bedrooms with private baths. Rooms carry the names of the owners' daughters. The Victorian-style parlor, filled with antiques and flowers, makes you feel welcome and at home. Enclosed porch with a swing. Nonsmoking establishment. No pets. Well-behaved children over the age of 12 are welcome. Beautifully decorated rooms. Ten-percent senior discount. Not handicapped accessible, as all the bedrooms are upstairs. Each room comes equipped with a phone and color TV. Heather's English Cottage has a queen-size bed and a full-size bed. Christy's Rose Garden, all in blues, has a bay window and a Murphy's chest, which opens out into an extra bed. Cassie's Carousel has a lavender claw bathtub and a charming window seat. Fawn's Victorian Fancy is decorated in soft pinks and off-white and features an old fireplace, a double bed, and a bath with a shower. Full breakfast provided from several menu choices. **1049 Center Street, Evanston, 82931; (800) 789-2069 or (307) 789-2787.**

Prairie Inn—$$–$$$

While this motel has standard accommodations, the rooms are large, comfortable, and clean. Continental breakfast. Plenty of parking. Handicapped accessible. Pets allowed for an additional fee. **264 Bear River Drive, Evanston, 82930; (307) 789-2920.**

Camping

Private Campgrounds and Cabins

Phillips RV Trailer Park has overnight full hookups, shade trees and grass, long pull-throughs, tent sites, hot showers, laundry facilities. Cable TV and e-mail access available. Pets allowed. Open April 1 to November 1. From I-80 take Exit 6. **225 Bear River Drive, Evanston, 82930; (307) 789-3805.**

Where to Eat

Last Outpost—$$–$$$$

Here's the place for a real buffalo steak, beef steak, or veal cutlet. However, if you prefer to sample Evanston's diverse ethnic cultures, try the Grecian Delight sandwich. Open daily 6 A.M. to 10 P.M. **205 Bear River Drive, Evanston, 82930; (307) 789-3322.**

Legal Tender Dining
(in the Dunmar Inn)—$$–$$$$

Elegant dining. Hearty portions for breakfast and dinner. Specialties include rib-eye steak, shrimp, crab, and veal. Children's menu. Handicapped accessible. Friendly hospitality. Open 5:30 A.M. to 9:30 P.M. daily, year-round. **1601 Harrison Drive, P.O. Box 768, Evanston, 82930; (307) 789-3770.**

Little America—$$–$$$$

The fast service and good food draw a substantial Sunday dinner crowd from Evanston. Three meals a day. Breakfast standards as well as lox and bagel platter, Spanish omelettes, and a dish called "Cheyenne"—scrambled eggs with diced ham, potatoes, and toast. For lunch, choose from salads, hot or cold sandwiches, burgers or entrées, such as chicken stir-fry or steaks. Or have a Wyoming-style dinner of prime rib or elk medallions. Also trout, vegetarian lasagna, or Shrimp Louie. Open 24 hours, seven days a week. **Route 80 Exit 68, Little America, 82929; (800) 634-2401 or (307) 875-2400, fax (307) 872-2666.**

New Garden Cafe—$$–$$$

A Chinese-food-lover's place where everything is made from scratch. The most popular dish, fried rice, is like no fried rice you will eat anywhere else. It's cooked in less than two minutes in a wok heated to 700 degrees. If you like it hot and spicy, dig into the Kung Pao shrimp or chicken. A respectable selection of American dishes is available, as well as meals for children. In the late 1930s, this same Chinese restaurant was called "The New Paris Cafe," so named because of the prevailing attitude toward the Chinese who came in with the railroad and mining. Open Tuesday through Saturday from 11 A.M. to 9:30 P.M., and on Sunday from 11 A.M. to 8:30 P.M. Closed Monday. **933 Front Street, Evanston, 82930; (307) 789-1256.**

Old Mill Restaurant &
Water Wheel Tavern—$$–$$$$

Constructed in 1892, the restaurant originally housed the Evanston Mill and Elevator Company and milled flour in Chinatown, which was close to the mill. Today, the Old Mill offers a wide selection of fine dinners, including Wyoming-raised lamb grilled to perfection, Idaho trout, Alaskan king crab, sirloin, and linguine. A pleasant wine list. Open Monday through Sunday from 4 P.M. to 10 P.M. **30 Country Road, Evanston, 82930; (307) 789-4040.**

Don Pedro's Family
Mexican Restaurant—$$–$$$

Authentic Mexican cuisine in a quaint cafe atmosphere. The spicy aroma teases your taste

15

buds the moment you open the door. For lunch, you can get a great combination plate; and for dinner, you might like the enchiladas a la crema or tortilla soup. Open Sunday through Thursday 11 A.M. to 9 P.M., and Friday and Saturday 11 A.M. to 10 P.M. **909 Front Street, Evanston, 82930; (307) 789-2944.**

Grazia's Giardino—$$–$$$

This is the place for pasta lovers. It's all homemade! There are also steak, veal, and chicken dishes. Open Tuesday through Saturday for dinner from 5 P.M. to 10 P.M., and Tuesday through Friday for lunch from 11 A.M. to 2 P.M. **125 10th Street, Evanston, 82930; (307) 789-8720.**

Services

Visitor Information

The **Evanston Chamber of Commerce** is centrally located in the heart of downtown on the corner of **10th and Front Streets** in Depot Square with the Chinese Joss House and the museum. **P.O. Box 365, Evanston, 82931-0365; (800) 328-9708** or **(307) 789-2757, fax (307) 789-4807. E-mail: chamber@-evanston.com. Website: www.evanstonwy.-com/chamber.**

Green River

Taking its name from the river that flows along the townsite, Green River sits in the shadow of the impressive red bluffs cut by the river. Sixty million years ago, the area was covered by a huge lake. At first, it was fresh water, but the level dropped after about a million years, cutting off its outlet to the ocean, and the water became saline like the Great Salt Lake for the next million years. Then the lake rose, and the water returned to being fresh. All the while deposits formed on the bottom of the lake. Once the lake disappeared entirely, the basin filled with volcanic ash. The spectacular rock formations you see today are the solidified lake sediments. Currently Green River is known as the "Trona Capital of the World." Refining the mineral ore trona produces soda ash, which goes into the manufacturing of baking soda, detergents, and glass.

Three locales in the vicinity received the designation of Green River—an encampment on the Oregon Trail approximately 34 miles from the current city, a stage station on the Overland Trail on the south side of the river where the Wyoming Game & Fish office is now located, and the present-day officially incorporated town on the north side of the river.

The Green River Historic Preservation Commission and the city coproduced an excellent self-guided tour of the historic town. They also publish "Nature's Art Shop," a driving tour to the incredible rock formations of the area. Be sure to pick up copies at the chamber of commerce office.

Flaming Gorge.

History

Unlike other towns along the Union Pacific (UP) railroad, the town now known as Green River began as a station on the Overland Trail and Pony Express routes. True settling, however, occurred shortly before the railroad. Land speculators like H. M. Hook, S. I. Field, and James Moore saw the potential for huge profits and gobbled up land that had been part of the Overland Mail Company through a congressional grant in 1862. In the winter of 1867, Charles Deloney set up a tie-hacking operation in the upper Green River country. The following spring, Judge William A. Carter also ventured into the lumber business, constructing his mill on the confluence of the Green River and Bitter Creek. When the railroad arrived in 1868, officials found a platted town with an established government and 2,000 people in residence. At first, the UP decided against locating its winter terminus in the town, but weather eventually forced the company to change its mind. By the 1930s railroad workers comprised so much of the population of the town that they passed the Green River Ordinance, a law that prohibited door-to-door salesmen from disturbing people during daylight hours so workers with unorthodox shifts could sleep uninterrupted.

In 1869 Major John Wesley Powell led his first expedition down the Green and Colorado Rivers, launching the exploratory trip from a point in the vicinity of the present-day city. The exact location remains unknown; however, his second trip in 1871 left from a campsite now named "Expedition Island" on the north side of town.

Festivals and Events

Flaming Gorge Days Celebration
late June

Celebrate summer fun with a three-on-three basketball tournament, concerts, a parade, a flea market, arm wrestling, horseshoe-throwing contests, and tug-of-war. On Thursday night, witness the Battle of the Bands. Children's entertainment and remote-control car races. Contact the chamber of commerce for all the details at **(307) 875-5711**.

Outdoor Activities

Boating

Twenty miles south of Green River on Hwy. 530, the reservoir at the **Flaming Gorge National Recreation Area** stretches over the countryside. World-class fishing includes brown, rainbow, and mackinaw trout; kokanee salmon; smallmouth bass; and catfish. The three marinas are spread out along the 375-mile-plus shoreline, so bring plenty of fuel, water, and food with you. In addition to water sports, take advantage of over 600 camping and picnic spots and 120 miles of hiking trails. Remember, you'll be traveling through a high

plains desert environment. Come prepared. Photo ops abound in the craggy cliffs (their fiery color is how the area got its name) that rise up to 1,500 feet above the water. Check out **Firehole Canyon** just above the confluence of the Black's Fork River and the Green. Stop in at one of the visitors centers for all the details. In winter, ice fish or take advantage of cross-country ski and snowmobile trails around the lake. Write **Flaming Gorge National Recreation Area, 1450 Uinta Drive, Green River, 82935; (307) 875-2871, fax (307) 875-1646. Buckboard Marina** rents boats and is open year-round. South of Green River 25 miles at Flaming Gorge. **Hwy. 530, HCR 65 Box 100, Green River, 82935; (307) 875-6927.**

Fishing

In addition to the spectacular fishing at the **Flaming Gorge National Recreation Area**, 60 miles northwest of Green River on Hwy. 372, you come across 139-foot-high earthen **Fontenelle Dam.** Besides regulating the flow of the river and generating electricity, the dam creates some excellent fishing and boating opportunities with 56 miles of shoreline and a 20-mile-long lake. **Seedskadee National Wildlife Refuge** also allows some fishing in a "blue ribbon" section of the Green River. Or fish in the river right in town at the public access areas on the **Greenbelt.** Contact **Wyoming Game & Fish, District #4 Office, 351 Astle, Green River, 82935; (307) 875-3223. E-mail: wgf@missc.state.wy.us. Website: www.gf.state.wy.us.**

Highland Desert Flies offers scenic and fishing trips on the Green and New Fork Rivers, as well as fly-fishing instruction. Half-day, all-day, and overnight trips. **79 North First East, Green River, 82935; (307) 875-2358. E-mail: hoghuntr@fascination.com.**

Four-Wheel-Drive Trips

In 1998 the Flaming Gorge Ranger District of the Ashley National Forest implemented a plan to better protect the region's natural resources. The "closed-unless-designated-open" policy affects off-road and off-trail use. Under this plan, all trails and roads have signs designating what sort of vehicular travel is suitable for the route. All other types of vehicles are not allowed. Nor is there any off-designated-road or off-trail travel. Still, the gorge provides a wide variety of four-wheel-drive and all-terrain-vehicle experiences. For the most current maps and travel designations, contact the **Flaming Gorge Ranger District, Ashley National Forest, P.O. Box 279, Manila, UT 84046; (435) 784-3445**.

Hiking and Backpacking

(See the Boating section, above.)

Horseback Riding

Horse corrals and an equestrian trail are part of the **Greenbelt** (see below) near the Jaycee ball field.

Skiing

Flaming Gorge National Recreation Area offers excellent nordic skiing. Trails range in elevation from 6,720 to 8,020 feet and show off southwestern Wyoming's unique beauty. Maps and the latest route information can be obtained from the **Flaming Gorge Ranger District, Ashley National Forest, P.O. Box 279, Manila, UT 84046; (435) 784-3445; or Flaming Gorge National Recreation Area, 1450 Uinta Drive, Green River, 82935; (307) 875-2871**.

Cross-Country Skiing

Canyon Rim Trail provides some wonderful wildlife-viewing opportunities on this easy-to-moderate six-mile one-way jaunt. Start at the Greendale Rest Area trailhead. Head west through the ponderosa pines and aspens and into the meadow. Along the way, you'll see Red Canyon and the Uinta, Little, and Richards Mountains. Cross the Skull Creek drainage. Here you'll meet the Canyon Rim campground and trailhead for a 2.5-mile loop.

Take an easy 5.5-mile trek round-trip at **Elk Park**. The trail leaves from the trailhead located on Hwy. 44. It weaves in and out of

stands of pines and aspens. Go west on Deep Creek Road to Elk Park, a large, flat, open meadow. From there, you can get a great view of the northern slope of the Uintas and usually see plenty of elk and maybe moose. While Elk Park is closed to snowmobiling, Deep Creek Road allows it, so be prepared to share the road.

Swett Ranch Trail offers some moderately difficult skiing conditions. A seven-mile round-trip, it takes off from the Greendale Rest Area parking lot and goes north for half a mile on the forest service road. At the three-way junction, head straight north. This will take you high above the historic Swett Ranch. Pass through the gate and down a short, steep slope. At the end, take a hard right turn and go southeast, gradually climbing the Allen Creek drainage and stands of trees. Another hard right leads you along a log fence, passing near some private homes before you go through another gate. Continue west past the road intersection and the turnoff to Swett Ranch. Ascend a slope and head west by an old log cabin and another section of fence. This will eventually loop back to the parking lot.

Snowmobiling

(See Four-Wheel-Drive Trips, above.)

Seeing and Doing

Greenbelt

A cooperative effort between the city and local businesses, this trail system meanders along the river and over several bridges. From the trail, which starts at Expedition Island, you'll see some spectacular geology, as well as natural and human history. Developed as well as natural trails, some with handicapped access. Picnic areas, boat ramps, playgrounds, and even a child-and-senior fishing pond. **Expedition Island** holds a monument to Major John Wesley Powell, who unraveled the mysteries of the Green and Colorado Rivers and left a lasting legacy of land-use policies as the first director of the U.S. Geological Survey. South 2nd East takes you to the island. Don't miss **Scott's Bottom Nature Area**, a half-mile loop that affords remarkable wildlife viewing through a riparian (water-abundant) habitat. **City of Green River, Parks and Recreation Department, Green River, 82935; (307) 875-5000, ext. 151.** Or call the chamber of commerce, **(800) FL GORGE (354-6743).**

Museums

Sweetwater County Historical Museum

If you're looking for a museum that offers ethnic diversity, look no further. It draws heavily from the town's ethnic mix. You'll find displays of striking Chinese tapestries, Sioux ledger art, contributions from Greek, Slovenian, Japanese, Native American, and European cultures, plus 100,000 photos of Sweetwater County's history. Open year-round from 9 A.M. to 5 P.M. **80 West Flaming Gorge Way, Green River, 82935; (307) 872-6435. E-mail: swchm@fiw.net.**

Scenic Drives

Seedskadee National Wildlife Refuge

To get there, take I-80 west to Hwy. 372 (toward La Barge). Go north about 28 miles to the refuge headquarters turnoff. This extremely remote area has no facilities, so bring plenty of water and food and don't forget to top off your gas tank before you head there. Picnic tables are provided, but no camping is allowed.

Managed by the U.S. Fish and Wildlife Service, the refuge covers 14,000 acres. Pronounced SEEDS-kee-dee, the Shoshone word means "sage chicken." It provides a home for

an incredible array of birds, including the peregrine falcon, Canada goose, prairie falcon, blue heron, and sage grouse, as well as crucial winter habitat for large animals such as moose, deer, and pronghorn. If you're lucky, you might spot sandhill cranes or trumpeter swans in the 800-acre wetland marsh created by the refuge.

Also of interest in the refuge is the Lombard Ferry Historic Site on Hwy. 28 next to the bridge. From 1843 well into the early 1900s, the ferry carried pioneers and other travelers across the Green River. During peak emigration months, the ferry ride cost up to $16 per wagon, a high price, but better than losing everything you owned—and possibly your life—in the swift current. Other remains of historic sites abound in the refuge, some of which require four-wheel-drive vehicles and/or walking to reach. Inquire at the headquarters about road conditions. **Route 372, P.O. Box 700, Green River, 82935; (307) 875-2187.**

Where to Stay

Accommodations

Sweet Dreams Inn—$$–$$$

Each of the 30 rooms at this inn are individually decorated. No run-of-the-mill motel furniture here! The inn features suites with whirlpool tubs, rooms with unique showers (to say the least), and a TV. Extra phone jacks let you plug in your laptop. There's also a full-service restaurant and lounge, and an arcade for kids. Handicapped accessible. Pets allowed. **1410 Uinta Drive, Green River, 82935; (307) 875-7554.**

Camping

In the National Forests

Buckboard Crossing at Flaming Gorge, 25 miles south of Green River on Hwy. 530, provides water, restrooms, an RV dump station, and camping pads that range from 21 to 70 feet. The marina next to the campground carries fuel and convenience items and has a public shower and a boat ramp. Open from May 1 to September 8 by reservation. To make reservations, call **(887) 833-6777.**

In the National Parks, Monuments, and Recreation Areas
(See Boating, above.)

Bureau of Land Management (BLM) Land
Fontenelle Reservoir offers four improved campgrounds with a total of 71 sites for tents and trailers, parking, shelters, grills, picnic tables, modern restrooms, and a boat ramp. Six miles north of the dam on the west side of the reservoir, you'll find **Fontenelle Campground. Weeping Rock Campground** lies below the dam on the west side of the Green River. **Tailrace** and **Slate Creek Campgrounds,** which also offer dispersed primitive camping (no maintenance and no water), are also located below the dam. Closes early October until early May (depending on weather). **Kemmerer Office of the BLM, 312 Hwy. 189 North, Kemmerer, 83101; (307) 828-4500. Website: www.blm.gov.**

Private Campgrounds and Cabins
Tex's Campground supplies sites for trailers and tents, showers, and laundry facilities. Open May 1 until October 1. Some off-season, weather permitting. **Hwy. 374, Green River, 82935; (307) 875-2630.**

Where to Eat

Embers Family Restaurant—$–$$
Open daily 6 A.M. to 10 P.M. for a hearty breakfast, hot or cold lunches (even a sack lunch to go), and an Embers steak dinner. Children's menu. Old-fashioned soda-fountain drinks. **95 East Railroad, Green River, 82935; (307) 875-9983.**

Services

Visitor Information

Green River Chamber of Commerce, 1450 Uinta Drive, Green River, 82935; (800) FL-GORGE (354-6743) or (307) 875-5711.

21

Laramie

Laramie, the "Gem City of the Plains," is a university town, but it has a frontier past that's about as Wyoming as it gets—everything from vigilance committees to gambling halls to hangings to Grandma Swain. On September 6, 1870, at age 70, Louisa A. "Grandma" Swain became the first woman to cast her vote in a national election. At least one of the vigilante hangings took place downtown with "Big Steve" strung up on a telegraph pole. See where a lot of local history happened by taking the historic architectural walking tours of the downtown area. A free booklet is available through the chamber of commerce, **(800) 445-5303.**

History

A trapper named Jacques La Ramee wandered through the lush valley in 1866. A corrupted version of his name resulted in many things in Wyoming being called "Laramie." (See Fort Laramie for more about Jacques.) Originally, the locale bore the name "Fort John Buford." That was a year before the railroad moved into the valley. At some point, the place became known as "Fort Sanders," after Brigadier General William P. Sanders, before it eventually took on its current name.

Laramie's checkered days of vigilantes resulted in the town becoming the site for the territorial penitentiary. It operated from 1872 until 1902, when the state penitentiary in Rawlins started receiving prisoners. During its tenure, the territorial prison housed a wide variety of outlaws, including Butch Cassidy and Minnie Snyder. She was convicted of manslaughter in 1896, after she killed a man who supposedly was trying to take away the land she owned with her husband. Strangely enough, once the prison closed, the University of Wyoming housed experimental farm livestock behind the prison walls for 60 years (to life?).

Festivals and Events

Jubilee Day Laramie
early July
Celebrate Independence Day and Wyoming Statehood Day at this community-wide event, including a parade, rodeo, downtown arts and crafts fair, the American West Art Show, and, on the Fourth of July, the "Fire in the Sky" fireworks. There's also plenty of country music, a barbecue, free pancake breakfast, a cattle drive, and a rendezvous. Call the **Laramie Chamber of Commerce** for details **(800-445-5303).**

Albany County Fair
early August
This is loads of fun. Demolition derby, 4-H exhibits (don't miss the goats and rabbits), cat and dog shows, handicrafts, foods, target shooting, photography, barrel racing, pedal-power tractor pull (another don't-miss), cook-off contests, and the Great Goat and Llama Trail Challenge, where a trained pack goat and llama compete against each other. Get all the details from the **Laramie Chamber of Commerce (800-445-5303).**

Outdoor Activities

Climbing

Vedauwoo Recreation Area
"Vedauwoo," pronounced VEE-da-voo, is an Arapaho word that means "earthborn." This distinctive rock formation is situated 20 miles east of Laramie just off I-80 in the **Pole Mountain** area of the **Medicine Bow–Routt National Forest.** In addition to camping, picnicking, mountain biking, and hiking, the rocks offer some of the most difficult climbing in the state, ranging from 5.0 to 5.14. Climb at your own risk and with your own equipment.

Biking

Mountain Biking

The gravel roads that head to the lakes off **Hwy. 130** in the **Snowy Range** provide some high-altitude mountain biking with unbeatable views and camping at most of the lakes.

Fishing

The Laramie area denotes fishing with many lakes and streams in the **Medicine Bow–Routt National Forest**, the **Laramie** and **Little Laramie Rivers**, and on **Lake Hattie**. Walleye and native cutthroat trout are local favorites. Ice fish in winter. You can also enjoy great windsurfing on Lake Hattie. In the Snowy Range, you'll find over 80 mountain lakes and numerous trout streams. **Wyoming Game & Fish** will point you in the right direction. **528 South Adams, Laramie, 82070; (800) 843-2352 (in state), (307) 745-4046 (out of state). Website: www.gf.state.wy.us.**

Fly Fishing Connection provides some unique fishing access on four ranch properties in the area with 15 miles of river fishing and two private lakes. Try for brownies, rainbows, and brook trout. **5711 Southview Road, Laramie, 82070; (800) 347-4775 or (307) 745-5795. E-mail: info@flyfishing-connection.com.**

Golf

Enjoy 18 holes and a driving range at the **Jacoby Golf Course, 30th & Willett; (307) 745-3111**. **Oasis Golf** offers miniature golf with one of the world's longest putting greens measuring 144 feet. If that isn't enough, how about a 12-foot waterfall? Open daily, Memorial Day through Labor Day. **15th and Skyline Drive, Laramie, 82070; (307) 745-7574.**

Hiking and Backpacking

In 1909 forest ranger J. H. Mullison described the terrain in the Medicine Bow Peak area of the **Snowy Range**: "Canyons and gorges are not frequent, slopes are easy, and as a rule streams are slow and traverse broad basins rather than valleys." Trailheads into the Snowy Range take off from **Hwy. 130** and lead to plenty of high-mountain fun. Explore the sub-alpine tundra. Wander through aspen groves. Play in the snow that dots the landscape year-round. Lakes located near the highway offer campgrounds, or you can camp in the backcountry. Check with the forest service office about restrictions and permits. Camping or picnicking within 500 feet of the Snowy Range Scenic Byway between the national forest boundary at Centennial and Road #103 (Cascade North Twin Road) is not permitted outside developed campgrounds.

Geology Museum of the University of Wyoming. Photo courtesy of the Wyoming Division of Tourism.

The **Medicine Bow–Routt National Forest** derives its name from a legend. Indian nations in the area found mountain mahogany in one of the mountain valleys. From it they made exceptionally high-quality bows. Various friendly nations would assemble there annually to construct weapons and hold ceremonies to cure the sick ("making medicine"). White mountain men bastardized the terms, as occurred often in western history, and "making medicine" and "making bows" resulted in their calling the place "Medicine Bow." The national forest provides some excellent short hiking trips. For maps and information, contact the **Medicine Bow-Routt National Forest, 2468 Jackson Street, Laramie, 82070; (307) 745-2300. Website: www.fs.fed.us/mrnf.**

Horseback Riding

Prairie horseback rides, wagon rides, and ride packages are available through **Prairie Rides** from June through mid-October. **190 Sprague Lane, Laramie, 82070; (307) 745-5095.** Rides are also offered through **Two Bars Seven Ranch (307-742-6072)** south of town. Each ride lasts about two hours, with two rides a day. You need to reserve a day or two ahead in summer.

Skiing

Downhill Skiing

Thirty-two miles from Laramie or just five from Centennial, ski 25 powder trails at the **Snowy Range Ski and Recreation Area**. Although it is primarily for intermediate skiers, this ski area offers some excellent long beginner runs and a few black diamonds. Snowboarders will enjoy Renegade Park, designed just for you. Five lifts. Ski and snowboard rentals, ski school, plus guided snowmobile tours. A children's ski and snow play school is also available. Lifts run from 9 A.M. to 4 P.M., late November through late spring, depending on the weather. **6416 Mountain Mist Court, Laramie, 82070; (800) GO-2-SNOW (462-7669) or (307) 745-5750, fax (307) 745-**

4113. **E-mail: skisnowy@aol.com. Website: www. snowyrange. com.**

Cross-Country Skiing

Nordic skiing is easily accessed throughout the Snowy Range Ski and Recreation Area into Medicine Bow–Routt National Forest's maintained trails at no charge. **Medicine Bow–Routt National Forest, 2468 Jackson Street, Laramie, 82070; (307) 745-2300.** You can rent skis from **Fine Edge, 1660 North Fourth, Laramie, 82070; (307) 745-4499.**

Seeing and Doing

Ames Monument

From the **Vedauwoo Exit**, turn south and view this 60-foot-high pyramid. The Union Pacific (UP) had the monument constructed in 1882, commemorating Oliver and Oakes Ames's contributions to the construction of the first transcontinental railroad—in spite of allegations of the brothers' misappropriations of funds. In addition, it pays tribute to the one-time railroad town of Sherman.

Lincoln Monument

The nation's first transcontinental road, called the Lincoln Highway, was completed during 1923 and paralleled the first transcontinental railroad, taking it through Laramie. In 1959, a Wyoming philanthropist named Dr. Charles Jeffrey commissioned construction of the 12.5-foot-tall bronze bust to commemorate the 150th anniversary of President Abraham Lincoln's birthday. Jeffrey had it erected on the road's highest elevation at Sherman Hill, 10 miles from town. However, when the interstate was built through there 10 years later, the 2,000-pound sculpture and its 30-foot granite base had to be moved 1 mile to its present location. The design and creation belong to Robert Russin, considered Wyoming's best-known sculptor and a former University of Wyoming art professor. Head east out of Laramie on **I-80** to the **Summit Rest Area and Visitors Center**. Open daily May through October.

Museums

Laramie Plains Museum

This elegant example of a Victorian home was built in 1892 by one of the first settlers in town. The house has been used in different ways since its construction. The original owner wanted it to appear worthy enough to house a governor—which he hoped to become. It was elaborately furnished and equipped with electricity and central heating, but it never became the governor's mansion. Next, it became a girls' boarding school. Then it was vacant and vandalized and almost turned into a parking lot. The community, however, saved it by raising enough money to turn it into a museum. It is well worth taking a guided tour. Kids are welcome. Open seven days a week in summer, open weekdays in winter, closed from mid-December through the end of January. Call for hours. Groups can make special arrangements by calling ahead. Small fee. **603 Invinson, Laramie, 82070; (307) 742-4448**.

University of Wyoming Art Museum

The building that houses this museum is a work of art in itself. Antoine Predock designed it to reflect Wyoming's spirit and history. Exhibits in the nine galleries include contemporary art, art from the eighteenth through twentieth centuries, Native American displays, and western memorabilia. The building also houses the American Heritage Center, a research facility with an extensive collection of family papers, historical documents, and rare photographs. Closed Monday, open Tuesday through Friday from 10 A.M. to 5 P.M., open Saturday from 10 A.M. to 5 P.M., and open Sunday from noon to 4:30 P.M. Free admission. Located on the University of Wyoming campus in the Centennial Complex. **2111 Willett Drive, P.O. Box 3807, Laramie, 82070; (307) 766-6622, fax (307) 766-3520.**

Wyoming Children's Museum and Nature Center

Hands-on exhibits mean lots of fun and discovery as young visitors explore the arts, humani-

Getting There

Laramie spreads out over the plains, 50 miles west of Cheyenne on I-80. You can fly into the **Laramie Regional Airport (555 General Brees Road, 307-742-4164)** via **United Express (800-241-6522).** Several companies rent cars at the airport. **Greyhound (800-231-2222** or **307-742-9663)** arrives at **4700 Bluebird Lane.** There is no local taxi service.

ties, and sciences. Learn about the Oregon Trail of the 1850s, sit in a Plains Indian tepee, take a GeoSafari. Plenty of programs, performances, and special activities for kids 3 through 12 and their families. Open Tuesday through Thursday and on Saturday. Call for hours. Small fee. **421 South 2nd Street, P.O. Box 51, Laramie, 82070; (307) 745-6332.**

25

Laramie Plains Museum. Photo courtesy of the Wyoming Division of Tourism.

Historic downtown Laramie.

Nici Self Museum

Experience Centennial's mining, ranching, lumbering, and railroad lifestyles through the museum's exhibits in the 1907 railroad depot. Open July 4 through Labor Day Friday through Monday. Call for hours. **Route 130, Centennial, 82055; (307) 742-7158.**

Scenic Drives

Snowy Range Road

Designated the nation's second scenic byway, **Hwy. 130** (known locally as the **Snowy Range Road**) leaves from historic downtown Laramie, elevation 7,165 feet, and heads to Centennial, elevation 8,076 feet, nestled at the base of the Snowy Range. Built in the 1870s as a wagon road, this route will give you a good taste of the meaning of the "Laramie Plains." It stretches for seemingly endless miles to the far mountains' edge—the heartland of the grassy plains and the true home of the cattle spread. Here animals survived winter incredibly well because the lush grass is more accessible during the snow months.

Eleven miles west of town, you'll cross paths with the Overland Trail. Ruts from the wagon traffic of the stagecoaches of the 1850s and the 1860s owned by the notorious Ben Holladay remain visible today. Getting closer to Centennial, the terrain becomes more mountainous with classic stands of pines and the hint of cold air in the breeze. The highway winds right through the heart of this quaint mining town founded in 1876.

Above the town, the road climbs into the mountains and enters the Medicine Bow–Routt National Forest. Five miles from Centennial sits the Snowy Range Ski and Recreation Area. Winter comes early in the Snowy Range. Generally this road closes just past this point in October and doesn't reopen until late May or in June. If you want to go "over the top" at the pass at Libby Flats, 10,830 feet above sea level, plan a summer trip. Words can't describe the incredible vistas seen from the summit. However, it may be snowing up there, even in the height of summer—they didn't call it the Snowy Range for nothing, you know! Bring a jacket. On clear days you can see the Zirco Wilderness in Colorado and the 12,000-foot towers of the Medicine Bow Peak.

On the descending side, you pass glaciers and glacier-cut lakes. The stark jutting rocks and brilliant blue waters will leave you breathless. Farther down, the forest gives way to ranch lands in the Upper North Platte River Valley, home of excellent trout fishing and rafting. Hwy. 130 turns right and goes to Saratoga, while left takes you on Hwy. 230 to Encampment.

Where to Stay

Accommodations

Brooklyn Lodge B&B—$$$$

Hoot Jones and Hattie Jones, friends of Buffalo Bill Cody, built the lodge now on the National Register of Historic Places at 10,200 feet from hand-hewn logs and used native stone in the fireplace. With only two rooms available (shared bath), make reservations well in advance. Other meals can be arranged for an additional fee. Children allowed. You can board your horse here, too, but not other types of pets. Nonsmoking establishment. **P.O. Box 292, Centennial, 82055; (307) 742-6916 or (307) 745-7874. E-mail: botycorbin@juno.com. Website: www.members.aol.com/botycorbin.**

Annie Moore's Guest House—$$$

Located next to the University of Wyoming, the house was built around 1910 by a rancher named Sayer Hansen. A post-Victorian Princess Anne-style house, it served as a sorority in 1928 and 1929 before becoming the residence and boardinghouse of Mrs. Annie Moore. "Aunt Annie," a widow, lived in the basement, rented out the upper floors, and served six meals a day to 50 or more people on the main floor. Many college students worked their way through school waiting tables or washing dishes for meals at Aunt Annie's between 1935 and 1949, when she retired. Enjoy cozy quarters amid antique furnishing in three guest rooms with shared baths. Each room has its own sink. Continental-plus breakfast. Smoke-free. No pets other than the resident cat. **819 University Avenue, Laramie, 82072; (800) 552-8992** or **(307) 721-4177.**

Prairie Breeze B&B—$$$

This Victorian classic built in 1888 originally belonged to the first secretary of the University of Wyoming. The B&B maintains the house's nineteenth-century charm with period antiques right down to the wallpaper. Four rooms each have a private bath. Kids (even babies) and pets are welcome, with prior arrangements. You'll find two dogs in residence that are quite popular with the guests, who even send the dogs postcards from home. Wake up to a hearty breakfast of homemade baked goods and fresh juices, or maybe a cinnamon waffle on Sunday. One block from the university. **718 Ivinson Avenue, Laramie, 82070; (307) 745-5482, fax (307) 745-5341. E-mail: prairiebrz@vcn.com.**

Ist Inn Gold—$$–$$$

Full-service, modern units. Handicapped accessible. Heated outdoor pool. Kids stay free. Pets welcome. **421 Boswell, Laramie, 82070; (800) 642-4212** or **(307) 742-3721.**

Guest Ranches

Vee Bar Guest Ranch—$$$–$$$$

Three months out of the year (summer) the Vee Bar guest ranch requires a three- or six-night minimum stay, with no minimum stay for its B&B. The ranch is located six miles from the Medicine Bow–Routt National Forest, with 800 acres to walk or bike on the ranch. The owners offer all the usual guest-ranch, Wyoming-style fun, but you must be over six years old to ride a horse. You'll eat well with a cooked-to-order buffet. Dinner extra with reservations when in B&B mode, September to May, but it's included during the summer. Stay in the Riverside Suite with two sleeping areas or stay in one of the cabins. Practice your catch-and-release techniques on the creek or stock pond. Go tubing in the Little Laramie River. Work the cattle, ride horses, hike, or just enjoy the hot tub. Near winter skiing and snowmobiling. No pets allowed. Open year-round. **2091 State Hwy. 130, Laramie, 82070; (800) 4-VEE-BAR (483-3227)** or **(307) 745-7036, fax (307) 745-7433. E-mail: Veebar@Lariat.org. Website: www.-vee-bar.com.**

Double Muleshoe Ranch—$$$

Two log cabins have fully equipped kitchen facilities that can sleep up to six. One cabin sleeps four. Both have private baths and no minimum stay. Bring your own food and feel like you've stepped back in time. The ranch, located eight miles south of Centennial, borders the Medicine Bow–Routt National Forest, so there's plenty of great hiking at the base of Sheep Mountain. Fishing or cross-country skiing and snowmobiling are in the area. Not handicapped accessible. No phones or TV. Children welcome. Pets allowed on a leash. **14 Fox Creek Road, Laramie, 82070; (307) 742-5629.**

Camping

In the National Forests

Try some high-mountain camping in the Snowy Range in the Medicine Bow–Routt National Forest. Half a dozen campgrounds located on the lakes are accessed via Hwy. 130. Most are open from late May through October. For location, contact the **Medicine Bow–Routt National Forest, 2468 Jackson Street, Laramie, 82070; (307) 745-2300.** Make reservations at specific campgrounds **(800-280-2267)**.

Private Campgrounds and Cabins

The **Laramie KOA,** just off Exit 310 on I-80, supplies 100 pull-through RV spots, as well as cabins, picnic sites, a tent area, and a rec room. Open April 1 to the end of October. **1271 West Baker Street, Laramie, 82070; reservations (800) KOA-4153, information (307) 742-6553.**

Where to Eat

Cafe Jacques—$$-$$$$

Elegant, fine dining for lunch or dinner can be had here in historic downtown. Delight to a "Banker's Burger" topped with Swiss cheese and sautéed mushrooms or spicy lamb Rappahannock. Open Monday through Saturday from 11 A.M. to 2 A.M. **216 Grand Avenue, Laramie, 82070; (307) 742-5522.**

The Overland Restaurant—$$-$$$

The killer quiche is a must-try! Enjoy the casual atmosphere or the summer day out on the patio. In addition to the homemade quiches, dive into one of the specialty sandwiches, fresh fish, or wild game dinners. Vegetarian selections and kids' meals. Wonderful homemade soups and even a delicious low-fat selection. Open daily, year-round, Monday through Saturday from 7 A.M. to 9 P.M. and Sunday from 8 A.M. to 8 P.M. **100 Ivinson, Laramie, 82070; (307) 721-2800.**

The Library Restaurant & Brewing Company—$-$$$

Yes, the decor looks like that of an open, airy, book-lined room with cozy study tables under a sunlight dome. Lunch is served at any time, dinner from 5 P.M. until closing. Veggie lovers will rave over the "Great Expectations" salad. In the sandwich department, try a "Catcher in the Rye" (you guessed it, a classic corned beef on rye). Dinner is definitely "The Godfather," penne pasta sautéed with a trilogy of peppers, prosciutto, and peas. And don't miss a "Great Gatsby" cheesecake topped with shaved chocolate or strawberry sauce. From the brewing company you might want to experience Dubliners Stout, a traditional stout that is heavily hopped and matches the roasted malts and chocolate flavors nicely. On the lighter side, get an "O.D.B." ("Over Due Brew"), an American-style wheat. Only "growlers" are available to go. Open Sunday through Wednesday from 11 A.M. to 9 P.M. and Thursday through Saturday from 11 A.M. to 10 P.M. **1622 Grand Avenue, Laramie, 82070; (307) 742-0500.**

The Chocolate Cellar—$-$$

This is a chocolate lover's location for take-home treats and lots of imported gourmet goodies. Indulge in a chocolate map of Wyoming! Open year-round Monday through Saturday from 10 A.M. to 5:30 P.M. **115 Ivinson, Laramie, 82070; (307) 742-9278.**

Services

Visitor Information

Laramie Chamber of Commerce, 800 South 3rd Street, Laramie, 82070; (800) 445-5303 or (307) 745-7339, fax (307) 745-4624. E-mail: lacc@lariat.org.

Medicine Bow

Here's the real thing when it comes to a western town. When you step out of your vehicle, it's like stepping back over 100 years into the past. Main Street is home to the hotel that also houses the saloon and cafe, a handful of stores, trains whistling as they pass through town, and a constant wind that blows the tumbleweeds around. Although the town's history seems inescapably linked to author Owen Wister's novel, *The Virginian*, the railroad kicked off this cowboy legend town 20 years before the author's arrival.

Wister Suite in the Virginian Hotel.

History

During the construction of the Union Pacific (UP), tie hackers floated railroad timber down the Medicine Bow River just east of town. The railroad brought the freight industry to town. In 1869 the U.S. Army established a supply depot at Medicine Bow. Supplies shipped via rail from the East were unloaded in town and transferred to freight wagons bound for Fort Fetterman and the Powder River region. Seventy-five men were garrisoned in town and charged with protecting the station. In the 1870s, cattle ranchers moved into the area. Soon the town boasted stockyards that handled cattle bound for the East. As many as 2,000 head a day were shipped out during the 1870s and 1880s. Then a writer came to town.

Owen Wister brought respectability to novels about the western way of life with the 1902 publication of *The Virginian*. He also put Medicine Bow on the literary map. When he first arrived in Wyoming and Medicine Bow in 1885, he wrote in his journal, "The place is called a town. 'Town' will do very well until the language stretches itself and takes in a new word that fits. Medicine Bow, Wyoming, con-

sists of 1 Depot house and baggage room, 1 Coal shooter, 1 Water tank, 1 Store, 2 Eating houses, 1 Billiard hall, 6 Shanties, 8 Gents and Ladies Walks, 2 Tool houses, 1 Feed Stable, 5 Too late for classification, 29 Buildings in all."

This passage shows up almost word for word in Wister's novel. Fortunately, the novel didn't describe his first night in Medicine Bow. The hotel had no vacancy, so he ended up sleeping on the counter at the general store.

Nowadays, the depot houses the museum. The cabin Wister lived in for a while at Jackson Hole has also been moved to the museum grounds, and the town is a bit larger, but it remains the perfect setting of Wister's novel.

The Virginian not only became a best-seller, it was turned into a play that ran for 138 performances. In 1914, Cecil B. DeMille made the story into a movie. Nine years later, a remake appeared on the screen. In all, three more remakes would continue the screen legend of *The Virginian*. Then from 1962 to 1970, NBC brought Wister's characters to life in the long-running TV series.

Festivals and Events

Medicine Bow Days
late June
Looking for a taste of real western Americana? Catch this celebration. Begin with the parade, complete with rodeo queens and clowns. Dig into the community picnic. Watch the Wyoming Rodeo Association-sanctioned rodeo. Boo the villain and cheer the hero of the melodrama, witness the hanging of Dutch Charlie at high noon. (He and an outlaw named Big Nose George supposedly murdered two deputies. Neither received a trial before hanging.) Or dance the night away. Don't miss the egg-tossing and wheelbarrow races or the "bull chip throwing" contest. Round it all off with the pie-eating contest. Get the schedule from the **Medicine Bow Area Chamber of Commerce, P.O. Box 456, Medicine Bow, 82329**; or call the **Medicine Bow Days Committee** at **(307) 379-2571**.

Seeing and Doing

Dinosaurs

Como Bluff
Due to the accessibility of the Jurassic Morrison Formation (river sediments 180 million years ago that rapidly buried the dinosaurs, preserving them in this bluff), more large dinosaur fossils have been dug out of the bluff than at any other Rocky Mountains site. Just looking at the east-west–running bluff, it's hard to imagine this was once the site of a full-scale feud—not over the usual western themes of water, grazing, or land ownership but over dinosaurs. In 1877, paleontologist Othniel Charles Marsh (the first professor of paleontology in the nation) opened several quarries at Como Bluff, unearthing several tons of high-quality dinosaur skeletons. News of a brontosaurus find brought Edward Drinker Cope. In the worst claim-jumping tradition, Cope and his crew staked out their own quarry at Como Bluff. The two men became bitter enemies, each trying to outdo the other. Sabotage and fighting abounded between the two camps. They dug a total of 14 complete dinosaur skeletons and a variety of other mammal bones out of Como Bluff. Today, all the fossils on the surface of the bluff have been removed and are housed in museums around the world. **County Road 610 (Marshall Road)**; no phone.

Fossil Cabin
Como Bluff is also the location of the world's oldest house, according to the owner. It was constructed out of dinosaur bones and is, therefore, millions of years older than conventional housing materials. It's now a private museum. You'll find it seven miles east of town on **Hwy. 30**.

Museums

Medicine Bow Museum
Located in the historic railroad depot building, the museum houses an interesting collection of railroad office equipment, World War I memorabilia, old-fashioned kitchens, rare books on Wyoming, and Owen Wister's cabin. It was relocated to the site from Jackson Hole as part of Wyoming's centennial celebration in 1990. Wister and his family spent many summers in the cabin. Be sure to take the time to tour this museum. It's full of little surprises. Open Monday through Friday, Memorial Day to Labor Day; hours depend on volunteers. **Main Street, Medicine Bow, 82329; (307) 379-2383**.

Nightlife
Diplodocus Bar
"The Dip Bar," as the locals call it, is about as authentic a Wyoming bar as you'll find. What

makes it unique is that it has what the chamber of commerce calls "the world's largest jade bar." The bar is a slab of jade, 40 feet in length, cut from a 4.5-ton chunk of the semiprecious stone found near Rock Springs. By the way, the Diplodocus was named after a type of dinosaur remains found in the area. Stop in and see it! Open Monday through Saturday from 10 A.M. to midnight, closed Sunday. **202 Lincoln Highway, Medicine Bow, 82329; (307) 379-2312.**

Getting There

About 60 miles northwest of Laramie, **Hwys. 30 and 287** run right through downtown Medicine Bow. Heading through Medicine Bow rather than going west on I-80, you will see some pretty countryside, ranches and rangeland, and millions of years of geologic history. **Greyhound** stops in town, and there is a 4,000-foot airstrip with no commercial service.

Where to Stay

Accommodations

The Virginian Hotel—$–$$$
In this world of chain motels where every room looks just like every other one, the Virginian Hotel stands out as a truly unique and very Wyoming place to spend the night. Built during 1911 by Medicine Bow's first mayor, the four-story structure once stood as the largest hotel between Denver, Colorado, and Salt Lake City, Utah. The historic rooms on the second and third floors take you back a century. All are furnished in a variety of antique pieces, with hardwood dressers, brass beds, and hardwood closets. The Owen Wister Suite and the Judge Garth Suite remind you of old-world elegance. Rooms in the original hotel have baths but share toilets. Rooms in the new addition are modern but not nearly so interesting. Unoccupied rooms are open for visitors to wander through and soak up the history. **Main Street, P.O. Box 127, Medicine Bow, 82329; (307) 379-2377.**

Where to Eat

The Virginian Hotel—$–$$$$
You can get a great stick-to-your-ribs breakfast or lunch in the cafe, and the Owen Wister Dining Room seats approximately 30 people for dinner. It's elegantly furnished with velvet draperies; oak and mahogany dining tables and chairs; a sideboard and china closet; chandeliers; white, maroon, and gold medallion wallpaper; and a photographic portrait of the famous author. Hearty, wholesome meals. Open daily 6 A.M. to 9 P.M. **Main Street, P.O. Box 127, Medicine Bow, 82329; (307) 379-2377.**

Services

Visitor Information

Contact the **Medicine Bow Area Chamber of Commerce, P.O. Box 456, 82329;** no phone. You can also request information from the **Rawlins-Carbon County Chamber of Commerce, 519 West Cedar, P.O. Box 1331, Rawlins, 82301; (800) 228-3547** or **(307) 324-4111.**

Rawlins

Walking through the downtown streets of Rawlins, you'll see the impact of the victors and the defeated in the economic expansion and contraction that prevailed throughout the town's history and much of the West.

On the military's survey for the railroad in 1867, Major General John A. Rawlins and his soldiers discovered a rarity on the sage-filled plains they traveled—an alkali-free spring that provided good drinking water. According to some accounts, after the general declared, "If anything is ever named after me, I hope it will be a spring of water," the commander of the expedition promptly marked the area "Rawlins Springs" on the maps. Other sources claim an early trapper called "Rawlins" or "Rawlings" gave the spring its name. Either way, the rail line the men had been sent to survey reached Rawlins Spring in 1868, giving birth to the town. When citizens incorporated it 18 years later, they shortened the name to Rawlins.

History

This "end-of-the-line town" thrived as a crossroads for supplies headed for the Wind River Indian Reservation in the north, the Ute White River Agency to the south in Colorado, and to far western points, first via the railroad and more recently the interstate.

Rich deposits of copper, coal, and iron brought entrepreneurs. When John C. Dyer discovered red hematite ore, his manufacturing of "Rawlins Red" paint at the Metallic Paint Company in the early 1870s contributed to the community's budding economy. A color still used today, "Rawlins Red" has coated many a barn, railroad car, and even the Brooklyn Bridge.

In spite of such business advances, the town remained a small oasis of civilization in a vast wilderness. In June 1873, the citizens of Rawlins received a pointed reminder that they still lived on the frontier. A raiding party of Arapaho warriors tried to steal some horses at the slaughter pens. The group wounded one settler just outside of town. The local sheriff immediately gathered together a posse that gave chase, killing four of the Indians. The incident turned into the so-called "Rawlins Massacre." ("Massacre" is usually the term applied when the Indians are victorious.) Regardless of who the townspeople claimed won the incident, a company of the Second Cavalry was stationed in town to protect the peace. Following the "Meeker Massacre" on the Ute White River Agency on September 24, 1879, Rawlins swelled again with an active military presence.

Next the cattle, then the sheep industries spread through the region, as did the population. Rawlins soon became a major wool-gathering and shipping center. Sheep ranches grew up along the railroad right-of-way and helped to keep the area alive during the lean years of the cattle industry after the Blizzard of 1886.

Two years later the town became the site for the state penitentiary, and Rawlins developed around and eventually surrounded the prison. Beginning about 1900, the buildings that would become the current Downtown Historic District started popping up on the horizon. Many of the structures utilized local materials, such as stones from the quarry north of town.

These thriving businesses drew more people to the town, which in turn affected the Union Pacific (UP) Railroad. Increased use of the rail line necessitated upgrading the depot, first built in 1868. The new brick and granite depot, completed in 1901, symbolized Rawlins's growing wealth and importance for nearly half a century. Elegantly designed, it housed segregated waiting rooms for men and women, a ticket lobby, ticket office, telegrapher's desk, restrooms, baggage room, and later a restaurant and lunch counter. The building is currently under extensive renovation and will again be a showpiece of history.

About the time of the railroad's decline, oil and gas fields started producing near Rawlins, with pipelines running into town. Fluctuating with the energy industry, Rawlins has managed to maintain its historic role as a cross-roads for commerce, ranching, and those just passing through on their way to other western destinations.

Festivals and Events

Old West Summerfest
mid-August
Held at the Frontier Prison, you can experience a variety of games, all sorts of food, a chili cook-off, arts and crafts booths, an art show, stagecoach rides, live music, tours of the prison, dancing, fireworks, and outhouse races! Contact the **Frontier Prison** for all the details and dates. **500 West Walnut, Rawlins, 82301; (307) 324-4422. E-mail: markset@trib.com.**

Outdoor Activities

Fishing

The reservoir at **Seminoe State Park,** located 40 miles northwest of town, provides 180 miles of shoreline and some of the best brown and rainbow trout fishing around—good wall-eyes, too, as well as ice fishing in winter. The largest of the state park reservoirs, Seminoe holds water from the North Platte River, up to 167 feet deep at the face of the dam. The park, as well as the nearby mountain range, takes its name from the corrupted version of a French trapper called "Basil Cimineau Lajeunesse." Boat ramps, picnic areas, playgrounds, and camping facilities dot the shore. **County Road 351, Rawlins, 82301; (307) 320-3013.**

Golf

Set amid the plains is nine-hole **Sinclair Golf Course (307-324-3918).** The North Platte River, which runs next to the course, supplies an oasis of green to play on. Open mid-April through mid-October.

Frontier Prison.

Seeing and Doing

Fort Fred Steele State Historic Site

Unlike other forts around Wyoming, few of Fort Steele's buildings remain intact. Those that still stand are too unstable to enter—mute testament to the passing of an era. Established on June 20, 1868, the fort lasted 18 years before the War Department deactivated it and sent the troops to other military facilities around the nation. Existing structures include the powder magazine, the bridge tender's house, the chimneys from the five enlisted-men's barracks, and the cemetery—minus its residents: The soldiers' and their dependents' graves were moved to Fort

McPherson National Cemetery in Nebraska during 1892. Open May 1 through September 15, dawn to dusk.

Museums

Frontier Prison

In preparation for statehood, the Wyoming territorial legislature voted to relocate the penitentiary to Rawlins in 1888. The facility, constructed of native sandstone, was supposed to cost $70,000. Originally laid out on 65.31 acres of land well north of town, the prison suffered from financial problems and structural changes that eventually brought expenditures up to $250,000 and delayed its opening until December 17, 1901. On that day, 40 prisoners were transferred from the old territorial prison in Laramie. They arrived in a specially prepared, converted baggage railcar called the "Jail Car." Forty more came the next day. Within three years the 104 cells brimmed with prisoners. Thirty-two more cells were built, but conditions didn't exactly improve.

Inmates referred to the prison as the "dungeon-house." The penitentiary opened without electricity or running water. Hot water was finally installed in 1978, three years before the Old Wyoming State Penitentiary closed its doors. Today, this institution, known as "Frontier Prison," offers visitors a tour through the spartan environment of cold, tiny cells that housed cattle rustlers, train robbers, and horse thieves from the turn of the century. Open daily during the summer call for hours or special arrangement out of season. **500 West Walnut, Rawlins, 82301; (307) 324-4422.**

Carbon County Museum

One of the most interesting items found at this small museum is the 1920 hook-and-ladder truck. You'll also find western lifestyle artifacts, such as a sheep wagon and cowboy gear. This free museum is open between May 1 and September 30 on Monday through Friday from 10 A.M. to 12 P.M. and 1 P.M. to 5 P.M., and between October 1 and April 30 on Monday, Wednesday, and Saturday from 1 P.M. to 5 P.M. **904 West Walnut, Rawlins, 82301; (307) 328-2740.**

Where to Stay

Accommodations

Bit O Country B&B—$$–$$$

Relax in one of two rooms with private bath in this 1903 Victorian mansion. For many years in the 1920s and beyond, the house was a series of apartments; it was recently restored to a single dwelling. You'll enjoy the close proximity of the historic downtown. Full buffet-style breakfast. No pets allowed, but you can arrange kenneling. No handicapped access. Discounts available, call for details. **221 West Spruce Street, Rawlins, 82301; (888) 328-2111** or **(307) 328-2111. Website: www.bandbonline.com.**

Rawlins Motel—$$

Some rooms are equipped with microwaves and refrigerators in this older-style but comfortable motel. Pets allowed for an extra fee. **905 West Spruce Street, Rawlins, 82301; (307) 324-3456.**

Camping

In Wyoming State Parks and Recreation Areas

Two campgrounds in **Seminoe State Park** offer shoreline camping at the reservoir. Contact the park on **County Road 351** for all the details; **(307-320-3013).**

Rawlins train depot.

Where to Eat

The Aspen House—$$-$$$$

Dine in a luxurious Victorian home built in 1905 by Dr. Raymond Barber. A nineteenth-century atmosphere with antiques, private dining rooms, and excellent service all add to the experience. The food is some of the best Wyoming has to offer. Excellent Italian (especially the cioppino—a stew with seafood), Asian dishes (Lena, co-owner, is a second-generation chef from Singapore), and authentic Cajun foods. Full bar. Vegetarian selections and kids' menu. This is the most popular eatery for many miles. Make reservations for dinner. Open year-round for lunch and dinner from 11 A.M. to 2 P.M. and 5 P.M. to 9 P.M., except on Saturday from 5 P.M. to 9 P.M. only. Closed Monday. **318 5th Street, Rawlins, 82301; (307) 324-4787.**

China Panda—$$-$$$

Head here for truly authentic Chinese food from mild to spicy hot. Try the hot and sour soup—it's excellent. Pleasant Oriental atmosphere with an unusual painted mural that's very Wyoming. Open Monday through Saturday from 11 A.M. to 2 P.M. for lunch and 4 P.M. to 8 P.M. for dinner. **1810 East Cedar Street, Rawlins, 82301; (307) 324-2198.**

Rose's Lariat—$$-$$$

The place resembles a tiny 1950s diner, but it offers dynamite Mexican food—the best you'll find anywhere. The chili verde is hot and hits the spot. Open every day from 11 A.M. to 7 P.M. There's likely to be a line, but it's well worth the short wait. **410 Cedar, Rawlins, 82301; (307) 324-5261.**

Getting There

Rawlins sits in the south-central part of the state along **I-80,** 100 miles west and slightly north of Laramie. It offers no air, taxi, or rental-car services; however, an **air strip** with a 7,000-foot asphalt runway can accommodate a midsize jet. The nearest commercial airport is in Laramie. **Greyhound,** however, does stop in Rawlins.

Services

Visitor Information

Rawlins-Carbon County Chamber of Commerce, 519 West Cedar, P.O. Box 1331, Rawlins, 82301; (800) 228-3547 or **(307) 324-4111.**

Rock Springs

Unlike the other Union Pacific (UP) towns that sprang up along the tracks, coal also played an important role in the development of Rock Springs, as did the water from the "rock springs." The town sits on the edge of the Red Desert, some of the most desolate land in Wyoming because it receives less than 10 inches of rain annually. However, the world's largest herd of pronghorns (antelope) call the Red Desert home.

The chamber of commerce carries maps for a self-guided walking tour of downtown. Not only will you see the distinct personality of the town, but you will discover the location of the butcher shop where Wyoming's infamous Mr. Cassidy got his nickname "Butch."

History

In 1861, Indians forced a Pony Express rider off the route, and he found a spring flowing out of the rocks. A year later, the Overland Stage Company built a stone stage station adjacent to the "rock springs," a sulfurous, bitter-tasting water supply, but one that provided an adequate source of water for travelers on the stage line, as well as Overland Trail emigrants. During the mid-1860s, a pair of stage station managers, Archibald Blair and Duncan Blair, began prospecting 1.5 miles southwest of the station, and the little community of "Blairtown" sprang up after the railroad arrived at the end of the decade.

The Union Pacific needed coal, so with the generous land grant the company received from the government for constructing the railroad, it quickly established UP coal mines and made it hard on the independent mines to compete. The UP charged outrageous freight fees for shipping independently mined coal, but trouble brewed for the UP. In 1875, the miners (at the time, all white) organized a local chapter of the Miners National Association and demanded better pay. The UP refused, and 500 men went on strike, bringing UP mining to a halt. Strikers threatened to set the mines on fire, so the UP asked the governor to send in troops. Soldiers warned strikers not to interfere with the 150 Chinese workers the UP was bringing in to work the mines. Tensions eased, the army left, many strikers returned to work and, with the Chinese, kept the mines operating for the next 10 years. By 1885, the UP controlled the water, the majority of the coal mines, a large part of the labor force (with company-provided housing), the price of shipping coal, and the notorious company store. The fact that the UP had continued to mine coal throughout the union strike appeared to have neutralized any unionized threat, but another problem arose—racism.

When another strike brewed that year, the scapegoat became the Chinese scabs brought in by the railroad. White miners, outnumbered two-to-one by the Chinese workers, rioted. They seized control of Chinatown, burning homes and killing an estimated 28 to 51 Chinese miners. The governor asked the president to send federal troops to restore peace. Soldiers ended up staying for the next 13 years after the "Chinese Massacre" of September 2, 1885.

Festivals and Events

Great Wyoming Polka & Heritage Festival
late August

This is a dance-to-it kind of festival with everybody getting in on the fun. Polka dance bands from around the nation come to play. Get the dates and details from the **Sweetwater County Events Complex, 3320 Yellowstone Road, Rock Springs, 82901; (307) 352-6789.**

Outdoor Activities

Fishing

(See Flaming Gorge Recreation Area in the Green River chapter of this region. It's located 60 miles from Rock Springs.)

Four-Wheel-Drive Trips

Wyoming's **Red Desert** presents a daring, harsh environment for exploration. Few roads exist into this expansion of sandy wilderness, covering more than two million acres. Travel shouldn't be taken lightly. When the area, which receives less than 10 inches of rain per year, does get a shower (which usually comes down in a torrential rain), the two-tracks and gravel "roads" become seas of mud that can leave you stuck until they dry out again. Travel them during the dry season of summer.

The nation's largest pronghorn herd calls the Red Desert home, as do the wild horses. Desert elk (the only herd in the nation) and deer also migrate across sections of this arid land. Sage grouse ("sage chickens" to the locals) strut their stuff by the hundreds in April along the Killpecker Creek area.

The Bureau of Land Management (BLM) oversees the Red Desert. There are no BLM-developed hiking trails or campgrounds in the Red Desert. Contact the BLM about conditions, access restrictions, and information about travel into the desert. Come prepared for lots of wind, harsh sunshine, and no water or other facilities. **Rock Springs District Office of the BLM, Hwy. 191 North, P.O. Box 280, Rock Springs, 82901; (307) 352-0256. Website: www.wy.blm.gov.**

Killpecker Sand Dunes

East of Eden (Wyoming, that is), just off Hwy. 191, will land you in the heart of what the locals simply call "the Sands"—Killpecker Sand Dunes. The colorful name comes from Killpecker Creek, so named by U.S. cavalrymen describing the effects of the minerals in the creek's water. Wind forms and constantly

A colt napping in the sun, one of the wild horses that roam in the Red Desert.

resculpts the dunes, forcing sand particles through a gap in the Leucite Hills, the remains of a Pleistocene volcanic flow roughly a million years old. The dunes stretch out into the basin for over 100 miles, rising as high as 150 feet. The moving sands are second only to the Sahara. To get to the dunes, take Hwy. 191 out of Rock Springs, heading north. Turn east on Tri-Territory Road, known locally as Chilton Ranch Road, about 10 miles out of town. Signs will tell you which areas are restricted from vehicle use.

Rock Formations

Within the Killpecker Sand Dunes region off Hwy. 191, Boars Tusk rises 400 feet into the air. Many Native Americans hold this volcanic monolith sacred.

Dinosaur Exhibit at Western Wyoming Community College. Photo courtesy of the Wyoming Division of Tourism.

Pilot Butte, located just outside Rock Springs off Hwy. 191, received its name because it acted as a beacon in the desert. Local tribes and mountain men used the landmark to orient themselves—as modern hikers do today.

Point of the Rocks along I-80 stood guard over a stage station on the Overland Trail. This rather moth-eaten-looking sandstone formation rises 1,100 feet. The sandstone station still stands. For a short period of time, the notorious Jack Slade ran the station for Ben Holladay. Slade made a reputation for himself as a fighter and man killer. Reportedly, he killed one of his teamsters on the stage route and brutally shot Jules Reni, telling him where each bullet would land before firing each time. Eventually, Montana vigilantes hung him, and his wife buried him in Salt Lake City in a zinc-lined coffin supposedly filled with whiskey.

Golf

Tee off to 18 holes of golf on the **White Mountain Golf Course** at the **Paul J. Wataha Recreation Area Complex (307-352-1415).** Take advantage of the driving range and pro shop. In addition, you'll find tennis courts, ball fields, a fishing pond, a picnic area, and a restaurant.

Seeing and Doing

Wild Horses

The BLM maintains a **holding facility for wild horses** rounded up in the Red Desert. Series of pens and a large corral have, depending on adoptions, a few to a few hundred horses in them. The roundup is generally in March, and the BLM tries to have the horses adopted and out of the pens by mid-December. They work the horses to get them used to humans. Visit them. Take Hwy. 191 south of the BLM office to Lion Kol Road and go 1.75 miles. It's on the left. **Hwy. 191 North, P.O. Box 280, Rock Springs, 82901; (307) 352-0256, ext. 208, fax (307) 352-0329. Website: www.blm.gov.**

Superior

Twenty-three miles northeast of Rock Springs on Hwy. 371 lies Wyoming's "largest ghost town." Superior, in its heyday, had over 3,000 inhabitants, one-tenth of today's population. However, the town appears much as it did during the mining boom days—storefronts on Main Street, handmade stone houses, the Union Hall. Wander through the interpretive park and learn what happened to the Swedish mining community. Handicapped accessible. Other than the two saloons in town, you're on your own for food and fuel. **Town of Superior, P.O. Box 40, Superior, 82945; (307) 362-8173.**

Reliance Tipple

If you don't know what a tipple is, then here's the place to discover it. Another UP mining town, Reliance was settled around the turn of the century. The tipple, one of two remaining in the state, housed coal that was graded and sorted by size, then loaded on railroad cars. A self-guided tour of the tipple will give you a good sense of its history and function. You can wander around the whole place but you can't get inside. Reach the tipple by driving north from I-80 on Hwy. 191. Three miles along the highway, turn east on Reliance Road; approximately 2 miles east on the right. Open daily during daylight hours. Handicapped accessible. Free admission. Write for information to the **Sweetwater County Historical Museum,**

Flaming Gorge Way, Green River, 82935. Reliance Interchange (Hwy. 191); (307) 872-6435 or (307) 352-6715. E-mail: swchm@fiw.net.

Dinosaurs

Western Wyoming Community College (WWCC) maintains one of the largest displays of dinosaur skeletons in this rich paleontologic region. Stroll around a stegosaurus, a Tyrannosaurus rex, a triceratops, a camptosaurus, a plesiosaur, and a huge fossilized fish named "xiphactinus." Fossils, a natural history museum, geolithic samples from the area—the whole ongoing collection is local. Donations are welcome. Tours are available, but you must call ahead, the day before if possible. Allow an hour. Children are welcome. Open school hours daily, year-round, closed holidays. **Western Wyoming Community College, 2500 College Drive, Rock Springs, 82901; (307) 382-1666.**

Museums

Rock Springs Historical Museum

The museum is located in the historic city hall building, and the structure commands as much attention as the museum pieces inside. Designed by M. D. Kern, the striking Romanesque Revival construction immediately grabs your attention. Built in 1894, the rusticated stone, arched windows and doorways, recessed doors, and turrets give the structure the look of a castle—quite unusual for Wyoming. Although the museum has changing exhibits, several mainstays will strike history buffs' fancies. Check out the American Indian trade-blanket collection. Of course, the jail is always popular with people coming to experience the real West and looking for outlaw history. In spite of the fact that "Butch" Cassidy lived in Rock Springs, he never ended up in the jail that's now part of the museum. He missed incarceration there by three years. Explore the small, but excellent, exhibit on the Chinese Massacre. Dig into the coal-mining display with themes related to the industry, the company-town way of life, the UP legacy, ethnic

diversity, and boom-period stories and photos. Open daily during the summer months (hours are changing) and Wednesday through Saturday from 10 A.M. to 5 P.M. the rest of the year. No admission charge. **201 B Street; mailing address: 212 D; Rock Springs, 82901; (307) 362-3138.**

Where to Stay

Accommodations

The Inn at Rock Springs—$$–$$$

Tour the lobby, and soak up the western atmosphere in the newly remodeled Wild West Museum. Swim in the indoor pool or relax in the spa. **2518 Foothill Boulevard, Rock Springs, 82901; (800) 442-9692 or (307) 382-9600, fax (307) 362-8846.**

Camping

Private Campgrounds and Cabins

Rock Springs KOA offers cabins, restrooms with hot showers, 106 pull-through sites, tent sites, convenience store, laundry, playground, heated pool, hot tub, and horse corrals. Children under six stay for free. Open April 1 through October 15. **86 Foothill Boulevard, Rock Springs, 82901; (307) 362-3063.**

Where to Eat

The Log Inn—$$–$$$$

The ambiance makes this an appealing restaurant. It's a genuine log structure, built in 1935.

Steak and fried shrimp rank among the most popular meals. The varied menu also includes pastas, chicken, and daily specials. The most unique dish has to be the deep-fried lobster tails—you have to taste them to appreciate the full, delicious effect! Open daily from 5:30 P.M. to 10 P.M. for dinner, except for major holidays. **12 Purple Sage Road, Rock Springs, 82901; (307) 362-7166.**

Ted's Supper Club—$$–$$$
If you thought there's only one way to fry a chicken, then try Ted's version. Steak lovers will enjoy a feast: steak marinated in garlic and soy sauce. A family-owned restaurant since 1960, Ted's is now into its second generation. Homey atmosphere. Great service. Open from 5:30 P.M. to 10:30 P.M. for dinner only, Monday through Saturday, closed Sunday, year-round. **9 Purple Sage Road, Rock Springs, 82901; (307) 362-7323.**

Services

Visitor Information
Rock Springs Chamber of Commerce, 1897 Dewar Drive, P.O. Box 398; (800) 46-DUNES (463-8637) or (307) 362-3771.

40

Saratoga and Encampment

Woodchoppers Jamboree. Photo courtesy of the Wyoming Travel Commission.

Although they are two distinctly different communities, Saratoga and Encampment often find themselves grouped together. Parts of their early history mesh, and their economies often intertwine. Indians hunted the forested mountains above and fished the rivers of the Platte Valley long before mountain men wandered through.

Saratoga began as a neutral territory for Native American nations who would come to heal the sick and wounded in the natural hot springs. The first permanent white settlement named the community "Warm Springs" in 1878. By 1884, the town wanted a more sophisticated name and changed it to Saratoga after the resort town of Saratoga Springs, New York.

Encampment saw white trappers working the streams in the valleys of the Sierra Madre Mountains for beaver pelts as early as 1834, calling the region "Camp le Grand," which translates into "Grand Encampment." The town, nestled in the gateway to the Sierra Madre, celebrated its centennial in 1997.

History

Demand for timber brought tie hackers into what is now the Medicine Bow–Routt National Forest around Saratoga and Encampment to cut trees to supply the railroad. The Union Pacific (UP) workers also needed meat. With this in mind, William H. Cadwell homesteaded land near current-day Saratoga's hot springs. However, the hot springs presented different business opportunities. He constructed a bathhouse and two crude lumber tubs, providing meals, hot baths, and a place where folks who came to soak in the springs could spread out their bedrolls.

The first permanent white settlement occurred in the 1870s with the tie-hacking industry in full swing. Ranchers also saw the possibilities of the valley and herded in cattle. But Encampment's big boom came with the discovery of copper. A sheepherder named Ed Haggarty started it all in 1897. He sold his initial claim in 1899 to his partner, George Ferris, for $30,000. At the turn of the century people thought Encampment would become the "Pittsburgh of the West," but the boom went bust in 1913, due to falling copper prices.

Saratoga, incorporated in 1900, experienced its own cycle of boom and bust, driven by copper mining in Encampment, a brief flirtation with gold prospecting in the Snowy Range, and coal extraction in the Hanna basin. Today ranching and tourism sustain both communities.

Festivals and Events

Donald E. Erickson Memorial Chariot Races
mid-February

It's *Ben-Hur* on snow! Well, not exactly. Instead of four horses pulling a Roman chariot, one horse pulls a cutter sled in Saratoga. But the pounding hooves and high excitement remain the same over two days of races with a calcutta (a cowboy auction where you can "buy" the teams) and prime rib banquet to round out the festivities. You'll want to bring a blanket to wrap up in and plenty of something hot to drink. Get dates and details from the **Saratoga-Platte Valley Chamber of Commerce** at **(307) 326-8855**.

Sierra Madre Winter Carnival
early February

Winter weather never stops Wyomingites from having great outdoor fun. Encampment hosts this gala tribute to the season with snowmobile races, snowshoe softball, sledding for kids, a chili dinner, a casino night, and, of course, some good ol' cowboy poetry! Bring your heavy coat, gloves, and a hat that will keep your ears warm, and join in. Call the chamber of commerce for event locations and information at **(307) 326-8855**.

Woodchoppers Jamboree
late June

If you've never seen lumber artists at work, you definitely don't want to miss this celebration of the timber industry. Events include pole climbing, log bucking, timed team sawing competitions for women and men, chopping through logs with axes, and more unusual occurrences such as chainsaw throwing and axe

throwing. In the evenings, boo the villain and cheer the hero in the wonderful locally produced and highly imaginative melodrama at the Historic Opera House. There are also parades, a barbecue, and an afternoon amateur rodeo. Contact the **Encampment-Riverside Lions Club (Encampment, 82325; 307-327-5465),** or call the chamber of commerce at **(307) 215-8855**.

Outdoor Activities

Biking

Mountain Biking

Many of the cross-country ski trails (see below) make perfect mountain-biking trails during the summer. In addition, the base of **Battle Mountain** presents some interesting treks along Great Mountain Falls and Black Hall Mountain Road. Head out Hwy. 70 to Battle Mountain. Also, check out the logging roads around **Hog Park Reservoir,** also out Hwy. 70 to Hog Park Road.

Fishing

The Saratoga Chamber of Commerce claims that it's the town "where the trout leap in Main Street." Well, the **North Platte River** does run right through town and lures fishing enthusiasts from around the world with its 65 miles of blue-ribbon trout fishing for browns, cutthroats, and rainbows. Know why the famed fishing magazine, *Orvis News,* considers the river "one of the fly fishing world's best kept secrets"? Over 2,300 fish per mile. Maybe it has something to do with the fact that it's one of the few rivers in the world that flows south to north. Whatever the case, this river is not stocked. It's one of a few rivers in the United States where you can fish in its natural state: Besides the healthy population of fish, the water isn't dammed for 141 miles.

Saratoga Lake, 1.5 miles north of town just off Hwys. 130 and 230, also supplies some fantastic fishing year-round. A special wintertime draw is the annual Saratoga Lake Ice

Fishing Derby in January. **Platt's Guides and Outfitters, Star Route Box 49, Encampment, 82325; (307) 327-5539. Website: www.ivacation.com/page5642.** offers guided fishing trips into the Medicine Bow–Routt National Forest. (See River Floating, below, for additional guided fishing tours.)

Cast for some dandy brook, brown, and rainbow trout in the **Encampment River** southwest of town on Hwy. 70, known locally as Battle Highway. Private lessons and guided fishing and float trips on the Encampment and North Platte Rivers can be arranged through **Medicine Bow Drifters, 102 East Bridge Street, P.O. Box 1642, Saratoga, 82331; (307) 326-8002. E-mail: jdobson@union-tel.com. Website: www.medbow.com. Hog Park Reservoir** also affords superb fishing, Hwy. 70 to Hog Park Road.

Check with **Wyoming Game & Fish** for current regulations and restrictions. **5400 Bishop Boulevard, Cheyenne, 82006; (307) 777-4601.**

Golf

The golfing at the nine-hole **Saratoga Inn Golf Course** draws top golfers from the world over, with its unsurpassed beauty and challenges galore on the 3,269-yard, par 36 course. Open to the public May 1 through the end of October. Full pro shop. **Pic Pike Road, Saratoga, 82331; (307) 326-5261.**

Hiking and Backpacking

Summer and fall afford the most favorable hiking and backpacking conditions in the high country. Equip yourself for all sorts of backcountry adventures in the **Medicine Bow–Routt National Forest**. Tackle everything from a half-mile jaunt at 10,800 feet on the **Lookout Mountain Trail** up to a 32-mile round-trip along the **Encampment River Trail** and everything in between. Get maps and travel advice from the **Brush Creek/Hayden Ranger District, Medicine Bow–Routt National Forest** at either **Hwy. 130 South, P.O.**

Box 249, Saratoga, 82331; (307) 326-5258; or 204 West Ninth, P.O. Box 187, Encampment, 82325; (307) 327-5481.

Looking for something a little less backcountry? Hike the 0.75-mile trail to the **"Indian bathtubs."** According to legend, Arapaho, Cheyenne, and Ute Indians took advantage of large depressions found in an outcrop of granite near the Encampment River when snow collected and melted into pools deep enough for bathing. The establishment of the trail to the "bathtubs" was part of the Wyoming Centennial celebration. Take Hwy. 230 South to Blackhall Road.

Horseback Rides

Platt's Guides and Outfitters offers day and multiday horsepacking trips into the Sierra Madre Mountains. **Star Route Box 49, Encampment, 82325; (307) 327-5539. Website: www.ivacation.com/page5642.**

River Floating

Thrill to Class III and IV whitewater in **North Gate Canyon**. In addition to seeing an abundance of wildlife, some as elusive as the bald eagle and bighorn sheep, you might spot the Indian petroglyphs. Canoe or raft rentals, as well as guided scenic float or fishing trips, are available through **Hack's Tackle and Outfitters, 407 North First, P.O. Box 1225, Saratoga, 82331; (307) 326-9823.** Half- to full-day guided fishing and scenic trips can be booked through **Great Rocky Mountain Outfitters, Inc., 216 East Walnut Street, P.O. Box 1677, Saratoga, 82331; (307) 326-8750, fax (307) 326-5390. E-mail: grmo@union-tel.com. Website: www.grmo.com.**

Head into some excitement on guided trips and overnight floats, as well as whitewater, scenic, fishing, and draft-fishing trips, plus private trophy pond fishing and five miles of river-leased fishing on the North Platte with **Platte Valley Outfitters, P.O. Box 900, Saratoga, 82331; (307) 326-5750. E-mail: pvo@union-tel.com.**

Skiing

44 Cross-Country Skiing

The Medicine Bow–Routt National Forest maintains separate cross-country skiing and snowmobiling trails. Explore over 6,000 acres of classic winter wilderness terrain. The **Brush Creek District** of the Medicine Bow–Routt National Forest offers several miles of cross-country ski trails and loops, primarily for easy to moderate skiing. The **Drinkard**

The Grand Encampment Museum.

Ridge Loop and the **Drinkard Trail** leading to it travel over steep hills and require more advanced skiing. All trailheads start from the Brush Creek Ranger Station.

Go from easy to very challenging backcountry skiing on the **Slaughterhouse Gulch** and **Bottle Creek Ski Trails**. Take Hwy. 70 for 5.5 miles out of Encampment. The trails begin at the end of the snow-plowed highway. (The forest service recommends the use of U.S.G.S. topographic maps for skiers on the Slaughterhouse Gulch Trail loop as only parts of it are marked.) Beginners will find some splendid cross-country skiing on the **Chimney Park Trail** system. Take Hwy. 230 for 7 miles above Woods Landing. No matter which trail you ski, follow the trail markers and enjoy some gorgeous Wyoming scenery. Perhaps you'll spot a variety of wildlife along the way. Call the **Forest Service district offices** in either Saratoga **(307-326-5258)** or Encampment **(307-327-5481)** for information and ski conditions before heading out.

Snowmobiling

Between the **Sierra Madre Mountains** and the **Snowy Range** you can experience over 411 miles of trails, 216 of them groomed. Peak snow falls from November through late May. Elevations range from 7,000 feet to 11,000 feet. Snowmobile rentals or guided trips are available from **Platte Valley Outfitters, P.O. Box 900, Saratoga, 82331; (307) 326-5750. E-mail: pvo@union-tel.com.**

For guided snowmobile trips (you provide your own machines), try **Platt's Guides and Outfitters, Star Route Box 49, Encampment, 82325; (307) 327-5539. Website: www.ivacation.com/page5642.**

Seeing and Doing

Saratoga National Fish Hatchery

Saratoga's first fish hatchery started in 1906. It moved to the present location in 1915. By the next year, the hatchery released 181,256

Saratoga and Encampment

brook trout into Wyoming's streams. Currently, the hatchery maintains a breeding population of lake and brown trout and houses the endangered Wyoming toad. Every year, millions of trout eggs are shipped to hatcheries around the nation. Open to the public Memorial Day through Labor Day daily from 8 A.M. to 4 P.M., and the rest of the year Monday through Saturday. It's free. **Hwys. 130 and 230, P.O. Box 665, Saratoga, 82331; (307) 326-5662. E-mail: 6ffa_sar@fws.gov.**

Hot Springs

For centuries this hot springs has attracted visitors seeking relaxation and rejuvenation. It's open 24 hours a day, every day, and everyone can enjoy the **Saratoga Municipal Hot Pool,** locally known as "the hot pool," free of charge. According to local history, Native Americans worried that the hot springs would become polluted with evil spirits, as white men moved into the area. Their fears seemed confirmed when the Indians tried to cure smallpox victims from the epidemic of 1874 by dipping the patients in the hot springs for a period of time, then rinsing them in the cold river. This treatment proved ineffective and most of the patients died. After that the natives believed the springs boiled with bad medicine and refused to come near the mineral waters, thus opening up the area to permanent white settlement.

Whites came to William Cadwell's bathhouse to treat "rheumatism, eczema, paralysis, stomach trouble, kidney diseases, nerves, and all forms of blood and skin disease." Whether or not the thermal waters cure all ills, the water temperature of 117 to 128 degrees feels wonderful. The pool sits behind the Saratoga municipal swimming pool at the end of **East Walnut Avenue.**

Museums

Grand Encampment Museum

A dynamite collection of local history, showing the boom-and-bust cycles of copper mining and nineteenth-century ranching and lumberjacking lifestyles of the upper valley,

awaits you in this museum. Wander back through time along the board sidewalk of the pioneer town behind the museum. Guided tours take you into the Lake Creek Stage Station, the one-room schoolhouse at Wolfard, a 100-year-old homestead house, past three towers from the original 16-mile-long aerial tramway that hauled copper ore from the Ferris-Haggarty Copper Mine to town, and much more. All these buildings are authentic and have been moved to the grounds to give you a great glimpse into frontier history. Don't miss the two-story outhouse! The museum also serves as a national repository for forest service artifacts. Check out the Slash Ridge Guard Town and the Webber Springs Guard Station, both relocated to the museum. Open daily from Memorial Day through Labor Day, 1 P.M. to 5 P.M. and some mornings, depending on volunteers. No admission charge. Out-of-season tours arranged by appointment only. **817 Barnett Avenue, P.O. Box 96, Encampment, 82325; (307) 327-5308.**

Saratoga Museum

Housed in the circa 1915 UP Railroad depot that was moved to the present location, the museum displays railroad memorabilia, the geologic history of the Platte Valley, exhibits of fossils, an archaeology room filled with arrowheads and other tools from sites in the Saratoga area, a rich exhibition of western saddles and spurs, dental equipment from 1935 to 1972 that will make you glad the stuff is not used today (like the foot-pedal drill), tie hack tools, a sheep wagon, and a beautiful pavilion presented by the George B. Storer Foundation that has become a popular site for weddings. Open daily Memorial Day through Labor Day, 1 P.M. to 5 P.M., free on Monday. Out-of-season tours by appointment only. **104 Constitution Avenue, P.O. Box 1131, Saratoga, 82331; (307) 326-5511.**

Scenic Drives

Sierra Madre Auto Tour

Discover the **Hayden District** of the **Medicine Bow–Routt National Forest** with the help of a self-guided vehicle tour. Take as little as half a day or make it an all-day trip—you decide. From Encampment, travel 5 miles west along Hwy. 70 to Hog Park Road. This leads to Battle Creek Campground, initially a Civilian Conservation Corps camp during the Great Depression of the 1930s. Workers who stayed there helped construct the Battle Highway. After crossing the North Fork of the Encampment River and passing the beaver ponds of Willow Park, you'll get a great view of Green Mountain from Deadhorse Park. Its barren hillsides are due to poor soil conditions. Halfway House was constructed in 1902 as a stopping point between Encampment and the tie hack camps of the Hog Park region. The road opens onto the broad expanse of Soldier Summit, where soldiers from Fort Fred Steele stood guard while tie hackers cut timber for the UP in 1868. Hog Park Reservoir was created in the 1960s to store water for Cheyenne. See Jessie Mine, one of countless mines located in the region by the end of the 1800s. Then it's on to Commissary Park where as many as 1,000 tie hackers lived and worked at the turn of the century. The trip returns to town along Rim Road and Blackhall Road. Pick up a guide booklet at the **Grand Encampment Museum** or have one sent from the **Hayden District, Medicine Bow–Routt National Forest, P.O. Box 187, Encampment, 82325; (307) 327-5481.**

Melodrama.

Where to Stay

Accommodations

Saratoga Inn Resort and Hot Springs Spa—$$$$

Stay in a haven for trophy fishing, complete with casting instruction if you so desire. Or indulge in a round of nine-hole golf. Play tennis. Soak in the 25-yard-long, on-site, outdoor mineral hot springs pool or in one of five individual pools. Sample one of the beers or root beer brewed at the inn. In the evening, curl up on a feather bed and watch a movie from the inn's selection. In the morning, enjoy the newspaper at your door, followed by breakfast in the dining room. For an additional fee, the sports package includes unlimited fishing, golf, horseback rides (children must be at least 16 years old). Handicapped accessible. No pets. **P.O. Box 869, Saratoga, 82331; (307) 326-5261, fax (307) 326-5109.**

Far Out West B&B—$$$–$$$$

An ideal location on the North Platte River. Stay in the main house in one of two guest rooms upstairs or three in back. There's also a separate cottage in back with a living room, equipped kitchen, and homey porch swing. Every room has its own bath and carries that personal touch of comfort you won't find in a motel. You'll find friendly interaction if you want it, peace and plenty of quiet if you prefer. Luxuriate in the library. Enjoy the large-screen TV and circular fireplace. Take advantage of the exercise equipment. The B&B is within walking distance to everything in Saratoga. Hot tub. Filling, wholesome breakfast. Children are welcome—any age. They will love the Hole-in-the-Wall playroom filled with toys, stuffed animals, puzzles, and books. No minimum stay. Handicapped accessible. No pets allowed, but boarding is available nearby. **304 North 2nd Street, P.O. Box 1230, Saratoga, 82331; (307) 326-5869, fax (307) 326-9864. E-mail: fowbnb@union-tel.com. Website: www.cruising-america.com/farout.**

Hotel Wolf—$$–$$$$

Frederick G. Wolf constructed his two-story red-brick hotel, the tallest building in town, during 1893. The "Grand Old Gal" quickly became a gathering spot for townspeople and tourists and the site of many gala affairs around the turn of the century. Renovated in 1977, the rooms still retain their quaint charm, and all contain private baths. Three suites were added with private sitting rooms. Excellent views. Comfy rooms. No pets allowed. Nonsmoking rooms. Not handicapped accessible. **101 East Bridge, P.O. Box 1298, Saratoga, 82331; (307) 326-5525.**

Grand and Sierra B&B—$$$

Glen Knotwell, a local guide, built this log home by cutting the timbers himself and dragging them out of the forest with his saddle horse. He peeled each log and did all the work on the house himself. It features two bedrooms with king-size beds and private baths and three rooms with semiprivate baths. Soak up the quiet on the deck that overlooks Encampment River Canyon. Relax in the outdoor spa. Staying here is like coming home. Pack, snow-mobiling, and dog-sledding trips can be arranged. Kids and pets allowed. Full country breakfast with homemade pancakes, French toast, and fresh-baked bread. **P.O. Box 312, Encampment, 82325; (307) 327-5200 or (307) 327-5107.**

Guest Ranches

Brush Creek Guest Ranch—$$$–$$$$

Built in the early 1900s, the *Orvis*-endorsed lodge provides a real western atmosphere on a 6,000-acre working cattle ranch. Nestled along the Sierra Madre Range next to Medicine Bow–Routt National Forest, the ranch provides a perfect setting of high-country meadows, prairie sage, and unparalleled stargazing well above the Saratoga Valley. Saddle up and participate in a variety of ranch chores during the summer months. The ranch can also arrange nearby riding, fishing, hiking, and jeep or float trips, with private fishing on three miles of Brush Creek. In winter, climb aboard a dogsled for a day tour, with lunch provided. See the winter landscape via a one-day guided snowmobile tour. Unguided snowmobiling also. Ice-skate on the private pond. Customized packages are available. American plan meals with a touch of the gourmet. Three-day minimum stay in summer, no minimum in winter. Open year-round except for November 15 to December 15. **Star Route Box 10; Saratoga, 82331; (800) RANCHWY (726-2499) or (307) 327-5241, fax (307) 327-5384. E-mail: kblumen@-csn.net. Website: www.duderanch.org/brush-creek.**

Medicine Bow Lodge and Guest Ranch—$$$—$$$$

Relish staying in the forest in renovated log cabins with private baths. Fishing, rafting, and hiking trips or horseback rides are available, as are a sauna, hot tub, and workout cabin. Guided snowmobile tours (with machines provided), and they even have cross-country skis for your use in winter. Handicapped accessible. Three meals are included with lodging. A two-night minimum stay is required on weekends and holidays. Open year-round except for the first three weeks of November. No pets. Group rates for over 25 people. **Star Route 8A, Saratoga, 82331; (800) 409-5439 or (307) 326-5439. E-mail: hpsally@aol.com. Website: medbowlodge.com.**

Camping

In the National Forests

The **Medicine Bow–Routt National Forest** provides several campgrounds. Some are primitive, others offer on-site bathroom facilities, fresh drinking water, and trailer spots. Generally **Battle Creek** is open from Memorial Day through October. Campgrounds at higher altitudes, like **Lake View** and **Lost Creek,** are open mid-June to October, depending on snow. Campgrounds on the **Snowy Range** may not open until July and close at the end of September. For details contact the **Medicine Bow–Routt National Forest District Office, 2468 Jackson Street, Laramie, 82070; (307) 745-2300. Website: www.fs.fed.us/mrnf.** To reserve forest campgrounds, call **(800) 280-CAMP (2267).**

In Wyoming State Parks and Recreation Areas

The **Saratoga Lake Campground** offers electrical hookups, restrooms, picnic tables, and drinking water. Open May 1 through October 30 and during the ice-fishing derby in January. Contact the **Town of Saratoga (307-326-8335)**.

Private Campgrounds and Cabins
Deer Haven RV Park provides large, shady spots along the North Platte River. Open May 1 through October 31. **706 North First Street, Saratoga, 82331; (307) 326-8746. Lazy Acres Campground** offers full or partial hookups for RVs and tent sites on the Encampment River. Showers, dump station, and laundry are also available. Open May 1 through November 1. **Hwy. 230 Riverside, P.O. Box 641, Encampment, 82325; (307) 327-5968.**

Where to Eat

Hotel Wolf Restaurant—$$-$$$$
Prime rib is the staple. Excellent steaks and pastas. Daily specials. Great homemade cheesecake and chocolate mousse. Kids' menu. Handicapped accessible. Summer hours: lunch from 11:30 A.M. to 2 P.M. and dinner 6 P.M. to 10 P.M., Monday through Saturday. Winter hours: Dinner from 6 P.M. to 9 P.M., Monday through Thursday, and from 6 P.M. to 9:30 P.M., Friday and Saturday. Sunday dinner available year-round from 5 P.M. to 9 P.M. **101 East Bridge Street, Saratoga, 82331; (307) 326-5525.**

Saratoga Inn Resort and Hot Springs Spa—$$-$$$$
Two dinning rooms for casual or fine dining. Classically trained chef. Breakfast and lunch buffet from 6:30 A.M. to 10: 30 A.M., lunch from 11 A.M. to 2 P.M., and dinner from 5:30 P.M. to 10 P.M. Handicapped access. **601 East Pic Pike Road, P.O. Box 869, Saratoga, 82331; (307) 326-5261.**

The Sugar Bowl—$-$$
Open daily for breakfast and lunch during the summer from 7 A.M. to 6 P.M. and Monday through Saturday the rest of the year from 7 A.M. to 5 P.M. Enjoy real old-fashioned soda-fountain drinks, tasty breakfast burritos, and taco salads. **706 Freeman, Encampment, 82325; (307) 327-5779.**

Services

Visitor Information
Saratoga-Platte Valley Chamber of Commerce, P.O. Box 1095, Saratoga, 82331; (307) 326-8855.

Oregon Trail Region

Fort Torrington. Photo courtesy of the Wyoming Travel Commission.

49

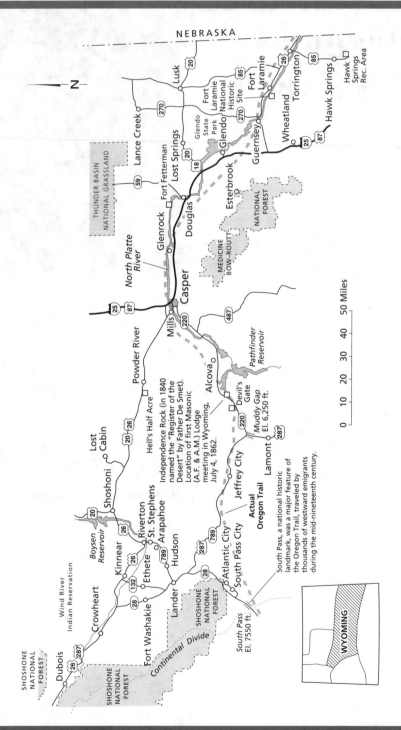

Casper

Nestled in Natrona County, Casper has a population of approximately 47,000, making it the largest city in Wyoming. With its central location, it serves as the state's business center, as well as its main commercial and transportation center. Casper was named after Lieutenant Caspar Collins (with an unfortunate misspelling of Caspar's name). It's a thriving place with big-city excitement and convenience, along with small-town charm, and it holds something for everyone. Contemplative solitude is easily found in the spectacular mountains, plains, rivers, lakes, and abundant wildlife around the city. Visitors can also find endless thrills in a city teeming with exciting things to do and see. Casper is guaranteed to please even the most skeptical of visitors.

History

In 1847, emigrating Mormons were the first to establish a base where Fort Caspar would eventually stand. They constructed and operated the first ferry across the North Platte River, which provided safe passage across the river for travelers and also generated essential revenue for new settlements in the Great Salt Lake Valley in Utah. The military eventually erected adobe buildings, tent barracks, and a telegraph station near the ferry base so troops could be dispatched to protect wagon trains traveling along the Oregon Trail. The base came to be known as North Platte Station.

The region, however, was a place of fierce and bloody sparring between the military and the Indians who lived there. At Sand Creek, Colorado, Colonel John Covington attacked Black Kettle's Southern Cheyenne village of 550 men, women, and children in November 1864, even though the camp was supposed to be under military protection. Most of the inhabitants were massacred. In response, Southern Cheyenne, Arapaho, and Powder

Wagons on the Oregon Trail.

51

River Sioux declared war. "The Bloody Year on the Plains" thus ensued with vigor.

The fighting was brutal and sporadic. During one battle on July 25, 1865, Lieutenant Caspar Collins was ordered to relieve a wagon train surrounded by Indian warriors. Collins thought it folly but obeyed orders and attempted the rescue mission. The young officer led his troops across the Platte Bridge, but before they could even reach the stranded train, they were surrounded by Indian warriors. Lieutenant Collins incurred a hip wound at the start but still attempted to come to the aid of one of his fallen men. He was killed, however, before he could reach the soldier. The battle lasted only 10 minutes, and most of the men were killed. All who managed to es-

Oregon Trail Region

cape ⌐ ⌐turn to the station were wounded. It was four days before troops managed to fend off attacking Indians long enough to return to the battlefield and retrieve the bodies of Lieutenant Collins and his men. All 21 bodies were buried where they lay.

Troops eventually reinforced the then-named Platte Bridge Station, which was renamed Fort Caspar in honor of Lieutenant Collins. The army dismantled and abandoned the site in 1867 and relocated to Fort Fetterman. Indian warriors burned the rest of the station. It wasn't until 1936 that a Works Progress Administration (WPA) crew rebuilt old Fort Caspar on the original site. Today it operates as a national historical site managed by the city of Casper.

The city of Casper itself grew at the terminus of the Fremont, Elkhorn & Missouri Valley Railroad. John Merrill, C. W. Eads, and Eads's children were its first settlers, establishing a townsite on June 8, 1888. Within a week, about 100 settlers were witnesses to the arrival of the first passenger train. Temporary structures or tents with earthen floors were erected quickly. Businesses were set up to haul lumber from Casper Mountain to construct buildings, and lots were sold for $200 to $250 each. The town of Casper was incorporated on May 6, 1889, just 14 months before Wyoming officially became a state. It was already known throughout the region as an oil hub, and from 1894 to 1895, the Pennsylvania Oil and Gas Company built a refinery in the area, capable of handling 100 barrels of oil per day.

With seemingly endless resources that would guarantee prosperity for Casper, its residents had the luxury of turning their attention to cultural and recreational pursuits, something other communities could not do. Electricity became available by 1900 and telephones in 1902. Office buildings, a hospital, hotels, bars, and businesses sprang up rapidly during the turn of the century, along with the arrival of automobiles, firmly linking Casper with the rest of the country.

Casper was a strategically placed settlement. It rested at the point of convergence for the Mormon, Oregon, California, Bridger, and Bozeman Trails, as well as the Pony Express route, and thus came to be known as "The Crossroads to the West." Much of western American history can be told through the lens of Casper, as nearly every emigrant searching for new land and a new life passed through this thriving little town. Much of this trail system, now a national monument managed by the National Park Service, the Bureau of Land Management, and the U.S.D.A. Forest Service, can be experienced while visiting Casper.

Festivals and Events

Cowboy State Games— Summer Sports Festival
mid-June

The first Summer Sports Festival was originally held in Cheyenne in 1986, and since moving to Casper it has grown from a single event with 700 participants to what has become two events, the Winter Sports Festival and the Summer Sports Festival, with 5,000 athletes competing annually. The games provide Wyoming residents an invigorating venue for positive personal development and Olympics-style amateur athletic competition. Both male and female athletes of all ages are welcome. Summer events include archery, canoeing/kayaking, cycling, diving, equestrian events, fencing, golf, judo, shooting, soccer, softball, swimming, tennis, track and field, and others. Come cheer on the athletes or watch a favorite event. **P.O. Box 3485, Casper, 82602; (307) 577-1125, fax (307) 577-8111. E-mail: csg@trib.com.**

Cowboy State Games— Winter Sports Festival
mid-February

The Cowboy State Games—Winter Sports Festival has been an annual event since 1990. Both male and female athletes of all ages can enter, even those from other states who do not have their own winter games competitions. Events include skiing, snowboarding, figure skating, basketball, indoor archery, a four-mile road race, ice hockey, indoor soccer, gymnastics, and others. The games last for four days. Come cheer on your favorite athlete, or enter as one if you're eligible. **P.O. Box 3485, Casper, 82602; (307) 577-1125, fax (307) 577-8111. E-mail: csg@trib.com.**

Central Wyoming Fair and Rodeo
early July

Enjoy fun-filled activities, carnival rides and games, and thousands of interesting exhibits nightly, along with cowboys competing for dominance in the Pro Rodeo & Cowboy Association (PRCA) Rodeo. For over 50 years, Casper's finest cowboys have dazzled the crowds with dangerous stunts to determine who is the best. Food and great midway entertainment even out the daily thrills. **1700 Fairgrounds Road, Casper, 82604; (307) 235-5775, fax (307) 266-4224.**

Powder River Sheepherders Fair, Lamb Recipe Cookoff, and Sheepdog Trials
early July

Visitors can experience a different sort of rodeo, the sheep ranchers' rodeo, where the best of the best compete with pride and sheepdogs are rated according to their herding ability. The skill involved is extensive and will delight those both familiar and unfamiliar with the sport. Hungry visitors can enjoy the best lamb anywhere. **P.O. Box 39, Powder River, 82648; (307) 472-7055, (307) 738-2522, or (307) 876-2778.**

Bear Trap Mountain Music Festival
mid-July

Casper Mountain holds a fantastic, fun-filled, bluegrass music festival for those wanting to experience the tunes held dear by Wyoming residents. Musicians come from all over the country, and the performers vary every year. A mountain bike race is held for those who appreciate the excitement and skill required for the sport. Kids will enjoy participating in the

Getting There

Access Casper via **I-25** (north and south) and **Hwys. 26 and 20** (east and west), 178 miles northwest of Cheyenne. Casper's **Natrona County International Airport** receives daily airline service through **Delta Airlines (800-221-1212** or **307-234-0607)** and **United Airlines (800-241-6522** or **307-472-5310).** A variety of rent-a-car companies are located at the airport. Call for a cab from **Tom's Taxi (307-237-8178).** Bus service is available through **Powder River Transportation (800-442-3682** or **307-266-1904).**

arts and crafts programs. Visitors can eat good food, dance to lively music, and cheer on the mountain bikers, all while surrounded by the spectacular backdrop of Casper Mountain. Bring lawn chairs or a blanket. **Natrona County Road, Bridges, Parks, Drawer 848, Mills, 82644; (307) 235-9311 (office)** or **(307) 235-9325 (information). E-mail: kellye@trib.com.**

PRCA Season Finale Rodeo
late October

The rodeo season rounds out with the last chance for professional cowboys to qualify for the national finals. Visitors can witness the excitement and suspense as the best athletes prove their agility and skill. **Casper Events Center, P.O. Box 140, Casper, 82602; (307) 235-8441, fax (307) 235-8445. E-mail: bobbip@trib.com.**

Outdoor Activities

Biking

Mountain Biking

The BLM has a physically challenging **Mountain Nature Trail** on **Muddy Mountain. Bureau of Land Management, 1701 East E Street, Casper, 82601; (307) 261-7600.**

Oregon Trail Region

Touring

A popular touring trip follows the Oregon Trail, leaving Casper on Hwy. 220 heading west, then taking Hwy. 287, which leads to Lander. Historic sights include Independence Rock, Devil's Gate, Martin's Cove, and Split Rock (see Seeing and Doing, below).

Climbing

Rock climbers will certainly relish the chance to scale the hundreds of feet of vertical walls of **Fremont Canyon**. Expect exceptional routes, some with roofs. Numerous routes are rated at class 5.13 (very difficult). The canyon is at the southwest end of Alcova Reservoir. **Split Rock** on **Hwy. 287** southwest of Casper on the Oregon Trail is also a cherished rock climbing spot. (See Seeing and Doing, below.) Get details, information, and regulations from the **Bureau of Land Management, 1701 East E Street, Casper, 82601; (307) 261-7600.**

Fishing

Part of the Oregon, Mormon, Pony Express, and California Trails runs right through the **North Platte River Recreation Area,** one of the finest in Wyoming. The picturesque river and its lakes accommodate rafters, boaters, anglers, and nature lovers, as well as over 200 species of wildlife. Between Alcova and Casper you'll find 20 public access fishing spots. **Natrona County Parks (307-234-6821)** or contact **Wyoming Game & Fish, 3030 Energy Lane, Suite 100, Casper, 82604; (307) 473-3400. E-mail: bolsen@missc.-state.wy.us. Website: www.gf.state.wy.us.**

Visitors can take advantage of the campgrounds, picnic areas, boat ramps, beaches, and hiking trails at the Bureau of Reclamation's **Alcova Reservoir.** Dinosaur bones that were discovered in the sandstone ledges of the Morrison Formation by fifth-grade science students from Casper can also be seen. Anglers will appreciate the walleye, rainbow, cutthroat, and brown trout available. For more about Alcova and the other reservoirs in the region, contact the **Bureau of Land Manage-**

ment, **1701 East E Street, Casper, 82601; (307) 261-7600.** Boat rentals and personal watercraft are available from **Alcova Lakeside Marina, 24025 Lakeshore Drive, Alcova, 82620; (307) 472-6666.** The marina is open daily April through October.

Flanked by the **North Platte River** and encompassing part of the historic Oregon, Mormon, Pony Express, and California Trails, **Edness Kimball Wilkins State Park** is located just six miles east of Casper. The river and a pond with its sandy beach become a serene escape. A cottonwood grove and open areas serve as optimal habitat for a variety of bird species, including yellow-billed cuckoos, cormorants, bald eagles, golden eagles, sharp-shinned hawks, and 16 species of ducks. Birdhouses and viewing areas allow for leisurely bird watching. Fishing, canoeing, rafting, swimming, and picnicking are also available. Exceptional amenities are also available to disabled visitors, such as a handicapped-accessible fishing pier and 2.8 miles of accessible hard-surfaced paths where wildlife can be observed. Open year-round. **P.O. Box 1596, Evansville, 82636; (307) 577-5150. E-mail: pthomp@missc.state.wy.us.**

Excellent fishing is also available at the **Platte River Parkway** in town, **Pathfinder Reservoir**, 47 miles southwest of Casper along Hwy. 220, and **Gray Reef Reservoir**, 10 miles beyond Pathfinder on County Road 412. The parkway also sports a delightful four-mile paved walking trail and a handicapped-accessible fishing pier.

Guided fly-fishing trips and boat rentals are available through **Wyoming's Choice Inc., 513 North Lennox, Casper, 82601; (307) 234-3870.** Guided fishing trips are available through **Platte River Fly Shop, 7400 Alcova Hwy. 220, Box 3, Casper, 82604; (307) 237-5997. E-mail: Platterat@aol.com.**

Four-Wheel-Drive Trips

You'll need high ground clearance and dry weather, but you can see some prime antelope habitat and high plains vistas on the **Alcova-Seminoe Byway.** Take Hwy. 220 southwest of Casper to Alcova. A locally paved road skirts the Alcova Reservoir, then turns to dirt as it heads south to Seminoe Reservoir. It's 64 miles one-way. Another 35 miles will get you to I-80 near Rawlins.

County Road 319 southwest of Mills traces portions of the Oregon, Mormon, Pony Express, and California Trails. It links up with Hwy. 220 near Martin's Cove. Expect over 30 miles of dirt after leaving the locally paved road.

The BLM oversees a backcountry byway 15 miles east of Casper on Hwys. 20 and 26 called the "South Bighorn Red Wall." Its 100 miles are a mixture of pavement and gravel that loops back to the highway at Waltman. Part of this route offers an alternative that goes up on top of Bighorn Slope where there are two semiprimitive four-wheel-drive campgrounds.

Head out into 200 acres of the **Poison Spider Off-Road-Vehicle Area** located 15 miles west of Casper on **Zero Road.** There are no designated roads and limited two-track use. Get the details from the **Bureau of Land Management, 1701 East E Street, Casper, 82601; (307) 261-7600.**

Golf

Play 27 holes, par 71, on the PGA **Casper Municipal Golf Course.** Lessons are available, as well as a driving range. Relax and replenish at the 19th Hole Restaurant and Lounge. Open March through October. **2120 Allendale Boulevard, Casper, 82601; (307) 234-1037.**

Get a club fitting on a computerized swing analyzer at **Paradise Valley Golf Club.** Tournament and group outings are welcome, as well as out-of-town guests. Guests can practice their swing on the driving range, and items are available at the pro shop. Open year-round except during January. **70 Magnolia, Casper, 82604; (307) 237-3673 or (307) 234-9146.**

Hiking and Backpacking

The **Lee McCune Nature Trail,** located on **Casper Mountain,** offers a unique hiking experience for the visually impaired. The trail runs along Elkhorn Creek in Skunk Hollow. A rope handrail and braille interpretive stations (also in English) help hikers interact with Wyoming's wild nature.

For a different type of hike, try the **Cottonwood Creek Dinosaur Trail** on the south side of **Alcova Reservoir.** Travel from the Sundance Era to the Morrison Formation, encompassing over 240 million years of the state's geological history.

Horseback Riding

An interesting way to get a better look at the scenery along the base of **Casper Mountain** is to take an hour or two-hour trail ride at **Happy Trails Stables.** Ride through quiet, secluded terrain where no vehicles are allowed. Thrill at the close-up glimpses of wildlife, especially the antelope. The season lasts from May 1 to November 1. **5223 Squaw Creek Road, Casper, 82604; (307) 234-7484 or (307) 235-5338. E-mail: happy@trib.com.**

Horseback or wagon rides along historic trails are available from **Historic Trails Expeditions.** Try three- to four-hour day rides, overnight, or multiday trips up to five days, as well as gold rush wagon train rides, or join the week-long wagon train trip over the South Pass. **P.O. Box 428, Mills, 82644; (307) 266-4868 or (307) 266-2746, fax (307) 237-6010. Website: www.HTrails.caspers.net.**

Skiing

Downhill Skiing

Winter can be fun and exciting while skiing at **Hogadon Ski Area.** Just a few minutes away from Casper, Hogadon offers competitive group rates, great runs for beginners and experts alike, double chairlifts, state-of-the-art snowmaking, a full lunch service and snack bar in the lodge, equipment rental, and ski lessons for all ability levels and age groups. Families can embark on a special package called the "Weekend Adventure," and young children, ages four to six, can participate in a special midweek class for four weeks. Weekdays are especially good for hitting the slopes when crowds are minimal. The season generally

55

Skiing at Hogadon. Photo courtesy of the Wyoming Division of Tourism.

opens late November, weather permitting, until the end of March or early April, Wednesday through Sunday. Also open on all holidays except for Christmas Day. The ski lodge is open from 8 A.M. to 4:30 P.M. Lifts are open from 9 A.M. to 4 P.M. The ski area is closed on Monday and Tuesday. **2500 West Hogadon Road, 1800 East K, Casper, 82601; (307) 235-8499.**

Cross-Country Skiing

Casper Mountain also offers 17 miles of groomed nordic trails that wind through forests and meadows. About a mile of the trail is lit for night skiing until 9 P.M. Season: mid-November to April. **Natrona County Parks** has all the ski information; **(307) 235-9325**. **Mountain Sports** offers cross-country equipment rentals. **543 South Center, Casper, 82601; (307) 266-1136.** Area **snow and road reports** are available at **(307) 235-8369.**

Snowmobiling

Zoom over 60 miles of groomed and 80 miles of ungroomed, mapped trails along the **Natrona County Parks Snowmobile Trail System** on Casper Mountain. The trailhead begins eight miles south of town on the **Casper Mountain Road**. Blaze through great snow and breathtaking scenery. Warm up at a number of huts and shelters along the way. Get hot food and drinks, as well. **Natrona County Parks, (307) 235-9325.**

Seeing and Doing

Independence Rock

One of the most important landmarks along the Oregon Trail, Independence Rock was so named by William Sublette, leader of the first wagon train to cross the new overland route. A celebration took place on July 4, 1830, and before a group of 80 pioneers, Sublette christened the rock in honor of the birth date of the United States. The name acquired a double meaning, however, because pioneers knew that if they reached the rock by July 4, they would likely cross the mountains safely before winter. Since then, thousands of pioneers, trappers, traders, and religious leaders and their followers have crossed its path, and many left their indelible marks. The rock is inscribed with hundreds of carved and chipped names and dates of people who were searching for a new life on the frontier. Experience a bit of history while viewing this "register of the desert" located on Hwy. 220. **P.O. Box 1596, Evansville, 82636; (307) 577-5150. E-mail: pthomp@missc.state.wy.us.**

Devil's Gate

About six miles to the west of Independence Rock on Hwy. 220 is Devil's Gate, another imposing feature of the Oregon Trail. Devil's Gate consists of a vertical slash in a 370-foot granite cliff. The chasm is 400 feet wide at the top but only 30 feet wide at the bottom, where the Sweetwater River rages. Some pioneers attempted to ride horses or walk through this passage, but the current most often proved too strong. The "Gate" was circumvented, and travelers followed the Sweetwater River for 93 miles to the Continental Divide or South Pass.

Martin's Cove

About 60 miles west of Casper, just past Devil's Gate, lies Martin's Cove, a south-facing cirque, surrounded by hills, that slopes toward the Sweetwater River. In 1856, the Martin Handcart Company, a group of Mormons pulling handcarts, crossed the Oregon, Mormon, Pony Express, and California Trails on their way to Salt Lake City. The people unfortunately left too late to beat the snow. A blizzard hit, stranding them, and a rescue party set out from Salt Lake City to help them. The group stayed five days at what could be called Martin's Cove, which offered protection from the heavy snowfall and subzero temperatures. Out of 576 people who left from Council Bluffs, one-fourth lost their lives along the way to Salt Lake City. The visitor center is open daily during the winter from 9 A.M. to 4 P.M. and from the first of May to September from 8 A.M. until sundown. **Mormon Handcart Visitor Center, 47600 West Hwy. 220, Alcova, 82620; (307) 328-2953.**

Split Rock

Fifteen miles across the prairie from Devil's Gate is Split Rock (accessed from Hwy. 287 southwest of Casper), the last of three Oregon Trail granite landmarks along the Sweetwater River. For a day or more, emigrants on the trail could look back at the V-shaped notch in the peak of the mountain with a summit of 7,305 feet. Today, Split Rock is a very popular climbing area.

Historic Trails Road— "Crossroads of the West"

Nearly every pioneer passed through what is now Casper, known as the "Crossroads of the West," because all five great routes to the West (Oregon, Overland, Pony Express, Mormon, and California Trails) converged there. All came together on the way to South Pass, which was the only accessible route through the mountains to Oregon, California, Salt Lake City, Utah, and other final destinations in the far West. Weather permitting, visitors can actually drive along the famous route on the Historic Trails Road, experience the grade rise while approaching the Continental Divide just as the pioneers did, and encounter significant marked sites on the trails. **Hwy. 287 West.**

Casper Planetarium

Built in 1966, the Casper Planetarium has provided valuable astronomical education to the students of Casper schools, as well as Casper College and the University of Wyoming. The planetarium also provides public programs, presented at various times of the year. Visitors can enjoy a multimedia program about everything from the latest frontiers of astronomical research and discoveries made to the exploration of historical astronomical knowledge, lore, and mythologies of our ancestors. Journey to the stars, nebulae, supernovae, galaxies, and black holes. The planetarium offers a gift shop where books, posters, games, science toys, and T-shirts can be purchased. Open Thursday night at 7 P.M. during the school year. During summer, daily programs start at 4 P.M., 7 P.M., and 8 P.M. Handicapped accessible. **904 North Poplar Street, Casper, 82601; (307) 577-0310. E-mail: stars@trib.com. Website: www.trib.com/-WYOMING/NCSD/planetimarima.**

Casper Troopers Drum and Bugle Corps

Known as "Wyoming's musical ambassadors," the Casper Troopers Drum and Bugle Corps delights spectators with flashy frontier cowboy and cavalry uniforms, shining instruments, and catchy tunes. Combine all that with flying flags, and crowd-pleasing performances are inevitable. Young people in the fourth grade through age 21 are invited to participate. The B Corps, grades 4 to 8, performs throughout Wyoming, while the A Corps travels all over the country. The best chance to see them in their own backyard is in the summer. **(307) 472-2141.**

The Wyoming Symphony Orchestra

Between September and May, the state's only professional orchestra performs eight concerts, often featuring world-class soloists, as well as local talent like the Casper Children's Chorale, the Casper Civil Chorale, and the

57

American Guild of English Handbell Ringers. The orchestra has performed continuously since 1948. Visitors can come in casual attire and listen to some of the finest music in the world, some the work of brilliant local composers. Performances are held at the Natrona County High School Auditorium. **111 West 2nd Street, Suite 103, P.O. Box 667, Casper, 82602; (307) 266-1478. E-mail: wso@coffey.com. Website: www.coffey.com/~wso/index.**

Hell's Half Acre

Located 45 miles west of Casper, Hell's Half Acre is a truly unique and breathtaking geological phenomenon. Surrounded by prairie, the formation consists of a 160- to 200-foot-deep depression that formed as a result of erosion and downcutting by a small intermittent stream, a tributary of the Powder River. The depression was formed some 50 million years ago when a tropical climate prevailed in the region. Red and yellow banks are ancient remnants of tropical soils. Once used as a buffalo trap and hunting ground by Indians, the area was known as "Burning Mountain" because vapors were seen rising from the ground. These have not been seen for some time, but the 320 acres of spectacular beauty still beckon. The site was used for the alien-planet backdrop in the 1997 movie *Starship Troopers*.

The Casper Troopers. Photo courtesy of the Wyoming Travel Commission.

Information kiosks are on the prairie above, and signs identify noteworthy geological formations. The cafe and motel by the site are open year-round. **P.O. Box 80, Powder River, 82648; (307) 472-0018.**

Dinosaurs

Tate Geological Museum

The Tate Geological Museum, part of Casper College's Earth Science Department, has become a major resource center for paleontological research and education. The museum currently houses a number of Jurassic-age fossils, including many that once roamed throughout the Wyoming region. There's also an extensive mineral collection on display, including samples of Wyoming jade. An interactive computer station and hands-on mineral and fossil displays allow for fun learning experiences. Closed on campus holidays. Open year-round Monday through Friday 9 A.M. to 4 P.M., and on Saturday from 10 A.M. to 3 P.M. Handicapped accessible. **Casper College, 125 College Drive, Casper, 82601; (307) 268-2447. Website: www.cc.whecn.edu/tate/webpage.**

Jurassic Treks

Dig dinosaur bones? Then you'll love this trek where you actually get to wander through some of the richest fossil beds in the nation, learning excavation and preparation techniques from experienced diggers working in the fields of paleontology and geology. Discoveries from the Morrison Formation of about 150 million years ago include allosaurus and stegosaurus, vertebrae from young brontosauruses, and stuff that hasn't been identified yet. Open year-round, depending on the weather. The site is located 30 miles west of town. **197 Indian Paintbrush, Casper, 82604; (307) 234-5791 or (307) 235-2921. E-mail: rmotten@trib.com.**

Museums

Fort Caspar Museum

In response to growing hostilities among settlers and Indians along the Oregon Trail, U.S.

troops entered the Casper region in 1855. At the critical trail crossing of the North Platte River, an outpost was established in 1859 that provided a bridge, a stage stop, a trading post, a Pony Express mail stop, and a telegraph office. This Platte Bridge Station was outfitted as a military post by 1861 to hold back an increasing number of Indian raids. In July of 1865, Sioux and Cheyenne, acting in retaliation for the Sand Creek Massacre, attacked a detachment of men led by Lieutenant Caspar Collins. Several were killed, including Lieutenant Collins, as he was attempting to rescue a wounded soldier. Soon after this event, the army officially changed the station's name, in honor of the fallen lieutenant, to Fort Caspar. The fort was abandoned in 1867. In 1936, the fort was reconstructed on the original site and turned into a museum and interpretive center. Today the fort buildings are open during the summer. The interpretive center is open Monday through Friday, year-round from 8 A.M. to 5 P.M. During winter it is open Monday through Saturday from 8 A.M. to 7 P.M. and on Sunday from 1 P.M. to 4 P.M. Between mid-May and early September it is open noon to 7 P.M. on Sunday. Handicapped accessible. **4001 Fort Caspar Road, Casper, 82604; (307) 235-8464.**

Nicolaysen Art Museum and Discovery Center

From humble beginnings in 1967 as a small collection displayed in a residence, the Nicolaysen Art Museum now houses an extensive collection of local, regional, and national art in a variety of media within an elegant modern building. Lectures, films, gallery tours, and concerts are all available at the museum. The Discovery Center is a unique educational component of the museum and allows visitors to take part in classes or just experiment with art materials. A fun learning experience for adults and kids alike. Open year-round Tuesday through Saturday from 10 A.M. to 5 P.M., Thursday nights until 8 P.M., Sundays from 12 P.M. to 4 P.M.; closed Mondays. Handicapped accessible. Fee. **400 East Collins Drive, Casper, 82601; (307) 235-5247, fax (307) 235-0923.**

Where to Stay

Accommodations

Bessemer Bend B&B—$$–$$$

Located less than half a mile from the uppermost crossing of the North Platte River on the Oregon Trail, this quaint little B&B overlooks the river and Bessemer Mountain. All three bedrooms are spacious—one room holds a queen-size bed, and the other two are equipped with a full-size bed and a twin-size bed—perfect for a family. Visitors can relax on the huge front porch and take in the breathtaking view or hike along the country roads to view the mountains and wildlife. A full breakfast is provided, and lunch or dinner is available with prior arrangements for an extra fee. The Bessemer Bend B&B is located just 10 miles west of Casper. Not handicapped accessible. No pets allowed. No smoking. Open year-round. **6905 Speas Road, Casper, 82604; (307) 265-6819. E-mail: stanopl@trib.com. Website: www.cruising-america.com/bestbend.**

Camping

In Wyoming State Parks and Recreation Areas

Natrona County Parks Campgrounds (Mills, 82644; 307-237-8098) at Alcova Reservoir, Pathfinder Lakes, Gray Reef Reservoir, Bear Trap, and Casper Mountain Parks provide a variety of camp facilities. Most have drinking water, picnic tables, and restrooms near tent and RV campsites. Gray Reef Reservoir has a handy fishing pier. Pathfinder Lakes and North Platte River are open year-round, others open May 15 through September. No water. Pets on leash. Handicapped accessible.

Bureau of Land Management (BLM) Land

The BLM maintains campgrounds at the **Muddy Mountain Environmental Education and Recreation Area** that are open from mid-June through the end of September and located 18 miles south of Casper. This 1,200-acre region sports two designated campgrounds, one developed, the other with some facilities but no water. The **Lodgepole Campground** has 15 sites, 2 pull-through spots for campers up to 45 feet, hardened surface sites and restrooms that are handicapped accessible, and water. The **Rim Campground** has six sites, a picnic area, restrooms, and 2.5 miles of loop trails that are handicapped accessible, with interpretive signs—all in an 8,200-foot subalpine/grassland environment. **Bureau of Land Management, 1701 East E Street, Casper, 82601; (307) 261-7600.**

Private Campgrounds and Cabins

The **Casper KOA** offers RV and tent sites, a miniature golf course, shuttle service to the mall, an outdoor pool, buffalo barbecue during the summer months, laundry, store, playground, camping cabins. Pets okay. Not handicapped accessible. Open year-round. **2800 East Yellowstone, Casper, 82609; (800) 423-5155 or (307) 237-5155.**

Fort Caspar Campground provides full hookups for over 90 RV sites, tent area, laundry, showers, dump site, playground, dog run, a half-mile river walk, a bird sanctuary, a convenience store, and a picnic area. Pets okay. Handicapped accessible. Open year-round. **4205 Fort Caspar Road, Casper, 82604; (307) 234-3260.**

Hell's Half Acre Campground offers 12 spaces with full hookups. Pets okay. Not handicapped accessible, except for the restaurant located on the site. **Hwys. 20 and 26, P.O. Box 80, Powder River, 82648; (307) 472-0018.**

Where to Eat

Bum Steer Steakhouse—$$–$$$$

Bum Steer Steakhouse offers fine dining with a touch of class at reasonable prices. Daily lunch and dinner specials are available, and the prime rib is delightful. An elegant happy hour takes place Monday through Friday in the Pump Room, with a chef's tray buffet. Open Monday through Friday from 11 A.M. to 10 P.M., Saturday from 5 P.M. to 10 P.M., and Sunday from 6 P.M. to 9 P.M. Kids' menu. Senior discounts available. Handicapped accessible. **739 North Center, Casper, 82601; (307) 234-4531.**

El Jarro's—$$–$$$$

This Mexican restaurant offers El Jarro potatoes—cottage fries with green chilies and sour cream. Try the Mexicali chicken with Monterey jack, beans, and rice in two deep-fried tortillas smothered in green chili sauce. The establishment serves American food, as well. Open daily 11 A.M. to 1:45 P.M. for lunch and 5 P.M. to 8:45 P.M. for dinner. Kids' menu. Handicapped accessible. **500 West F, Casper, 82609; (307) 577-0538.**

Goose Egg Restaurant—$$–$$$$

Fine dining in a comfy country feel of a living room with nice draperies and artwork. Fried chicken is the specialty. Kids' menu. Bathrooms not handicapped accessible, as the building was built in 1936. Open Tuesday through Saturday from 5:30 P.M. to 9:30 P.M. **10580 Goose Egg Road off Hwy. 220, Casper, 82604; (307) 473-8838.**

Services

Visitor Information

Casper Area Visitors Bureau and Convention Center, 500 North Center, P.O. Box 399, Casper, 82602; (800) 852-1889 or (307) 234-5311, fax (307) 265-2643. E-mail: cacc@trib.com. Website: www.casper-ets.com.

Douglas and Glenrock

The towns of Douglas and Glenrock line the banks of the North Platte River with the Laramie Mountains on one side and the Thunder Basin National Grassland on the other. Douglas was named after Stephen A. Douglas, Abraham Lincoln's debate opponent. It has been home to the Wyoming State Fair since the first one in 1905. Emigrants on the Oregon Trail camped in a rocky glen at the edge of what is now Glenrock, giving the town its name.

History

Although the Douglas townsite was surveyed in 1886, the Fremont, Elkhorn and Missouri Valley Railroad, which owned the townsite, refused to allow people to stake out land until the railroad arrived in August of that year. Undeterred, people built a tent town a few miles from Douglas and waited. As soon as the first passenger train arrived, the tent owners moved their town, constructed on wheels, to Douglas and set up the community within three days. The town officially incorporated during 1887.

Douglas became a shipping point for the growing sheep and cattle industry that had taken advantage of the prime grasslands and high mountain meadows in the region. When the army abandoned Fort Fetterman in the 1880s, civilians bought the buildings and a small community flourished until the railroad decided it wouldn't run a line there. After that, many of the people and building materials from the old fort merged into Douglas.

Seventy years later, uranium deposits and coal mining brought another boom to Douglas's

Near Ayres Natural Bridge, Douglas. Photo courtesy of the Wyoming Division of Tourism.

and Glenrock's economy, followed by oil and gas exploration during the 1970s.

Glenrock went from a stopover on the Oregon Trail to a Mormon station on the Mormon Trail during the 1850s. After the Mormons abandoned it during the 1857 Mormon War, an Indian agent named Thomas Twiss moved his base of operation from Fort Laramie to the deserted Mormon buildings—without the military's permission. Twiss had served in the military with distinction before joining the Indian Bureau. During 1859, he suggested a reservation system for the Plains Indians. Meetings were held with the Indian nations and a formal treaty was proposed to Congress in 1859. As part of this treaty, the Oglala Sioux were to receive a reservation along Deer Creek. Congress, however, refused to ratify the treaty, feeling the terms were too liberal and allowed the Indians to keep too much prime land. Many have speculated, after the fact, that if Congress had ratified this treaty, the Indian Wars might have been averted. Twiss, disappointed by the failed treaty negotiations, resigned in 1861 and moved to Nebraska under a cloud of distrust, due to a misappropriation of the annuity goods he was supposed to have distributed among the Indians.

Coal mining later boomed around Glenrock. Coal from a mine 10 miles north of town now fuels the huge Dave Johnston Power Plant, one of the largest coal-fired electricity plants in the Rocky Mountains.

Festivals and Events

Wyoming State Fair (Douglas)
mid-August

Douglas hosted the first Wyoming State Fair in 1905. It's the big one. Things get started with a demolition derby. Then you can enjoy a ranch rodeo, all-girl rodeo, and PRCA rodeo. If that's not enough horsepower, watch the motorcycle races and the dressage horse show. The exhibit buildings have something for everybody.

Wyoming State Fair. Photo courtesy of the Wyoming Division of Tourism.

There are livestock-judging contests, a dog show, a dairy goat show, sheep shows, a volleyball tournament, a kids' parade, a carnival, concerts, Native American dances, and much more. Get all the details from the **Wyoming State Fair, Drawer 10, Douglas, 82633; (307) 358-2398, fax (307) 358-6030. E-mail: wystfair@coffey.com. Website: www.coffey.com/~wystfair.**

Deer Creek Days (Glenrock)
mid-July

A 5K run/walk across Deer Creek kicks off festivities that include a parade, an art show, kids' games, a raft race on the North Platte River, a street dance, a pancake breakfast, a talent show, mud volleyball, and a golf tournament. The **Glenrock Chamber of Commerce** has all the details. **(307) 436-5652.**

Outdoor Activities

Biking

Mountain Biking

The **Douglas Ranger District** oversees the management of over 750,000 acres of the **Medicine Bow–Routt National Forest** and **Thunder Basin National Grassland.** Check with them for which trails allow mountain biking at **2250 East Richards Street, Douglas, 82633; (307) 358-4690.** Bike rentals are available through **Curley's Leisure Sports, 219 West Yellowstone Hwy., Douglas, 82633; (307) 358-9394.**

Bicycle Touring

On Yellowstone Street, cycle along the **Heritage Trail Bike Path** through Douglas on a four-mile, well-maintained path that winds along the North Platte River.

Fishing

The Medicine Bow–Routt National Forest offers excellent fishing. Catch rainbow, brook, and brown trout in forest streams such as

LaBonte, LaPrele, Deer Creek, Beaver Creek, and Wagonhound, and rainbow trout, walleye, perch, catfish, and crappies around the North Platte River and Glendo Reservoir. The Douglas Ranger District, Medicine Bow–Routt National Forest, carries excellent information at 2250 East Richards Street, Douglas, 82633; (307) 358-4690.

The reservoir at Glendo State Park was created out of the damming of the North Platte River. Enjoy 12,500 acres of fishing, boating, water skiing, sailing, jet skiing, and swimming just 20 miles southeast of Douglas. Seventy-eight miles of shoreline even sports a large sandy beach for sunbathing. Boat ramps, camping facilities, and a complete marina. Rent fishing or pontoon boats from May to the end of September and slips on Glendo Reservoir. Tackle, bait, gas, licenses, and supplies are all available. Glendo Marina, 383 Glendo Park Road, Glendo, 82213; (307) 735-4216.

In Douglas, fish right in town at Riverside Park, with handicapped access right to the water. Great fishing abounds just six miles out of Glenrock at the northern edge of the Laramie Mountains.

Only 10 minutes southeast of Glenrock, Boxelder Canyon beckons. Its steep walls guard some dandy fishing in Boxelder Creek. County Road 18 through the canyon is open year-round and goes out to the south recreation area, where you can picnic. There's also an RV dump station.

For additional fishing information and regulations, contact Wyoming Game & Fish, 431 North 4th, Douglas, 82633; (307) 358-3249.

Curley's Leisure Sports rents canoes, rafts, fishing boats, and float tubes and offers a fishing guide service with advance notice. 219 West Yellowstone Highway, Douglas, 82633; (307) 358-9394.

Golf

Tee off for 18 holes at par 71 at the Douglas Municipal Golf Course east of the river. Enjoy

Getting There

Douglas is located 54 miles east of Casper, and Glenrock is 30 miles east of Casper on I-25. The Converse County General Aviation Airport (307-358-4924) is equipped with lights and an instrument landing system. Bus service to Douglas/Glenrock is available on Powder River Transportation (800-442-3682).

lessons, a clubhouse, a 250-yard driving range, and rental carts. Open daily during the summer from 7 A.M. to 7 P.M. and April 1 to October 15, depending on the weather. 64 Golf Course Road, Douglas, 82633; (307) 358-5099.

Hiking and Backpacking

63

Laramie Peak in the Medicine Bow–Routt National Forest stands 10,274 feet high, dominating the horizon for 100 miles. Twin Peaks Trail offers a fun two-mile hike that starts at the Esterbrook Campground. Take Hwy. 91 west of Douglas to Esterbrook Road. After three miles, take a left onto Hwy. 91. The pavement ends 25 miles down the road, and it becomes Converse County 24. The trailhead is 11 miles down Converse County Road 24. The starting elevation is 7,600 feet and climbs from there. Stay on the trail. The first half-mile is on private land. Hike 3.5 miles east to Black Mountain Lookout, where you can climb the tower between June and the end of October for a fabulous view of the region. It's wide, windy, and steep. For more details, contact the Douglas Ranger District, Medicine Bow–Routt National Forest, 2250 East Richards Street, Douglas, 82633; (307) 358-4690.

Snowmobiling

You can snowmobile 25 miles away on Casper Mountain. (See Casper, page 56.)

Seeing and Doing

Fort Fetterman State Historical Site

Fort Fetterman is an old army outpost built in the 1800s during the Indian uprisings. Be sure to watch the short film about the fort—it is the best interpretation among any of the forts in Wyoming of the events leading to the Indian Wars. Some of the old buildings have been restored, and each year the fort hosts Fort Fetterman Days, which features mountain men, black-powder-rifle enthusiasts, and cavalry in authentic dress. The fort is located eight miles northwest of Douglas on Hwy. 93. No fee. Open daily from Memorial Day weekend through Labor Day from 9 A.M. to 5 P.M. and during the winter by appointment only. Handicapped accessible. **752 Hwy. 93 Douglas, 82633 (mailing address: P.O. Box 520, Story, 82842); (307) 358-2864** and **(307) 684-7629** in winter.

Douglas Railroad Interpretive Center

The interpretive center grew out of the site of the depot for the Chicago and Northwestern Railroad. Wander through railroad history as well as the railcars. Climb aboard a steam locomotive, taste the nostalgia of the Silver Salver, the stainless-steel Zephyr dining car. Get cozy in the sleeper car. Learn the railroad's role in the development of Douglas. Tours available Saturday in summer, 10 A.M. to 4 P.M. **121 Brownfield Road, P.O. Box 74, Douglas, 82633; (307) 358-9684.**

Ayres Natural Bridge

Five miles off I-25 (Exit 151) on paved County Road 13, this natural bridge spans LaPrele Creek, 150 feet long and 50 feet high. The creek cut away the banks both up- and downstream, leaving the resistant ridge of rock from the Casper Sandstone Formation, which formed over 286 million years ago. The bridge gets its name from Alva Ayres, who settled the land near the natural wonder in 1882. Alva's son donated the land to the county in 1920 to create the park. Open April 1 through October

31 from 8 A.M. to 8 P.M. **208 Natural Bridge Road, Douglas, 82633; (307) 358-3532**.

Jackalope Square

Douglas is home to the famed jackalope—a cross between a jackrabbit and an antelope. Jackalopes are shy and quite rare and sing during thunderstorms, according to locals. Check out the statue of the jackalope in the square. Covered picnic tables, handicapped-accessible restrooms. **Third and Center Streets.**

Rock of the Glen

Pioneers on the Oregon Trail camped on this spot 1.5 miles west of what would become Glenrock on Hwys. 26 and 20. The relatively flat site protected by a rock outcropping sheltered the weary travelers. A few of the 1800s wayfarers carved their names in the rocks.

Scenic Drives

Rochelle Hills Loop

Travel 35 miles north from Douglas on Hwy. 59 to the town of Bill. Turn right just past Bill onto Steinle Road and follow it for 12 miles to Dull Center Road. Turn left and follow it for eight miles, then take another left onto Rochelle Hills Road. Eleven miles down the road, take a left onto Piney Canyon Road. Stay on it for 11 miles, then take another left onto paved Hilight Road. Follow it for 12 miles back to Hwy. 59. Although the unpaved roads are maintained gravel roads, there are a few places where passenger cars with low ground clearance might hit a few snags. It takes 3.5 hours of driving time to complete the loop.

On this loop you might encounter a wide variety of wildlife. **Thunder Basin Grassland** is home to antelope, deer, elk, coyotes, jackrabbits, prairie dogs, 17 species of eagles and hawks, owls, and rattlesnakes, to name a few. The route also takes you through lots of human history. Old homesteads are scattered through the grassland, all protected by state and federal laws. You will also pass through the Antelope Coal Mine area on your way back to Hwy. 59.

Private land intermingles with U.S.D.A. Forest Service and Bureau of Land Management lands, so before heading out, be sure to pick up a map of the Thunder Basin Grassland from the **Douglas Ranger District, Medicine Bow–Routt National Forest, 2250 East Richards Street, Douglas, 82633; (307) 358-4690.**

Dinosaurs

Glenrock Paleontological Museum

In 1994 Glenrock resident Sean Smith discovered a dinosaur bone in an ancient river channel across the North Platte River on land owned by Merle and Mona Dunham. Working with the Tate Museum at Casper College, Smith and other volunteers eventually recovered a complete skeleton of a Triceratops prorsus, which Smith named Stephanie. The Dunhams have donated all the fossils excavated on their property to the children of Glenrock, with the only stipulation being that the remains stay in Glenrock. Thus, the museum and education center began. Currently, Stephanie's brain case and prepared horn core are on display in the museum along with nodosaur armor, Tyrannosaurus rex teeth, a complete skeleton of a prehistoric horse, and other fossils. The rest of Stephanie's skeletal remains are in the lab at the museum, being painstakingly cleaned and assembled for future display—the process takes years. Open in summer Monday through Saturday from 1 P.M. to 5 P.M. and in winter on Tuesday and Thursday from 1 P.M. to 4 P.M. and Saturday from 10 A.M. to 4 P.M. **152 Mustang Trail, Glenrock, 82637; (307) 436-2667** or **(307) 436-2259. E-mail: seandsmith@yahoo.com.**

Museums

Wyoming Pioneer Memorial Museum

Located on the Wyoming state fairgrounds, the museum's collection began in the early 1900s when a group of old-timers, who became the Wyoming Pioneer Association, met during the state fair. As an important aspect of this annual gathering, they brought mementos from the early days of statehood (1890). The museum explores rodeo roots with the memorabilia of Bill Pickett, employed by the 101 Ranch Wild West Show. He created the bulldogging event seen in modern-day rodeos. See the elaborate Chinese loveseat from the Higgins Hotel in Glenrock, the 1914 bar from the LaBonte Inn, period clothing, Johnson County War artifacts, and a tepee used in the movie *Dances with Wolves*. Open year-round, 8 A.M. to 5 P.M., Monday through Friday. In summer, Saturday 1 P.M. to 5 P.M. as well. The museum hosts the Platte River Primitive Skills Rendezvous during late July. See demonstrations of flintnapping, braintanning, the use of black-powder weapons, and lots more. Handicapped accessible. **400 West Center Street, P.O. Drawer 10, Douglas, 82633; (307) 358-9288, fax (307) 358-9293.**

65

Where to Stay

Accommodations

Two Creek Ranch—$$$$

While nestled between La Bonte and Wagonhound Creeks and the North Platte River, you can experience life on a 25,000-acre working cattle ranch. Join in a 75-mile cattle drive the last 10 days in May, June 2 through 10, or the last 10 days in October. At other times of the year, enjoy participating in such other cowboy activities as moving cattle, branding, and horseback riding. Open April through October. Stay in the bunkhouse or in the main house. Some accommodations have shared baths. No pets. Not handicapped accessible. **800 Esterbrook Road, Douglas, 82633; (307) 358-3467, fax (307) 358-4193. E-mail: 2creekranch@chalk-buttes.com.**

Deer Forks Ranch—$$–$$$$

Board your horse and your family at one of three modern guest houses. Fully equipped kitchens. Trailer hookup. Enjoy guided trail rides for guests only, trout fishing on your own, wildlife watching, and participating in activities associated with a working sheep and cattle ranch. Children welcome. Located 25 miles into the country. Closed the end of November to May. Bring your own food, or the ranch will supply meals for an extra fee. Several eating plans are available. Not handicapped accessible. **1200 Poison Lake Road; Douglas, 82633; (307) 358-2033. E-mail: deerfork@coffey.com.**

Higgins Hotel—$$-$$$

If you want to indulge yourself in Wyoming's past and, at the same time, pamper yourself with comforts, stay at the Higgins Hotel. Built in 1916, the hotel retains its original grandeur. Each room has its own delightful touches of history and homeyness. Walk into the lobby and step back through time. The hotel has remained in continuous operation since the day it opened. A delightful breakfast comes with the rooms, served in sunny nooks or the gorgeous dining room. Handicapped accessible. No pets. **416 West Birch, Glenrock, 82637; (800) 458-0144** or **(307) 436-9212, fax (307) 436-9213.**

Esterbrook Lodge—$$

Nestled in the Laramie Range of the Medicine Bow–Routt National Forest, this lodge contains three rustic cabins with shared bath, mobile homes, and the main building with a dining room, lounge, and dance hall. There are also RV hookups. Handicapped accessible. Pets okay on leash. Open year-round, except for Thanksgiving Day and Christmas. **32 Pine Esterbrook, Douglas, 82633; (307) 358-6103.**

Guest Ranches

Cheyenne River Ranch—$$$$

While isolated on the plains of eastern Wyoming, relish the peace and quiet, as well as an unbelievable view, on this 8,000-acre working sheep and cattle ranch. Sign on for a cattle drive between June and August. Help out on the ranch, branding and working livestock, take trail rides, or participate in other family-oriented ranch activities. Stay in one of two

bunkhouses with private baths or in the main house with shared baths. Guest ranch rates are from Sunday to Saturday, or a three-day minimum stay. Not handicapped accessible. No pets allowed, as there are ranch dogs and sheep. No drinking, and the owners prefer no smoking. **1031 Steinle Road, Douglas, 82633; (307) 358-2380. E-mail: ccranch-@coffey.com. Website: www.cruising-america.com/riverranch.**

Camping

In the National Forests

Maintained campgrounds at LaBonte Canyon, Campbell Creek, Cold Springs, Esterbrook, Friend Park, and Horseshoe Creek provide potable water, fire pits, and restrooms. Open May through October, depending on the weather. **Douglas Ranger District, Medicine Bow–Routt National Forest, 2250 East Richards Street, Douglas, 82633; (307) 358-4690.**

In Wyoming State Parks and Recreation Areas

Ayres Natural Bridge Park, located 15 miles west of Douglas, provides beautiful overnight camping spots; however, you must obtain written permission of the caretaker to camp there. Three nights maximum; permission must be renewed daily by the caretaker. Handicapped accessible. Pets okay. No hookups, no water, but there are restrooms and a playground. Dandy fishing on-site, and swimming and tubing. A large picnic shed with electricity is available for cooking; you must reserve it ahead of time. **208 Natural Bridge Road, Douglas, 82633; (307) 358-3532.**

Campgrounds at **Glendo State Park** offer sites along the reservoir, some with drinking water, picnic tables, restrooms, and playgrounds. **383 Glendo Park Road, Glendo, 82213; (307) 735-4216.**

Private Campgrounds and Cabins

Lonetree Village RV Park provides a laundry room, showers, full RV hookups, and some tent sites. Open year-round for monthly stay in winter only. Monthly rates available. Overnighters April through October or November. Pets okay.

Handicapped accessible. **1 Lonetree Tree Drive, Douglas, 82633; (307) 358-6669.**

Jackalope KOA Kampground offers RV and tent sites, restrooms, showers, dump station, pay phones, laundry, propane, groceries, a heated pool, game room, and playground. Open from March 15 through November 1. Handicapped accessible. Pets okay. Some discounts. **168 Cold Springs Road, P.O. Box 1190, Douglas, 82623; (307) 358-2164.**

Deer Creek Village RV Campground provides full hookups, tent sites, laundry, on-site fishing, and a clean, modern bathhouse. Weekly rates and camper rentals available. Handicapped accessible. Pets okay. Open from April until November. Located behind the city park. **302 Millar Lane, Glenrock, 82637; (307) 436-8121. E-mail: LDRCREEK@-aol.com.**

Riverside Park in Douglas offers free, 48-hour camping in town along the North Platte River. Water, showers, restrooms, and a dump station. For information, call the city of **Douglas** at **(307) 358-9750.**

Where to Eat

Madame Clementines—$$–$$$$
The western atmosphere is what makes Madame Clementines a unique dining experience—including the old bathtub salad bar and the great fireplace. Try the Mother Lode prime rib and mud pie for dessert. Handicapped accessible. Kids' menu. Open Monday through Thursday from 11 A.M. to 9 P.M., Friday and Saturday from 11 A.M. to 11 P.M., and Sunday from 11 A.M. to 9 P.M. In summer open daily from 11 A.M. to 10 P.M. **1199 Mesa Drive, Douglas, 82633; (307) 358-5554.**

Paisley Shawl Restaurant and Highlander Bar—$$–$$$$
A gourmet's delight, the restaurant takes its name from a family heirloom, a hand-loomed shawl from Paisley, Scotland, brought to Wyoming in 1903. Located in the historic Hotel Higgins, the restaurant offers Old World elegance, as well as some of the best meals you'll find anywhere in Wyoming. Try a Paisley

Paisley Shaw Restaurant in Glenrock.

Shawl reuben for lunch or fettuccine with clam sauce. Savor the five-course continental dinners, such as coconut-chutney shrimp or veal Madeira creme. Nightly specials. An international dinner featured from different countries every Friday night. Open daily from June 1 to September 1 and Tuesday through Saturday the rest of the year from 11:30 A.M. to 1:30 P.M. for lunch and 6 P.M. to 9:30 P.M. for dinner. The Highlander Bar comes well stocked with a variety of interesting brews and microbrews, as well as an impressive wine list, all in a small, cozy Scottish atmosphere. Ask about the history of the photos on the walls. Handicapped accessible. **416 West Birch, Glenrock, 82637; (800) 458-0144** or **(307) 436-9212, fax (307) 436-9213.**

Services

Visitor Information
Douglas Chamber of Commerce, 121 Brownfield Road, P.O. Box 74, Douglas, 82633; (307) 358-2950. E-mail: jackalope@chalkbuttes.com. Website: www.-chalkbuttes.com/Jackalope.

Glenrock Chamber of Commerce, 110 South 4th, P.O. Box 411, Glenrock, 82637; (307) 436-5652, fax (307) 436-3418.

67

Dubois

The Shoshone and Sheepeater Indians, who originally lived and hunted here, favored this land for its forgiving weather, calling it the "Valley of the Warm Winds." Pioneers later settled next to the Wind River in this stunning and uncharacteristically warm valley. During its early days, the place took on a rather unattractive reputation as home to working men who didn't seem to work hard enough to sweat. The town was dubbed "Never Sweat," a name the U.S. Postal Service refused to use when they put in an office. The postal service picked the name "Dubois" in honor of an Idaho senator of the time who was very generous, acquiring funding for the postal service. Dubois is now home to some of the finest outdoor recreation wilderness in the West. This small, rustic community of log cabins and ranches is nestled among some of the most unique landscapes in Wyoming. But don't pronounce the name of this town with a French pronunciation. It's DUE-boys.

History

During the early part of the nineteenth century, little was known about the vast mountain ranges that seemed to rise up along the west-ern horizon forever. Indigenous Shoshone and Sheepeater Indian nations made frequent forays into the Wind River Mountains, often using a natural low point in the range, later to be called Union Pass, that allowed easier access to the Green River Basin on the west side of the Continental Divide. The pass, just west of Dubois, was probably used by early explorers, including John Colter, Captain Bonneville, and numerous other mountain men who journeyed through here in search of furs. Along this time-honored trail is the headwaters of this country's mightiest rivers; the Mississippi, Columbia, and Colorado all start with the snow that falls along these peaks.

Early settlement of Dubois began sometime in the late 1800s as the entire Wind River Valley was opened to settlement with the formation of more wagon roads and the end of potential hostilities with the creation of the Wind River Indian Reservation. Timber harvesting soon became a major part of the growing settlement's activity and income, with the abundant pine forests covering the surrounding mountains.

Around the turn of the century, Scandinavian settlers came to this richly forested area. Beginning in 1914, these stout, brawling men with broadaxes in hand started cutting railroad ties out of solid logs to accommodate the Chicago and Northwestern Railroad. When the Wind River swelled with spring melt, the tie hacks would float the heavy ties out of the mountains via an elaborate flume system, remnants of which can still be seen within the hills today. The logs would enter the Wind River and continue their journey down to Riverton, 80 miles away.

Festivals and Events

Dubois Pack Horse Races
late May
This annual Memorial Day event gets summer rolling with a rugged 14-mile packhorse race, starting at the town arena and climbing up into the parched badlands before returning in a flurry of dust and leather to the arena. Partici-

Horsepacking races in Dubois.

pants demonstrate the skills of packing up an entire camp and stowing it in traditional panniers on their pack animals, then leading them out of the arena to travel into the "wilderness" of the race course. Plenty of western fun and excitement are always a part of this unique event. The chamber of commerce has the details **(307-455-2556)**.

Whiskey Mountain Buckskinners Rendezvous
mid-August

Colorful characters from all over the region gather in period costumes and paint to re-create the historic fur trapper and Native American gathering that took place in this area over a century and a half ago. Buckskinners demonstrate the old arts of flint fire starting, leather working, and black-powder riflery. Held on **Jakey's Fork,** four miles southeast of town. Also check out the Buffalo Barbecue the same weekend (always the second Saturday in August). **(307) 455- 2837, (307) 455-3493,** or **(307) 455-2568.**

Outdoor Activities

Biking

Mountain Biking

Mountain biking on **Union Pass** (see below) presents excellent physical challenges, as well as great beauty in the wilderness. Rent a mountain bike or take guided bike tours on Union Pass with **Bob's Bike Corral, 8 Stalnaker Street, P.O. Box 673, Dubois, 82513; (307) 455-3193. E-mail: bike@-wyoming.com.**

Dog Sledding

Washakie Outfitting offers a variety of three-hour trips (9 A.M. to 12 P.M. or 1 P.M. to 4 P.M.) on Togwotee Pass, on its own trails north of the lodge at Cowboy Village, with a stop halfway for hot drinks and snacks. Try a half-day trip out of the ranch north of Dubois. Full-day

Dinwoody glacier. Photo courtesy of the Wyoming Travel Commission.

69

trips in the Brooks Lake area include a great lunch at Brooks Lake Lodge, a side trip to Bonneville Pass, or a great day on private, secluded runs at the ranch. The latter has more dog sledding and a lunch on the trail, cooked over an open fire. Overnight trips go from afternoon to the next morning to Double Cabins and are for the extreme adventurer, because they involve winter camping! Great family fun! Get as involved as you want. Drive the sled or jump in and enjoy the ride. Open Thanksgiving to mid-April. Kids welcome. **Hwy. 287, P.O. Box 1054, Dubois, 82513; (307) 455-2616.**

Fishing

Excellent brown, rainbow, cutthroat, and brook trout fishing are found along the **Wind River**'s five miles of public access near Dubois on Hwys. 287 and 26. **Brooks Lake,** approximately 23 miles northwest of town on Forest Road 515, offers rainbow and brook trout, as well as splake fishing opportunities. The **Jakey's Fork** and **Torrey Creek** drainages—both accessed from the Fish Hatchery Road three miles east of town—are a little more off the beaten path. Take a left onto Forest Road 257 and head to some dandy trout, lingcod, and splake fishing at **Trail Lake**. The local **Wyoming Game & Fish** office **(260 Buena Vista in Lander, 307-332-2688)** can help you plan the perfect fishing trip.

Four-Wheel-Drive Trips

A few miles west of Dubois along **Hwys. 26 and 287,** the vast **Dunoir Valley** opens up to the north, offering an extraordinary view of Ramshorn Peak and the beginning of the Absaroka Mountains (pronounced ab-SOR-ka). On the other side of the highway from the Dunoir is **Union Pass Road,** an improved gravel road that traverses the northern end of the Wind River Range, eventually leading to the Green River Basin on the western side to connect with Hwy. 352 north of Pinedale. This pass was used for centuries by frontier explorers, trappers, and local tribes. Today, the road can be traveled in good weather up and over the Continental Divide, where three of this country's major rivers have their headwaters. A shorter loop down **Warm Springs Creek Road** will lead down through beautiful forests and overlooks back to the highway. A vehicle with high ground clearance is a very good idea, as the road gets rougher as it goes along.

Goatpacking

Goats, like humans, can put in 8 to 10 miles a day in rough country. In the plains of the Red Desert, they can trek 15 to 20 miles per day. One goat can usually carry about 70 to 75 pounds. Does carry only about 25 to 30 pounds but give a real treat in the backcountry—fresh milk! And goats make excellent hiking companions. They love company and will stay right with you. On the trail you can't tell their tracks and droppings from those of deer, antelope, or

bighorn sheep. **Wind River Pack Goats** offers day and multiday trips into the Wind River Range and the Red Desert. **6668 Hwy. 26, Dubois, 82513; (307) 455-2410.**

Golf

Antelope Hills Golf Course offers a nine-hole course adjacent to the stunning red hills of the Wyoming Badlands half a mile west of Dubois along the main highway to Jackson. This is a private club, but the public is welcome. **P.O. Box 96, Dubois, 82513; (307) 455-2888.**

Hiking and Backpacking

Over two million acres of **Shoshone National Forest** and some of the most extensive wilderness areas surround Dubois. The Wind River Mountains (known locally as "the Winds") alone offer 800 miles of trail systems. Most of the trails lead quickly into the mountains at elevations ranging from 8,000 to 11,000 feet. An easy hike that still gives a taste of the Winds is the **Brooks Lake Trail.** Travel northwest from Dubois on Hwys. 287 and 26 approximately 23 miles to Brooks Lake Road. The trail begins 5 miles down the road at the lake to the west of the boat ramp at the campground. The trail is 3.5 miles in length and gains 100 feet in elevation from a start at 9,050 feet.

A more moderate hike is the **Whiskey Creek Trail.** This 3.5-mile trek goes from 7,850 to 10,450 feet. Head south out of Dubois on Hwys. 187 and 26 to Trail Lake Road. Continue on it for 2.5 miles to the Whiskey Basin/Trail Lakes junction. Proceed east on Trail Lakes Road a quarter of a mile to the first junction on the right, then along the fence, following the road until it bends to the southwest about three-eighths of a mile. This is bighorn sheep country.

Wyoming's highest mountain, **Gannett Peak,** rising to 13,804 feet, is the centerpiece of the deep wilderness country for serious backpackers. Access it from the Trail Lake roadhead on Forest Road 257, only a few miles south of Dubois off Hwys. 287 and 26.

70

Obtain map, hiking, and backcountry camping information about the Shoshone National Forest from the **Wind River Ranger District, 1403 West Ramshorn, P.O. Box 186, Dubois, 82513; (304) 455-2466.**

Horseback Riding

Many of the trails into the Wind River Range allow horsepacking. Check with the **Wind River Ranger District, 1403 West Ramshorn, P.O. Box 186, Dubois, 82513; (307) 455-2466.**

Larry Stetter's outfit offers overnight horsepacking fishing trips, drop trips for climbers and hikers, and long-term horse rentals for a week or even a month. Trail rides by the hour, half day, or full day are also available through **Larry Stetter General Outfitters, 656 Horse Creek Road, P.O. Box 695, Dubois, 82513; (307) 455-2725.**

Skiing

Cross-Country Skiing

Winter snow turns Dubois into a wonderland of cold-weather recreation with over a million acres perfect for backcountry skiing on **Togwotee Pass,** 40 miles northwest of Dubois on Hwys. 287 and 26. Many consider it to have the best snow conditions and scenery in the nation. **Union Pass** also offers good nordic skiing, but it is generally crowded with snowmobilers. Groomed trails are at **Falls Campground** and **Brooks Lake** in the Shoshone National Forest. Get details from the **Wind River Ranger District, 1403 West Ramshorn, P.O. Box 186, Dubois, 82513; (307) 455-2466.**

Snowmobiling

Over 380 miles of snowmobile trails in the Dubois area await your pleasure. Only 59 of those miles are ungroomed. Head up and over **Togwotee Pass** or over **Union Pass** to Pinedale. Explore the **Gros Ventres** and the **Goosewing.** You'll find fuel, food, lodging, and restrooms along the way.

Getting There

Dubois nestles in the mountains 86 miles southeast from Jackson or 78 miles northwest from Riverton along **Hwys. 287 and 26.** Although Dubois has an air strip, there is no commercial service. Fly into Jackson on **American (800-443-7300)** or **United Express (800-241-6522).** A variety of rental cars are available at the Jackson Hole Airport. Or fly into Riverton on United Express.

Snowmobilers rank **Togwotee Pass** among the country's top terrain. The powder riding, whether on or off the trail, is the best in the state. The **Continental Divide Trail** connects snowmobile thoroughfares in Yellowstone and around Jackson Hole to Togwotee Pass for some incredible scenic adventures. Togwotee Pass's two million acres allow plenty of room to play and some challenges for every skill and age level. The area receives an average of 600 inches of snowfall over the course of a season. Any wonder that it draws everyone from the first-timer to the pros, and even snowmobile manufacturers? Togwotee Pass lies approximately 40 miles from Dubois on Hwys. 287

Snowshoeing on Togwotee Pass.

and 26 North. **Wyoming State Snowmobile Program; (307) 777-3680.**

Togwotee Mountain Lodge offers daily guided and unguided snowmobile adventures through gorgeous mountain meadows, challenging mountainsides, and snow cornices. It also provides a great lunch and interpretive tours. **P.O. Box 91, Moran, 83013; (800) 543-2847.**

Timberline Ranch (4127 Hwy. 26, Dubois, 82513; 307-455-2513) offers guided snowmobile tours and rentals. **Snow Adventures (20 Kingfisher Road, P.O. Box 666, Dubois, 82513; 307-455-2210)** offers guided trips and rentals.

Washakie Outfitting offers guided day and overnight snowmobile trips. **Hwy. 287, P.O. Box 1054, Dubois, 82513; (307) 455-2616.**

Seeing and Doing

Ramshorn Peak

A stunning spire of ancient volcanic sediment, this peak is a local favorite and symbol of Dubois's scenic resources. The peak soars 11,635 feet into the sky. The best view of it comes at the western edge of town from the scenic overlook. The improved gravel road winds sharply up a hill that affords an incredible view of not only Ramshorn Peak but also the Wind River Range and the Absarokas.

Dubois Badlands

The intriguing badlands meet the town on the east. Variegated red and gray bands of prehistoric lake and stream sediments characterize this natural wonder. Hwys. 187 and 26.

Tie Hack Memorial

Approximately six miles northwest of town on Hwys. 287 and 26 stands a monument to a special breed of logger, the tie hacker. From 1914 until the early 1950s, these men cut and hand-hewed logs into railroad ties, then floated them down the Wind River to Riverton. During the peak year of 1947, they cut 700,000 ties.

Museums

Dubois Museum

Displays showcase the indigenous Sheepeater Indians, the tie hack industry that helped shape the town, and samples of the local geology and wildlife. Authentic outbuildings depict aspects of western life, such as Dubois's first one-room schoolhouse and its original saddle shop. The museum also has a ranger station and an early gas station. Movie buffs will enjoy learning about Clark Gable's resort lodge. A 1905 house serves as a children's museum. Special programs, designed especially for kids, include candle making, soap making, and storytelling. Check out Dubois's first fire truck, a converted Willys jeep that was in use until the late 1950s. It still runs! The Dubois Museum is open daily between Memorial Day and Labor Day from 9 A.M. to 7 P.M. The remainder of the year it is closed, except for special, pre-arranged tours. Modest fee. **909 West Ramshorn, P.O. Box 896, Dubois, 82513; (307) 455-2284**.

National Bighorn Sheep Interpretive Center

Just on the outskirts of Dubois lies the Whiskey Mountain Wildlife Habitat Area. This beautiful region among the foothills of the Wind River Range serves as natural habitat for the nation's largest wintering herd of Rocky Mountain bighorn sheep. It's only fitting that the town of Dubois is home for the National Bighorn Sheep Interpretive Center, a modern museum of natural history devoted to the study and appreciation of this classic western American animal. Exhibits and interactive displays explore the biology of bighorn sheep, other wild sheep of the world, the role of the Sheepeater Indians in Wind River history, and wildlife conservation and management issues. The interpretive center is open throughout the summer daily from 9 A.M. to 8 P.M., and during fall from 9 A.M. to 5 P.M. Has been closed November to May 1, but call for winter hours, since they may be changing. Guided tours to Whiskey Basin available during winter. **National Bighorn Sheep Interpretive Center,**

907 West Ramshorn, Dubois, 82513; (307) 455-3429. Website: www.wyoming.com/ndte/wildlife-museums/nbisa.

Scenic Drives

Dubois to Togwotee Pass

Travel **west along Hwys. 26 and 287** for approximately 40 miles along a gradually climbing highway that crests at the Continental Divide at 9,668 feet. The colorful, dry badlands and sagebrush of Dubois give way along this meandering drive to lush mountain conifer stands and stunning rock cliffs. It's not uncommon to see deer or an occasional moose browsing in the woods or open meadows within yards of the highway. The road to Brooks Lake turns off the highway about 23 miles west of Dubois. The lakes and surrounding cliffs of ancient volcanic sediment are spectacular scenery to enjoy while hiking or fishing.

Trail Lake Road

A short **three miles east of Dubois on Hwys. 26 and 287,** a right on to Fish Hatchery Road, then a quick left (Forest Road 257) starts you on an improved journey on gravel road toward one of the most popular and scenic roadheads leading into the Wind River Mountains. Three glacial-carved lakes that all provide excellent fishing are situated just off the road. The bighorn sheep wintering range spans the high hills rising out of the narrow valley. Explorers with a keen eye may find some of the many petroglyphs etched among the rock cliffs thousands of years ago.

Horse Creek Road

A "blink-and-you'll miss-it" dirt road that cuts north right out of the heart of Dubois leads into some of the most scenic and varied country in the area. **From Hwy. 287 south,** Horse Creek Road follows its namesake waters through multicolored badlands, then it crosses over to follow the Wiggins Fork, slowly giving way to green aspen groves and lodgepole pines and eventually leading to the edge of the Shoshone National Forest. Pinnacle-like peaks

mark the end of the road but the beginning of the foot trails for travelers so inclined.

Where to Stay

Accommodations

Brooks Lake Lodge—$$$$

Nestled within the pristine Absaroka Mountains along the shore of Brooks Lake, this lodge provides elegant accommodations among some of the most beautiful vistas that Wyoming has to offer. Trail rides, fishing trips, and family-style dinners are featured. Cross-country skis, snowshoes, and snowmobiles are available for overnight guests only. Open from late December through the end of March and July 1 through late September. During the summer there is a three-night minimum stay. Open in winter for lodging Wednesday through Sunday. Make reservations. The owners don't plow the road, so the only way to access the lodge in winter is via snowmobile, and the owners will snowmobile out to get you. Parking is available off Hwys. 287 and 26. Kids welcome. No pets. The restaurant is open to the general public during the winter only on Thursday through Monday from 11 A.M. to 3 P.M. Dinner and breakfast are included with lodging; lunch is also provided in summer. Standard lunch fare and a great buffalo burger. Not handicapped accessible. **458 Brooks Lake Road, Dubois, 82513; (307) 455-2121. Website: www.brookslake.com.**

Jakey's Fork Homestead B&B—$$$–$$$$

Heated by a wood-burning stove and large brick fireplace, this rustic home set against the Wind River Mountains offers cozy warm nights and hospitality. Enjoy scenic views from the bedroom windows or from the 1889 historic cabin where Butch Cassidy once enjoyed Christmas dinner. Shared bath. Jacuzzi and sauna. Hiking right out the door. Fishing a quarter mile down the road. Full, delicious breakfast with sourdough pancakes, biscuits and gravy, and homemade granola with yogurt. Lots of coffee available from 5:30 A.M. on. Get

73

some and enjoy sipping it outside while you dine overlooking the lovely landscape. No pets. Not handicapped accessible. Open year-round. Get co-owner Justin Bridges to show you his Wind River Knives operations. They are one of a kind in more ways than one! **Fish Hatchery Road, P.O. Box 635, Dubois, 82513; (307) 455-2769.**

Togwotee Mountain Lodge—$$$–$$$$

This lodge is an expansive, three-story facility located along Togwotee Pass between Dubois and Jackson. Its ideal location among pristine forests provides an incredible view of the Teton Mountains. Lodge activities include trail-ride cookouts, western music, horse trail rides, entertainment, and naturalist talks. The lodge is open during the winter to accommodate snowmobile and backcountry ski enthusiasts. Nightly stays or winter packages are available. The latter include a four-night minimum stay, dinner and breakfast, social hour every evening, guide service, snowmobiles, and airport pickup at Jackson Hole. You can also get guided dogsled tours, rent skis or snowshoes, or take horse-drawn sleigh rides. Soak in one of four hot tubs. Convenience store and gas on-site. Handicapped accessible at the lodge and cabins. No pets. Open mid-November to mid-April and June 1 to mid-October. **Hwys. 26 and 287, P.O. Box 91, Moran, 83013; (800) 543-2847 or (307) 543-2847, fax (307) 543-2391. Website: www.cowboy-village.com.**

Guest Ranches

Lazy L&B Guest Ranch—$$$$

If you love to ride horses, this is the place for you. Ranch-style meals and lots of horseback riding are specialties at this ranch tucked away in the beautiful valley along the East Fork of the Wind River. The ranch staff offer riding lessons on the trail for children and adults. Riding every day. Fishing on the ranch's stocked pond or in the Wind River, which runs through the ranch. Leather-working shop and petting farm on-site. Hiking every morning

before breakfast. Attend square dances in town. Weekly program Sunday to Saturday. Minimum stay of six nights (one week) during July and August. No pets. Solar-heated pool. Jacuzzi. **1072 East Fork Road, Dubois, 82513; (800) 453-9488 or (307) 455-2839. Website: www.ranchweb.com/lazyl&b.**

Triangle C Guest Ranch—$$$$

Three-day minimum stay. Situated right along the Wind River for easy access to fishing. Western hospitality includes comfortable cabins, hot tubs, western dances, and sightseeing trips to Yellowstone and Grand Teton National Parks. Trail rides, hiking trips, rafting, snowmobiling, and rodeos are also available. Kids' activities. Family oriented. No pets. Handicapped accessible. Closed April and May only. **3737 Hwy. 26, Dubois, 82513; (307) 455-2225. E-mail: info@triangle.com. Website: www.trianglec.com.**

Camping

In the National Forests

The forest service maintains a variety of wilderness campgrounds, most offering tent and trailer sites, picnic tables with grates, and restrooms. **Dickinson Park**, off Hwy. 287, is open July through September. Contact **Washakie Ranger District, 333 East Main Street, Lander, 82520; (307) 332-5460**. **Horse Creek Campground** and **Double Cabin Campground,** accessible from Horse Creek Road, are open June through September. Off Hwys. 287 and 26 northwest of Dubois are campgrounds at **Brooks Lakes, Pinnacle Falls, Brooks Creek Falls,** and **Wind River Lake,** which are generally open mid-June to mid-September. **Wind River Ranger District, 1403 West Ramshorn, P.O. Box 186, Dubois, 82513; (304) 455-2466.**

Private Campgrounds and Cabins

Located 20 miles west of Dubois, **Pinnacle Lodge and Campground** is a family-run lodge and campground that offers modern rooms in a lodge with full-size beds, private baths, and TV. The campground has full hookups, tent sites, water, and electricity. There's a nearby gas station, general store, and restaurant. Pets okay. Not handicapped accessible. Open year-round, but you need four-wheel drive to get into the campground in winter. **3577 U.S. Hwy. 26 West, Dubois, 82513; (307) 455-2506.**

Where to Eat

The Old Yellowstone Garage—$$$–$$$$

When you step inside, the place looks like a 1930s lodge in Yellowstone—lots of dark wood and a wood-burning oven in the center of the dining room. It's great! The menu changes nightly, depending on what's fresh and in season, but the seafood is always excellent. So are the Italian dishes. Food is delivered here from around the world. Local ingredients appear in dishes such as venison ravioli. The grilled quail is tops. Handicapped accessible. Open daily during the summer for dinner from 5 P.M. to 10 P.M.; in winter, Thursday through Saturday from 5 P.M. to 10. P.M. and Sunday 6 P.M. to 9 P.M. for wood-oven pizza. **112 East Ramshorn, P.O. Box 1436, Dubois, 82513; (307) 455-3666.**

Togwotee Mountain Lodge—$$–$$$$

Try the baby back ribs, the prime rib, the venison, the buffalo sausage, or the dandy fresh trout. Kids' and seniors' menus. Handicapped accessible. Enjoy a breakfast buffet in winter.

Open daily from mid-November to mid-April and June 1 to mid-October from 6:30 A.M. to 9:30 A.M. for breakfast, 11 A.M. to 2:30 P.M. for lunch, and 5:30 P.M. to 9 P.M. for dinner. Sandwiches available in between at the Red Fox Saloon. **Hwys. 26 and 287, P.O. Box 91, Moran, 83013; (800) 543-2847 or (307) 543-2847, fax (307) 543-2391. Website: www.cowboyvillage.com.**

Cowboy Cafe—$$–$$$

Daily specials. Charbroiled steaks and burgers. Not handicapped accessible. Kids' and seniors' menus. Open in winter from 6:30 A.M. to 8 P.M. and in summer from 6 A.M. to 9 P.M. or later. **115 East Ramshorn, Dubois, 82513; (307) 455-2595.**

Ramshorn Bagel and Deli—$$

Open 9 A.M. to 3 P.M. daily, closed Monday. Handicapped accessible. Good deli sandwiches. **202 East Ramshorn, Dubois, 82513; (307) 455-2400.**

Services

Visitor Information

Dubois Chamber of Commerce, 616 West Ramshorn Street, P.O. Box 632, Dubois, 82513; (307) 455-2556. Website: www.-duboiscc.wyoming.com.

75

Fort Laramie

Fort Laramie played a primary role in the frontier epic of the United States. As early as the 1820s, the area became the site for rendezvous for fur trappers, including trapper Jacques La Ramee. A corruption of his name appeared later on many things in Wyoming. Within a decade, the fort provided a focal point for the fur trade, an oasis for westward-bound emigrants and gold seekers headed both west and north, a headquarters for military campaigns on the northern plains, a place of peace for the great Indian councils, and a location to observe the closing of the frontier and the fulfillment of Manifest Destiny.

History

In 1834, a couple of fur traders named William Sublett and Robert Campbell constructed the first structure of several to be located near the headwaters of the Laramie and North Platte Rivers. They named it Fort William, and it quickly became an important base of operation for traders and trappers. The partners sold the fort to the American Fur Company in 1836. The post was renamed Fort John after John B. Sarpy. At some point the log structure rotted and was replaced with an adobe blockhouse. A clerk shortened "Fort John on the Laramie" to "Fort Laramie," and the name eventually stuck.

During 1842, pathfinder John C. Frémont suggested Fort John would make a good military post for protecting pioneers headed toward the Far West. Three years later, Congress authorized the establishment of military posts along the Oregon Trail, but it wasn't until 1849 that Congress authorized the purchase of Fort John for $4,000. Fifty thousand people had already passed through Fort Laramie on their way to Oregon. Over the next 20 years, emigrants camped, repaired their equipment, and bought provisions at the fort. Between 1851 and 1868, the fort hosted many treaty talks between the Indians and the government. As many as a hundred tepees dotted the landscape around the fort during these talks.

Unfortunately, the government failed to keep the treaties and asked for more and more concessions from the Indians, until things degenerated into the Indian Wars. Fort Laramie became a staging point for the army campaigns that eventually subdued the Northern Plains nations.

After the Indian Wars, the railroad moved in, but it bypassed the fort, choosing Cheyenne as its base. The army abandoned Fort Laramie in 1890. The buildings and land were auctioned off to local citizens. Over 50 structures were moved elsewhere, demolished, or dismantled. The remaining 20 buildings fell into disrepair until 1937, when the state of Wyoming purchased the site. A year later, ownership was transferred to the National Park Service and Fort Laramie became a national historic monument. Congress redesignated it a national historic site in 1960.

Festivals and Events

Frontier 4th of July
4th of July weekend
The fort puts on a bang-up celebration of Independence Day, re-creating various aspects of festivities of the national holiday as celebrated in 1876. Participate in games, enjoy programs and watch demonstrations of military and garrison life.

Military Encampment and Moonlight Tour
mid-August
This tour focuses attention on specific events in the fort's military history. There are solider camps, firing demonstrations, and special programs. Moonlight tours are all first-person living-history programs that explore particular

themes, such as the Connor Expedition, the incident of the hanging of two Indians at the fort, or occurrences on the Bozeman Trail. Reenactors dress in period clothing and will talk with you about all aspects of history.

Fur Trade Fort Laramie
Labor Day (early September)
Living history involving 20 trappers, traders, and Indians from the fur trade era explores the 150-year history of the early fort. Wander through a trading camp circa 1834 to 1849, see mountain-man demonstrations and other presentations. An evening program on Saturday night starts at 8 P.M.

Outdoor Activities

Fishing
Anglers will love the game fishing at **Hawk Springs State Recreation Area**. Prime months are June and July for walleye, but try your luck anytime for largemouth bass, yellow perch, channel catfish, and black crappie. Good ice fishing can be had in winter; however, the roads to the park are not plowed, so getting there can be tricky. **C/O Guernsey State Park, P.O. Box 429, Guernsey, 82214; (307) 836-2334. Wyoming Game & Fish** in **Torrington (307-532-2433)** has more details.

Fifteen minutes from Wheatland, **Grayrocks Dam and Reservoir** contains 104,000 acre-feet of water recreation. Free camping. Drinking water is available, but no hookups. Take **Exit 80 off I-25.**

Sheltered by cliffs and canyons, the reservoir at **Guernsey State Park** is a scenic place to enjoy some excellent catfish, bluegill, crappie, largemouth bass, or walleye fishing. A great place to windsurf! A full marina; picnic and camping sites, too. **Guernsey State Park, P.O. Box 429, Guernsey, 82214; (307) 836-2942.**

Horseback Riding
Play cowboy at the **Diamond Guest Ranch**, established in 1880. Participate in trail rides

Old Bedlam.

by the hour, breakfast rides, supper rides, and hayrides. Lodging, camping, and fishing trips are also available. **P.O. Box 236, Chugwater, 82210; (800) 932-4222** or **(307) 422-3564, fax (307) 422-3310. E-mail: diamon4632@aol.com. Website: www.-diamondgr.com.**

Seeing and Doing

The Fort
The fort offers daily programs, tours, and specialty talks in the summer, as well as an excellent 16-minute orientation film. Make your first stop the museum and visitor center. **Hwy. 160, HC 72 Box 389, Ft. Laramie, 82212; (307) 837-2221. Website: www.nps.gov/fola.**

Old Bedlam, constructed in 1849, saw service as everything from military headquarters to bachelors' quarters to married officers' quarters. **Sutler's Store,** built in 1848, carried necessities and even a few luxuries of life. Sutler's Store and Old Bedlam are the two oldest existing structures in Wyoming. Other buildings to see and wander through when they are open include the **Officer's Quarters,** the **Cavalry Barracks,** the **Old Guard House** with a scary, tiny jail, and the **Bakery.**

Oregon Trail Ruts National Historic Landmark

This national monument, just west of Register Cliff, pays tribute to the thousands of people who crossed the country in search of a better life. Ruts (locally called the "Guernsey Ruts") cut into the sandstone, up to five feet deep in places, were cut by wagon wheels. Pioneers and later freighters traversed the rock rather than the valley, which was boggy and thus harder to get across. To walk in the ruts is an experience you won't forget. **One mile south of Guernsey on Wyoming Avenue.**

Register Cliff State Historic Site

The sandstone cliff rises over 100 feet above the valley floor of the North Platte River, a nineteenth-century landmark for travelers on the Oregon Trail. Countless emigrants inscribed their names, dates, origins, and even

Travelers carved their names at Register Cliff.

messages on the soft rock surface. Travelers camped in the shadow of the chalky Register Cliff their first night out of Fort Laramie. Many of the names carry dates from the 1840s and 1850s with them. The earliest known date reads, "1829 This July 14" and is thought to belong to a French trapper or explorer commemorating Bastille Day. The graveyard at the site attests to the hardships of travel. Charles A. Guernsey, a pioneer cattleman and the person the town was named after, established a ranch near the cliff in the 1890s. His successor, Henry Frederick, donated the historic site to the state. **South Guernsey Road, Guernsey.**

Museums

Fort Laramie Museum

Fort Laramie was the last outpost of civilization in the Oregon Trail days. See the military of the West and experience the hardships of life in the frontier army. Share the joys and burdens with soldiers' families stationed far from home. During the summer, stop in at the Enlisted Men's Bar for a sarsaparilla. You can feel the presence of the ghosts! Open daily year-round, in winter from 8 A.M. to 4:30 P.M., and in summer from 8 A.M. to 7 P.M. Grounds open from dawn to dusk. **Hwy. 160, HC 72, Box 389, Fort Laramie, 82212; (307) 837-2221. Website: www.nps.gov/fola.**

Guernsey State Park Museum

Housed in a building constructed in 1930 by the Civilian Conservation Corps (CCC), this free museum features displays of the CCC crews and their work at Guernsey State Park. Other buildings and recreation facilities are available. Open daily May through Labor Day from 10 A.M. to 6 P.M. **Hwy. 26 north of Guernsey; 429 Hwy. 26, Guernsey, 82214. Call (307) 836-2900** for the museum and **(307) 836-2942** for boating and camping.

Homesteader Museum

Housed in the old 1925 Union Pacific Depot, this dandy little museum displays the richness and harsh reality of the pioneering life on the prairies of Goshen County. The fly nets from the Old 4A Yoder Ranch built in 1880 by Phillip and Cinderella Yoder testify to the conditions. Visit the Union Pacific caboose gallery filled with railroad memorabilia; see the Bordeaux Trading Post, once located near Fort Laramie; learn about the area's Native Americans through the Potter Family's Indian Artifact Collection. Open Memorial Day to Labor Day Monday through Saturday from 10 A.M. to 4:30 P.M., and Sunday 1 P.M. to 4:30 P.M. In winter, Monday through Friday from 10 A.M. to 4 P.M. Handicapped accessible for the most part. **495 Main, P.O. Box 250, Torrington, 82240; (307) 532-5612.**

Western History Center

The Western History Center offers a peek into the area's prehistoric past. See the 10-foot mammoth tusk, one of the recent discoveries unearthed by archaeological teams working near the center. Hands-on learning experiences. Interesting displays. Located four miles east of the town of Fort Laramie. Small fee. Call for hours. **Fort Laramie, 82212; (307) 837-3052.**

Where to Stay

Accommodations

Kings Inn—$$–$$$

Relax in quiet, comfortable rooms, some equipped with HBO. Pool and hot tub. King-size waterbeds available. Senior discounts. Weekly rates. Pets okay. Handicapped accessible. **1555 Main Street, Torrington, 82240; (307) 532-4011, fax (307) 532-7202.**

Vimbo's Motel—$$–$$$

Thirty-eight motel units—large rooms with queen-size beds. Small pets okay. Take the South Wheatland exit. **203 16th Street, P.O. Box 188, Wheatland, 82201; (307) 322-3842.**

The Bunkhouse Motel—$$

Interesting western decor with comfy rooms. Some rooms come equipped with refrigerators. Weekly rates available. Pets okay with a

Getting There

Fort Laramie is located off **Hwy. 160,** 105 miles north of Cheyenne. Wheatland, Guernsey, and Torrington all have airports that offer no commercial flights. Fly into **Cheyenne Municipal Airport** on **United Express (307-635-6623)** or use **Sky Harbor Air Charter Service (307-634-4417).** A variety of rental cars are available at the Cheyenne airport. **Powder River Transportation** also services the area **(800-442-3682 or 307-635-1327).**

refundable deposit. Handicapped accessible. **350 West Whalen, P.O. Box 310, Guernsey, 82214; (307) 836-2356, fax (307) 836-2328.**

Maverick Motel—$$

A nice small motel, with smoking and non-smoking rooms available. Twenty miles to Fort Laramie on the west edge of town. Across from a convenience store. One room has a kitchenette. Small pets okay. Not handicapped accessible. **Route 1, Box 354, Torrington, 82240; (307) 532-4064, fax (307) 532-2577.**

Guest Ranches

Grant Ranch—$$$$

Take a cattle ranch vacation, complete with hands-on ranching adventure. This 1890s ranch provides seasonal activities of branding in early June, moving cattle from July through September, hayrides, fishing, horseback rides, hiking, roping lessons, and special events. Open May through September. No minimum stay. **P.O. Box 459, Wheatland, 82201; (307) 322-2923. E-mail: migrant@wyoming.com. Website: www.grand-ranch.com.**

Camping

In Wyoming State Parks and Recreation Areas

Take pleasure in camping at the **Hawk Springs State Recreation Area,** 44 miles from Fort

Laramie. Twenty-four RV sites, tent sites, boat ramps, picnic areas with fire grills, restrooms, and drinking water. Open from Memorial Day through Labor Day. **C/O Guernsey State Park, P.O. Box 429, Guernsey, 82214; (307) 836-2942. Website: www.wywebb.-state.wy.us.**

Fort Laramie Municipal Park has no hookups. Overnight parking. Restrooms. Open year-round. **South Main, Fort Laramie, 82212; (307) 837-2711.**

Larson Park has electricity and water. Open mid-May until Labor Day. **Wyoming Street, Guernsey, 82214; (307) 836-2335.**

Private Campgrounds and Cabins

Chuckwagon Campground offers full hook-ups, tent sites on the lawn, and restrooms with showers just three miles from the fort. Pets okay on leash. Handicapped accessible. Open April to October. **Box 166, 306 Pioneer Court, Fort Laramie, 82212; (307) 837-2828.**

Where to Eat

Vimbo's Restaurant—$–$$$

A la carte dining. Decent food. The cooks cut their own steaks and roasts and make a tasty hamburger and chicken-fried steak. Open in summer Monday through Saturday from 5:30 A.M. to 10 P.M. and Sunday from 6 A.M. to 9 P.M. Open in winter Monday through Thursday from 6:30 A.M. to 9 P.M., Friday and Saturday until 10 P.M., and Sunday from 6 A.M. to 9 P.M. Closed Thanksgiving and Christmas. Handicapped accessible. **203 16th Street, P.O. Box 188, Wheatland, 82201; (307) 322-3725.**

Services

Visitor Information

The Fort Laramie Visitor Center is open between October and April daily from 8 A.M. to 4:30 P.M. From mid-May to October, the hours are 8 A.M. to 6 or 7 P.M. Interpretive programs and fort tours during the summer run from 9:30 A.M. to 5:30 P.M. **Fort Laramie National Historic Site, Hwy. 160, HC 72, Box 389, Fort Laramie, 82212; (307) 837-2221. Website: www.nps.gov/fola. Guernsey Visitors Center, P.O. Box 667, Guernsey, 82214; (307) 836-2715. Goshen County Chamber of Commerce, 350 West 21st Street, Torrington, 82240; (800) 577-3555 or (307) 532-3879. Platte County Chamber of Commerce, 65 16th Street, P.O. Box 427, Wheatland, 82201; (307) 322-2322, fax (307) 322-3419. Website: www.wyoming.com/~platte/.**

Lander

As you crest the hill coming into Lander, the Wind River Mountains recede into a blue, snow-capped horizon. Dropping into the basin, you can easily imagine descending through time into the land the Shoshone called the "valley of the warm winds." The Crow Indians also utilized the Wind River Valley because it furnished the best wintering grounds and provided clear, sweet water, as well as plenty of antelope, moose, deer, bighorn sheep, and buffalo.

Lander sits at one of the main access points into the Wind River Mountains. Like many places in the West, the Wind River Mountains received their name from an English translation of the Indian name—in this case, the name for the river that swells up from snow melt in the northern part of the mountain range. An almost year-round current of wind flows down the river of the "Big Wind" between the Shoshone and Wind River Ranges. At times, this prevailing, often spirited breeze amounts to a gale force, sweeping snow and frigid temperatures before it, but most of the time it lends the basin a more agreeable climate than the surrounding areas.

Likewise, the Popo Agie River (pronounced po-PO-zuh), which streams through Lander, comes from the Crow language—*popo* meaning "head" and *agie* meaning "water." The Middle Fork (the main branch of the Popo Agie) and its two sidekicks, the Little Popo Agie and the North Fork, originate in these rugged mountains.

The chamber of commerce stocks a walking-tour booklet for $1 each. The tour lasts about half an hour and covers over a hundred years of architecture and business history of Lander's historic downtown.

History

A historical marker in town states that trappers visited the valley in 1811. Possibly this date connects with the Pacific Fur Company

The Rise at Sinks Canyon.

overland journey bound for Astoria the year before the one mentioned above entered Wyoming from the West Coast. A party of 65 men, 82 horses, 1 woman, and 2 children (the family of the Indian interpreter) supposedly followed the Wind River through the valley. This group gained recognition for being the first to cross the continent after the famed Lewis and Clark Expedition. Just to complicate matters, a few historians suggest this Astorian party traversed the Winds through Union Pass (Dubois) and went down into the Green River Valley, then up to Jackson Hole, bypassing the Lander Valley by nearly a hundred miles.

Regardless of when they came, the trappers caught every beaver they could. By 1840 the cornucopia of fur animals had disappeared. The same historic marker mentions 1829, 1830, and 1838 as the dates when the

Lander Valley hosted the fur-trading tradition—a rendezvous.

The actual dates when people settled in the basin remain obscure. Modern Lander has been associated with four names. "Pushroot" seems an unlikely name for a settlement, but one report says residents swore it accurately described the windy weather that appeared to push the plants out of the soil in spring. It then became Camp Augur. Named for Brigadier General Christopher C. Augur, the commanding officer of the Department of the Platte, the post sat on the present city block between 5th and 6th Streets. The camp started up as part of an arrangement made with Chief Washakie when the government created the Wind River Indian Reservation for the Shoshone Nation in 1868.

In June 1870, the army renamed the post Camp Brown in honor of Captain Frederick Hallam Brown, who died during the Fort Fetterman Fight at the close of 1866. Later the camp moved to its present location—now named Fort Washakie.

Some historians contend the town surrounding the camp was settled in the 1870s. The official town of Lander, Wyoming, received incorporation in 1890.

Festivals and Events

Wyoming State Winter Fair
early February
This is the biggest wintertime trade show in the state, held indoors. In addition to continuous entertainment during the trade show, enjoy the two-day horse show; livestock shows that include pigs, sheep, steers, and llamas; and the Winter Fair Queen contest. Nashville performers headline the Winter Fair Dance held on Saturday night following the fair. **C/O Marlene Young, P.O. Box 162, Lander, 82520; (307) 332-4011.**

Wyoming Single Action Shooters
early May
Located at Hart Ranch Hideout, the site where oil was first discovered in Wyoming. At "high noon" the Wyoming Single Action Shooters, dressed in authentic western period clothing, gather to reenact historical and cinematic shoot-outs with timed, target contests. **7192 Hwys. 789 and 287, Lander, 82520; (307) 332-3836. E-mail: hartranch@campwyoming.com. Website: www.campwyoming.com.**

Outdoor Activities

Biking

Mountain Biking
Well-marked, established trails in the Shoshone National Forest just outside of town provide excellent mountain biking. The **Loop Road** (see Seeing and Doing, below) makes for a challenging bike ride. Bike rentals are available from **Freewheel Ski & Cycle, 258 Main, Lander, 82520; (307) 332-6616.**

Climbing

The **Granite Buttress**, about a quarter mile from the start of the **Popo Agie Falls Trail**, presents some interesting challenges for all climbing levels, as does the very popular south-facing wall of the **Limestone Buttress** at the start of **Sinks Canyon.** Climbs range in difficulty from class 5.9 (difficult) to 5.13+ (very difficult). **Wild Iris Climbing Area** in the **Limestone Mountains,** about 30 miles south of Lander on Hwy. 28, offers 150 climbing routes for skill levels ranging from class 5.7 to 5.14. Climb with your own gear at your own risk.

Fishing

The **Little Popo Agie River** teems with brown trout and some rainbow trout in the upper reaches. One stretch of it offers about three miles of public access with a couple of parking areas. The **Middle Fork** of the Popo Agie River, primarily its upper reaches, also has rainbow and brown trout. In the valley it has some public access fishing areas above and in town. Downstream from town is mostly private. The **North Fork** of the Popo Agie River provides brown and rainbow trout fishing. Lower portions are mainly on private land, but there are some public fishing accesses near the town. Large portions in the upper part of the **Sweetwater River** are unproductive due to runoff from the mountains, but as the river flows downstream it gains in productivity, offering some brook and rainbow trout fishing. It offers quite a lot of public access on Hwy. 28 and along the stretches of BLM land in Sweetwater Canyon that provides good rainbow and brown trout. Downstream from there it's private land. The **Wyoming Game & Fish District Office** has all the information to make your fishing experience the best. **260 Buena Vista Drive, Lander, 82520; (307) 332-2688.**

Rocky Mountain Horseback Vacations offers five-day mountain horsepacking trips and will pack in the whole camp, including all the food and gear, and move camp each day, so you get to see lots of the high country and get in plenty of trout fishing in pristine lakes. View wildlife, scenic vistas, and wildflowers! Fishing trips are available on the Continental Divide and in the Wind River Range at glacier lakes above timberline. The company will also set up camp and let you fish for five days straight in ideal trout environments at over 12,000 feet. Dozens of lakes and streams are within half a mile from base camp. The rest of the family can enjoy mountain trail rides while you fish. Five-day Outlaw Trail adventures also available. Customized trips for small groups. Flexible schedules. **P.O. Box 592, Lander, 82520; (800) 408-9149 or (307) 332-8535, fax (307) 335-8626. E-mail: edabney@rmisp.com. Website: www.willowcreekranch.com.**

Golf

Enjoy 18 holes at par 71 on a hilltop overlooking the town at the **Lander Golf Club.** Watch out for wildlife wandering onto the green! Monday is kids' day until noon. Wednesday is ladies' day, and Thursday is men's day, but women can play on Thursdays and men can play on Wednesdays. There are no restrictions.

Getting There

Lander is located next to the Shoshone National Forest, the largest of 16 national forests in the Rocky Mountains and the first to be set aside by the Yellowstone Timberland Reservation Act of March 3, 1891. The town is located in the central part of the state, 160 miles southeast of Jackson Hole. Get there via **Hwy. 287.** Lander only has a small, noncommercial air field, so fly into Riverton 25 miles to the northeast on **United Express (800-241-6522)** and rent a car at the airport from **Avis (800-331-1212 or 307-856-5052)** or from **Hertz (800-654-3131 or 307-856-2344).** The **Wind River Transportation Authority** provides bus service to Lander from the **Riverton Airport (800-439-7118).**

Club rentals and a driving range are available. Open June through August from 7 A.M. until dark every day, and open March, April, and October (depending on the weather) from 9 A.M. until dark. **1 Golf Course Drive, P.O. Box 417, Lander, 82520; (307) 332-4653.**

Hiking and Backpacking

A relatively easy way to gain a taste of Wyoming wilderness lies along **Popo Agie Falls** on the Middle Fork of the Popo Agie River. It makes a great introductory hike into elevation, climbing 600 feet in less than two miles. The hike follows the river, gradually gaining in altitude. There is one steep switchback, but the view of the falls more than makes up for it. Relax on a bench set in the shade before the return trek or sit on the edge of the rock overlook.

The **Middle Fork Trail,** which travels beyond Popo Agie Falls, provides the main access into the southern Popo Agie Wilderness. An arduous trek of 16 miles, the trail leads to Shoshone Lake, Sweetwater Gap, and Three Forks Park.

The trailhead for both these hikes begins at the Bruce's Bridge picnic area on Sinks Canyon Road just before the Loop Road (see Seeing and Doing, below) begins.

Oregon Trail Region

Along the Loop Road about 23 miles from Lander, hikers can take advantage of **Silas Lake Trail** and **Christina Lake Trail,** which leave from the Fiddlers Lake Campground. About a mile from the trailhead, the trail divides. Silas Lake goes to the right. To the left takes travelers to Gustave Lake or to Christina Lake. Some worn-out hiker scratched "100 more miles" into the wooden sign next to the mileage for Christina Lake. Nine miles can seem like a hundred in the high-altitude backcountry. Nevertheless, both trails wander through the essence of the Wyoming wilderness and lead to great fishing lakes.

The **Washakie Ranger District of the Shoshone National Forest** carries excellent hiking information and will help you tailor a trip to suit your abilities and time frame. The office is open year-round, Monday through Friday, from 8 A.M. to 4:30 P.M. **333 East Main Street, Lander, 82520; (307) 332-5460.**

Horseback Riding

Rocky Mountain Horseback Vacations will supply a very unique, very Wyoming horse ride. Try a historic reenactment trip on the Oregon Trail—70 miles worth, averaging about 15 miles a day. You'll cross the Continental Divide and South Pass and ride through Atlantic City and South Pass City, heading west each day, skirting the foothills of the Wind River Range. The trip is done as authentically as possible with outfitters and wranglers, in period clothing, cooking and camping in mid-1800s style. Trips last from Sunday to Friday afternoon. Local historians visit the camp and tell about the history of the area, including certain aspects of regional Native American and women's history. As an option, you'll be given weapons (and shown how to use black-powder rifles safely with no lead balls) with which to defend yourself against an Indian attack or to prevent being held up by outlaws. These events are nonscripted, so no one knows when or how they will take place. You can have a similar reenactment trip to the Hole-in-the-Wall country as a member of the Wild Bunch eluding a posse, trying to make it back to Butch Cassidy's famous hideout, or trying to make peace with the Indians. (See Powder River Region, Buffalo, Accommodations, Willow Creek Ranch at the Hole-in-the-Wall.) Leave the ranch headquarters on Monday morning, camp in a different location each night, and make it to the Hole-in-the-Wall site Wednesday afternoon. Tour the "Wall" on Thursday and head back to the ranch on Friday. These are time-travel, educational experiences that offer insight into Wyoming lifestyles of the 1800s. Make reservations. **P.O. Box 592, Lander, 82520; (800) 408-9149 or (307) 332-8535; fax (307) 335-8626. E-mail: edabney@rmisp.com. Website: www.willowcreekranch.com.**

Horseback rides by the hour, half day, or full day are available from **Wyoming Country Outfitters.** Cross-country rides over South Pass on Monday-through-Saturday trips average 15 miles a day and include reenactments with Indians and outlaw attacks. The Hole-in-the-Wall rides, also Monday through Saturday, travel into Butch Cassidy's territory with reenactment of outlaws, sheriff posses, and shoot-outs. Special reservations required for custom trips. All rides must be booked ahead of time. **7696 Hwy. 287, Lander, 82520; (307) 332-9149.**

For the more adventurous, try horsepacking trips from **Allen's Diamond Four Wilderness Ranch.** Besides lots of riding, on this two-week, hands-on pack trip you'll learn how to pack in gear and you'll practice wilderness skills, mountain fishing, plant identification, and map reading. Daring routes! Small classes. Not for the faint-hearted. You will learn the full spectrum, then hit the trail! Guided wilderness trips into the Popo Agie Wilderness, Wind River Range, and Dickenson Park in the Shoshone National Forest. Trips available June through September. **P.O. Box 243, Lander, 82520; (307) 332-2995, fax (307) 332-7902. Website: www.wyoming.-com/~dmndfour.**

Western Encounters provides one-week horseback riding and camping adventures between May and September on the Outlaw and Pony Express/Oregon trails, in the Great

Divide Basin, and on cattle drives through the foothills of the Big Horn Mountains. **24 Birchfield Lane, Lander, 82520; (800) 572-1230, phone/fax (307) 332-5434. E-mail: dashley@wyoming.com. Website: www.horseriders.com.**

Llama Trekking

Looking for a unique wilderness experience? Try llama packing in the Wind River Mountains. **Lander Llama Company** will fix you up with a scheduled trip or one of your own creation (four-person minimum). Both are guided treks and can last from three to seven days. Experience Sweetwater Canyon, Popo Agie Canyon, the Wind River and Absaroka ranges, and the Red Desert. Or plan a three-day fishing trip on the Sweetwater River in combination with staying at The Bunk House (see below). **2024 Mortimore Lane; (800) 582-5262** or **(307) 332-5624, fax (307) 332-5624. E-mail: woodruff@wyoming.com. Website: www. landerllama.com.**

Skiing

Cross-Country Skiing

The forest service maintains two cross-country ski trails in Sinks Canyon. The **Sage Draw Loop Trail** is a gentle 1.7 miles, and the **Moose Gulch Trail** offers more challenges on its 1.4 miles. **Washakie Ranger District, 333 Hwy. 789 South, Lander, 82520; (307) 332-4560.** Ski rentals are available from **Freewheel Ski & Cycle, 258 Main, Lander, 82520; (307) 332-6616.**

Snowmobiling

Head into deep powder on 95 miles of groomed trails in the Lander area. As part of the **Continental Divide Snowmobile Trail** system, trails connect Lander to Pinedale, Jackson, Grand Teton National Park, and Yellowstone National Park. It all begins at the southeast end of Lander. The variety of terrain, snow, and scenery will leave you awestruck. This system is *the* trail to ride! Get maps and

Lander Llamas.

information from the **Washakie Ranger District, 333 Hwy. 789 South, Lander, 82520; (307) 332-4560.** Be sure to pick up a copy of the city's snowmobile regulations at the Lander Chamber of Commerce.

85

Seeing and Doing

The Oregon Trail

(For information about the Oregon Trail, see the Casper chapter in this section.)

Scenic Drives

Loop Road

From downtown Lander, head south on 5th Street. Turn right on Fremont Street (Hwy. 131), which curves to the left, becoming Sinks Canyon Road. Go through the park and into the Shoshone National Forest on what locals refer to as the Loop Road (Forest Road 300). Head up the switchback past Frye Lake, beyond the south edge of Fiddlers Lake, around Louis Lake, and into the heart of the forest. Great wildlife viewing, scenic vistas, fishing, and picnicking opportunities. The improved gravel road, which gets rough in several spots, comes out on Hwy. 28 between the roads that lead to South Pass City and Atlantic City. Closed in winter.

Sinks Canyon

Follow the directions for traveling to the Loop Road (see page 85). Sinks Canyon State Park, known locally as just "the Sinks," received its name because the Middle Fork of the Popo Agie River disappears (it sinks) into a cave about halfway through the canyon. A quarter mile farther, it emerges into a large, calm pool, called "the Rise," on the opposite side of the canyon. The water takes two hours to travel that quarter mile. Something odd occurs at the Rise: More water comes out of it than flowed into the Sinks, plus the water of the Rise is warmer than that of the Sinks. While in the canyon, look for bighorn sheep. A herd of about 50 were reintroduced into the canyon from Whiskey Mountain at Dubois during the 1980s. The Sinks Canyon Visitors Center, open between Memorial Day and Labor Day from 9 A.M. to 7 P.M., has a nice little (free) museum about the geology, natural history, and human development of the canyon. **Hwy. 131, Lander, 82520; (307) 332-6333.**

Red Canyon

This national natural landmark is located 11 miles south of town on Hwy. 28. It is a winter range for elk, and the canyon's beauty spreads out from a scenic overlook. Once a wagon road called "Red Grade," the road showcases the deep red stone of the Triassic Chugwater Formation set against the Jurassic nugget sandstone cliff on the mountains.

Where to Stay

Accommodations

The Resort at Louis Lake—$$$–$$$$
In the Shoshone National Forest by Louis Lake, this resort offers rustic living in five one-room cabins with small kitchens, propane stoves, and a shared bathhouse. No phones, no TV, but plenty of quality fishing, hiking, mountain biking, or just relaxing. Rent a canoe or fishing boat. Guided snowmobile trips available. Handicapped accessible. Pets okay. Kids welcome. Open year-round, by reservation only in the winter. **1811 Louis Lake Road, Lander, 82520; (888) 4-A-CABIN (422-2246) or (307) 332-5549. Website: www.Wyoming.com/~louislake.**

Blue Spruce Inn—$$$
Surround yourself in western hospitality in this turn-of-the-century Arts and Crafts–style house built in 1920 by Lander's mayor, Frank Brower. Four large rooms have private baths. Relax in the glassed-in sunporch or the library filled with books. There's a lovely flower garden in the summer and a rec room. No minimum stay. Not handicapped accessible. No pets. Children over 12 welcome. Open year-round. Full, big breakfast. Nothing wimpy here! The Popo Agie River is a block from the house. The inn also offers a special-occasion package with dinner, wine, and a night's stay. Reduced rates for a stay of three of more nights. Two-day minimum stay over the 4th of July. Off-street parking. **677 South 3rd; (888) 503-3311, (307) 332-8253. E-mail: bluespruce@rmisp.com. Website: www.blue-spruce.com.**

The Bunk House—$$$
Settle into a rustic cabin filled with home comforts located at the Lander Llama Company. Refrigerator is stocked with all sorts of healthy foods and homemade cinnamon rolls. Fully equipped kitchenette to cook your own breakfast whenever you like, plus evening snacks provided. Sleep up to six people (using extra beds in the loft). Private bath. Get acquainted with the resident, friendly llamas! A delightfully quiet and secluded place to stay. **2024 Mortimore Lane; (800) 582-5262, fax (307) 332-5624. E-mail: woodruff@wyoming.com. Website: www. lander-llama.com.**

Piece of Cake B&B—$$$
Stay in one of three log cabins or two rooms in the main house. Each offers a private bath. The cabins have a refrigerator and a microwave and private porches for lots of peace and quiet. Located five miles from Lander in the foothills of the Winds, the B&B property covers 34 acres, surrounded by BLM land, so there's

plenty of secluded hiking and mountain biking available. Full breakfast with homemade muffins and breads—you'll go away full. Close to snowmobiling. No minimum stay. Pets okay. Kids welcome. During the spring and autumn, a Native American study tour is available. Open year-round. **2343 Baldwin Creek Road; (307) 322-7608. E-mail: pieceofcake@-wyoming.com.**

Guest Ranches

Allen's Diamond Four Wilderness Ranch—$$$$
Here is a wilderness experience unlike any other. Mountain ranch vacations in Dickenson Park in the Wind River Range is where guests really rough it. Spend a week in cabins with no electricity, but the shower house does have hot and cold water. At 9,200 feet, it's the highest ranch in Wyoming. The cost includes lodging, three meals a day, and guides. Ranch staff also provide guided, catered trips for fishing, supplying a cook, a fishing guide, the horses, and all the camping supplies. All you need to bring is your sleeping bag, fishing rods, and personal items. There is also a kids-only trip for 9- to 15-year-olds. Open June through September. **P.O. Box 243; Lander, 82520; (307) 332-2995, fax (307) 332-7902. Website: www.wyoming.com/~dmndfour.**

Three Quarter Circle Ranch—$$$$
Want to try cattle ranching? Then plan on vacationing here for a week-long authentic cattle vacation. You catch up (catch, bridle, and saddle) your horse at sunrise, check cattle on the open range, participate in roundups, learn to work with a cow horse, and stay in mobile homes with showers where the Oregon Trail crosses the Continental Divide. The ranch has 35,000 acres and over 1,000 head of cattle. With no more than six to eight guests per week and a cowboy-to-guest ratio of one to two, you can't ask for a better experience. Daily riding is all work-related: pushing cows and cutting out cattle on the open range. Prior riding experience is mandatory! You'll learn safety and have an opportunity to improve your riding skills, regardless of your skill level. Bring your own horse, if you want. This vacation is not for everybody, but it's fantastic for those who love to ride. Three meals a day and airport pickup included. Come whenever you'd like between May and June and September and October. **P.O. Box 243, Lander, 82520; (307) 332-2995, fax (307) 332-7902.**

Camping

In the National Forests
Forest Service Sinks Canyon Campground just beyond the state park offers nine tent and trailer sites, picnic tables with grates, restrooms, and drinking water. Good fishing. Open May through October. **Hwy. 131, Lander, 82520; (307) 332-6333.**

Louis Lake Campground has nine sites for tents and trailers for up to 16 days, then you must move five miles away. Drinking water, tables and grates, and restrooms. Fishing and hiking. Open July through September. **333 East Main Street, Lander, 82520; (307) 332-5460.**

Ray Lake Campground offers a variety of tent sites, 10 full RV hookups. Drinking water, tables with grates, restrooms. Not handicapped accessible. Open May 1 to September 30. **39 Ray Lake Road, Lander, 83530; (307) 332-9333.**

Fiddlers Lake Campground, 23 miles from Lander on the Loop Road, has 13 tent and RV sites, drinking water, restrooms, and picnic tables with grates. Great fishing and boating on the lake. Handicapped accessible. Open early July through mid-September. **(307) 332-5460.**

In Wyoming State Parks and Recreation Areas
Sinks Canyon State Park supplies 10 tent sites and 30 sites for trailers for up to two weeks. Restrooms, water, tables with grates, handicapped-accessible sites. Fishing, hiking, rock climbing. Open May through October. Visitors center hours Memorial Day through Labor Day: 9 A.M. to 7 P.M. **Hwy. 131, Lander, 82520; (307) 332-6333.**

Private Campgrounds and Cabins
Lander City Park offers seven trailer sites (no

87

hookups) and unlimited tent camping for up to three days. Restrooms and drinking water available. Utilize the picnic tables with grates and a fun playground. Open May through September. **405 Fremont Street, Lander; (307) 332-4647.**

A scenic location nine miles south of Lander, **The Hart Ranch Hideout RV Park & Campground** provides full hookups, restrooms, laundry, horse corrals, fire rings, a playground, tent sites, rustic cabins, and a good store with fishing and RV supplies. Free coffee in the mornings at the store. Group, weekly, and monthly rates. Open May 1 to mid-October. **7192 Hwys. 789 and 282, Lander, 82520; (307) 332-3836. E-mail: hart-ranch@campwyoming.com. Website: www.campwyoming.com.**

Where to Eat

Hitching Rack—$$–$$$$
Located on the hill overlooking town, "the Hitch," as people call it, offers good steaks in a steakhouse atmosphere. Kids' and seniors' menus available. A big salad bar and fresh fish on the weekends. Try the Swedish cream for dessert—it's fantastic! Open year-round from 4:30 P.M. until folks leave, closed Sundays. **Hwy. 287 South, P.O. Box 1033, Lander, 82520; (307) 332-4322.**

Big Noi Restaurant—$$–$$$$
Fried rice is the house special recipe. Discounted kids' meals and half orders available. American foods as well. Handicapped accessible. Discount for seniors. Open daily, 8 A.M. to 9 P.M. **8125 Hwy. 789, Lander, 82520; (307) 332-3102 or (307) 332-8214.**

Breadboard—$–$$$
Sandwiches; soups; chili; and the Piggyback, made with Canadian bacon, smoked bacon, and provolone cheese—all on fresh-baked breads. Open in winter Monday through Friday from 11 A.M. to 7 P.M., and the rest of the year daily from 11 A.M. to 4 P.M. Freshly cut meats and vegetables prepared to order. You can enjoy a great view of the mountains from the restaurant, and historic photos of the last 120 years of Lander decorate the walls. Drive-up window. Handicapped accessible. **1350 Main, Lander, 82520; (307) 332-6090.**

Hooligan's—$–$$
The place to enjoy the goodies from Hooligan's is just outside the door beside the creek in a quiet, shady little alcove. In addition to good sandwiches and fries, try the Disaster—12 scoops of ice cream and everything else they can find to put in it! Handicapped accessible. Open Tuesday through Thursday 10 A.M. to 8 P.M., Friday 10 A.M. to 10 P.M., Saturday noon to 8 P.M., and Sunday noon to 10 P.M. **351 Main, Lander, 82520; (307) 332-5050.**

Services
Lander Area Chamber of Commerce, 160 North First Street, Lander, 82520; (307) 332-3892, fax 332-3893. E-mail: lander-chamber@wyoming.com. Website: www.landerchamber.org. You can also contact the **Wind River Visitors Council, P.O. Box 1449, Riverton, 82501; (800) 645-6233.**

Riverton

Riverton is the crossroads between the sagebrush prairies and the Wind River Mountains. When every motel and campground along Hwys. 287 and 26 north toward Yellowstone National Park is booked solid, which happens every year, it makes a good alternative location to use as a base.

History

Since the early 1800s, legendary mountain men braved these mountains, exploring and trapping for fur. Often they wouldn't see another person until the annual rendezvous where trappers, Indians, and traders came together to swap goods and tell stories. Riverton is known to be home to the only documented site of the rendezvous, taking place in 1830 and 1838 near the confluence of the Big and Little Wind Rivers.

The Wind River Indian Reservation, a prominent feature of the area, was established in 1868 to ease tensions with the Plains Indians during the period of encroaching white settlement. The site of Riverton was once part of this reservation. As part of a 1903 treaty, the resident Indian nations relinquished this land north of the Wind River, leaving it open to white settlement. The railroad completed a line into Riverton in 1906, founding the town and encouraging a flood of settlers who set up tents and wagons within recently surveyed plots. For a while the place was known as "Tent City." Most settlers came to work the land, as the temperate climate in the Wind River Valley and open land were considered good farming country.

Riverton was also key in the timber "tie hack" industry, receiving the hand-hewn logs that were floated 80 miles down the Wind River from Dubois to supply the growing railroads at the turn of the century.

Castle Gardens. Photo courtesy of the Wyoming Division of Tourism.

Festivals and Events

Mountain Man Rendezvous
early July

This famous celebration of the old tradition takes people back in time more than 160 years to when the region was home to the Shoshone Indians and a few brave explorers and trappers. This festival takes place on the site of the original 1838 rendezvous. Participants dressed in period costumes of the fur-trade era—buckskins and fur hats. Along Traders Row, vendors display and sell furs, shirts, wool goods, beads, and other antique and reproduction wares that fit the era. Native American displays and demonstrations of mountain-man backcountry skills are part of the tradition. Come evening, there's usually a big council fire, encouraging stories and songs. **1838 Rend Association, P.O. Box 1838, Riverton, 82501; (307) 856-3210.**

Wild West Winter Carnival
early February
This celebration of winter recreation is held at Boysen State Reservoir. Festivities include races on snowmobiles, all-terrain vehicles (ATVs), bikes, and dogsleds. Ice sculpting and an ice-fishing derby aren't all the ice pursuits. How about a miniature golf tournament and softball games on the ice and, of course, ice hockey? Also enjoy a demolition derby, volleyball matches, and a dance. For more information call **(307) 856-7783.**

Outdoor Activities

90

Ballooning

The skies over Riverton are full of color during the third week of July from the **Balloon Rally.** During the rally, dozens of balloons rise up in the early morning and gently float over the town against the backdrop of the Wind River Mountains. There's plenty to do besides watching or riding in the balloons. Enjoy fireworks, a dance, a vaudeville show, pig wrestling, a rodeo, and stock-car races. There's also a money grab for envelopes with bucks in them on top of a 30-foot pole. **Riverton Rendezvous, P.O. Box 299, Riverton, 82501; (307) 856-4285** or **(307) 856-4801.**

Biking

Mountain Biking

Rails to Trails has turned 25 miles of land along the old railroad line through town to Shoshoni into an excellent path for biking. Mainly gravel, some portions in town are paved.

Fishing

Boysen Reservoir is a large and popular boating area north of Riverton, just west of the town

of Shoshoni. The 36,480-acre-foot reservoir is located at the mouth of a gorgeous canyon cut by the Wind River over the course of roughly 600 million years of Wyoming's geologic history. There's great walleye, crappie, burbot, bullhead, western sauger, perch, ling, trout, and bass fishing north of Riverton in Boysen Reservoir and the Wind River. (For more information, see Big Horn Region, Thermopolis.)

Ocean Lake, 15 miles northwest of town just off Hwy. 26, supplies some great bluegill, perch, bass, and crappie fishing. June is a hot fishing month on this lake. In winter check out the ling fishing. Contact **Wyoming Game & Fish (307-332-2688).**

Golf

Riverton Country Club's 18-hole, par-72 course is private but open to the public for a modest fee. This championship-quality course is ranked one of the best in Wyoming. **Riverview Road, Riverton, 82501; (307) 856-4779.** Or try a great course at **Renegade Golf, Hwy. 26 West, Riverton, 82501; (307) 857-0117.**

Hiking and Backpacking

(See the Lander and Dubois chapters for hiking and backpacking opportunities in this region.)

Snowmobiling

(See information on Boysen Reservoir in Fishing, above, and in the Thermopolis chapter of the Big Horn Region.)

Swimming

Riverton Aquatic Center offers indoor swimming and diving areas, jacuzzi baths, and steam and sauna rooms. **2001 West Sunset, Riverton, 82501; (307) 856-4230.**

Seeing and Doing

Castle Gardens

In earlier times, Native Americans roamed the Wind River country, hunting and camping in the valleys. Castle Gardens, 40 miles east of Riverton, preserves a wealth of prehistoric petroglyphs depicting images sacred to those ancient peoples. Castle Gardens extends six miles and is a mile in width. Petroglyphs dot the landscape with drawings appearing on a series of vertical cliffs, highly eroded, rising 10 to 100 feet above the valley floor. Castle Gardens gets its name from the way the landscape looks like a medieval castle and gardens. Located on a dirt road **just off Hwy. 136.**

Sage and Prairie Chicken Strutting Grounds

April visitors have the opportunity to see something rare, the strutting ground of the sage and prairie chickens in the Gas Hills off Hwy. 137. Tours can be arranged through **Wyoming Game & Fish (307-332-2688).**

Museums

Riverton Museum

Unique displays tell the story of pioneering in the area. See the drugstore, a schoolroom, household goods, and farm equipment artifacts, as well as a collection of Indian items from the Shoshone and Arapaho tribes. Most of the items in the museum come from the Riverton area. The old newspaper print shop is a working exhibit that shows visitors what a newspaper shop of the 1920s through the 1950s was like. Old radios and phonographs from the 1900s through the 1930s are also demonstrated for visitors. Special tours can be arranged in advance. No fee. Open year-round, 10 A.M. to 4 P.M., Tuesday through Saturday, closed holidays. **700 East Park Avenue, Riverton, 82501; (307) 856-2665.**

Where to Stay

Accommodations

Tomahawk Motor Lodge—$$–$$$

An excellent, comfortable, family-run lodge that delivers on real western hospitality. Large, cozy rooms. Wake up to coffee or tea in

Getting There

Riverton spreads along the edge of the Wind River Indian Reservation in the central part of the state 25 miles northeast of Lander and 120 miles west of Casper. Travel to Riverton along **Hwys. 26 and 789.** Or you can fly into Riverton on **United Express (800-241-6522)** and rent a car at the airport from **Avis (800-331-1212 or 307-856-5052)** or **Hertz (800-654-3131 or 307-856-2344).** The **chamber of commerce** has a list of area day-care centers at **(307) 856-4801.**

your room; coffee and tea are also available in the lobby. Airport transportation. No pets. **208 East Main, Riverton, 82501; (800) 637-REST (7378)** for reservations or **(307) 856-9205, fax: (307) 856-2879.**

Cottonwood Ranch B&B—$$–$$$

Located on a working 250-acre ranch. Three rooms, one shared bath and one half bath. There's a butte behind the house; you can hike to the top for a fantastic view. Watch the cattle roundup. Not elegant, just homey. Great food! Within 20 minutes of rivers and lakes for fishing and the mountains. Good rockhounding. Full farm-style breakfasts served with homemade breads and preserves. Not handicapped accessible. Pets okay outdoors and in the outbuildings. Kids welcome under supervision. Open year-round. **951 Missouri Valley Road, Riverton, 82501; (307) 856-3064.**

Guest Ranches

Strathkey Wranglers—$$$$

This working ranch offers trail rides and trailing cows. Work with wranglers, rounding up and branding strays. For small groups of no more than four people. Big trail drive in November and December, moving cattle from the summer to the winter pasture. Kids welcome. Includes meals, rooms, and horses, or bring your own horse. Open year-round. **189 Yound Road, Riverton, 82501; (307) 856-2194.**

Camping

In Wyoming State Parks and Recreation Areas

(See the Thermopolis chapter in the Big Horn Region for camping at Boysen Reservoir.)

Private Campgrounds and Cabins

Riverton RV Park offers full hookup and pull-through sites. Grills, picnic tables, a dump station, laundry, and even tepees are available. Full telephone service and phone jacks available for Internet access. Pets okay. Open year-round. **1618 East Park Avenue, Riverton, 82501; (800) 528-3913 or (307) 857-3000, fax (307) 856-9559. E-mail: jpepper@wyoming.com. Website: www.-campwyoming.com.**

Fort Rendezvous Campground provides full hookups for self-contained spaces only. Pets allowed if kept on a chain. **10368 Hwy. 789, Riverton, 82501; (307) 856-1144.**

Owl Creek Campground offers full hook-ups, tent sites, restrooms, a store, rec room, swings, showers, laundry. Pets okay on a leash. Partially handicapped accessible. Open mid-May to mid-September, depending on the weather. **11124 Hwys. 26 and 789, Riverton, 82501; (307) 856-2869.**

Where to Eat

The Depot La Estacion—$$–$$$$

Taste the seafood enchiladas. Some American foods. Mexican decor with hand-laid Mexican-tile tables. Located in the historic train depot.

Open in winter Monday through Saturday from 11 A.M. to 9 P.M., in summer until 10 P.M. Kids' dishes that they will love. Ten-percent discount for seniors. Not handicapped accessible. **Depot Building, First and Main Streets, Riverton, 82501; (307) 856-2221.**

The Bull Steakhouse—$$–$$$$

Steaks, seafood, and good prime rib. Kids' and seniors' menus. No handicapped restroom. Open daily for lunch and dinner, 11 A.M. to 2 P.M. and 5 P.M. to 10 P.M. Daily specials. Cocktails. **1100 West Main, Riverton, 82501; (307) 856-4728.**

Yellowstone Drug Store—$

This is *the* place for the best malts and milk shakes in the state! Made with real ice cream at an old-fashioned soda fountain. The one-day record is 624 malts and shakes made to order, and there's a running number in excess of 55,000 using 11,802 gallons of real ice cream. Wyomingites traveling through this section of the state always stop in for a malt or shake. **127 Main, Shoshoni, 82649; (307) 876-2539.**

Services

Visitor Information

The Riverton Area Chamber of Commerce, 101 South First Street, Riverton, 82501; (307) 856-4801, fax (307) 857-0873. E-mail: rivertoncc@wyoming.com. Website: www.wyoming.com/~rivertoncc.

92

South Pass City and Atlantic City

Historic South Pass City. Photo courtesy of the Wyoming Division of Tourism.

South Pass is not exactly a mountain pass in the traditional sense of a narrow break between two mountains. It is actually a huge plateau of sage flats, buttes, and Red Desert sand that rises gradually to the Continental Divide at 7,400 feet. On top of this plateau, the southern end of the lofty Wind River Mountains gives way to the flat expanse of the Great Divide Basin. During the gold rush years, South Pass City took on the pass's namesake, while Atlantic City was named for the side of the divide it was founded on. South Pass City and Atlantic City nearly disappeared into legend, but both have been revived, and their histories restored for the public to explore and enjoy.

History

South Pass, acting as a natural break in the Rocky Mountains chain, was used by American Indians for many years. It was first utilized by white explorers, trappers, and traders in the early 1800s. The pass proved critical for virtually all of the emigrant traffic that was to follow along the Oregon Trail throughout the mid-1800s. It's estimated that during the height of the westward migration nearly 350,000 settlers crossed South Pass on their way to California, Oregon or Utah. Pioneers encountered the "Parting of the Ways," a point that marked the split in trails toward respective destinations, a bit west of South Pass City. The Oregon Buttes, flattop sandstone hills rising out of the plateau, signaled the splitting of the trails.

Gold was first discovered in the South Pass area in 1842. Prospectors worked the clear waterways for nuggets for years following the first strike. By 1867, disenchanted miners returning from the California rush tried their luck at South Pass and found more gold. Henry Reedal put in the first mining claim on what become known as the Carissa Lode. The Carissa Mine, a hard-rock mining operation, produced over six million dollars' worth of gold from a 400-foot shaft. This triggered a boom for the region that created mines at South Pass City and Atlantic City and populated the area with almost 3,000 people at its peak in 1869. The rush didn't last long, and by 1872 both towns were all but deserted. A few gold booms occurred later, but South Pass City essentially became a ghost town, and Atlantic City remained a small town and cozy home to ranchers.

South Pass City was home to Esther Hobart Morris, who made national history by becoming in 1870 the first woman to hold office as justice of the peace. Morris held the position for eight and a half months, serving up justice in her bailiwick of 460 people. Historians disagree about the number of cases she tried, but no higher court ever overturned any of her 26 to 50 case decisions. Regardless of her record, Morris received no reappointment and subsequently retired, but her role in women's suffrage would change and grow with the passage of years. Many feel she was also crucial in setting the stage for women being granted voting privileges in Wyoming in 1869. Wyoming became the first state or territory to grant women's suffrage in the United States, hence Wyoming's motto: "The Equality State."

A few more boom-bust eras seized the South Pass area throughout the nineteenth century. During the 1960s, the area was prospected for iron ore and a large strip-mine operation was built to extract the metal. Today, only a few hopeful prospectors still pan the Sweetwater River for the precious gold.

Outdoor Activities

Climbing

Climbers flock to the **Cirque of the Tower,** a semicircle of jagged pinnacles of rock rising up from Lonesome Lake at the headwaters of the North Fork of the Popo Agie River. The most prominent formation in "the Cirque," the shortened name the locals use, is Pingora Peak. It ranks as a favorite among ambitious climbers, shooting up from the lake like a gargantuan tree stump. Supposedly, Pingora derives its name from the Shoshone language and means "high, rocky, inaccessible peak." Access the Cirque from the Big Sandy Opening off Hwy. 28 south of the South Pass near Farson.

Allen's Diamond Four Wilderness Ranch will carry supplies and/or climbers into and out of the mountains. **P.O. Box 243; Lander, 82520; (307) 332-2995, fax (307) 332-**

7902. **Website: www.wyoming.com/ ~dmndfour.**

Fishing

The **Sweetwater River** runs cold and clear along the high plateau. Brown and brook trout swim in those waters. Public access is available just off Hwy. 28.

Hiking and Backpacking

The **Red Desert** is a harsh environment for human and nonhuman alike. The basin is grassland to thousands of antelope and one of the last remaining herds of wild horses. Indian artifacts, Wyoming jade, and a variety of fossils are abundant in this region. If you are properly trained and prepared, the desert can be a worthwhile experience. The basin is located south of South Pass and is accessed from Hwy. 28, Hwy. 191, and I-80. There are no marked trails, no facilities, and, for the most part, very little water. (For more on the Red Desert, see the Rock Springs chapter in the Union Pacific section.)

Horseback Riding

(See the Lander chapter in this section for outfitters who offer horseback and wagon rides around South Pass.)

Skiing

Cross-Country Skiing

The forest service maintains a cross-country ski trail system near South Pass. The trailhead starts from Hwy. 28 just south of South Pass City. **Willow Creek Trail,** the main access trail, is a difficult 0.9 mile with some downhill. **Miners Delight Loop,** 0.8 mile, and **Duck Soup Loop,** 1.7 miles, require some advanced skiing. **Aspen Glide Loop** is an easy 0.7 mile through a forest of aspens. **Horse Feathers Loop** is another scenic, easy 0.5 mile. **Washakie Ranger District, 333 Hwy. 789 South, Lander, 82520; (307) 332-4560.**

Snowmobiling

Atlantic City is the southern end of the extensive **Continental Divide Trail** system, offering excellent snowmobiling among the foothills of the Winds. (See the Lander chapter in this section for more about snowmobiling along the Continental Divide Trail system in this area.)

Seeing and Doing

South Pass City State Historical Site

The journey to South Pass City is a beautiful drive up out of the Wind River Basin onto the high desert plateau of sagebrush and grass sprawling out from the southern terminus of the Wind River Mountains. The gold mining boom-bust town of South Pass City is now one of the most authentic historic sites enrolled on the National Register of Historic Places. Thirty of the original structures have been restored, housing thousands of artifacts that are authentic to the site. The buildings are now open to the public. Explore the entire town as one large, 39-acre, open-air museum of nineteenth-century western living. Some of the key buildings to explore are the respectable **South Pass Hotel,** which featured front-door stagecoach service and postal service. The **Exchange Bank** opened in 1868 to assess prospectors' raw gold and purchase the metal. This building later became a saloon that was frequented by Butch Cassidy. The **Esther Morris Memorial Cabin** is a reconstruction of the one she lived in with her family when she served as the first woman to hold political office in the nation as justice of the peace for South Pass City in 1870. There's also **Smith's General Store,** a **variety theater, blacksmith shop, livery stable, newspaper office,** the **Sweetwater County Jail,** and several more buildings and artifacts to see. Travelers are greeted at a small visitors center/fee station equipped with restrooms. A concession, operated by the Friends of South Pass, offers refreshments at the Smith Sherlock Store. Historic South Pass City is open from mid-May

Getting There

South Pass City and Atlantic City skirt the edge of the Wind River Mountains on an **improved gravel road just off Hwy. 28,** 30 miles south of Lander. The nearest airport is in Riverton over 60 miles away. Fly into Riverton on **United Express (800-241-6522).** Rental cars are available at the airport.

through mid-October. South Pass City is 2 miles off Hwy. 28, 35 miles south of Lander. **South Pass City State Historical Site, 125 South Pass Main, South Pass City, 82520; (307) 332-3684, fax (307) 332-3688.**

Atlantic City Mercantile & Historic Site

Known locally as "the Merc," this historic steakhouse and saloon has become a legend for its gourmet dining, local entertainment, authentic rustic atmosphere, and scenic location. German entrepreneur Lawrence Giessler came to Wyoming in 1873 to be a cowboy. At that time Atlantic City had become all but a ghost town with the gold rush going bust in the area. In 1893, Giessler opened the mercantile during another surge of gold fever that seized the area. That gold boom ended quickly, too, but the mercantile remained as ranching continued near the Sweetwater River and Red Desert. Today, the mercantile is a national historic site, retaining much of its original darkwood interior and Old West charm. (See Where to Eat, below.) **100 East Main Street,** Atlantic City, 82520; (888) 257-0215 or (307) 332-5143, fax (307) 332-9376.

Where to Stay

Camping

In the National Forests

Forest service campgrounds are available along the **Loop Road** out of Lander. (See the Lander chapter in this section for more details.) **Washakie Ranger District, 333 Hwy.**

95

789 South, Lander, 82520; (307) 332-4560.

Bureau of Land Management (BLM) Land

Atlantic City Campground and **Big Atlantic Gulch Campground** are located on an improved gravel road just off Hwy. 28 South on the way to Atlantic City. Both are open June 1 through October 31 and offer trailer and tent sites, picnic tables with grates, restrooms, and drinking water. **BLM Lander Resource Office, 1335 Main Street, P.O. Box 589, Lander, 82520; (307) 332-8400.**

Where to Eat

Atlantic City Mercantile—$$–$$$$

Steaks are cooked over aspen logs to juicy perfection on the dining-room grill. Drinks are served at the classic western bar, and someone's usually plinking away at the saloon-style upright piano in the corner. During the summer months, the mercantile is open seven days a week and often hosts local bands who play country-and-western favorites on Friday and Saturday nights. Steak nights are Thursday through Sunday. Basque Night on Wednesdays, featuring a seven-course old-country sheepherders' dinner, is a real treat. Lunches are served all day, making this a great place to stop before or after visiting South Pass City, only two miles away. The mercantile is open during the winter Friday through Sunday from 11 A.M. to 9 P.M. to serve snowmobile enthusiasts and hardy backcountry skiers taking advantage of the marvelous trails along the foothills of the Wind River Mountains. The mercantile also offers four reasonably priced A-frame cabins for lodging. Open daily May through October, Monday through Saturday from 11 A.M. to 11 P.M. and open December through April, Friday through Sunday from 11 A.M. to 9 P.M. Dinner served Sunday 6 P.M. to 10 P.M. **100 East Main Street, Atlantic City, 82520; (307) 332-5143, fax (307) 332-9376.**

Services

Visitor Information

South Pass City Historical Site is administered by the Wyoming Department of Commerce's Division of State Parks and Historic Sites. **The Friends of South Pass City** also provide information about the site. **(307-332-3684.)** General tourist information is available through the **Lander Area Chamber of Commerce, 160 North First Street, Lander, 82520; (307) 332-3892, fax (307) 332-3893. E-mail: landerchamber@wyoming.com. Website: www.landerchamber.org.**

96

Wind River Indian Reservation

About 8,000 Shoshone and Arapaho share the Wind River Indian Reservation. Originally the reservation was set aside for the Shoshone and Bannock; however, the Bannocks received their own reservation in Idaho. The Arapaho, traditional enemies of the Shoshones, were to have their own reservation, but the government asked if the Arapahos could spend one winter on the Shoshones' reservation. That was in 1877. The two Indian nations have been forced to share the reservation ever since. Each nation has its own government, and both tribal governments have headquarters in Fort Washakie, located 15 miles outside Lander. Fort Washakie has the distinction of being the only United States military installation ever named after an Indian chief.

History

Historically, the Eastern Shoshones have occupied the Wind River Valley since the early to mid-1800s. The Shoshones' first contact with whites came through Sacajawea, a Shoshone woman who helped guide the Lewis and Clark Expedition of 1805. Her presence helped guarantee the success of the expedition, making it easier for the whites to obtain supplies and places of safe passage through Indian lands.

Washakie became a principal chief of the Shoshone Nation in 1840. He strongly believed in maintaining the peace with the whites. During the 1850s, he and the U.S. government struck an unofficial bargain in Lander, whereby the Shoshones would help emigrants. The treaties began in 1863, and they permitted whites to cross the Shoshones' ancestral lands unharmed and allowed for the building of the railroad. Four treaties and five years later, the government once again came to the Shoshones with a treaty, this one setting up the Shoshone and Bannock Indian Reservation, which extended from the Wind River Valley all the way to Fort Bridger. Discoveries of gold at South Pass and coal at Rock Springs quickly decreased the reservation boundaries.

That same 1868 treaty called for the establishment of a military camp to protect the Shoshone and Bannock Indian Reservation against the wandering hostile Indian enemies of these two nations. The protection was also extended to the miners of the nearby Sweetwater region (South Pass, where gold had been discovered). Fort Augur, later Fort Brown, was built at present-day Lander in

1869. Two years later Fort Brown was relocated to the fork of the Little Wind and was renamed Fort Washakie in 1878.

During the final Indian Wars, many Shoshones enlisted with the army and served as scouts. They participated in a number of engagements against the Sioux, Cheyenne, and Arapahos. In 1883 Reverend John Roberts founded the Shoshone School for Indian Girls and oversaw the erection of the mission in 1889. Reverend Roberts baptized Chief Washakie shortly before the chief's death in 1900. He was buried with full military honors. The military abandoned Fort Washakie in 1909.

Festivals and Events

Wind River Pow Wows
various locations all summer

Clothed in colorful outfits that reflect their tribes' customs, Native Americans honor centuries-old traditions through dance and song at annual pow wows. When tribes gathered to trade, a "pow wow" rounded out the social interaction. Modern pow wows include dance competitions, contests, and Native American arts and crafts demonstrations and sales, as well as traditional Indian food. For times, locations, and dates, contact the **Shoshone Tribal Cultural Center, 31 First Street, P.O. Box 1008, Fort Washakie, 82514; (307) 332-9106.**

Shoshone Indian Days All-Indian Rodeo
late June

Held in Fort Washakie, this rodeo is the most unique you will see. All participants are Indians. In addition to standard rodeo events, there are daring Indian horse races. Get all the details from the **Shoshone Tribal Cultural Center, 31 First Street, P.O. Box 1008, Fort Washakie, 82514; (307) 332-9106.**

Outdoor Activities

Fishing

The reservation is not public land. The land, lakes, and streams belong to the Shoshone and Arapaho tribes. Fishing is only allowed in specific areas. Fishing on the reservation also requires a special permit obtained from the **Tribal Fish and Game Office,** which has maps showing where public fishing is permitted. Get one. **P.O. Box 217, Fort Washakie, 82514; (307) 332-7207.**

Horseback Riding

Idgie Poo Outfitters offers horsepacking trips into the mountains that emphasize fishing and riding into two camps. The lower one can be driven into with a four-wheel-drive vehicle; you get to do a lot of riding there. From that camp, you horsepack to the upper one, about 10,000 feet in elevation. The outfitters furnish everything and cook meals for you. All you need to bring are your personal items. Sleep in comfortable beds in wall tents or tepees. Three-day minimum stay. Most are five-day trips. For four to six people. **P.O. Box 582, Crowheart, 82512; (307) 486-2261.**

River Floating

Wind River Canyon Whitewater trips take you rafting through Wind River Canyon, either the upper half from the campgrounds to the convenience store or from the store to the lower end of the canyon. If you're really jazzed, do both—with lunch provided. Trips last two to three and a half hours for the half sections, five and a half for the full canyon. The season runs Memorial Day through Labor Day. Fishing trips at any time, year-round. Make reservations. **P.O. Box 592, Crowheart, 82512; (307) 486-2253.** During the whitewater season: **210 Suite 5, Hwy. 20 South, Thermopolis, 82443; (307) 864-9343.**

Seeing and Doing

Wind River Indian Reservation Tours

The best way to get the feel of the reservation, as well as travel to places you wouldn't otherwise get to see, is to go on an individual or group tour with Wind River Indian Reservation Tours. Guides are from the reservation and have a unique perspective to offer visitors. Tours last approximately three hours. Wear your walking shoes, as this is no drive-by kind of tour. History comes alive as you wander through Fort Washakie's historic district. Buildings take on deeper meaning than just structures constructed for military purposes in the 1800s or as part of the Indian Agency occupancy. The tour also includes a trip to the tribal complex for the Shoshone and Arapaho tribal governments, the old block house, the Arapaho Cultural Museum, St. Michael's Mission, Chief Washakie's and Sacajawea's grave sites, and the Eastern Shoshone Tribal Cultural Center. Tours can include such events as pow wows and Indian meals. Reservations required. **P.O. Box 903, Fort Washakie, 82514; (307) 332-7076.**

Crowheart Butte

This lone butte near the small town of Crowheart remains visible for quite a distance along Hwys. 287 and 26. According to legend, the claystone and sandstone formation received its name from a battle fought in 1866 between the Shoshones and Crows for the right of the rich hunting grounds found in the Wind River Basin. Neither side seemed to be gaining the upper hand, so Washakie, the Shoshone chief, and Big Robber, the Crow chief, met in single combat to the death. The victor won the war. Washakie defeated Big Robber and ate his heart during a victory celebration held on top of the butte.

Hot Springs

Chief Washakie Plunge

Located east of Fort Washakie along Ethete Road (pronounced E-the-tee). Jacuzzi, slide,

Getting There

The Wind River Indian Reservation borders Lander, Thermopolis, Riverton, and Dubois and encompasses a portion of the Shoshone National Forest. Hwys. 287, 26, and 789 go into the reservation. There is no commercial air service to any of the towns on the reservation. The nearest airport is in Riverton. Fly in on **United Express (800-241-6522)**. Rental cars are available at the airport from **Avis (800-331-1212 or 307-856-5052)** or from **Hertz (800-654-3131 or 307-856-2344)**.

private baths, and a kiddie pool. Open in winter Wednesday through Sunday from 9:30 A.M. to 5:30 P.M. and in summer Tuesday through Sunday from 9 A.M. to 9 P.M. Senior, student, and handicapped discounts. Children under seven admitted free. Lockers available. Towel and swimsuit rentals. Handicapped accessible. **206 Ethete Road, P.O. Box 538, Fort Washakie, 82514; (307) 332-4530.**

Museums

Eastern Shoshone Tribal Cultural Center

Gain a greater understanding of the Wind River Indian Reservation and the Eastern

Crowheart Butte.

Ethete Episcopal Church.

100

Shoshone tribe at the cultural center. Open year-round Monday through Friday from 9 A.M. to 4 P.M. (closed for lunch from noon to 12:45 P.M.) or by appointment on the weekend. **House #31 First Street., P.O. Box 1008, Fort Washakie, 82514; (307) 332-9106.**

Shoshone Episcopal Mission

The mission was established in the late 1800s. The original chapel building was built in 1899. The baptismal font is where Father John Roberts baptized Chief Washakie. Next to it is a pictorial museum history of the Shoshone tribe. The old Shoshone girls school is located on the site as well. You can also see the remains of the old orchard where the girls raised their own food. Father John Roberts was responsible for building most of the Episcopal churches in Wyoming. Not handicapped accessible. View by appointment only. **P.O. Box**

175, Fort Washakie, 82514; (307) 332-7925.

Arapaho Cultural Museum

This is an excellent small museum for gaining an understanding of Arapaho traditions and way of life. Lovely beadwork, quillwork moccasins, and parfleches with traditional geometric designs. A good collection of black-and-white photos of historic and contemporary tribal leaders and modern families. Histories of chiefs such as Sharp Nose and Yellowcalf. Open year-round. Call for hours. **c/o Doris Wagon, St. Michaels Circle, Ethete, 82520; (307) 332-8117.**

Where to Stay

Camping

Private Campgrounds and Cabins

For a campsite with a mountain view, try the **Rocky Acres Campground,** 4.5 miles northwest of Lander on the reservation. Twelve full hookups, 40 tent sites, shower, laundry, restrooms. Pets okay. Not handicapped accessible. **5700 Hwy. 287, Lander, 82520; (307) 332-6953. E-mail: rockyacres@rmisp.com.**

Where to Eat

Choke Cherry Cafe—$-$$

Come hungry for very generous portions. The homemade fry bread, served hot and fresh, is spectacular! Homemade pies and cinnamon rolls. Try the Puppies in the Straw! Daily specials. In summer, open from 11 A.M. to 11 P.M., Tuesday through Saturday. In winter, open from 11 A.M. to 9 P.M. and Saturday from noon to 9 P.M. Closed Sunday and Monday. **460 Ethete Road, Ethete, 82520; (307) 332-3680.**

Wind River Indian Reservation

Services

Visitor Information

Shoshone Tribal Cultural Center, P.O. Box 1008, Fort Washakie, 82514; (307) 332-9106.

Shoshone and Arapaho Tribes, 15 North Fork Road, Fort Washakie, 82514; (307) 332-3040.

Wind River Visitors Council, P.O. Box 1449, Riverton, 82501; (800) 645-6233. Website: www.wind-river.org/.

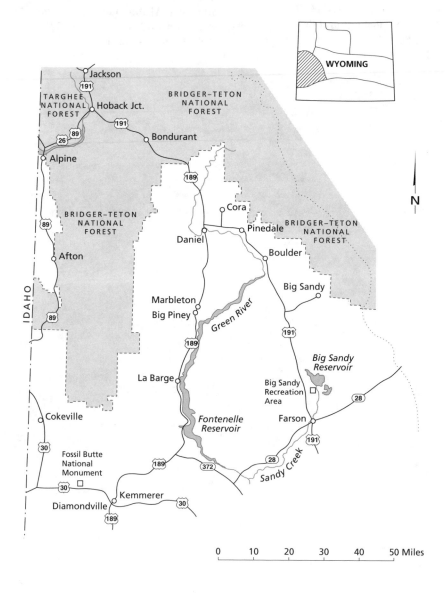

Rendezvous Region

Rendezvous
Region

The historic Green River Rendezvous Pageant. Photo courtesy of the Wyoming Travel Commission.

103

Fort Bridger

Getting There

Fort Bridger is nestled 32 miles from Evanston in the Bridger Valley. Take I-80 east to Exit 34. It will take you right to the fort.

Shoshone and Bannock tribes frequented the Fort Bridger region long before it became a rendezvous site for mountain men in 1834 and afterward a fort. Today, Fort Bridger's living-history programs let you experience the ways of the mountain men, fur traders, and frontier military life. Wander through restored buildings and a reconstruction of the original trading post that the Mormons burned down in 1857. See the trader's store, schoolhouse, icehouse, commanding officer's quarters, and cemetery. Find out about Thornburgh, the dog, and visit his grave.

104

History

Jim Bridger, a veteran mountain man, decided there was more money to be made in trading than trapping and built a trading post on the Black's Fork of the Green River in 1842. It opened for business the following year. Bridger and his partner, Louis Vasquez, did well, thanks to the strong migrations of people across the Oregon Trail and the Mormon Trail—both traveling right past the trading post. Bridger had no competition until Mormon leader Brigham Young instructed some of his followers to construct Fort Supply, a trading post about 12 miles from Bridger's location. Depending on whose account you read, Bridger either left of his own accord or was forced out by the Mormons, but either way, the Mormons, headed by Lewis Robinson, a quartermaster in the Utah militia, took over Bridger's store and controlled the position until the Mormon War in 1857. U.S. troops advanced on the site and the Mormons burned it and Fort Supply before retreating back to Salt Lake City.

Under U.S. occupation, many of the buildings you see today were constructed. Troops stationed there protected the Overland Stage Route and the Union Pacific Railroad, and oversaw the signing of the treaty with Shoshone Chief Washakie, which established the Wind River Indian Reservation.

No troops were stationed at the fort between 1878 and 1880, due to the Indian Wars with the Northern Plains nations; however, unrest on the Uinta Reservation and the White River Agency (Utes) in Colorado brought a renewed army presence at Fort Bridger. The military post closed for good on November 6, 1890.

Festivals and Events

Mountain Man Rendezvous
Labor Day weekend
The rendezvous tradition dates back to the early 1800s when mountain men and Native

Re-created Bridger Trading Post.

Americans gathered to trade furs for necessities and other goods, test skills with black powder rifles, throw tomahawks and knives, dance, and have a rip-roaring good time! People come from all over the country to set up camps authentic to the era, wear period clothing, and sell their wares. This particular rendezvous ranks at the top of the list as one of the largest in the West. Enjoy cannon shoots, muzzle-loader contests, Indian dancing, cooking contests, and loads of activities for kids. Contact the **Fort Bridger Rendez-vous Association** for all the details. **P.O. Box 198, Fort Bridger, 82933; (307) 782-3842.**

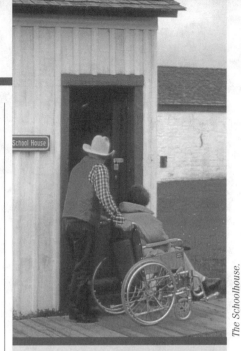

The Schoolhouse.

Services

Visitor Information

Fort Bridger State Historic Site and Museum is open daily from May through September for weekends in April and October, and it's closed November through March. Much of the site is handicapped accessible. Pets must be on a leash. The park charges a $1 per person entrance fee for ages 18 and older. Annual passes (good at all Wyoming state parks) cost $25.

During the summer, the **Fort Bridger Historical Association** sponsors guided tours.

Contact the association to arrange one. **P.O. Box 112, Fort Bridger, 82933; (307) 782-3842.**

For general information, contact the **Fort Bridger State Historic Site, P.O. Box 35, Fort Bridger, 82933; (307) 782-3842, fax (307) 782-7181.**

Jackson Hole

Jackson Hole looks like a tourist town—which, of course, it is. The place would never have survived without the industry that has brought in "the dudes" since the early 1900s. You can spot "dudes" quickly. They're the ones who call the town "Jackson"—its shortened name on the map. Technically, Jackson Hole refers to the entire valley. Locals, however, see the town and its surroundings as one community. And underneath the area's touristy image lurks an authentic western settlement.

Encircling the square is the historic downtown, complete with board sidewalks first installed by the all-woman town council (the nation's first) in the early 1920s. The **Jackson Hole Museum** and **Teton County Historical Society (307-733-9605)** offer a self-guided walking tour of the area that starts at the museum with its collection that displays Jackson Hole's history from prehistoric Native American artifacts through 200 years of white colonization.

Other downtown stores tender everything from western art and jewelry to live musical theater, bona fide soda-fountain drinks, designer western apparel, and antler furniture. Local artisans create and produce many of the items found in these shops.

History

Before John Colter wandered onto the scene around 1806, Sheepeater Indians dwelled in the region. They hunted bighorn sheep, hence the tribe's name, and lived off the land much like the trappers who descended upon the beaver-filled "hole"—a pelt hunter's term for such high mountain valleys—throughout the early 1800s. In all, six mountain ranges frame Jackson Hole—the Tetons, Gros Ventres (pro-

nounced grow-VONTS), Snake River, Wind River, Absaroka (pronounced ab-SOR-ka), and Wyoming.

Folklore tells of a trapper named David "Davey" E. Jackson who spent so much of his time trapping in the valley that his partners in the Rocky Mountain Fur Company called the locale "Jackson's Hole." (Not until the town was incorporated in 1901 did it become just Jackson.)

Hearty homesteaders next appeared to wrestle a living out of the harsh environment where winters could (and still do) last six months. When railroads connected points west, Jackson Hole remained isolated. The nearest track was 75 miles away, and deep snows clogged Teton and Togwotee (pronounced TOE-ga-tee) passes, making it virtually impossible to get into or out of the valley for months at a time. This made the town a safe haven for outlaws and other assorted hellraisers well into the first decades of the twentieth century.

Settlers brought the first cattle herds into the valley in the mid-1800s and raised beef and hay. Working ranches continue those traditions, with a turn-of-the-century twist. Today, guest ranches give tourists a taste of wrangling horses, punching cows, and even chuckwagon cooking. Packers, whether with horses, mules, goats, llamas, or backpacks, still trek through the pristine wilderness of the high country.

Controversy shadows another type of venture sought by travelers to Jackson Hole's mountains. Debate continues over who first successfully ascended Grand Teton, a popular climb these days for mountaineers. Members of the Hayden Expedition, which surveyed Yellowstone in 1872, claimed to have reached the top first. However, an 1898 ascent by William O. Owen suggested that descriptions of scenery by earlier attempts were not accurate, as seen from the summit. Later climbers disagree.

Winter enlivens the area with newer traditions. Although mail delivery first began to arrive in Jackson Hole via snowshoes and skies, the first ski resort came into existence in 1946. Nowadays, the mountains provide some of the most extreme black diamond skiing found in the West, along with cross-country skiing, snowmobiling, mushing with sled dogs, and sleigh rides through herds of elk. For a more relaxing experience, there's soaking in the hot springs, drifting over the Tetons in a hot-air balloon, and, of course, the rodeo.

Festivals and Events

Elk Antler Auction
late May
All antlered animals grow a new set of antlers every year, shedding the old ones over winter. In April each year, members of the local Boy Scouts chapter collect shed antlers on the National Elk Refuge for an auction. Funds raised benefit the scouts and the refuge. People from around the world attend the auction, buying the antlers for a wide variety of reasons—Asian aphrodisiacs, furniture, wall mounts, gun racks, candle holders, and even as decorations in dried floral arrangements. Contact the **National Elk Refuge** for information **(307-733-9212)**.

Old West Days
late May
Old West Days includes performances by famous singers, cowboy poets, authors, and musicians; black powder shoots; a parade; Indian dances; a rodeo; a cutting horse competition; a barn dance; tomahawk throws; and a carriage-driving competition. The **Jackson Hole Visitors Council** has all the details **(307-733-3316)**.

Shriner's All American Cutter Races
mid-February
If you're in the mood for a *Ben-Hur* kind of event, you won't want to miss the horse-drawn cutter races, the West's version of chariot races. Teams run two abreast for a quarter mile of raw excitement, thundering hoofbeats, and flying snow. The **Jackson Hole Shriners**

Dog-sledding. Photo courtesy of the Wyoming Division of Tourism.

107

Club sponsors the horse races. Proceeds go to the Shriners Hospital for Crippled Children in Salt Lake City, Utah. For details, call **(307) 733-8853**.

Outdoor Activities

Ballooning

Every clear morning of the year the **Wyoming Balloon Company** meets up to nine passengers at flight headquarters at 5:45 A.M. While that may sound horribly early, the sunrise over the mountains as the balloon fills with air is quite a sight to behold! Flights last approximately an hour and will give you an unforgettable view of Jackson Hole. Take plenty of film

Trail ride near Teton Village.

108

for your camera, for you'll be able to get spectacular pictures of the mountains, the Snake River, and wildlife. Drifting on the air currents, there's little sensation of movement. You'll see wildlife without spooking them. If you're worried about safety, all balloonists are FAA-certified, licensed pilots. Like planes, balloons must pass a yearly safety inspection. Flights end with a champagne breakfast (a flying tradition). Reservations required. **335 North Cache Street, P.O. Box 2578, Jackson, 83001; (307) 739-0900. E-mail: abreffei@wyoming.com.**

Biking

Mountain Biking

With multiple mountain ranges to choose from, Jackson offers the expert or novice great mountain biking opportunities. Taking the chairlift uphill at **Snow King Mountain** and riding down the dirt roads is a fun way to see the sights without too much high-altitude effort. For more of a challenge, pedal over 8,400-foot **Teton Pass** or take the vertical dare of 4,139 feet straight up.

For chairlift/bike tours or mountain bike rentals, contact **Hoback Sports' Fat Tire Tours, 40 South Millward, P.O. Box 8910, Jackson, 83001; (307) 733-5335.**

Dog Sledding

Glide silently past incredible snow-covered mountain scenes and abundant wildlife located around Granite Hot Springs, the Gros Ventres, or the Bridger-Teton National Forest with **Jackson Hole Iditarod Sled Dog Tours.** After an orientation session where you become acquainted with each dog and learn basic commands and how to drive a team, you're off mushing with one guide for every four clients. It's hard to describe the relationship that develops between the dogs and the mushers. Half- and full-day trips include lunch. Custom tours are also available. Mushing season begins around the end of November and usually runs into April. Don't forget to dress warmly and in layers. Contact the tour company for information or reservations. **11 Granite Creek, P.O. Box 1940, Jackson, 83001; (800) 554-7388 or (307) 733-7388, fax (307) 734-1163. Website: www. jacksonnet.com or www.jacksonhole.com.**

If you're lucky enough to be in western Wyoming between the end of January and mid-February, you can catch the **International Rocky Mountain Stage Stop Sled Dog Race.** Mushers from around the world head out from Jackson, traveling through Moran, Dubois, Pinedale, Evanston, Alpine, Lander, Kemmerer, and back to Jackson's Teton Village in this *Tour de France*–style 11-day race. The field is limited to 30 teams, which cover 420 miles. There are official starts and finishes each day. You can watch anywhere along the route or in one of the towns. **Jackson Hole Iditarod Sled Dog Tours** has the details. **P.O. Box 1940, Jackson, 83001; (800) 554-7388. Website: www.wyomingstage-stop.org.**

Fishing

Fly fishers love the **South Fork River** and the **Snake River,** claiming they "teem with trout." **Flat Creek** in the National Elk Refuge offers some excellent Snake River trout fishing. For more information call the **National Elk Refuge** at **(307) 733-9212.**

Located four miles north of Jackson, the **Jackson National Fish Hatchery** produces eggs and stocking fish for the area's lakes and streams. Each year, the hatchery raises close to half a million native Snake River cutthroat and lake trout, which range in size from one to eight inches. You can see these trout in the hatchery's aquarium. Open daily year-round from 8 A.M. to 4 P.M. Call to set up a tour or take the self-guided tours. All free. **1500 Fish Hatchery Road, Jackson, 83001; (307) 733-2510; fax (307) 733-8616. Website: www.usgs.com.**

John Henry Lee Outfitters arranges transportation to and from the Snake River, and provides the boats, rain gear, and basic fishing equipment for day trips on the river, or fishing trips up to 10 days in Yellowstone National Park or the Bridger-Teton Wilderness. **P.O. Box 8368, Jackson, 83001; (800) 3-JACKSON, (800) 352-2576, or (307) 733-9441.**

Jack Dennis Fishing Trips provides rental equipment, hourly fly-casting instruction, and one-day fly-fishing seminars. **P.O. Box 3369, Jackson, 83001; (307) 733-3270. E-mail: bjames@blissnet.com. Website: www.jacksonwy.com/jackdennis.**

Half- or all-day trips down to the Green River and New Fork in Pinedale, with all equipment provided for two, is the specialty of **Mangis Guide Service. P.O. Box 3165, Jackson, 83001; (800) 850-1220 or (307) 733-8553. E-mail: kmangis@wyoming.com.**

Golf

Looking for a unique golfing experience? Try the Arnold Palmer Golf Course at the **Teton Pines Country Club and Resort.** This 18-hole, signature-design course has four different tee boxes that allow for different abilities on the course. There are also acres of water and wooden bridges. Open to the public. **3450 North Clubhouse Drive, Jackson, 83001; (307) 733-1773.** You can also try the par-72 Robert Trent Jones Jr. Championship Course at **Jackson Hole Golf and Tennis Club, 500 Spring Gulch Road, Box 250, Jackson, 83001; (307) 733-3111.**

Hiking and Backpacking

The **Bridger-Teton National Forest** (BTNF) began as one of four divisions of the Yellowstone Timberland Reserve, created in 1891 as the nation's first forest reserve, and set up as part of Congress's forest conservation policy. The system became the National Forest System in 1907. The reserve originally encircled Yellowstone National Park, taking up approximately 9,500 square miles (just about double the size of the state of Connecticut), and encompassed portions of Idaho and Montana, as well as Wyoming. The Teton section of what would become the Bridger-Teton National Forest began in 1908 with 1,694,574 acres. In 1911, a presidential executive order established the Bridger division, named after mountain man Jim Bridger. It contained 744,702 acres. The two merged in 1973 for a total of 3.4 million acres, making it the second largest national forest outside Alaska. BTNF has some of the best hiking in Wyoming. Ecosystems range from sagebrush deserts to aspen or lodgepole pine forests to subalpine and alpine meadows. Short hikes begin from **Granite Hot Springs** and **Hoback Canyon.** Longer, more challenging hikes that take most of a day lead to great places like **Shoal Falls** and **Deer Ridge.**

For more information, maps, and trail conditions, contact the **Forest Supervisor's Of-**

109

fice, 340 North Cache Street, P.O. Box 1888, Jackson, 83001; (307) 739-5500, fax (307) 739-5010. E-mail: btnsinfo@-sisna.com. Website: www.fs.fed.us/btnf/-welcome.

Expect rugged and steep trails leading to wonderful vistas while hiking around Jackson. **Snow King Mountain** presents the most accessible hiking right in downtown Jackson. Part of BTNF, Snow King's nature loop trail wanders through a sagebrush meadow and patches of forest, or follow the service road up the face of the mountain. Plan on two to four hours for the hikes, and take plenty of water to drink! For details, contact the **Snow King Ski Resort, P.O. Box SKI, Jackson, 83001; (800) 522-KING (5464), fax (307) 733-4086. E-mail: snowking@wyoming.com. Website: www.snowking.com.**

For a breezy way to view the mountains, take the aerial tram at Jackson Hole Mountain Resort, 12 miles outside of Jackson, to the top of **Rendezvous Mountain.** A 20-minute ride whisks you straight up 2.5 miles of steep mountainside. You can't beat the view from the peak, encompassing Housetop Mountain (10,537 feet), Marrion Lake, Grand Teton National Park, Fossil Mountain (10,916 feet), Mount Bannon (10,966 feet), Granite Canyon, Prospectors Mountain (11,241 feet), Mount Hunt (10,783 feet), Grand Teton Peak (13,770 feet), Buck Mountain (11,938 feet), Static Peak (11,303 feet), Jackson Lake, the Teton Wilderness, the Absaroka Range, Mount Leidy (10,326 feet), Blacktail Butte (7,688 feet), Lower Slide Lake, the Gros Ventre River, Sheep Mountain (11,190 feet), the Bridger-Teton National Forest, the Gros Ventre Range, Jackson Peak (10,707 feet), Cache Peak (9,730 feet), the town of Jackson, Snow King Mountain (8,005 feet), the Snake River, and the Snake River Range.

This is also the starting point for several day or overnight hikes. **Summit Loop** is an easy 20-minute walk around the top of Rendezvous Mountain. In about two hours you can take a moderate hike to the **Granite Canyon** trailhead or head for the **Green River Over-**

look. The **Cody-Rock Springs Loop** takes from four to six hours to complete. For a challenge, take off for a 7-mile hike from **Rendezvous Mountain** to **Teton Village. Rendezvous Mountain** to the **Granite Canyon** trailhead is 11.5 miles, and a loop to **Marrion Lake** is 12 miles. Hiking information and maps can be obtained through the **Jackson Hole Ski Corporation, P.O. Box 290, Teton Village, 83025; (307) 739-2753; fax (307) 733-2660. E-mail: info@jacksonhole.com. Website: www.jacksonhole.com/ski.** Call **(888) DEEPSNO (888-333-7766)** for a snow report. Overnight campers must get a permit from Grand Teton National Park **(307-739-3399).**

The HOLE Hiking Experience provides guided hikes for all levels of physical ability. Choose from interpretive day hikes, all-day treks, or four-hour walks at sunrise or sunset for small groups or families. Private hikes and overnight backcountry trips are also available. All trips are guided by local naturalists. Discuss flowers, geology, local history, birds, and animals. Lunch and snacks, transportation, nature guides, backpacks, rain ponchos, and water bottles are supplied. All you need is proper clothing and good shoes. Half- or full-day winter snowshoe tours; look for animal tracks and signs and discuss shrews. Trips throughout the year. **P.O. Box 7779, Jackson, 83002; (307) 739-7155 or (307) 609-HIKE (4453). E-mail: wholehike@tetonvalley.net. Website: www.jacksonholenet.com/wholehike/.**

Horseback Riding

Spend the day in a saddle and you'll see Jackson Hole the way the settlers did. Take a guided horseback or wagon ride at the **Spring Creek Ranch.** Ranch staff offer one- or two-hour rides, half-day trips, and even a one-hour ride with a delicious breakfast or dinner cookout. Rides with breakfast must be reserved by 8 A.M., dinner rides by 2 P.M. the day before the ride. **W.W. Guides, P.O. Box 3154, Jackson, 83001; (307) 733-9209, fax (307) 733-1524.**

Llama Trekking

Llama trekking makes a great alternative to lugging a heavy pack through the wilderness. Not only do you get minimum-impact camping, but you get fresh food and other comforts as well. **Jackson Hole Llamas** offers three- to five-day, fully guided expeditions into the Yellowstone area or the Jedediah Smith Wilderness of the Tetons, as well as custom trips and drop camps (they take you to a campsite and pick you up there some days later). **P.O. Box 12500, Jackson, 83002; (800) 830-7316** or **(307) 739-9582. E-mail: jhllamas-@blissnet.com. Website: jhllamas.com.**

River Floating

(See Grand Teton National Park chapter in the Yellowstone section.)

Skiing

Welcome to world-class downhill skiing! Wyoming's first ski resort, Snow King, began operation in 1939 and really caught on after World War II ended in 1945. Snow King rises above the heart of downtown Jackson (ever so convenient for skiing over a lunch break). Jackson Hole Mountain Resort is just 12 miles from town in Teton Village.

Downhill Skiing

Snow King Resort generally opens in late November and closes about the first of April. In addition to being the first ski resort in the state, it alone offers night skiing. Snow King can supply you with a full line of rental equipment. Resort staff can repair skis as well, and they run schools for both alpine and nordic skiing. Mountain elevation ranges from 6,237 feet to 7,808 feet with approximately 400 acres of skiable terrain. Half of this can be skied at night. (No night skiing on Sunday and Monday.) Three hundred acres are machine-groomed. While more than half the runs are geared toward advanced skiers, there's plenty of excitement for beginners and intermediate skiers. You can also snowboard and telemark.

Downhill skiing. Photo courtesy of Woodall/McKay, the Wyoming Division of Tourism

Check out the snow-tubing park for a wild ride. Indoor ice skating rink, skate rentals, and lessons. **P.O. Box SKI, Jackson, 83001; (800) 522-KING (5464), fax (307) 733-4086. E-mail: snowking@wyoming.com. Website: www.snowking.com.**

Jackson Hole Mountain Resort, called "Teton Village" by the locals, usually opens early in December and closes about the beginning of April. In addition to offering the best view of the Teton Range, not to mention incredible extreme skiing, Teton Village provides the nation's greatest vertical rise, 4,139 feet. Two mountains, Apres Vous and Rendezvous, make up the Jackson Hole Mountain Resort. It receives an average yearly snowfall of approximately 400 inches. That's 38 feet of mostly dry powder! A temperature inversion on the mountain means it's about 20 degrees warmer on the upper slopes than in the valley. From the base at an elevation of 6,311 feet, the aerial tram takes you up to 10,450 feet. Teton Village has 2,500 acres of skiable terrain, and 22 miles of it are machine-groomed. Only about 10 percent of the terrain is suitable for beginners, and half meets the demands of advanced skiing. Besides an excellent ski school, you'll find all the necessities in rentals, clothing, maps, food, and lodging. **P.O. Box 290, Teton Village, 83025; central reservation—(800) 443-6931, main switchboard at the re-**

sort—(307) 733-2292, ski conditions—(888) DEEPSNOW (888-333-7766), fax (307) 733-1286 or (307) 733-2660. E-mail: info@jhsnow.com. Website: www.jh-snow.com.

Helicopter Skiing

If your idea of hitting the slopes includes jumping out of a helicopter into virgin, deep, powder snow, then you'll love heli-skiing in Jackson Hole! **High Mountain Heli-Skiing** provides a full day of helicopter skiing from mid-December through mid-April starting at 8:30 A.M. with your pickup at Teton Village. The pilot drops four clients and a guide on top of a mountain with 12,000 to 15,000 vertical feet worth of skiing opportunities. While you need not be an expert skier, intermediate skills are highly desirable. High Mountain Heli-Skiing carries fat boards especially designed for extreme conditions: They are shorter and twice the width of regular skis, allowing for better balance and easier handling in turns. Bring your own snowboard if you like. High Mountain will also set up three- to seven-day packages. Make six runs each day, with the option of additional runs, transportation to and from the heli-pad, a Heli-Deli lunch, snacks, and drinks. **P.O. Box 173, Teton Village, 83025; (307) 733-3274, fax (307) 733-0645. E-mail: heli-ski@wyoming.com. Website: www.-skitvs.com.**

Snowmobiling in the Bridger-Teton National Forest. Photo courtesy of the Wyoming Division of Tourism.

Cross-Country Skiing

You can telemark at both Snow King and Jackson Hole Mountain resorts or strike out on your own with backcountry skiing in the Bridger-Teton National Forest (BTNF) or on a variety of groomed trails. Check with **BTNF** for restrictions or permits you might need **(307-739-5500)**. To obtain the latest **weather and avalanche conditions** for backcountry skiing, call **(307-733-2664)** or log onto **www.fs.-fed.us/btnf/welcome**.

Ski 22 kilometers of groomed trails at the **Jackson Hole Ski School and Nordic Center,** or head out over a self-guided nature trail or on the gently rolling backcountry. Open early December through mid-April, the center offers telemark lessons on alpine slopes and guided mountain tours. **7658 Teewinot, P.O. Box 290, Teton Village, 83025; nordic center—(307) 733-2292, ski school reservations—(307) 739-2610, fax (307) 733-2660. E-mail: info@jacksonhole.com. Website: www.jacksonhole.com.**

Tour 14 kilometers of trails or take an individual guided backcountry trip with **Spring Creek Ranch Touring.** Full-moon twilight ski tours, too. **P.O. Box 3154, Jackson, 83001; (307) 733-1004.**

Glide over 13 kilometers of skiing and skate tracks at the **Teton Pines Resort and Ski Center,** open for skiing between December and April. **3450 North Club House Drive, Jackson, 83001, or P.O. Box 14090, Jackson, 83002; (307) 733-1005. E-mail: info@tetonpines.com. Website: www.teton-pines.com.**

Nordic and telemark skis and snowshoe rentals are available from **Wilson Backcountry Sports** **(307-733-5228)**. All types of ski equipment and snowshoes can be obtained from **Hoback Sports (307-733-5335)** and you can rent nordic and backcountry skis at **Skinny Skis (307-733-6094)**.

Snowmobiling

Snow conditions usually bring on the snowmobiling season in early November. It lasts through April. The snow becomes packed toward the end of the season, making it ideal for beginners. You can expect to plow through drifts at elevations that range from below 7,000 feet to well over 10,000 feet, so be prepared for some extremes in weather and environment.

Granite Hot Springs makes a fantastic destination when snowmobiling. Where else can you shed your snowsuit for a bathing suit and a 110-degree natural hot spring? The 10-mile ride takes you over a groomed trail in the Gros Ventres to the springs. Grab a hot lunch and a soak, then head back to town. You'll find the trailhead at unplowed **Granite Creek Road** about 10 miles south of Hoback Junction on Hwy. 191.

Several businesses offer guided snowmobile tours for beginners and experts alike. Most also create day or overnight trips. **Rocky Mountain Snowmobile Tours** supplies a continental breakfast, lunch, snowmobile clothing, and group rate with its tours. **Box 820, Jackson, 83001; (800) 647-2561 or (307) 733-2237.**

Seeing and Doing

Town Square

Gunfire rings in the town square—usually right around 6:30 P.M. Residents and actors gather to perform one of several 20-minute melodramas based on some tale or actual event in Jackson Hole's past. The chamber of commerce hosts these Old West shoot-outs that take place every evening during the summer months except Sunday.

The town square, officially named the George Washington Memorial Park in 1932 in honor of the president's 200th birthday, also sets the stage for stage rides, craft fairs, art shows, and the annual antler auction. The Rotary Club constructed the arches at each corner of the park from shed elk antlers collected in the National Elk Refuge by the local Boy Scouts.

Jackson Hole Stagecoach Rides

Between Memorial Day and Labor Day you can climb aboard a part of the West's unique history—the old Overland Mail Stagecoach. The 100-year-old stagecoach pulled by a pair of horses leaves from the stage stop on the corner of the town square for 10-minute rides through the streets of downtown Jackson. For details contact the **Jackson Hole Chamber of Commerce (307-733-3316).**

National Elk Refuge

The Shawnee Nation calls the North American elk *wapiti* (pronounced WHA-pa-tee), which means "white rump." The elks' natural migration patterns brought them out of the high mountains and into the Jackson Hole valley for hundreds of years before the whites settled the land and cut the elk off from their winter food supplies. The elk starved by the thousands before photographer Stephen Nelson Leek, dubbed "The Father of the Elk," focused the nation's attention on their plight. His turn-of-the-century photos started a conservation movement that resulted in the formation in 1912 of the National Elk Refuge, the winter home of the world's biggest free-ranging elk herd. Congress appropriated money for the purchase of 1,760 acres north of town, and a series of presidential executive orders between 1914 and 1916 set aside an additional 1,000 acres from the public domain.

The main mission of the National Elk Refuge is to preserve and manage the elk's winter range. As part of this mission, the refuge is working to enhance the natural ecosystem, providing habitat for endangered and threatened species of animals and plants. Biologists performed the first successful transplant of four endangered trumpeter swan cygnets to the refuge in 1938. Now you can see up to 300 tundra and trumpeter swans migrating through the refuge each year.

The refuge currently contains 24,700 acres. This is about one-fourth of the elk's historic winter range. Elk have been known to migrate up to 65 miles to reach the refuge. The land supplies natural feed for about half of the 11,000 to 12,000 elk that winter in the refuge. Supplemental feeding in the form of alfalfa hay pellets has led to one of the most unique events in Jackson—the elk sleigh ride (see page 114).

A wildlife viewing area pull-off is on Hwys. 191, 89, and 26 as you come into town from the north. Just down the same highway, you can wander through the wildlife interpretive center at the visitors center that houses National Park Service, Wyoming Game & Fish, forest service, National Elk Refuge, and chamber of commerce information. The center is open year-round, from 8 A.M. to 5 P.M. with extended hours during the summer from 8 A.M. to 8 P.M. daily. **P.O. Box 510, Jackson, 83001; (307) 733-9212. E-mail: r6rw_ner@-mail.fs.gov. Website: www.fws.gov.**

Elk Refuge Sleigh Rides

Daily (except for Christmas) from mid-December through the end of March, you can spend approximately 45 minutes riding through the 11,000-plus elk herd on either a sleigh or wagon, depending on the amount of snow. The refuge offers 10 to 15 rides a day between 10 A.M. and 4 P.M. No reservations are necessary. You can get tickets for the sleigh ride or for a ride/wildlife museum combination at the **National Museum of Wildlife Art, 2820 Rungius Road, P.O. Box 6825, Jackson, 83002; (307) 733-5771 or (307) 733-9212.**

Jackson Hole Playhouse

Constructed in 1916, the Jackson Hole Playhouse building provides the perfect setting for Jackson's oldest original live theatre. When you walk into the nineteenth-century-style lobby, which looks like a grand Victorian parlor, get a whiff of the sarsaparilla and popcorn—you'll feel like you've stepped back in time. And you have. Broadway shows with Old West themes such as *Seven Brides for Seven Brothers*, *Paint Your Wagon*, and *The Unsinkable Molly Brown* offer a wonderful family experience. Settle in for a live performance every Monday through Saturday from Memorial Day through Labor Day. Reservations. Group rates available. **145 West Deloney, P.O. Box 2788, Jackson, 83001; (307) 733-6994.**

Hot Springs

(See **Granite Hot Springs** under Snowmobiling, above, and **Astoria Hot Springs** under Camping, below.)

Museums

Jackson Hole Museum

Although the displays change from year to year, the Jackson Hole history themes never disappear from the museum. Items date back to prehistoric times with a collection of hunter-gatherer stone tools and utensils. In the Native American room you will see rare Sheepeater artifacts, as well as Plains Indian ceremonial dresses and glass trade beads. For the kids, there's a family of paper dolls and a "touch me" display of tools and essentials from the mountain-man era. Learn about Jackson's all-woman government in the 1920s. See a fully furnished guest ranch room. View life on the Hayden Expedition into Yellowstone. Open Memorial Day through early October from 9:30 A.M. to 6 P.M. on Monday through Saturday and from 10 A.M. to 5 P.M. on Sunday. Downtown walking tours on Tuesday, Thursday, and Friday filled with 14 blocks of town history! Small fee. Family, senior, and student rates available. **105 North Greenwood, P.O. Box 1005, Jackson, 83001; (307) 733-2414.**

National Museum of Wildlife Art

The National Museum of Wildlife Art focuses on first-rate wildlife-related art. The collection contains over 2,000 paintings, sculptures, photos, and drawings by over a hundred distinguished artists from the nineteenth and twentieth centuries. Reflect on the works of George Catlin, Albert Bierstadt, John James Audubon, Charles M. Russell, Frederick Remington, and Carl Rungius. Located across from the National Elk Refuge, the museum houses 12 galleries, an interactive gallery for children, two classrooms, an auditorium, a cafe, a gift shop, and a library/archives. Open daily in summer and in winter from 9 A.M. to 5 P.M. In spring and fall it is open 10 A.M. to 5 P.M. on Monday through Saturday and 1 P.M. to 5 P.M. on Sunday. **2820 Rungius Road, P.O. Box 6825, Jackson, 83002; (307) 733-5771, fax (307) 733-5787. E-mail: info@wildlifeart.org. Website: www.wildlifeart.org.**

Nightlife

Million Dollar Cowboy Bar

This place must be seen to be believed! It personifies the western watering hole. Amid gambling memorabilia from the days the gambling chips clinked as fast as the whiskey glasses, pool tables, and the dance floor, you can step into a real saddle at the bar, have some genuine Cowboy Bar beer, and learn how the bar got its name from the locals. Open from 2 P.M. to 2 A.M. Tuesday through Thursday, and noon to 2 A.M. on Friday and Saturday. **25 North Cache Street, Jackson, 82301; (307) 733-2207.**

Jackson Hole Pub and Brewery

Called locally "the Brew Pub," the Jackson Hole Pub and Brewery "double brews" their beers for great taste and consistent quality. Watch them make everything from pale ale to stout in their glass-enclosed, two-story brewery. You can also sample Wapiti Wheat, a malted wheat lager with a touch of clove; Custer's Last Ale, an India pale ale; Buffalo Brown Ale, full of American malts; Bald Eagle Bock, Bavarian-style lager; and of course, Snake River Lager, a festive Oktoberfest-style brew. Send a six-pack anywhere! If you're hungry, try a dandy wood-fired pizza and tasty soft pretzels with out-of-this-world mustard-seed sauce! Open year-round every day, except for Thanksgiving and Christmas, from noon to midnight. Dinner is served from 6 P.M. to 11 P.M. **265 South Millward, Jackson, 83001; (307) 739-BEER (2337). E-mail: brewpub@sisna.com. Website: www.snakeriverbrewing.com.**

Mangy Moose

The **Mangy Moose** in Teton Village is the quintessential mountain skiing bar. Huge open spaces have incredible views of the mountains both inside and out on several levels. Take the

time to wander through it, paying attention to what's hanging from the ceiling. Open during the summer and ski season from 5:30 P.M. to 10 P.M. **Teton Village, 83025; (307) 733-4913.**

Scenic Drives

Driving anywhere around the Jackson area is taking a scenic drive, but if you want to get some fantastic mountain views, take **Hwy. 22** west out of Jackson and head up **Teton Pass**, elevation 8,429 feet. (However, think twice about this if it's snowing and the road is slick. It might give you a heart condition.) The road winds and weaves through forest and open meadows that must be experienced to get the full effect. The highway more or less follows the route pioneers took coming into the valley with wagons filled with homesteading goods. You'll also see why the pioneers cut huge logs and chained them behind their wagons to help slow them down when descending into the valley that would become Jackson.

(For other scenic drives see **Togwotee Pass** in the Dubois chapter and the **Grand Teton National Park** chapter.)

Where to Stay

Accommodations

Davy Jackson Inn—$$$$

The inn is within walking distance of downtown, making it a convenient place to stay. The 12 guest rooms, one handicapped accessible, with private baths, phones, and cable TV with HBO, are quite comfortable. Then there's an outdoor hot tub. Some rooms also include a steam shower, fireplace, or jacuzzi. There is no minimum stay. No pets allowed, except in the guest cottage. In the B&B style, you'll get a full breakfast, plus afternoon tea. Dinner for special groups, as well as a Christmas and New Year's dinner and buffet. Try the homemade cinnamon buns and sourdough buckwheat pancakes. **85 Perry Avenue, P.O. Box 20147, Jackson, 83001; (307) 739-2294.**

A Teton Tree House B&B in Wilson.

E-mail: DavyJackson@wyoming.com. Website: www.davyjackson.com.

116 ## Huff House Inn—$$$$

Built in 1917, the Huff House originally belonged to the town doctor. The rooms served as his office and hospital. The house was one of the first in town to have plumbing and electricity. Dr. Huff had these luxuries installed during his term as mayor. Although the house has been remodeled and now functions as a B&B, it retains the essence of a more relaxed era. The five guest rooms and four guest cottages all have private baths. Enjoy the outdoor hot tub or sunporch in back. Family-style breakfasts. Children welcome, provided they are well-behaved. Because there is a step up into each of the cottages, the inn is not considered handicapped accessible. No pets allowed. **240 East Deloney, P.O. Box 1189, Jackson, 83001; (307) 733-4164, fax (307) 739-9091. E-mail: huffhousebnb@blissnet.com.**

Spring Creek Ranch—$$$$

Originally the 1893 homestead of William Preston Redmond, this resort sits on top of East Gros Ventre Butte and has an incredible view of the Tetons. In addition to a variety of delightfully cozy hotel rooms, it also has studios, suites, and condominium lodges, all with fireplaces, executive refrigerators, lodgepole furnishings, and a private deck or balcony. A fantastic place to sit and take in the scenery 1,000 feet above Jackson Hole. **1800 Spirit Dance Road, P.O. Box 4780, Jackson, 83001; (800) 443-6139 or (307) 733-8833. E-mail: info@springcreek.com. Website: www.springcreekranch.com.**

A Teton Tree House—$$$$

Ninety-five steps take you up to this charming B&B set on the side of a hill overlooking Jackson Hole. Its location on Heck of a Hill Road is infinitely appropriate and gives you a delightful feel of mountain living. All the rooms have private baths and fantastic views out every window. Bookcases are well stocked with a wide selection of books (including regional history and guides), and private decks and an outdoor hot tub help you relax amid the wilderness, all while you sip one of Denny's tasty fruit-juice concoctions. You can even go for walks with Denny's two goats. During July and August there is a four-night minimum, the rest of the year a three-night minimum. Open year-round. The best time to come is during April and May or October and November, which is off-season in Jackson. Tasty homemade breakfasts. Package deals that include hiking, canoeing, and sight-seeing trips can be arranged. Not handicapped accessible. No pets allowed as a cat and dog are in residence. **P.O. Box 550, Wilson, 83014; (307) 733-3233, fax (307) 733-0713. E-mail: treehouse-@wyoming.com. Website: www.cruising-america.com/tetontreehouse.**

Painted Porch B&B—$$$-$$$$

You'll enjoy the wide-open feel of this B&B located in a 1901 farmhouse nestled in the quaking aspens. Four rooms, two with private baths. You can relax in the Japanese soaking tubs. Children over the age of six are welcome. Enjoy a full breakfast with fresh fruit and hot main dishes. Six miles from Grand Teton National Park. No pets. Not handicapped accessible. **3755 Moose-Wilson Road (Hwy. 390), P.O. Box 6955, Jackson, 83002; (307) 733-1981. Website: www.jacksonhole-net.com/JH/Lodging/SBB/PP.**

Jackson Hole

Twin Trees B&B—$$$–$$$$

Here's a B&B to feel perfectly at home in. All the comforts, including private baths and even house cats to get cozy with. (Unfortunately, the kitties don't allow other pets.) Healthy, hearty breakfast. Close to Snow King ski area. The beautiful windows provide an excellent view of two of Jackson's oldest events, the April World Championship Snowmobile Hillclimb and the Fourth of July fireworks display. Children over 15 welcome. There's a minimum stay of two nights during the summer months but none in winter. **575 South Willow, P.O. Box 7533, Jackson, 83002; (800) 728-7337 or (307) 739-9737, fax (307) 734-1266. E-mail: twintreesbb@rmisp.com. Website: www.-jacksonholebnb.com.**

Guest Ranches

Crescent H Ranch—$$$$

If your dream vacation is to fish, here's a guest ranch that caters just to you. The Crescent H was built in 1927 and in the 1970s became the first Orvis Endorsed Lodge. Designed for 20 to 22 guests per week between June and the end of September, the ranch provides fishing from Saturday to Saturday in July and August. There are also horseback riding and other activities for family members, as well as fishing lessons and a pond stocked with over 50,000 wild Snake River cutthroat hatchlings for the beginning angler. **P.O. Box 347, Wilson, 83014; (307) 733-3674, fax (307) 733-8475. Website: www.crescenth.com.**

Lost Creek Guest Ranch—$$$$

During your seven-night stay, you'll encounter the western life of yesteryear. Horseback riding, Snake River floats, a half-day hike into Grand Teton National Park, full-day tours in Yellowstone National Park, evening entertainment, and more! An intimate ambiance with no phones or TVs in rooms. However, there are phones in the lodge. Ten cabins can accommodate up to 64 people. Kids welcome. No pets. Handicapped accessible. Open the first week in June through October. **P.O. Box 95, Moose, 83012; (307) 733-0945, fax (307) 733-1954. Website: www.lostcreek.com.**

Moose Creek Ranch—$$$–$$$$

During the summer, Moose Creek Ranch offers a Sunday-to-Sunday program with trail rides, whitewater floats on the Snake River, guided fishing, hiking, and camping trips. In winter, the ranch functions as a B&B and can set up snowmobile trips. Located 18 miles west of Jackson on the edge of the Jedediah Smith Wilderness. You'll experience some of the area's most unique terrain. Relax in the indoor pool in summer or the hot tub year-round. There is no minimum on age for kids riding, as long as they are able and willing, and there are plenty of other things for kids to do. Individual cabins available. No pets in buildings. **P.O. Box 3108, Jackson, 83001; (800) 676-0075, fax (208) 787-2284. E-mail: moosecreekranch@pdt.net. Website: www.webfactor.com/mooscrk.**

Heart Six Dude Ranch—$$–$$$$

This ranch, built in 1910, will customize a summer trip for you into the heart of the Tetons. A minimum stay of six days in summer gives you plenty of time to explore the forest, fish the creeks, float the Snake River, have fun on a hayride, and brush up on your country-dancing skills. September through May, the Heart Six offers nightly stays that can include three meals and snowmobile trips into Yellowstone and along the Continental Divide Trail. No pets allowed. Children three and under are not allowed to ride, but staff will instruct older kids in riding techniques. **P.O. Box 70, Moran, 83013; (888) 543-2477 or (307) 543-2477. E-mail: heartsix@-wyoming.com. Website: www.heartsix.com.**

Camping

In the National Forests

Many forest service campgrounds populate the Jackson area. Some allow reservations. The remainder are on a first-come, first-served basis. A small fee is charged at most campgrounds between Memorial Day and Labor Day. Expect rustic conditions, meaning no showers, electrical hookups, or sewage. You will find picnic tables, fire grates, drinking water, and garbage pickup. Pets are permitted, provided they are on a leash. After summer, campgrounds are generally free, but no water or garbage service is available. All are closed in winter. To check which are on the reservations system or to make a reservation, contact the **BTNF Visitor Center (800-280-2267 or 307-739-5500).**

Private Campgrounds and Cabins

Astoria Hot Springs has a naturally heated pool with an average temperature of 95 degrees, as well as a kiddie pool, playground, 102 campsites, full and partial hookups, showers and restrooms, tent campsites, a snack bar, sand volleyball, horseshoes, and hiking. It's located 17 miles south of Jackson. Fish along a mile of river on the Snake. Handicapped accessible. Pets okay on leashes (except in pool area). No minimum stay. Open May 1 through September; pool open June through August. **12,500 South Hwy. 89, Star Route Box 18, Jackson 83001; (307) 733-2659.**

Wagon Wheel Campground has 33 full RV hookup sites, 11 tent sites, and hot showers. Open May through October. Pets okay with restrictions. Handicapped accessible. **505 North Cache, P.O. Box 1463, Jackson, 83001; summer phone—(307) 733-4588, winter phone—(307) 733-2357.**

Where to Eat

Bar J Chuckwagon and Western Show—$$$-$$$$

Dinner and western-style entertainment that just can't be topped! From Memorial Day through the end of September, come rain or sunshine, the Bar J feeds barbecued beef and grilled chicken with all the fixings every night to about 600 people. And they do it in 20 minutes. No kidding. Then the fun begins. The Bar J Wranglers will make you laugh with their ranch humor, as well as sing cowboy songs, treat you to some yodeling, and recite cowboy poetry. Handicapped accessible. Get reservations early! "Lap-size" kids eat free. **P.O. Box 220, Wilson, 83014; (307) 733-3370.**

Blue Lion—$$$-$$$$

Close to the town square, enjoy a casual elegant atmosphere and delicious meals. You can't beat the Wyoming beef Tournedos Au Blue, medallions of beef tenderloin sautéed with crab and artichoke hearts and served in a brandy–blue cheese cream sauce. Vegetarian and kids' menus. Early-bird specials in summer. Open in winter Wednesday through Monday from 6 P.M. to 10 P.M., daily during the summer from 5:30 P.M. to 10 P.M. Not handicapped accessible. **160 North Millward, P.O. Box 1128, Jackson, 83001; (307) 733-3912, fax (307) 733-3915.**

Nani's Genuine Pasta House—$$-$$$$

You might not think of Jackson as the place where you can get truly authentic regional Italian food, but you can taste some of the best cuisine from Italy at Nani's. The menu changes each month with the food of a different region of Italy featured and everything made from scratch in the restaurant's kitchen. You can't go wrong with any dishes, such as Malloreddus, a homemade saffron and flour gnocchi tossed in a fresh tomato sauce and served with Parmesan and Romano cheeses, and the to-die-for desserts. Open for dinner only, 5 P.M. to 10 P.M. Closed Sunday and Monday. Handicapped accessible. Kids' menu. Make reservations. **242 North Glenwood, P.O. Box 1071, Jackson, 83001; (307) 733-3888, fax (307) 733-3957. E-mail: cparker@wyoming.com. Website: www.nanis.com.**

The Sweetwater Restaurant—$$-$$$$

Dine amid antiques in this historic log cabin. Great moussaka, the Middle Eastern casserole of layered eggplant and spiced ground beef; a cheese soufflé; and salad topped with the Sweetwater's own feta herb garlic dressing. Open for lunch, 11:30 A.M. to 3 P.M. (2 P.M. in winter), and for dinner, 5:30 P.M. to 9:30 P.M. (10 P.M. in summer). Reservations for dinner. **P.O. Box 3271, Jackson, 83001; (307) 733-3553. Website: www.focusproductions.com.**

The Granary at Spring Creek Ranch—$–$$$$

Enjoy one of the most spectacular views while dining. The Granary serves an excellent bagel and smoked salmon breakfast and tasty elk steaks for dinner. Open daily from 7 A.M. to 10 P.M.; however, closed between 10:30 A.M. and noon. Make reservations for dinner. **1800 Spirit Dance Road, P.O. Box 4780, Jackson, 83001; (307) 733-8833.**

Jedediah's Original House of Sourdough—$–$$$

If you've never tasted sourdough pancakes or bread, definitely put Jedediah's on your list of things to do in Jackson. All sourdough products are made on-site using a hundred-year-old sourdough starter. Take home some fresh sourdough starter from the 50-gallon crock. Besides great sourdough pancakes, try a buffalo burger on a sourdough bun or the sourdough carrot cake. The log house the restaurant is located in just adds to the nineteenth-century atmosphere of the place. Be sure to pick up a copy of the *Mountain Rendezvous Times* while you're there. Hours are 7 A.M. to 2 P.M. for breakfast and lunch. Kids' menu. Handicapped accessible. **135 East Broadway, P.O. Box 3857, Jackson, 83001; (307) 733-5671.**

Services

Visitor Information

Contact the **Jackson Hole Chamber of Commerce** at **P.O. Box E, Jackson, 83001; (307) 733-3316, fax (307) 733-5585.** You can also receive information packets from the **Jackson Hole Visitors Council, P.O. Box 982, Jackson, 83001; (800) 782-0011. E-mail: info@jacksonholechamber.com. Website: www.jacksonholechamber.com.**

Kemmerer

In 1847, Elizabeth Dixon Smith Geer, a traveler on the Oregon Trail, mentioned fossils in her diary. "This large waste of country in my opinion has once been a sea. My husband found on the top of a mountain sea shells petrified to stone. The crevices in the rocks show the different stages of the water." Trappers discovered fossilized fish, marine animals, insects, berries, and palm fronds during 1897, and a man named E. W. Holland was the first to cash in on the artifacts from what is now a portion of Fossil Butte National Monument. Buried within the Eocene Epoch formation of 45 to 50 million years ago, Fossil Butte rises 1,000 feet. Fossil hunters have unearthed such finds as a 13-foot alligator, 6-foot garfish, a variety of plants and other freshwater fish, and even a bird that resembles a modern-day chicken. And the upper Cretaceous Period left the region with another legacy—coal.

History

The turn-of-the-century town received its name from M. S. Kemmerer, the president of the Kemmerer Coal Company. By 1902, the community of 900 took care of business at the bank, the barber shop, and the company store, and many frequented the 14 saloons and two brothels. That same year, however, the son of a Baptist minister opened a dry-goods store that would become the first in the still-going-strong retail-chain—the J. C. Penney store.

James Cash Penney believed in serving customers from daybreak until the streets emptied for the night and charging a fair price, rather than an inflated one, to any and all customers. This philosophy gave the Kemmerer company store a real run for its money. Penney's store earned $466.59 on opening day. Not bad, considering a top-notch man's suit carried a price tag of less than $10 and a good pair of shoes cost only half a dollar.

Today the area's coal mines still operate, and so does the J. C. Penney store.

Festivals and Events

Turn of the Century Days
late July
Kemmerer is one of the few communities that celebrates summer with Turn of the Century Days. Enjoy food and craft booths, live entertainment, a carnival, street dances, a teen dance, and much more. Contact **the Kemmerer Chamber of Commerce** for dates and details **(888-300-3413).**

Oyster Ridge Music Festival
late August
Get into the swing with bluegrass music, mandolin and fiddling contests, banjo solos, and other country-and-western entertainment from around the nation. The chamber of commerce has all the information **(888-300-3413).**

Outdoor Activities

Fishing

Sixteen miles north of Kemmerer the **Kemmerer Reservoir** and **Lake Viva Naughton** offer some angling challenges and wonderful rainbow trout fishing. Boat launch and rentals at the marina. The five-mile-long and two-mile-wide lake also provides good sailing and windsurfing. **Hwy. 233, (307) 877-9669.** **Solitary Angler** offers fly-fishing excursions in the region. **P.O. Box 363, Kemmerer, 83101; (307) 877-9459.**

Hiking and Backpacking

For a clearer picture of the area's incredible geological history, hike the trails at **Fossil Butte National Monument.** All the trails afford some fantastic views, and a few physical demands, as they wind through 50 million years of deposits. **Fossil Lake Trail** wanders over 1.5 miles of history through lush terrain filled with aspen groves and water. **Quarry Trail**'s 2.5 miles spread out along the more desertlike south-facing slope. Be warned: It's a more strenuous trail, although worth it, for the vistas can't be beat! You won't see lots of fossils on these hikes. Most have long since been removed. Nevertheless, the area's natural history is incredible, and there's plenty of wildlife. If you like, you can take a guided hike in the morning or afternoon during the summer to the experimental quarry and participate in the dig. However, you won't be allowed to take anything you find. The trails are open as long as weather permits. (The road to the trail is not plowed in winter.) Also, there is positively *no* fossil or other artifact collecting allowed in the park. Open between Memorial Day and Labor Day from 8 A.M. to 7 P.M., and the rest of the year from 8 A.M. to 4:30 P.M. **Fossil Butte National Monument, 864 Chicken Creek Road, Hwy. 30 West, Box 592, Kemmerer, 83101; (307) 877-4455.**

Snowmobiling

You'll find all the ingredients for a fun day of snowmobiling in the **Lake Viva Naughton** area—70 miles' worth of groomed trails, over 100 miles ungroomed, and scenery galore! A groomed snowmobile trail connects to the Bridger-Teton National Forest.

Seeing and Doing

J. C. Penney Mother Store

James Cash Penney, along with his wife and two sales assistants, opened a Golden Rule Store in Kemmerer on April 14, 1902, in a wood-frame building. By 1913, he renamed the booming business the J. C. Penney Company. The store outgrew its building twice, finally being moved to its present location in 1928. The mother store for the entire chain is still in operation today. **722 J. C. Penney Drive, Kemmerer, 83101; (307) 877-3164.**

Fish from Fossil Butte. Photo courtesy of the Wyoming Division of Tourism.

121

J. C. Penney Home

The Penneys spent many years in Kemmerer. The J. C. Penney Foundation restored the entrepreneur's home and moved it from its original site to the one across from Herschler Triangle Park. A guided tour shows you family memorabilia and turn-of-the-century furnishings. Notice the floorboards Mr. Penney cut out so he could put his money box under the bed, where he kept the money he brought home from the store. Open daily in summer and by appointment during the winter. Call for hours. **107 J. C. Penney Drive, Kemmerer, 83101; (307) 877-4501.**

Lincoln County Restored Courthouse

Constructed in 1925, the courthouse and jail now serve as a repository of fossils from the

Rendezvous Region

Fossil Butte National Monument. Photo courtesy of the Wyoming Travel Commission.

region, including a large turtle shell, a six-foot petrified palm tree complete with a portion of trunk and fronds, and three floors of fossilized fish. All are on display during courthouse hours of 8 A.M. to 5 P.M. weekdays. **925 Sage Avenue, Kemmerer, 83101; (307) 877-9056**.

Tynsky's Fossil Fish Center

If you want to do some fossil hunting, try this privately owned fossil quarry. Guided tours that last between two and four hours take you to the quarry and instruct you how to dig and what to look for. You get to keep what you unearth. The most notable find so far was a Knightia fish from the Eocene Epoch. Open generally from May to October, 8 A.M. to 5 P.M. **716 J. C. Penney Drive, Kemmerer, 83101; (307) 877-6885**.

Dinosaurs

Fossil Butte National Monument

Ten miles west of Kemmerer, Fossil Butte rises 1,000 feet above Twin Creek Valley, revealing some of the nation's best fossilized fish deposits in its limestone layers. The unique thing about this butte is that it produced an entire fossilized system here—from microscopic specimens up to the larger end of the food chain. Scientists dug up fish still in their eggs; seeds of plants; insects; and remains of bats, gar, and alligators—all well preserved, providing a study of Eocene ecology. The national monument, established in 1972 by the National Park Service, is located on 13 square miles. Open daily year-round, except holidays and when the roads are too bad. In addition to the trails mentioned in the hiking section, one that is handicapped accessible leads to the picnic area. The information center offers a great interpretive museum with videos that explain the area's history. Open 8 A.M. to 4:30 P.M. Open 8 A.M. to 7:00 P.M. Memorial Day to Labor Day. **864 Chicken Creek Road, Hwy. 30 West, Box 592, Kemmerer, 83101; (307) 877-4455**.

Museums

Fossil Country Frontier Museum

If you really want to get a good perspective on the region and learn how geology ties the fossils and coal industry together, make this museum your first stop. Explore a wonderful mine mock-up by going right inside a simulated underground coal mine in the corner of the gallery. Learn about various jobs and tools used in the mine. Trace the mining industry on a map of coal towns in the area—most no longer exist because gases stopped underground mining. Dabble in the moonshine still exhibits. See the famous Coletti stovetop still—a tiny still designed to sit on top of a stove to make moonshine. There are also a copper boiler and a replica of a bigger still. "Kemmerer Moonshine" was served in the famous Stork Club in Chicago. Supposedly Al Capone loved it and took it everywhere with him. There's a great children's discovery room where kids can touch everything. There are even rocks available that they can create their own petroglyphs on. Indian tepees display different types of hides used in their construction. Learn about Annie Richie, the petticoat rustler known as "Queen Annie." This ravishing beauty was the first woman to be convicted as a rustler. Her ranch is now the housing development called "Twin Creeks." View the original

Catholic church stained glass that weighs 250 pounds. Note the dinosaur footprint taken from a big pit in the coal mine just outside of town. In the summer, enjoy campfire chats on local history in nearby Archie Neil Park every Thursday evening. Open daily year-round. Free admission. Call for hours. **400 Pine Avenue, P.O. Box 854, Kemmerer, 83101; (307) 877-6551. E-mail: museum@hamsfork.net.**

Where to Stay

Accommodations

Energy Inn—$$–$$$
The Energy Inn awaits with all the standard motel amenities, including cable TV with free Showtime and HBO. Kitchenette units available. You'll also find coffee in the lobby. Plenty of parking space. Handicapped accessible. No pets allowed. Located at the junction of Hwys. 30 and 189. **360 Hwy. 30, P.O. 554 Diamondville, 83116; (307) 877-6901.**

Camping

Private Campgrounds and Cabins
Lake Viva Naughton Marina includes lakeshore RV camping areas and a permanent camping area where you can leave trailers year-round. Tent sites. Electrical hookups. A-frame cabins for rent. Showers available. There's a restaurant with good food and a busy bar located at the marina. Open year-round. **Hwy. 233, Kemmerer, 83101; (307) 877-9669.**

Riverside Mobile Home & RV Park has self-contained RV hookup sites. Sewer and water. No showers. No tent sites. No restrooms. Pets okay. **216 Spinel, Hwy. 189 North, Kemmerer, 83101; (307) 877-3416.**

Getting There

Kemmerer is located along **Hwy. 189,** 50 miles north of Evanston. You can charter a flight into the **Kemmerer Municipal Airport (307-828-2370),** but there is no commercial service. No taxi, bus, or rental cars are available.

Where to Eat

Luigi's—$$–$$$$
This is not the average burger restaurant. It's definitely upscale. Dine on Cajun prime rib, steak, or Chicken G (a pasta dish with chicken, artichoke hearts, olives, and a luscious cream sauce) in semiformal surroundings Wednesday through Saturday nights year-round, 5 P.M. to 9 P.M. Fun, different, delicious foods. Unique old pictures of Diamondville on the walls. Handicapped accessible. No kids' menu, but there is a seniors' menu. Stop by. You'll be surprised. **819 Susie Avenue, Diamondville, 83116; (307) 877-6221.**

Busy B Cafe—$–$$
Get fixed up here with a hearty, homemade breakfast or lunch. Open year-round 6 A.M. to 2 P.M. **919 Pine Avenue, Kemmerer, 83101; (307) 877-6820.**

Services

Visitor Information

Kemmerer/Diamondville Chamber of Commerce, Herschler Triangle Park, 800 Pine Avenue, Kemmerer, 83101; (888) 300-3413 or (307) 877-9761. E-mail: chamber@avicom.com. Website: www.kemmerer.org.

Pinedale

Lush mountain meadows of the Wind River Range (known locally as "the Winds"), a glaciation-created lake, and rivers teeming with wildlife drew Indians and later mountain men to this area long before anyone thought of settling permanently in this gorgeous valley. Nicknamed the "City Beautiful," Pinedale has recently experienced a population explosion due to its proximity to the ever popular Jackson Hole. Nevertheless, Pinedale has maintained its own historical identity. The Pinedale Area Chamber of Commerce offers a self-guided tour of the town's historic district. Call for a brochure **(307-367-2242)**.

History

Sixty-one members of John Jacob Astor's American Fur Company, along with their guides Pierre Dorion and his Indian wife and the couple's two young sons, were supposedly the first whites to enter the region around modern-day Pinedale. The Astorians, as they were called, crossed the Rocky Mountains and set up a camp approximately 28 miles north of Pinedale in September 1811. They hunted buffalo, jerking the meat, and traded with an Indian nation they called the "Snakes" (the Shoshones). Astorians misinterpreted the Indians' sign language for their tribal name. What the whites saw as a serpentinelike motion actually was a weaving gesture that described the type of grass lodges the Shoshone Nation was known for.

In 1835, famed mountain men Jim Bridger and Kit Carson respectfully sat in on the reportedly first Protestant sermon in the Rocky Mountains, held in almost the same spot as the Astorian camp location 24 years before. However, when some buffalo roamed into view, the mountain men dashed to their horses and gave chase before the preacher could end the service. A full belly ranked much higher than a church service to men who had faced starvation time and again in their travels.

The first permanent settlement came with the cattle industry. Pinedale began as Bob Graham's ranch. It also served as the post office for the area starting in May 1899. After the town incorporated during 1912, anyone who promised to put up a building received two town lots. The cattle business, and the town's status as county seat, kept Pinedale alive through much of the twentieth century.

Festivals and Events

Green River Rendezvous Pageant
mid-July

"Meet me on the Green" became the password of mountain men throughout the region. Pelt hunters, traders, and Indians gathered just west of Pinedale for six summers between 1833 and 1840 to rendezvous—that is, to have a huge party with drinking, dancing, fighting, games of chance, contests, and horse races. They also conducted business related to the fur trade. Beaver pelts or "plews" brought good money, as the felt made from the fur was in high demand for men's hats at the time.

Nowadays, the Pinedale community gathers at the Rendezvous Grounds to reenact this tradition. The **Sublette County Historical Society** has hosted the celebration since 1936, although not every year, due to such interruptions as World War II. Step back in time, surrounded by authentic costumes, lodging, and crafts in the reenactment village. Enjoy mountain-man games such as black-powder shoots, axe throwing, and knife throwing. The **Museum of the Mountain Man** hosts "Rendezvous Days" in conjunction with the pageant weekend, offering living-history programs, the Pelt and Plew Social and Buffalo Feast (pit-roasted buffalo is deliciously melt-in-your-mouth tender), and a family concert. For details, contact the museum and historical society at **(307) 367-4101.**

Outdoor Activities

Biking

Mountain Biking

The **Bridger-Teton National Forest** allows mountain biking, except in the Bridger Wilderness. Summer and early fall, take to the ski trails at **White Pine Recreational Area.** Hit the back roads or logging road in the forest. Head out across the open sage desert between Pinedale and Boulder. Expect elevations to range from 7,175 to 10,000-plus feet. The forest service office will give you some solid route information to suit your pedal level. **Pinedale Ranger District of the Bridger-Teton National Forest, 29 East Fremont Lake Road, P.O. Box 220, 82941; (307) 367-4326. Website: www.pinedaleonline.com** or **www.fs.fed.us/btnf/welcome.htm.** Additional information can be obtained from the **Bureau of Land Management, Pinedale Resource Area, 432 East Mill Street, P.O. Box 768, Pinedale, 82941; (307) 367-5300.**

Climbing

Pinedale furnishes one of the main entrances into the Wind River Range at **Elkhart Park,** located 14 miles up Skyline Drive from town. From there, mountain climbers can access Wyoming's highest peaks and glaciers via the **Island Lake Trail** and **Titcomb Basin.** Gannett Peak (13,804 feet), Warren Peak (13,722), Helen Peak (13,620), Sacajawea Peak (13,569), and Woodrow Wilson Peak (13,502) present varied and challenging ice and snow climbing. Fremont Peak (13,745 feet) offers a walk-up route that requires only an energetic, adventurous spirit and a good pair of hiking boots. None of these, however, are the type of trips that involve a day in, a day climbing, and a day out. None are suggested for novice climbers or hikers. Consult with the forest service before attempting these peaks **(307-367-4326).**

Taking a break at Warbonnet Peak.

125

Fishing

The **Bridger Wilderness** in the Wind River Mountains, accessed from trailheads near Pinedale, has been called "The Land of 1,300 Lakes." In addition, the town sits near a group of lakes and the **New Fork** and **Green Rivers,** which are all easily accessible and offer rich recreational opportunities.

Just northeast of town you'll find **Fremont Lake,** named after the famed pathfinder John C. Frémont. This natural lake formed when glacial action shoved a huge pile of debris out of the mountains during the "Pinedale Glaciation" 70,000 to 15,000 years ago. Boulder moraine created a dam that captured snowmelt and creek runoff from the heart of the mountains. The lake is 600 feet at its deepest.

Fremont Peak in the Wind River Mountains.

126

Twenty-two miles of shoreline give you ample opportunity to explore, fish, picnic, or camp. Besides excellent fishing (especially mackinaw and rainbow trout), you can swim or waterski. There is a boat ramp. Remember, as with all mountain-snow- and water-fed lakes, the water is incredibly cold, even in the height of summer.

Willow Lake, known for its rainbow and mackinaw trout, also supplies camping, boating, swimming, and hiking trailheads. **Half Moon Lake** (three miles from Fremont Lake on a dirt road) also has a boat ramp, camping and picnic areas, and places to swim and do some great fishing. **Soda Lake** offers more rugged pleasures with undeveloped camping and lively fishing for better-than-average-size brook trout and brownies. For more details about recreation at these area lakes and winter ice fishing, contact the **Pinedale Office, Wyoming Game & Fish, 117 South Sublette, Pinedale, 82941; (307) 367-4353.**

The Great Outdoor Shop offers guided fishing and backpacking trips, as well as fly-fishing instruction. Open year-round. **332 West Pine, P.O. Box 787, Pinedale, 82941; (307) 367-2440. E-mail: greatos@-wyoming.com. Website: www.greatoutdoorshop.com.**

Hiking and Backpacking

From the trailhead at **Elkhart Park** you can access the Bridger Wilderness of the Bridger-Teton National Forest. This is rugged, near-pristine hiking at its best. It's also a popular starting point for horsepackers. The forest service runs a visitors center at the trailhead. You'll also find a corral, drinking water, restrooms, and camping facilities. Trailheads from Elkhart Park travel deep into the Winds; however, day hikes abound as well. Try the **Sacred Rim Trail** for a four-mile round-trip or **Miller Park** in about seven miles round-trip.

Other trails for adventurous day hikes include the **Half Moon Trail,** which takes you around Half Moon and Fayette Lakes. The **Sweeney Creek Trail** leads to **Kelly Park Trail,** which leads to **Fortification Mountain.** Better plan on this one taking all day to get there and back.

Come prepared and well equipped to hike in the Winds. Speak with the forest service office **(307-367-4326)** about routes, bear-camping techniques, rerations, and maps prior to heading out.

The Great Outdoor Transportation Company offers trailhead service for cars and people, as well as transportation to and from the airport. **332 West Pine, P.O. Box 787, Pinedale, 82941; (307) 367-2440. E-mail: greatos@wyoming.com. Website: www.greatoutdoorshop.com.**

Horseback Riding

O'Kelley Outfitting can design a wilderness horsepacking trip, educational tour, or a combination riding, hiking, and fishing excursion. **155 South Bench Road, P.O. Box 833, Pinedale, 82941; (307) 367-6476. Website: www.pinedaleonline.com/okelley.**

Llama Trekking

Mountain dwellers in Peru have long utilized llamas to pack everything from trade goods to personal possessions. A llama carries approximately 75 pounds—enough for one person's equipment in the backcountry and then some. Llamas, while quite gentle, don't like to be touched or petted. They can walk faster and can handle mountainous terrain better than humans, but llamas behave well on a lead. (Forest service regulations require all pack animals to be on lead ropes.) Like other pack animals, if they get loose, they will head back to the trailhead.

In addition to five- to seven-day guided llama treks into the Wyoming Range, you can rent pack llamas and try your hand at this alternative to backpacking. **High Plains Llamas** has a training arena, as well as all the necessary tack and gear. **31 Blair Road, P.O. Box 84, Boulder, 82923; (307) 537-5292. E-mail: hpllamas@wyoming.com. The Great Outdoor Shop** also offers instruction and gear. **332 West Pine, P.O. Box 787, Pinedale, 82941; (307) 367-2440. E-mail: greatos@wyoming.com. Website: www.-greatoutdoorshop.com.**

River Floating

The **Fort William Guest Ranch** at the **Fort William Recreational Area,** eight miles east of Pinedale, provides kayaking as well as float trips. **308 Fall Creek Road, P.O. Box 1588, Pinedale, 82941; (307) 367-4670.**

Skiing

Downhill Skiing

White Pine Recreational Area, located between Fremont and Half Moon Lakes, supplies uncrowded skiing just 15 minutes from Pinedale. Ski 900 vertical feet on one of four runs. There's one lift and little waiting. A great place for beginners and intermediates. Contact the **Bridger-Teton National Forest** office at **29 East Fremont Lake Road, P.O. Box 220, Pinedale, 82941; (307) 367-4326. Website: www.fs.fed.us/btnf/welcome.htm** or **www.pinedaleonline.com.**
·

Cross-Country Skiing

White Pine Recreational Area also offers 35 miles of marked cross-country ski trails. Just about four miles of that is groomed. Contact the **Bridger-Teton National Forest** office at **29 East Fremont Lake Road, P.O. Box 220, Pinedale, 82941; (307) 367-4326. Website: www.fs.fed.us/btnf/welcome.htm** or **www.pinedaleonline.com.**

127

Snowmobiling

Leaving right from town, you can snowmobile vast areas in the forest and BLM lands; however, the Gros Ventre and Bridger Wilderness areas allow no motorized vehicles within their boundaries, and rangers will hit you with a large fine for transgressions. Groomed trails around the **Upper Green River** and the **Green River Lakes** area connect with trails that lead into Dubois on the other side of the Winds and into Jackson Hole. Right in the Pinedale area, 185 miles of maintained trails present every type of winter scenery and conditions.

Then there's the granddaddy of them all—the **Continental Divide Trail**—655 miles of snowmobiling adventure through the heart of Wyoming, 591 miles of it groomed. From Pinedale, you can ride through the mountains and open prairies to South Pass, staying in lodges and stopping at restaurants you can ride right up to. The experience beats any other snowmobiling trek! On clear days, vantage points expose approximately 150 miles of scenic panoramas at a time. The trail drives through dense forest and high mountains in six to eight feet of snow, but be warned: There's one stretch of 90 miles that has no fuel stops along it.

Get maps and information from the **Wyoming State Snowmobile Program (307-777-3680). Avalanche conditions** can be obtained from the Avalanche Center **(307-733-2664).** You can rent a snowmobile from **Bucky's, 146 South Lincoln Avenue, P.O. Box 668, Pinedale, 82941; (307) 367-2833.**

Seeing and Doing

Trapper's Point

A registered historic landmark, Trapper's Point overlooks the valley of the Green River, the 1835 rendezvous site, and Fort Bonneville, where 5,000 Indians once camped (where the town of Daniel currently is located). The point is the site of the impact of the fur trade on Native American and mountain-man history. It's located on the south side of **Hwy. 187,** six miles west of Pinedale, opposite the Cora Road exchange. The point is located on the ridge separating the Green River valley from that of its largest tributary and running parallel to the New Fork River.

Trappers Point. Photo courtesy of the Wyoming Division of Tourism.

Kendall Warm Springs

Thirty-one miles northeast of Pinedale past the spot where Hwy. 352 turns to gravel, Kendall Warm Springs lies tucked away in the Wind River Range. Although the forest service prohibits swimming, wading, and bathing, it does so to protect the Kendall Warm Springs Dace, a rare, two-inch-long (full grown) fish you will see only in these waters. A forest ranger found this now endangered fish at the springs in 1934. While dace, related to minnows, are known to inhabit warm waters, this particular species appears to have evolved separately from other cold-water dace found in the area.

The springs, elevation 7,840 feet, maintain a year-round temperature of 85 degrees Fahrenheit. Water from springs and snowmelt filter through a ridge of limestone that heats the water and adds calcium. The heated water pools up in a travertine shelf built from centuries of calcium deposits. Eventually the springs water drops over the shelf, falling into the Green River 10 feet below. Scientists speculate that Kendall Warm Springs' water has stayed isolated from the river for thousands of years, allowing the unique dace to develop. Contact the **Bridger-Teton National Forest** office for more about the dace and a map to the springs **(307-367-4326).**

Museums

Museum of the Mountain Man

One section of the museum entitled "The Hat that Opened the West" sums up the mountain-man era pretty well. World fashion demanded the luxurious underfur of the beaver for the best hats that money could buy. Mountain men combed the countryside for beaver and took back tales of the West's rich land and resources, paving the way for Manifest Destiny to bring settlers in by the thousands. Dedicated to the approximately 16-year period of U.S. history between the 1820s and 1840s, the museum focuses on the tools and techniques of beaver trapping, the Native American role in the fur trade era, daily life for mountain men, a trapper hall of fame, the mountain men who went on to become the guides for wagon trains headed West, and, of course, the rendezvous. There's also a hands-on children's corner with stuffed animals from the region and videos. Open daily between May 1 and October 1 from 9 A.M. to 4 P.M. and by appointment the rest of the year. Small fee. Call for group rates. **700 East Hennick; P.O. Box 909, Pinedale, 82941; (307) 367-4102, (307) 367-4101 for appointments; fax (307) 367-6768.**

Scenic Drives

Green River Lakes

Six miles west of Pinedale take Highway 352 north into the Bridger-Teton National Forest. The pavement ends, becoming gravel that, at times, is better suited to four-wheel-drive vehicles than cars. Check road conditions with the forest service **(307-367-4326)**. However, the drive is well worth it. It winds 50 miles into the Wind River Mountains, the range containing the highest point in the state—Gannett Peak, elevation 13,785 feet. You'll get a great view of the high peaks that form the home of the Dinwoody Glaciers, the Lower 48's largest group of active, alpine glaciers. You also pass the Kendall Warm Springs (see Seeing and Doing, above) and the remains of the Billy Wells Ranch, one of Wyoming's first guest ranches. The road dead-ends at the **Green River Lakes,** the headwaters of the Green River. You can fish, camp, picnic, boat, or head up to one of the wilderness access trailheads. From the lakes, the Clear Creek Falls Trail makes an excellent day hike filled with wildlife and some great photo ops.

Where to Stay

Accommodations

The Chambers House B&B—$$$–$$$$

Stay in a unique log home built in 1933 out of old-style cut logs. Yet it's pretty classy inside! Two of the four bedrooms have fireplaces.

Large log home furnished with antiques and modern furnishings. Nonsmoking facility. Full, hearty country breakfast. Handicapped accessible. Open year-round. Children welcome. Dogs allowed for an extra fee. **111 West Magnolia Street, P.O. Box 753, Pinedale, 82941; (800) 567-2168, fax (307) 367-4209 (call fax number before sending a fax).**

Window on the Winds B&B—$$$

A warm fire and friendly folks await you at this B&B located on the Continental Divide Snowmobile Trail. Stroll the balcony and drink in an incredible view of the Winds. Four bedrooms, two with shared baths. Sleep in queen-size lodgepole pine beds. Soak in the hot tub amid a sunroom filled with plants. Fill up on a healthy full breakfast. Not handicapped accessible. Children and pets welcome. Open year-round. **10151 Hwy. 191, P.O. Box 996, Pinedale, 82941; (888) 367-1345 or (307) 367-2600, fax (307) 367-2395. E-mail: lmcclain@wyoming.com. Website: www.-cruising-america.com/windowonwinds.**

Pole Creek Ranch B&B—$$–$$$

Rustic charm nestled within sight of the Wind River Range. Sleep inside in one of two bedrooms that share a bath and den, one room with a private bath, or spend a night in the tepee. Cots and extra bedding are available to accommodate large families. Experience a ride in a wagon, buggy, or sleigh, or on horseback. Evening campfires. Horse boarding. Allows all sort of pets—cats, dogs, even rabbits! Flexible scheduling of horsepacking courses, but you do need to plan them ahead of time. Outdoor hot tub. Not handicapped accessible. Kids under six stay free. Monthly horse boarding available. **244 Pole Creek Road, P.O. Box 278, Pinedale, 82941; (307) 367-4433. Website: www.bbonline.com/wy/polecreek.**

The Rivera Lodge—$$–$$$

All different log cabins, some fancy with private phones, TV, some simple cabins. All with private baths. Located on Pine Creek. Pets okay. Open May to October. **442 West Marilyn, P.O. Box 896, Pinedale, 82941; (307) 367-2424.**

Guest Ranches

DC Bar Guest Ranch—$$$$

Located 30 miles north of Pinedale, next to the Bridger-Teton National Forest. This historic ranch is located at 8,000 feet where the aspen and pines come together in alpine meadows. It was started by five brothers at the turn of the century. The DC Bar, named after owners Cita Dew and Dick Dew, was quite popular back in the 1920s. Cita used to go to the East every winter to promote the ranch at women's universities to attract them as the clientele to come to the West. The young women took the train to Rock Springs; from there they boarded wagons (later vehicles) that delivered them to the ranch for the entire summer. For two weeks, the girls practiced riding horses, learned how to pitch tents, and slept on the ground. They headed out on a 45-day pack trip in the wilderness. The ranch sent a chef, a doctor, and plenty of chaperons. There were five cowboy wranglers on the trip, so there were five chaperons—one to watch each cowboy. Still, the girls fell in love with the cowboys. However, they returned East to finish school before coming back to marry their cowboys. Many stayed in the area and started businesses. In fact, this was how the valley got populated in the first place. Now, old people come up the road to see how the ranch looks, and they delight that it still looks the same as when they left all those years ago. Individual cabins have been preserved to maintain the atmosphere of those early days. No TV or boom boxes allowed! Minimal electricity use. Cabins, which are scattered throughout the trees, use propane and oil lights. They allow only 24 to 28 people, which makes for a secluded vacation. This is a get-into-the-woods-and-learn type of experience where you'll see a last glimpse of the wilderness that is rapidly disappearing. Take nature walks through fields filled with wildflowers in summer. Bask in the morning and evening sun. Watch the moose, deer, and elk in the yard. Listen to the coyotes howl at night. No pets. Kids welcome. In fact, the ranch hands will tell stories around the campfire at night. Horseback riding onto unmarked trails adjacent to the forest that has no roads. A different route each day.

Seven springs and a beaver pond make for a healthy trout population. Guides will teach you to fly fish. Float trips on the Green River or one of the lakes. Not handicapped accessible. Three days and nights minimum stay, all meals included. With six nights, get an overnight pack trip. **P.O. Box 561, Pinedale, 82941; (888) 803-7316 or (307) 367-2268. E-mail: singewald@aol.com. Website: www.bwo.com.**

Camping

In the National Forests
(See Fishing, above.)

Private Campgrounds and Cabins
Lakeside Lodge Resort & Marina on Fremont Lake provides RV camping with hookups. Closed in winter. **P.O. Box 1819, Pinedale, 82941; (307) 367-2221.**

Pinedale Campground on the west end of town offers electric hookups, heated restrooms, hot showers, a dump station, drinking water, and a convenience store. Closed in winter. **204 South Jackson Avenue, P.O. Box 248, Pinedale, 82941; (307) 367-4555.**

Where to Eat

McGregor's Pub—$$–$$$$

Enjoy the rustic decor of knotty pine, western art, and memorabilia while feasting on such delights as garlic shrimp, grilled chicken breast, or pepper steak. And all their soups, sauces, and desserts are homemade. There's a kids' menu and seniors' portions called "inbetweeners." Take advantage of the outdoor deck in the summer. Lunch served Monday through Friday, 11:30 A.M. to 2 P.M. Open for dinner year-round, except for the week before and week of Thanksgiving, 5:30 P.M. to 10:30 P.M. Not handicapped accessible. **21 North Franklin, P.O. Box 99, Pinedale, 82941; (307) 367-4443. E-mail: jcrandal@wyoming.com.**

The Della Rose—$$$

Home of the biggest hamburger in town, a half-pounder! Great pastas like Carbonara fettuccine with ham, greens, and bacon. A good family-dining, diner-type atmosphere. Very comfortable. Handicapped accessible. Open Monday through Saturday, 9:00 A.M. to 6:30 P.M. **120 West Pine, Pinedale, 82941; (307) 367-2810.**

Services

Visitor Information

Pinedale Area Chamber of Commerce, 32 East Pine Street, P.O. Box 176, Pinedale, 82941; (307) 367-2242. E-mail: chamber@pinedaleonline.com. Website: www.pinedaleonline.com.

131

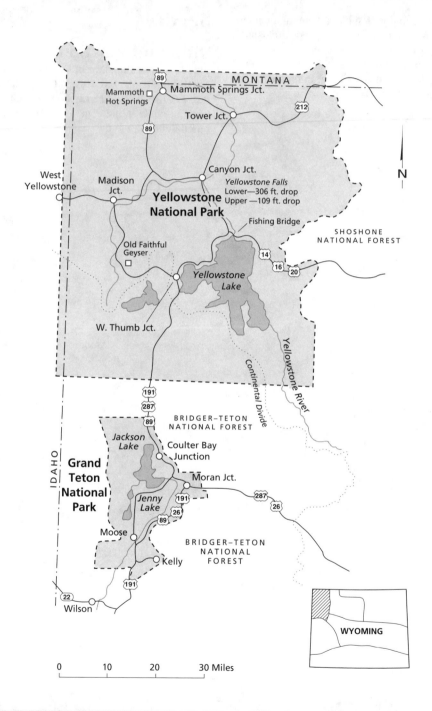

MONTANA

89 Mammoth Springs Jct.

Mammoth □
Hot Springs

212

Tower Jct.

89

Canyon Jct.

West
Yellowstone

Madison
Jct.

**Yellowstone
National Park**

Yellowstone Falls
Lower—306 ft. drop
Upper —109 ft. drop

Fishing Bridge

SHOSHONE
NATIONAL FOREST

Old Faithful
Geyser □

*Yellowstone
Lake*

14

16 20

W. Thumb Jct.

Continental Divide

Yellowstone River

191
287
89

BRIDGER–TETON
NATIONAL FOREST

*Jackson
Lake*

Coulter Bay
Junction

**Grand
Teton
National
Park**

Moran Jct.

287

26

*Jenny
Lake*

191

26

IDAHO

89

Moose

Kelly

BRIDGER–TETON
NATIONAL
FOREST

22

191

Wilson

WYOMING

0   10   20   30 Miles

N

Yellowstone Region

Yellowstone Region

The Snake River.

133

Grand Teton National Park

Grand Teton National Park (GTNP) offers visitors 485 square miles (310,521 acres) of hiking, camping, packing, mountaineering, biking, floating, boating, fishing, skiing, snowshoeing, homesteading history, and wildlife viewing. The park has gone through as many name changes as the mountains themselves.

Mountain men used natural landmarks to navigate the wilderness. The Tetons' three most distinctively jagged peaks made a perfect marker that they named "Pilot Knobs." Indian nations of the area referred to them as *Teewin-ot*, currently the name of one of the peaks in the Teton Range. Later French *voyageurs* called the three pinnacles *les trois tetons* (the three breasts) and the name stuck—not just for the peaks now known as Grand, Middle, and South but for the entire mountain range.

While looking at the flower-filled meadows and sparkling water of the Snake River that wind their way beside the base of the spectacular Teton Range, it's hard to imagine that the section of highway running along the Tetons was once cluttered with a collection of unsightly buildings and glaring billboards that all but obscured this incredible view. Yet the desire to preserve the scenic mountain vista led to one of the hottest controversies in the country.

History

Horace Albright, the superintendent of Yellowstone National Park from 1919 to 1929, wanted to add the Teton Range and surrounding forest lands (which were part of the nation's first national forest) to Yellowstone National Park. Citizens of Jackson, area ranchers, and employees of the forest service were all outraged by Albright's proposal. It would mean the loss of income, tax revenue, grazing land, jobs, and control over the land.

Nevertheless, in 1925 Pierce Cunningham, one of Jackson's pioneering citizens, petitioned the government to preserve the mountain range "for the education and enjoyment of the Nation as a whole." A year later John D. Rockefeller Jr. and his family vacationed in Yellowstone, and Albright took Rockefeller on a tour of the Teton valley, outlining his idea. Rockefeller was so taken with the area that he set up the Snake River Land Company to begin purchasing ranches and other properties along the Tetons as they came onto the market.

In 1929, a bill passed in Congress, setting aside six lakes at the base of the Tetons and the national forest lands that surrounded them as Grand Teton National Park. Many local residents were not happy about this. At the time Rockefeller's land company had spent over a million dollars purchasing 35,000 acres from 320 different landowners. When Rockefeller announced his intentions of donating this land to the park, things really heated up. Accusations of cheating people out of their property, forcing sales, and paying less than market value brought on a senate investigation into the practices of the land company, but the government found no wrongdoing. In fact, the land company had paid above market value in many cases. However, Wyoming's congressmen managed successfully to stop Rockefeller from adding the Snake River properties to the park.

So Rockefeller went around Congress. With the help of the secretary of the interior, he persuaded President Franklin D. Roosevelt to issue an executive order in 1943, creating the Jackson Hole National Monument adjacent to Grand Teton National Park. The monument included not only Rockefeller's holdings but also 211,936 acres of the Teton National Forest and other federally owned lands. The outrage went national. Congressional bills passed in both houses, calling for the abolishment of the monument. Roosevelt vetoed them. It took until 1950 to settle things. Congress finally created an expanded Grand Teton National Park that included Rockefeller's holdings and the other lands from the monument.

Festivals and Events

Arts for the Parks Awards
mid-September

In 1986 the National Park Foundation and the National Park Academy of the Arts began sponsoring the annual Arts for the Parks competition. Artists from around the country submit works that depict a site in one of the country's 370 national parks, historic sites, or monuments. Every year a different distinguished panel of judges composed of directors of museums, art magazine editors, and well-known artists select the top 100 paintings. These are displayed at Jackson Lake Lodge in Grand Teton National Park during the third week of September as the kickoff to the annual nationwide tour, designed to raise public awareness and support of the national park system. The tour also gives artists a chance for national exposure. The panel of judges chooses the winners by considering artistic merit, content, and how well the portrait captures the feel and essence of the park, site, or monument. Through the course of the tour, a silent auction is held with part of the proceeds going to the national park system for maintenance and preservation.

The grand-prize–winning artist receives $50,000. The National Park Foundation donates the winning work of art to the park it depicts. The display is open to the public. However, if you'd like the opportunity to meet many of the artists, plan to attend the Saturday night banquet at Jackson Lake Lodge where the winners are announced and cash awards given. Festivities get under way with a reception where you can enjoy some tasty treats while viewing the spectacular high-quality art and rub elbows with the artists. The banquet follows at 6 P.M. For people interested in entering, the deadline is June 1. For information, banquet tickets, or entry forms, contact **Arts for the Parks, P.O. Box 608, Jackson, 83001; (800) 553-2787. E-mail: artsforthepark@blissnet.com. Website: www.artsforthepark.com.**

Chapel of the Transfiguration.

Outdoor Activities

Biking

Mountain Biking

Expect breathtaking scenery, glimpses of wildlife, and fascinating natural features while you bike through Grand Teton National Park. **Antelope Flats Road** just off Hwys. 26, 89, and 191 goes to Mormon Row, part of the valley's homesteading history.

Teton Mountain Bike Tours offers some fantastic guided trips in GTNP where you'll not only see the sights, but gain a great understanding of Mormon Row's homesteading his-

Elk near Mount Moran in Grand Teton National Park. Photo courtesy of the Wyoming Division of Tourism.

136

tory and learn about the area's wildlife and ecology. Yellowstone National Park tours also available. They have half-day, full-day, and custom multiday trips with transportation to and from the tour area. Child carriers provided on request. **P.O. Box 7027, Jackson, 83002; (800) 733-0788 or (307) 733-0712, fax (307) 733-3588. E-mail: wybike@wyoming.com. Website: www.tetonmtbike.com.**

Bike tours are also available from **Spring Creek Ranch Touring Center** in summer **(307-733-1004).** Mountain bike rentals are available **from Wilson Backcountry Sports (307-733-5228)** or **Hoback Sports, 40 S. Millward, Jackson, 83001; (307) 733-5335. E-mail: hobacksports@hobacksports.com.**

Climbing

The **Teton Range** rises 1.5 miles straight up from the valley floor with no foothills to ease you into the mountains. A young range formed of old rock, the Tetons were thrust onto the scene approximately nine million years ago. That sounds old, until you compare it with the neighboring Wind River Range at approximately 60 million years old! The rock is estimated to be three billion years old and is quite

hard and relatively free of slides. The product of a geological fault, the Teton Range continues to rise, while the Jackson Hole valley drops. Most of the earthquakes that result from this constant seismic activity, however, remain too small to notice. The Moose Visitor Center contains some interesting displays about earthquakes and scientific studies in the Tetons.

Seventeen named points jut into the sky, carrying colorful names like Cloudveil Dome, Maidenform Peak, the Jaw, and Bivouac Peak. The highest peak in the range, Grand Teton, towers above it all at 13,776 feet and summons climbers to scale it. Mountaineers call Grand Teton the "American Matterhorn."

Several people have claimed to be the first to reach Grand Teton's summit. A man named William O. Owen was one of the most persistent in making this claim. He demanded credit after his successful ascent on August 11, 1898, even petitioning the Wyoming legislature to "officially" name him as the first. Nevertheless, historical journals tell a story far different from Owen's. Sidford Hamp, a 17-year-old member of the 1872 Ferdinand V. Hayden Expedition into Yellowstone, wrote a detailed and accurate account of a Grand Teton climb to the summit on July 29, 1872. Hamp's descriptions of the terrain, as well as an article about the climb that appeared in the June 1879 issue of *Scribner's Monthly,* written by the group's leader, Nathaniel Langford, accurately depict the view from the summit that later climbers would verify. Then there's "The Enclosure," a stone structure the Sheepeater Indians were credited with constructing on the summit of Grand Teton's west spur long before the Langford group completed their ascent.

Today, climbers at any skill level will find a challenge in the Tetons. Difficulty ranges from 5.2 to 5.10. Beginners should gain some basic techniques at a climbing school before attempting a Teton climb. The park has some regulations regarding climbs, and you must apply for a permit. **GTNP, P.O. Drawer 170, Moose, 83012; (307) 739-3399. Website: www.nps.gov/grte/.** The office is open daily, from June through Labor Day, 8 A.M. to 7 P.M., and the rest of the year from 8 A.M. to 5 P.M. Closed Christmas Day.

Jackson Hole Mountain Guides & Climbing School guides small groups year-round. Classes instruct intermediate and more advanced climbers in summer mountain snow techniques, protection placement, and other skills for high peak ascents. There is no age limit; however, they require prior mountaineering experience. They offer guided nontechnical day climbs, two-day major peak ascents, and extended trips up to 12 days. **P.O. Box 7477, Jackson, 83001; (307) 733-4979.**

Exum Mountain Guides lead one- to four-day climbs throughout the year in the Tetons. No prior experience is necessary before attending their basic school. They also offer instruction for intermediate and advanced climbers, as well as snow climbing and women's classes. Exum also provides private guides and porters. Classes and climbs are limited to small numbers. **P.O. Box 56, Moose, 83012; (307) 733-2297, fax (307) 733-9613. E-mail: exum@wyoming.com. Website: www.exumguider.com.**

Skinny Skis rents some mountaineering and climbing gear, as well as camping equipment, sleeping bags, stoves, rock climbing shoes, and snow and ice climbing boots. **65 West Deloney Street, P.O. Box 3610, Jackson, 83001; (307) 733-6094. E-mail: skinnyskis@blissnet.com.**

Fishing

In addition to GTNP's many lakes, the **Snake River** grants anglers a rare opportunity to fish for the Snake River cutthroat trout. The Snake River cutthroat is the only trout native to GTNP. The park encourages catch and release of the small cutthroat, so it will continue to thrill anglers in the future. Other game fish include rainbow, mackinaw, brown, and brook trout, as well as the Rocky Mountain whitefish. Contact the park for special regulations and restrictions at **(307) 739-3300.**

The **Colter Bay Marina** offers a full-service marina for Jackson Lake. Rent a boat. Get fishing licenses, tackle, groceries, and fuel.

137

Getting There

Grand Teton National Park is **adjacent to Yellowstone National Park**'s southern entrance. It is accessible either through Yellowstone or between Moran Junction and Jackson on **Hwy. 390.** Jackson is 13 miles south of GTNP. The **Jackson Hole Airport,** the country's only airport to be located within the boundaries of a national park, offers daily commercial flights on **American (800-443-7300)** or **United Express (800-241-6522).** A variety of rental cars are available at the Jackson Hole Airport. Taxicab services includes **All Star Taxi (800-378-2944), Alltrans (307-733-3135),** and **Buckboard Cab (307-733-1112).**

Scenic lake cruises are available between early May and mid-September. **(307) 543-2811, fax (307) 543-3143. Website: www.gtlc.com.**

Guided fishing trips by the hour are available on **Jackson Lake,** as well as scenic lake cruises with or without breakfast or dinner included. Guided fly-fishing and boat rentals, too. **Grand Teton Lodge Company, P.O. Box 240, Moran, 83013; (800) 628-9988** or **(307) 543-3100.**

Signal Mountain Lodge rents canoes, deck cruisers, pontoon boats, pleasure boats, and fishing boats. **P.O. Box 50, Moran, 83013; (307) 543-2831. Website: www.foreverresort.com. Teton Boating** cruises around Jenny Lake and ferries people to the far side of the lake, so they can hike up to Hidden Falls. They also rent fishing boats. Located at the south end of Jenny Lake. **P.O. Box 1553, Jackson, 83001; (307) 733-2703.**

Hiking and Backpacking

Welcome to day hiker's heaven! Terrain in GTNP presents something for everybody, regardless of what shape you're in or how acclimatized you are to the higher altitude. The **Lakeshore Trail** at **Colter Bay** is a great easy introduction to the Teton Range. The two-mile round-trip trail wanders east and north along the shoreline, leaving from the north end of the Colter Bay Visitor Center. It follows the perimeter of a lodgepole pine-forested peninsula that juts into Jackson Lake. Then there's the great panorama of the northern section of the Tetons.

The **String Lake Trail,** just over 3 miles round-trip, and **Leigh Lake Trail,** 2 miles round-trip, also offer exciting vistas and easy hiking. A more moderate hike to **Two Ocean Lake,** about 6.5 miles round-trip, gains 80 feet in elevation while traversing conifer forests along the south shore and aspen groves and beautiful meadows on the north shore. If you're looking for strenuous activity, try the **Amphitheater Lake Trail.** It's just over 9.5 miles with a difference of 2,958 feet in elevation over the course of the hike. The trail climbs up to glacial lakes and wanders through subalpine meadows.

138

Trailhead parking in the park becomes a factor in the peak hiking months of July and August. Lots fill up quickly, and illegally parking outside of designated lots will result in an expensive ticket. So if you plan to hike in GTNP during these months, figure on starting out early. Besides, nippy early mornings offer some excellent wildlife viewing. If you plan an overnight backpacking trip, you'll need to get a free backcountry use permit from the Moose Visitor Center. They are on a first-come, first-served basis between June 1 and October 1. Between January and the end of May the park does offer some limited reservations on backcountry camping sites. As always, check with the park officials about trail conditions and any restrictions before heading out on the trail. **GTNP, P.O. Drawer 170, Moose, 83012, (307) 739-3300. Website: www.nps/gov/grte/.**

Horseback Riding

Embarking on a wilderness horsepacking trip means seeing the country in the same way as the early explorers. Outfitters supply horses for riding and packing, basic camping equipment, delicious meals, and guides for either sight-seeing, photography, or fishing adventures.

Located inside GTNP, the **Triangle X Ranch** provides a true roughing-it-style vacation in the Tetons. The daily itinerary is geared to the client's interests, whether it's photography, wildlife watching, fishing, or simply exploring. They only use mountain-wise horses. Pack trips begin in mid-June and continue through early September with a four-day minimum. **Hwys. 26, 89, and 191, Moose, 83012; (307) 733-2183, fax (307) 733-8685. E-mail: johnaturner@blissnet.com. Website: www.trianglex.com.**

One-, two-, or three-hour rides or half-day trips are available, as well as breakfast and dinner horseback or wagon rides. **Grand Teton Lodge Company, P.O. Box 240, Moran, 83013; (800) 628-9988 or (307) 543-3100.**

River Floating

The **Snake River,** dubbed "The Mad River" by French trappers in the early 1800s, shifts from serene to swift-flowing water and rapids with little or no warning. Its typical depth of 4 feet and an average flow rate of 3,000 cubic feet per second increases to about 15,000 cubic feet per second when the mountain snows melt and run off during the summer.

Whitewater

The Snake is famous for its whitewater rafting. It's thrill-a-second, heart-in-your-mouth adventure at its best! Come prepared to get soaking wet. Several outfitters guide summer whitewater excursions. **Mad River Boat Trips** specializes in guided whitewater trips. **P.O. Box 2222, Jackson Hole, 83001; (800) 458-RAFT (7238), fax (307) 733-7626.** **Sands Wild Water River Trips** also includes eight miles of scenic floating and lunch on their whitewater trips. They offer overnight trips, too. **P.O. Box 696B, Wilson, 82014; (800) 358-8184, fax (307) 734-9064.** **Lewis & Clark River Expeditions** provides scenic and/or whitewater trips with a meal option. **P.O. Box 720, Jackson, 83001; (800) 824-5375, fax (307) 733-0345.**

Scenic Floats

For those not quite ready for the adrenaline rush of whitewater, the Snake's scenic floats represent unsurpassed beauty, close encounters with wildlife (even a glance at a bald eagle if you're lucky), and the time to soak it all in instead of getting soaked.

Take a 10-mile sunrise or evening float with **Triangle X Float Trips.** They also offer five-mile floats, which are great for parents with small children. No kids under four years old allowed. They cannot fit into the life preservers properly. Options also include 20-mile and special fishing floats. **Moose, 83012; (307) 733-5500, fax (307) 733-8685. E-mail: johnaturner@blissnet.com. Website: www.trianglex.com.** Other 10-mile float trips are available through **Barker-Ewing Scenic Tours, P.O. Box 100, Moose, 83012; (800) 365-1800, fax (307) 739-1800.** Scenic lunch or dinner trips are available through **Grand Teton Lodge Company, P.O. Box 240, Moran, 83013; (800) 628-9988 or (307) 543-3100.**

Skiing

Cross-Country Skiing

To truly experience winter in **GTNP,** cross-country ski its trails. Trails are not groomed, but they are usually well packed. Most are marked with orange flagging, tags, or blazes on trees. Unplowed roads, on the other hand, generally aren't flagged. Stay alert for snowmobilers.

Jenny Lake Trail's nine easy round-trip miles loop around Cottonwood Creek. The trail begins at the Taggart Lake parking area where the plowed road ends. The trail crosses large meadows and climbs a low ridge of glacial moraine, skirting the base of the Tetons, and shows off a lovely view of the lake. **Swan Lake-Heron Pond Loop** offers another easy three miles of scenic wonder near the Colter Bay Visitor Center.

For a more challenging route, take the six-mile round-trip **Flagg Canyon Trail.** It begins across from Flagg Ranch Resort on the John D. Rockefeller Jr. Memorial Parkway between Yellowstone and GTNP. The trail follows the

Kayaking whitewater on the Snake River. Photo courtesy of the Wyoming Travel Commission.

edge of the Snake River through meadows, then along the volcanic rock wall canyon. It gets steep in a few spots.

Several areas in the park are closed to oversnow use, or other regulations may be in effect. Check with the park **(307-739-3300)** when planning any ski trip.

Spring Creek Ranch Touring Center (800-733-0788 or 307-733-1004) has a guided ski excursion into GTNP for either a half day or full day. Custom trips; pickup at your hotel; helmets provided; lunch on full-day trips. **Skinny Skis** specializes in nordic equipment and rental. **65 West Deloney Street, P.O. Box 3610, Jackson, 83001; (307) 733-6094. E-mail: skinnyskis@bliss-net.com.**

Snowmobiling

Explore a different world in winter in GTNP via snowmobile on designated, unplowed roads. Among them are the **Jenny Lake Loop** road, the **Signal Mountain** road, sections of the **Moose-Wilson** road, and a number of forest service access roads. Expect inclines and dips through majestic mountain valleys. Or be brave and skate Jackson Lake on a snowmobile—when weather conditions permit, of course! Winter park permits are required for unguided snowmobile trips in GTNP, and a variety of regulations apply to snowmobiling, including giving the wildlife a wide berth! Contact park officials for all the details and maps. **P.O. Drawer 170, Moose, 83012; (307) 739-3300. Website: www.nps/gov/grte/.**

139

Grand Teton Park Snowmobile Rental offers guided tours to Old Faithful with a continental breakfast and lunch at Old Faithful. Pickup in town is included on these full- or half-day trips. Also included are snowsuits, boots, hats, and gloves. Tours and rentals available from mid-December through April. **17800 East Hwys. 26 and 287, P.O. Box 92, Moran, 83013; (800) 563-6469 or (307) 733-1980. Best Adventures Snowmobile Tours** offers multiday guided trips. **(800) 851-0827 or (307) 733-4845. Website: www.yellowstonerv.com.**

Snowshoeing

Park rangers offer a two-hour, 1.5-mile nature tour on snowshoes every day except Wednesdays, starting in late December until spring, at 2 P.M. You must make reservations in person at the **Moose Visitor Center** or by calling **(307) 739-3399.** The park provides the snowshoes. Participants must be eight years old or older.

Seeing and Doing

Cunningham's Cabin

Pierce Cunningham and Margaret Cunningham, among the early homesteaders in the area, established the 160-acre Bar Flying U Ranch in 1890. For the first five years, they lived in the two-room dog-trot-style log cabin that still stands today. The open veranda between the two single-room square cabins offered a cool, shaded breezeway in summer and a place to store firewood to keep it dry and handy in winter. Mr. Cunningham played a prominent role in Jackson's early history, and the cabin was the site of a strange murder that went under the guise of catching some horse thieves. The cabin is down a short dirt path from the turnout and parking lot on **Hwys. 26, 89, and 191.**

Chapel of the Transfiguration

The Chapel of the Transfiguration nestles between the Teton Range and the Snake River in probably the most scenic location of any church built in the country. Constructed of native lodgepole pine logs, the church set the pattern for construction in the Rocky Mountain region. The chapel originally served the employees and guests of the outlying dude ranches at the turn of the century. Sunday services are still held in this chapel during the summer. The church is located just past the **Moose Visitor Center** entrance to the park.

Menor's Ferry

Around 1894, William D. "Bill" Menor began ferrying passengers and goods across the highly unpredictable Snake River, which divided the Jackson Hole valley. Most of the residents lived on the east bank. The best access to timber, hunting, and wild food, such as huckleberries, was on the west side.

Menor employed a cable system to pilot his ferry, a sharp-prowed double pontoon boat with a flat platform that resembles a catamaran without a sail. Menor charged 50 cents for a wagon and team, 25 cents for a horse and rider. Pedestrians could cross for free—provided Menor happened to be ferrying over a wagon at the same time.

Menor also built a homestead on the bank near his ferry. But by 1918, he had grown tired of the business and sold it. The ferry continued operation until the first bridge was built near the ferry site in 1927. The homestead and ferry site are located just **north of the Moose entrance.**

Museums

Colter Bay Indian Arts Museum

This museum exhibits a small, very impressive collection of Native American relics. Touring the displays offers insight into the daily lives of many Indian cultures. Laurance S. Rockefeller and Jackson Hole Preserve, Inc., assembled the collection and donated it to the museum. See moccasins, baskets, shields, and pipes that date back to early contact between Plains Indians and whites. The photomurals are intriguing as well. Located half a mile from the Colter Bay Junction on Hwys. 89, 191, and 287, the Colter Bay Museum is free and open daily from the beginning of June to the beginning of September from 8 A.M. to 8 P.M., and during May and the rest of September from 8 A.M. to 5 P.M. Closed the rest of the year. **Colter Bay Village; (307) 739-3300.**

Murie Memorial Museum

Housed in the Teton Science School, the Murie Museum displays and holds the extensive natural history collection that belonged to world-renowned naturalists and field biologists Adolph, Olaus J., and Mardy Murie. The Muries devoted their lives to the study of North American birds and mammals. Their collections include over 1,000 mammal skulls and skins and 600 birds, a number of them rare specimens, as well as samples of bird and mammal scat and tracks Olaus used in compiling *A Field Guide to Animal Tracks,* first published in 1954.

The Murie Museum is free to the public, but you need to call ahead to arrange an appointment to tour the facility. Located 18 miles north of Jackson, off Hwys. 26, 89, and 191. **c/o Teton Science School, P.O. Box 68, Kelly, 83011; (307) 733-4765, fax (307) 739-9388. Website: www.info@tetonscience.org.**

Scenic Drives

Mormon Row

Mormon Row offers a level, scenic route through a lush valley overshadowed by the Teton Range. The row is not marked on park maps, or talked about in brochures. In fact, as with other aspects of human (as opposed to natural) history, some park officials have expressed a desire to rid the park of such human intrusions. Fortunately, more understanding heads higher up have prevailed, so visitors can see this significant part of GTNP.

Turn onto **Antelope Flats Road** from Hwys. 26, 89, and 191 approximately two miles north of Moose Junction. Mormon Row is the first dirt road on the right. It is a decent, two-lane, straight road that runs through the heart of historic Mormon Row and then connects to the paved Gros Ventre River Road. Turn right to go back to the highway.

The **Andy Chambers Homestead Historic District** stands as the last nearly intact ex-

ample of the homestead ranches on the once densely settled Mormon Row. During 1908, officials of the Teton National Forest returned some lands north of the Gros Ventre River to the public domain. Mormons soon settled the area east of Blacktail Butte.

Residents of Mormon Row patterned their growing community after the Mormon line village in Grouse Creek, Utah, hence the nickname "Mormon Row." Andy Chambers built his home near what turned out to be the center of the settlement.

Across the road from the Chambers homestead sits the **Moulton Barn,** the most photographed barn in the region. It has come to be the symbol of Jackson Hole. Thomas Alma (T. A.) Moulton and his brother John (whose barn still stands at the end of the row) claimed land back in 1907. T. A. began building his barn in 1913. It took 20 years to complete.

The Chambers and Moulton families tried for years to get the park to allow the families and friends to restore the structures that nature (and the park's lack of enthusiasm and outright neglect) threatened to destroy. Finally, starting in 1995, the park granted the families permission to make limited repairs over a period of years.

Wildlife Safari!

Here is one very different sort of scenic drive through GTNP, put on by the **Great Plains Wildlife Institute.** Wildlife biologists and naturalists teach the principles of ecology and ethical wildlife observation techniques through actual field experience. All of the institute's programs endeavor to keep any negative impact on wildlife to a minimum. From open-roofed safari vehicles, view animals with the assistance of 22x spotting scopes and binoculars provided by the institute. Depending upon the time of year, participate in a variety of projects, actually helping to collect data, such as taking a census of trumpeter swans, sage grouse, elk, wild horses, or the nests of birds of prey such as osprey and bald and golden eagles. Document bighorn sheep lambing in the Teton Range. Monitor the reintroduction of the black-footed ferret. Listen in on the radio tracking of elk, mule deer,

141

Yellowstone Region

bats, raptors, pronghorns, or bighorn sheep. Or participate in coyote and pronghorn research. Wildlife Discover tours are 8 to 10 hours long and go from 7 A.M. to 4:30 P.M. daily. Sunrise or sunset tours last 4 hours in either of two seasons: from December 20 through April or from the last week in May to the first week in October. Wolf Weekend tours are only in May. On these two-day tours, you'll see bears and wolves. Great Parks Safaris are week-long programs. Half- and full-day excursions, as well as multiday trips, start at 7:00 A.M. in summer and 8:00 A.M. in winter. Come away with a greater understanding of how the ecosystem works and how we all fit into it. Reservations required. Pickup at your hotel. **P.O. Box 7580, Jackson, 83002; (307) 733-2623. E-mail: safari@blissnet.com. Website: wildlifesafari.com.**

Other sight-seeing tours of GTNP or a combination of GTNP and Yellowstone are available through **Jackson's Hole Adventure (P.O. Box 2407, Jackson Hole, 83001; 800-392-3165)** and **Grand Teton Lodge Company (P.O. Box 240, Moran, 83013; 800-628-9988 or 307-543-3100).** Day or multiday trips for individuals and groups are provided by **Gray Line of Jackson Hole National Park Tours, P.O. Box 411, Jackson, 83001; (800) 443-6133 or (307) 733-3135, fax (307) 733-2689. E-mail: alltrans@sisna.com. Website: www.jacksonholenet.com.**

Where to Stay

Accommodations

The Inn at Buffalo Fork—$$$–$$$$
The unique thing about this B&B is its location, just six miles from the Moran entrance to GTNP. And you have a killer view of the Tetons! Plus, the B&B is surrounded by a working ranch. Five rooms with private baths and a hot tub outside. Hearty hot breakfasts with fresh fruit and often a side meat—enough to get you energized for sports. Third-generation homesteader and fishing guide on-site. Take day trips from the B&B into either Grand Teton or

Yellowstone National Park. Winter adventures include cross-country skiing or snowmobiling nearby. Horse boarding available in summer. No other pets allowed. Dinner with prior arrangement available in winter. Open year-round. Not handicapped accessible. **18200 East Hwy. 287, P.O. Box 311, Moran, 83013; (307) 543-2010, fax (307) 543-0935. E-mail: innatbuff@blissnet.com. Website: www.cruising-america.com/buffalofork.**

Jenny Lake Lodge—$$$$
Thirty-seven duplex cabins. Room rates include breakfast and dinner and the use of bicycles. Jackets and elegant dress at dinner are required. No pets. Opens the end of May to early October. **Grand Teton Lodge Company, P.O. Box 240, Moran, 83013; (800) 628-9988 or (307) 543-3100.**

Jackson Lake Lodge—$$$–$$$$
Rooms with a view in a historic lodge built to house tourists back in the 1920s! What more could you ask for? Cottages and suites. No pets. Open mid-May through mid-October. **Grand Teton Lodge Company, P.O. Box 240, Moran, 83013; (800) 628-9988 or (307) 543-3100.**

Signal Mountain—$$$–$$$$
Enjoy lakefront apartments, log cabins, or motel units on Jackson Lake. Rustic one- or two-room units, some with fireplaces. Two-room units can sleep up to six. Motel rooms come equipped with queen- or king-size beds. Apartments have kitchenettes. Some rooms are handicapped accessible. Pets okay. Kids welcome, no extra charge. A marina on-site offers boat rentals—canoes, pontoons, deck cruisers—as well as guided lake fishing and scenic float trips on the Snake River. Be sure to ask how Signal Mountain got its name! Open mid-May through mid-October. **P.O. Box 50, Moran, 83013; (307) 543-2831. Website: www.foreverresorts.com/signalmt.**

Guest Ranches

Triangle X Guest Ranch—$$$$
This early 1900s ranch is located within Grand Teton National Park. The Triangle X offers a great Wyoming-style family vacation with

horseback riding, horsepacking trips into the Teton wilderness, fishing or scenic floats along the Snake River, cookouts, western dancing, and hiking. They also arrange cross-country skiing, snowshoeing, and snow-mobiling tours over Togwotee Pass or in Yellowstone. Or just soak the winter away in the outdoor hot tub. Special programs and events for little wranglers 5 to 12. Open mid-May through mid-November and mid-December through the end of March. There is a four-night minimum stay between mid-May and June 10 and between September 15 and mid-November, and a two-night minimum during winter. They prefer no pets. Rates include three meals a day. In summer, expect family-style meals; gourmet menu with selections cooked to order in winter. Handicapped accessible. **Hwy. 89, Moose, 83012; (307) 733-2183, fax (307) 733-8685. E-mail: johnaturner@bliss-net.com. Website: www.trianglex.com.**

Turpin Meadow Guest Ranch—$$–$$$$
Located two miles from the Moran Junction entrance to GTNP, this ranch dates back to the early 1920s, making it one of the longest continuously running dude ranches in Wyoming. The ranch features cabin accommodations and home-cooked buffet-style meals. During the summer, explore the mountains on horseback on a wilderness pack trip or just a trail ride. Participate in a uniquely Wyoming gymkhana where everybody gets to demonstrate their equestrian talents! Cowboy cookouts, covered-wagon rides, and, in winter, snowmobiling. Open year-round. Handicapped accessible. Pets allowed for an extra fee. **P.O. Box 10, Moran, 83013; (800) 743-2496 or (307) 543-2496, fax (307) 543-2850. E-mail: turpinmeadow@wyoming.com. Website: www.turpinmeadow.com.**

Camping

In the National Parks, Monuments, and Recreation Areas
Colter Bay Village provides service stations, a marina, general store, food court and snack bar, launderette, and public showers. **Colter Bay Village Cabins** offers one-room cabins

with either semiprivate or private baths. Open from late May to late September. **Colter Bay Tent Cabins** are available from the end of May to the beginning of September. The **Colter Bay RV Park** opens late May and closes in late September. **Grand Teton Lodge Company, P.O. Box 240, Moran, 83013; (800) 628-9988 or (307) 543-3100.**

Private Campgrounds and Cabins
Dornen's **Spur Ranch Cabins** are located along the Snake River near the park entrance at Moose. The new log cabins come with fully equipped kitchens and western-style lodgepole furnishings. Enjoy a tranquil view of the Tetons. Sit on the deck or porch and watch the mountains. Jackson is close but not the bustle. Open year-round. Handicapped accessible. No pets. No smoking. Three-night minimum stay June through September. **P.O. Box 39, Moose, 83012; (307) 733-2522, fax (307) 739-9098. E-mail: spur@sisna.com. Website: www.dornans.com.**

Grand Teton Park RV Resort supplies electrical hookups year-round, but there is no water in winter. Tent sites and camping cabins. The campground is partially handicapped accessible. Pets allowed, if on a leash. **17800 East Hwys. 26 and 287, P.O. Box 92, Moran, 83013; (800) 563-6469, (307) 543-2483, or (307) 733-1980; fax (307) 543-0927. E-mail: gtprv@blissnet.com. Website: www.yellowstonerv.com**

143

Where to Eat

Jackson Lake Lodge Mural Room—$$$–$$$$
This restaurant provides one of the best views of any in the state. The windows present a grand view of the Tetons in all their splendor. Open for breakfast from 7 A.M. to 9:30 A.M., lunch from noon to 1:30 P.M., and dinner 6 P.M. to 9 P.M. Make reservations for dinner. Box lunches are available from the Pioneer Grill at the lodge, which is open from 6 A.M. to 10 P.M. for standard breakfast items, sandwiches, salads, and ice cream. **Grand Teton Lodge Company, P.O. Box 240, Moran, 83013; (800)**

628-9988 or (307) 543-3100.

The Aspens Dining Room and Lounge and the Cottonwood Cafe—$$–$$$$

Located at Signal Mountain. Enjoy a continental menu, wild game, pasta dishes, or fresh seafood. The dining room is open from 7 A.M. to 10 P.M. The cafe has sandwiches, burgers, salads, and a kids' menu. The cafe is open from 5 A.M. to 10 P.M. **P.O. Box 50, Moran, 83013; (307) 543-2831. Website: www.forever-resorts.com/signalmt.htm.**

Dornan's Chuck Wagon—$$–$$$

Genuine chuckwagon meals since 1948. The Dutch ovens are about the size of individual hot tubs. The food is extra tasty because it has been cooked over a fire, and the panorama of the Snake River and the Tetons spread out in front of you only adds to this unique dining experience. To top it off, Dornan's is "all you can eat," so come hungry! Barbecue short ribs, roast beef, vegetable beef stew, cowboy beans, and potatoes and gravy come with a salad, fresh sourdough bread, and coffee, tea, or lemonade. For breakfast, try the sourdough pancakes, also "all you can eat." Look for the huge tepees, used for dining out of the sun or during bad weather, on Hwys. 26, 89, and 191. Open from mid-June through Labor Day. Handicapped accessible. Dinner menu for kids. Kids five and under eat for free. Steak and prime rib or chicken night with all-you-can-eat buffet on Wednesday, Saturday, and Sunday. **P.O. Box 39, Moose, 83012; (307) 733-2415, ext. 300, fax (307) 733-3544. E-mail: dornans@dornans.com. Website: www.dornans.com.**

Services

Visitor Information

You will pay a fee to get into Grand Teton National Park. As of this writing, a daily pass, which is good for up to seven days in both GTNP and Yellowstone, costs $20 per vehicle, $15 for motorcycles, and $10 for bicycles, horseback, on foot, or if you're over 62. A one-year pass to both parks is $40. A Golden Eagle Pass, which is good for every national park in the country for an entire year, costs $50.

Roads into the park generally open in mid-May and close at the end of October. Unpaved roads usually close by mid-October. But keep in mind, road and park opening and closure dates are approximate and are subject to the weather. GTNP oversnow use areas (snowmobiles, skis, snowshoes, etc.) are closed along the Snake River floodplain from the Buffalo Fork downstream to Menor's Ferry north of Moose between the end of December and the end of March to allow wildlife undisturbed access to critical winter habitat. The Willow Flats area, Buffalo Fork River, Kelly Hill, and Uhl Hill are closed from mid-December to mid-April.

The Moose Visitor Center located on Teton Park Road half a mile from Moose Junction is open daily, May 19 to June 1 from 8 A.M. to 6 P.M.; June 2 to September 1 from 8 A.M. to 7 P.M.; and the rest of September and May 10 through May 18 from 8 A.M. to 5 P.M. Call **(307) 739-3399.**

Colter Bay Visitor Center located on Hwys. 89, 191, and 287 half a mile west of Colter Bay Junction is open daily, May 19 to June 1 from 8 A.M. to 7 P.M.; June 2 to September 1 from 8 A.M. to 8 P.M.; and the rest of September and May 10 through May 18 from 8 A.M. to 5 P.M. Call **(307) 739-3594.**

Jenny Lake Visitor Center located 8 miles north of Moose Junction on Teton Park Road is open daily, June 2 to September 1 from 8 A.M. to 7 P.M.

The Flagg Ranch Information Center is located at Flagg Ranch Resort, 15 miles north of Colter Bay on Hwys. 89, 191, and 287. It is open daily, June 2 to September 1 from 9 A.M. to 6 P.M.

For general information about Grand Teton National Park, contact the headquarters at **Drawer 170, Moose, 83012; (307) 739-3300, (307) 739-3399 (general information), or (307) 739-3600 (for a packet of information). Website: www.nps/gov/grte/.**

144

Yellowstone National Park

Grand Canyon of the Yellowstone River.

Yellowstone. The very name conjures up images of strange natural forces, mystery, majesty, and wonder. Fortunately for everyone, a few farsighted people fought to save and preserve this incredible natural resource that has changed little since the last glacier in the area receded around 10,000 years ago.

145

History

Geologists believe volcanic eruptions began occurring in the park 2.5 million years ago, creating the Yellowstone Plateau. Eruptions persisted until approximately 70,000 years ago, producing a series of volcanic craters known as calderas.

Archaeological evidence shows that Indians hunted and fished in the region of the Yellowstone Plateau for over 11,000 years. Their descendants described the extraordinary marvels to the members of the 1803–1805 Lewis and Clark Expedition, but the troop skirted around what is now Yellowstone National Park, leaving the wonders for John Colter to see.

Colter, a member of the Lewis and Clark Expedition who stayed in the country after the others headed back to the United States, became the first white man to travel the valleys of the "stinking water" and hear the earth rumble like thunder. He returned to civilization in 1807; however, nobody believed his "tall tales" for 65 years, until the first official government-sponsored survey of the Yellowstone Plateau authenticated Colter's stories.

Dr. Ferdinand V. Hayden, director of the U.S. Geological Survey, headed the government survey to Yellowstone in 1871. Two people in the group of 34 would be instrumental in the creation of the national park—Thomas Moran, whose painting *Grand Canyon of the Yellowstone* was hung in the U.S. Capitol building, and photographer William Henry Jackson, whose photos of Yellowstone's geysers, waterfalls, hot springs, and wildlife were captioned and bound in volumes and handed to every member of Congress. On March 1, 1872, Congress set aside over 2.2 million acres (3,472 square miles) of land "as a public park or pleasuring ground for the benefit and enjoyment of the people" as attested to by President Ulysses S. Grant, Vice President Schuyler Colfax, and Speaker of the House James G. Blaine.

Fishing the Firehole. Photo courtesy of the Wyoming Division of Tourism.

Festivals and Events

146

Park rangers and naturalists offer guided walks and campfire programs throughout the summer, covering a wide range of topics. Contact the ranger's office for more details. **P.O. Box 168, Yellowstone National Park, 82190; (307) 344-2120; Website: www.nps.gov/yell.**

Outdoor Activities

Biking

Biking is prohibited in the backcountry or on trails and boardwalks. It is permitted on established public roads, parking areas, and designated routes. Narrow roads, the lack of road shoulders to ride on, large potholes, and the large volume of motorized traffic, however, generally make biking less than fun in the park.

Fishing

Originally called Lake Eustis and Lake Riddle, **Yellowstone Lake** became the official name on maps published in 1838. In 1889, the grand tour of Yellowstone included a sailing excursion on Yellowstone Lake aboard the steam-boat *Zillah,* a 40-tonner measuring 81 feet in length and 14 feet in width at its beam. It ferried 120 passengers between the stagecoach lunch station at Thumb Bay and the Lake Hotel, making a stopover on Dot Island so passengers could see the animals' enclosure where the steamboat's owner, E. C. Waters, had corralled elk, deer, and buffalo.

Today, you can't top fishing the waters of Yellowstone Lake for North America's largest inland population of wild cutthroat trout! Enjoy 110 miles of shoreline and 136 square miles of surface area at an elevation of 7,733 feet. The season opens in mid-June. Guided expeditions are available through the Bridge Bay Marina, as well as outboards and rowboat rentals, mid-June through mid-September. **Amfac Parks & Resorts, Reservations Department, P.O. Box 165, Yellowstone National Park, 82190; (307) 344-7311, TDD (307) 344-5395.**

The fishing season on the **Yellowstone River** and its tributaries starts mid-July. Most other places the season runs from Memorial Day Saturday until the first Sunday in November. There are detailed regulations for lake trout and Yellowstone cutthroat trout. Contact the **Chief Ranger Office** for all the details. **P.O. Box 168, Yellowstone National Park, 82190; (307) 344-2120.**

Hiking and Backpacking

Yellowstone is a backpacking paradise with over 1,100 miles (1,771 km) of hiking trails with 85 trailheads. Old Faithful, Norris Geyser Basin, and Mammoth Hot Springs have handicapped-accessible boardwalks.

A terrific easy hike is the **Canyon Rim Trail.** This 7.4-mile round-trip trek begins at the North Rim Road, a mile from Canyon Village, and ends at Artist Point, revealing awe-inspiring vistas all along the way, and, of course, the grand view of the Grand Canyon of the Yellowstone.

Although the **Mount Washburn Trail** is only 5.5 miles, it wanders through gradually increasing elevation, 1,380 feet worth of a climb. Once an old road that led to the top of Mount Washburn, the trail begins five miles north of Canyon Village on the Tower Junction

Road at Dunraven Pass. Allow half a day for the trip up and back down the road. It's a great one for seeing wildlife and wildflowers.

An all-day hike to **Hellroaring Creek** follows a dirt road once used by the Yellowstone stagecoach rides through the park. Start at the Roosevelt Lodge at Tower Junction. It's 10 miles with a 450-foot drop down to the Yellowstone River. This is true Yellowstone backcountry.

Backcountry overnight hikes require a permit obtained at any ranger station. Bear camping procedures are in effect throughout the backcountry. As a side note: Climbing is not recommended in the park and is illegal in the Grand Canyon of the Yellowstone.

Horseback Riding

Ride by the hour, day, or two days through Yellowstone's incredible scenery. Available from Mammoth Hot Springs Hotel mid-May through late September, from Roosevelt Lodge from mid-June through early September, and from Canyon Lodge from late June through mid-September. Or try a bit of a twist on it and climb aboard a stagecoach ride, also leaving from Roosevelt Lodge between mid-June and early September. Old West cookout dinner rides on horseback or wagons with a western buffet meal leave from the Roosevelt Lodge between mid-June and early September. **Amfac Parks & Resorts, Reservations Department, P.O. Box 165, Yellowstone National Park, 82190; (307) 344-7311, TDD (307) 344-5395.**

John Henry Lee Outfitters provides personalized pack trips into Yellowstone National Park and the Teton Wilderness area. **P.O. Box 8368, Jackson, 83002; (800) 3-JACKSON (800-352-2576) or (307) 733-9441.**

Skiing

Cross-Country Skiing

The first winter expedition into Yellowstone was during 1887. All unplowed roads, as well as the trails, are open to cross-country skiing and snowshoeing. Unfortunately, unplowed roadways are also shared with snowmobiles.

Getting There

Yellowstone National Park is located in the northwestern corner of Wyoming, 52 miles west of Cody on **Hwys. 14, 16 and 20**; and 56 miles north of Jackson on **Hwys. 191, 89, and 287.** Commercial flights arrive in West Yellowstone, Montana, three miles from the entrance and into Jackson and Cody. Rental cars are available from major car companies at all of these airports. **Powder River Transportation (800-442-3682)** services the park from Cody.

So watch out! Two of the most intriguing winter skiing destinations are Old Faithful and the Canyon Rim Trail. Ski rentals are available at Mammoth Hot Springs Hotel and Old Faithful Snow Lodge Ski Shops.

Snowmobiling

147

One hundred fifty miles of roads are available for snowmobiling in the park. Snowmobiling is allowed in the park between mid-December and early March. Rent snowmobiles, suits, boots, helmets, and gloves at Mammoth Hot Springs Hotel and Old Faithful Inn. Full-day rentals only. Or take a full-day guided snowmobile tour on Sundays from Mammoth Hot Springs. Fuel is available at Old Faithful, Canyon, Fishing Bridge, and Mammoth Hot Springs. Off-road travel or sidehilling is illegal in the park. If wind and snow in your face is not quite your idea of fun, opt for a snowcoach tour. Day trips or multiday excursions. **Amfac Parks & Resorts, Reservations Department, P.O. Box 165, Yellowstone National Park, 82190; (307) 344-7311, TDD (307) 344-5395.**

National Parks Adventures (P.O. Box 2665, Jackson, 83001; 800-255-1572. E-mail: nps1@juno.com) and **Old Faithful Snowmobile Tours (P.O. Box 7182, Jackson, 83002; 800-253-7130; E-mail: oldfaithfultours@wyoming.com. Website: www.jacksonwy.com/oldfaithful)** provide snowmachine tours in the park. **Flagg Ranch Resort (P.O. Box 187, Moran, 83013; 800-443-2311 or 307-543-2861, fax 307-543-**

Old Faithful. Photo courtesy of the Wyoming Division of Tourism.

2356) offers snowcoach trips in addition to snowmobiling.

Snowshoeing

148

Take a winter walk with a three-hour guided snowshoe tour of Old Faithful Geyser Basin or the terraces around Mammoth Hot Springs. Available Thursday and Sunday. Bring your own snowshoes or rent them for the tour. **Amfac Parks & Resorts, Reservations Department, P.O. Box 165, Yellowstone National Park, 82190; (307) 344-7311, TDD (307) 344-5395.**

Seeing and Doing

Old Faithful

No one knows how many geysers erupt in Yellowstone; nevertheless, the Upper Geyser Basin holds at least 70 (approximately one-fourth of the world's geysers). Home of Old Faithful, the basin's recent earthquakes have disturbed Old Faithful's eruption schedule, changing it from an average of every 65 minutes to about every 75 minutes.

Fountain Paint Pots

These clay and silica mud pots bubble and boil and spit blobs of mud, because they lack

enough water to create a geyser. The acids in the water break down the rock, making the mud, which is colored by the variety of minerals in the rock. The pinks, blues, and oranges resemble containers of paint.

Firehole Canyon Drive

Originally part of the old highway through Yellowstone, the one-way drive takes you by 800-foot-high lava cliffs, the 40-foot-high Firehole Falls, and the Cascades of the Firehole.

Black Dragon's Caldron

In 1948, what would become known as the Black Dragon's Caldron broke open and blew pitch-black mud into the nearby trees. Since then, the Caldron has moved approximately 200 feet from where it first started bubbling up.

Grand Canyon of the Yellowstone River

Yellowstone has 150 waterfalls; however, the best known, and certainly among the most spectacular, is in the Grand Canyon of the Yellowstone. The canyon runs 24 miles long, 4,000 feet at its widest point, and 1,200 feet at its deepest. The Yellowstone River carved the canyon out of volcanic rock that had been weakened by the geyser basin's hot water and acidic gases. The canyon's striking colors come from oxides and minerals leaching out of the decaying rocks. Two falls roar through the canyon—Upper Falls (109 feet) and Lower Falls (308 feet).

Petrified Tree

One of Yellowstone's lesser known wonders is in an area where a petrified redwood forest dating back millions of years once stood. A volcanic eruption approximately 45 million years ago buried the forest in ash and debris. "Human erosion" pillaged all but one fossilized tree stump, which is now protected by a tall iron fence.

Mammoth Hot Springs

Mammoth Hot Springs spills out 700 gallons of water daily, spreading out over a colorful and much photographed travertine terrace that stairsteps into the side of the mountain. The hot springs add approximately two tons of new deposits every 24 hours, which translates into approximately eight inches of new rock every year. The U.S. Army stationed in the park between 1886 and 1916 kept visitors from carrying away chunks of the formation as souvenirs.

Museums

Museum of the National Park Ranger

Explore the development of the park ranger profession. See Yellowstone's history as an army camp where soilders trained. National Park Service history, as well. Located at Norris. Open 9 A.M. to 6 P.M. between Memorial Day and Labor Day and 9 A.M. to 5 P.M. early September to late May **(307-344-7353)**.

Norris Geyser Basin Museum

Learn about the park's geysers and geothermal events. Also located at Norris. Open 8 A.M. to 7 P.M. between Memorial Day and Labor Day and 9 A.M. to 5 P.M. early September to late May **(307-344-2812)**.

Scenic Drives

The Loops

Yellowstone's road system makes two loops that form a figure eight. The Upper Loop takes in Mammoth Hot Springs, Sheepeater Cliff, the Obsidian Cliff, Roaring Mountain, Norris Geyser Basin, Dunraven Pass, Mount Washburn, Tower Falls, the Petrified Tree, Floating Island Lake, Phantom Lake, and Undine Falls. The Lower Loop includes Yellowstone Lake, the falls at the Grand Canyon of the Yellowstone, the Norris Geyser Basin, Gibbon Falls, Firehole Canyon Drive, Fountain Flat Drive, the Lower Geyser Basin, Fountain Paint Pots, Firehole Lake Drive, Great Fountain Geyser, Midway Geyser Basin, Biscuit Basin, Upper Geyser Basin, Black Sand Basin, Old Faithful, Kepler Cascades, Scaup Lake, Craig Pass, and Lewis Lake. The Lower Loop Road is 96 miles.

Mammoth Hot Springs. Photo courtesy of the Wyoming Division of Tourism.

The Upper Loop Road is 70 miles. The combined total is 142 miles (the loops overlap at points).

Various full-day sight-seeing tours can be arranged between late May and the end of September (depending on location and weather). **Amfac Parks & Resorts, Reservations Department, P.O. Box 165, Yellowstone National Park, 82190; (307) 344-7311, TDD (307) 344-5395.**

149

Where to Stay

Accommodations

Old Faithful Snow Lodge—$$$$

Newly built, this lodge was designed to complement the nearby historic Old Faithful Lodge. It's beautifully constructed with heavy timbers, hardwood floors, and wrought iron accents. Some of the timbers were recycled from other buildings in the park. A balcony overlooks the lobby from the second floor. Also, check out the chairs in the lobby with carved wildlife on the backs; and you'll be asking where you can get one of the lamps for yourself. Two big fireplaces; one separates the lounge and dining area and the other is in the lobby. The kids will enjoy the skiing bears they might find in the lodge! Fifty-two rooms and some cabins, as well as family-style restaurant, gift shop, and lounge. Wyoming microbrews available in the lounge. Some rooms have cozy window seats with spectacular views. Handicapped accessible. No pets are allowed in the cabins. Guided snowshoe and ski tours available. Cross-country ski lessons also available for anyone over the age of six. An on-site retail outlet/ski shop rents cross-country skis, snowshoes, and snowmobiles. In winter, you can only reach the lodge via an oversnow vehicle, which can be booked (in addition to room cost) from West Yellowstone, Mammoth, or Flagg Ranch. Regular runs or groups can charter a run. The lodge is open May through October and mid-December through March. **Amfac Parks & Resorts, Reservations Department, P.O. Box 165, Yellowstone National Park, WY, 82190; (307) 344-7311, TDD (307) 344-5395. Website: www.travelyellowstone.com.**

Old Faithful Inn—$$–$$$$

Stay in a gorgeous inn built in 1903 that has been designated a national historic landmark. Wander through it, even if you aren't staying there. Designed by Robert Reamer, the inn incorporates what was considered a radical idea for its day. Reamer believed a structure should heighten rather than divert the spirit of the wilderness that surrounded it. His philosophy of architectural sensitivity to the environment set the standard for construction by the National Park Service for succeeding decades. Some rooms available with baths down the hall. Open May through October and mid-December through early March. Handicapped accessible. No pets. **Amfac Parks & Resorts, Reservations Department, P.O. Box 165, Yellowstone National Park, 82190; (307) 344-7311, TDD (307) 344-5395.**

Flagg Ranch—$$$–$$$$

Cabins with two to four rooms. Dining room in lodge. Open summer, mid-May through mid-October, and in winter late December through early March. Pets okay for an extra fee. Some handicapped accessible rooms. Rent snowmobiles in winter. Campground open, depending on weather, from June 1 through September 30. Float trips available, three hours long, one-hour-long whitewater trips. Fly-fishing trips on the Snake River. Horse rentals by the hour in summer. **P.O. Box 187, Moran, 83013; (800) 443-2311 or (307) 543-2861, fax (307) 543-2356. E-mail: info@flaggranch.com. Website: www.flagg-ranch.com.**

Lake Yellowstone Hotel & Cabins—$$$–$$$$

Originally built in 1891 and renovated back to its 1920s look, the hotel has some luxurious suites with parlors. Cabins are available on-site as well as at the Lake Lodge Cabins, within walking distance of the hotel. Open mid-May through October for the hotel, mid-June through mid-September for the Lake Lodge Cabins. The hotel is handicapped accessible. No pets in the hotel, cabins only. **Amfac Parks & Resorts, Reservations Department, P.O. Box 165, Yellowstone National Park, 82190; (307) 344-7311, TDD (307) 344-5395.**

Mammoth Hot Springs Hotel & Cabins—$$–$$$$

This hotel dates back to 1937, with one wing built in 1911. A convenient place to launch into winter activities in the park. In addition to hotel rooms, there are cottage-type cabins, some with private hot tubs. Open May through October and mid-December through early March. Not handicapped accessible. No pets in hotel rooms. Pets okay in the cabins. **Amfac Parks & Resorts, Reservations Department, P.O. Box 165, Yellowstone National Park, 82190; (307) 344-7311, TDD (307) 344-5395.**

Canyon Lodge & Cabins—$$–$$$

Only half a mile from the fabulous Grand Canyon of the Yellowstone on the Yellowstone River. The main lodge offers hotel-style rooms. All cabins come equipped with private baths. Open June through mid-September. Handicapped accessible. Pets allowed in cabins only. **Amfac Parks & Resorts, Reservations Department, P.O. Box 165, Yellowstone National Park, 82190; (307) 344-7311, TDD (307) 344-5395.**

Roosevelt Lodge Cabins—$$–$$$

Named after President Teddy Roosevelt's favorite camping location, the rooms are all rustic-looking cabins, some without baths. Open mid-June through early September. Not handicapped accessible. Pets okay. **Amfac Parks & Resorts, Reservations Department, P.O. Box 165, Yellowstone National Park, 82190; (307) 344-7311, TDD (307) 344-5395.**

Camping

In the National Parks, Monuments, and Recreation Areas

Campgrounds in Yellowstone come equipped with restrooms, drinking water, and picnic tables with fire grills. Pets are allowed on a leash. Parking space, however, can be rather limited.

The **Fishing Bridge RV Park** is for hard-sided campers only, no more than 40 feet in length. The park, located along Yellowstone Lake, has a shower, laundry, full hookups, dump station, and a store. **Madison Campground,** 14 miles east of the West Yellowstone entrance, offers no hookups or shower; however, there is a dump station. **Canyon Campground** at the Grand Canyon of the Yellowstone provides a pay shower, laundry, dump station, and restaurant, but no hookups. **Bridge Bay Campground** on the northern edge of Yellowstone Lake has a marina, boat launch, dump station, and a store. A pay shower and laundry are located four miles away. **Grant Village Campground** on the southwestern edge of Yellowstone Lake offers a dump station, pay shower, laundry, a store, and a restaurant.

Make reservations well in advance. All reservations for Yellowstone accommodations are handled through **Amfac Parks & Resorts, Reservations Department, P.O. Box 165, Yellowstone National Park, 82190; (307) 344-7311, TDD (307) 344-5395. Website: www.travelyellowstone.com.**

Private Campgrounds and Cabins

Flag Ranch Resort offers full hookups, tent sites, laundry, restrooms, showers, and a grocery store stocked with camping and fishing supplies. **P.O. Box 187, Moran, 83013; (800) 443-2311 or (307) 543-2861,** fax **(307) 546-2356.**

Where to Eat

The dining rooms at the lodges all have similar menus and services. They offer good prime rib and chicken dishes in historic and/or scenic surroundings. Daily specials. Vegetarian meals. Open for breakfast, lunch, and dinner. See each individual lodge listing above for the season each restaurant is open and for handicapped accessibility. General hours are from 6 A.M. to 9 P.M. Dinner reservations required, and you might want to dress for dinner. Meal cost: **$$$–$$$$.**

Services

Visitor Information

Yellowstone National Park offers 20,000 rooms. Summers are busiest. Reservations should be made as far in advance as possible to get the type of room and the location that you desire. However, if you don't mind possibly rustic accommodations and the location doesn't matter, the park can generally accommodate most visitors with rather short notice. If there is nothing available, Cody, Thermopolis, Dubois, and Powell are within reasonable driving distance. Jackson and Grand Teton National Park are also generally booked in advance, but might present an alternative.

For lodging and restaurant reservations, contact **Amfac Parks & Resorts, Reservations Department, P.O. Box 165, Yellowstone National Park, 82190; (307) 344-7311, TDD (307) 344-5395. Website: www.travelyellowstone.com.**

For general information on the park, contact **Yellowstone National Park, National Park Service Office, P.O. Box 168, Yellowstone National Park, 82190; (307) 344-7381. Website: www.nps.gov/yell.** Road information in the park is available by calling **(307) 344-7381.**

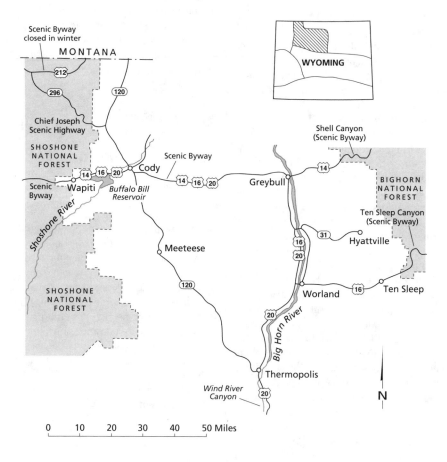

Scenic Byway
closed in winter

MONTANA

212

296

120

Chief Joseph
Scenic Highway

SHOSHONE
NATIONAL
FOREST

Scenic Byway

14   16   20   Cody

14   16   20   Greybull

14

Scenic
Byway   Wapiti

Buffalo Bill
Reservoir

Shoshone River

Shell Canyon
(Scenic Byway)

BIGHORN
NATIONAL
FOREST

Ten Sleep Canyon
(Scenic Byway)

Meeteese

16   31   Hyattville

16

20

SHOSHONE
NATIONAL
FOREST

120

Worland   16   Ten Sleep

20

Big Horn River

Thermopolis

Wind River
Canyon   20

N

0   10   20   30   40   50 Miles

WYOMING

Big Horn Basin Region

Big Horn Basin Region

Shell Canyon Falls.

153

Cody

Two things make this century-old community unique among western towns. It received its name from William Frederick Cody, known throughout the world as Buffalo Bill. And, as if that's not enough, Cody guards the eastern gate to Yellowstone, the country's first official national park, accessed through the Wapiti Valley of the Shoshone National Forest, the country's first national forest.

Although Buffalo Bill guided hunting parties, and even Yale archaeologist/fossil hunter O. C. Marsh, through the Yellowstone and Big Horn Basin area from as early as 1871, he only played a limited role in the actual founding of the town that would eventually bear his name (at his insistence), a place he envisioned as "the next Eldorado of the West."

History

Although fur trapper John Colter first traveled through here in 1807, trading with the Native American tribes who inhabited the region, settlers didn't begin to filter in for over 70 years. By 1885, the area loosely went by the name DeMaris Springs after homesteader Charles DeMaris, who started trailing cattle through the Big Horn Basin in the late 1870s. This became the first of several names the community would have.

DeMaris Springs, also referred to as "Needle Plunge," went unnoticed until 1894 when George T. Beck and his financial backer Horace C. Alger cast a speculative eye on the basin. Cody's son-in-law, Horton Boal, was among the surveyors sent to check out the possibilities. Buffalo Bill learned from Boal about the plans for the Shoshone Land and Irrigation Company, and he joined the partnership.

In the initial phase, the company laid out the first real townsite during the autumn of 1895, but a bit of a land dispute prompted Beck to insist on moving the town about a mile downriver from DeMaris Springs to the present site in 1896. Early names included "Shoshone" (after the river) and "Richland" (what the partners hoped the irrigation ditch they built would turn the ground into) before finally becoming Cody, so named because Buffalo Bill's reputation would bring settlers.

Sure enough, the showman proved to be the growing little community's greatest asset. Buffalo Bill's personal involvement in the town stemmed from a genuine love for the region and a desire to invest profits from his Wild West Show into ventures that would support his retirement.

Fifty years old himself the year the town of Cody was born, Buffalo Bill planned to create the perfect city in the Rocky Mountains—a place that offered sophistication to world travelers and, at the same time, a business hub that accommodated ranchers and rural settlers. This utopia would need more than just the usual saloons, general store, and crude lodgings, and he would supply them—in the process leaving a legacy!

Buffalo Bill charmed the Burlington Railroad into building a 70-mile-long spur to the town, completed in 1901, and some accounts claim he invested in a stagecoach line that would ferry visitors from the railroad to Yellowstone National Park 52 miles to the west, stopping at his two strategically placed lodges—Wapiti Inn and Pashaska Teepee.

Legend has it that toward the end of his life, Buffalo Bill and White Beaver, a friend of long standing, made a death pact. Bill would be buried on Cedar Mountain and White Beaver on Red Butte, so their spirits could stand guard over the valley and the town of Cody that lay between. But this was not to be. Bill died while on a trip in Denver, and he was buried on Lookout Mountain. Some accounts insist that Bill's wife, Louisa, was paid ten thousand dollars by a man named Harry Tammen to have Buffalo Bill laid to rest in Colorado.

However, as the showman foresaw, tourism would become the town's lifeblood. And Buffalo Bill's mark can be seen in just about every facet of life in modern-day Cody.

Festivals and Events

Cody Nite Rodeo
nightly all summer

Cody is billed by the chamber of commerce as the "Rodeo Capital of the World," and the Cody Nite Rodeo, the longest running rodeo in the United States, dates back to 1938. About dusk every evening between June and September, cowboys step on high rollers (big leaping bucking horses), dally (wrap the rope end around the saddle horn), tie a hooey (half hitch used in calf roping), and try not to dog-fall (illegal wrestling move in downing a steer) or pull leather (bronc rider's free hand touches the saddle during his ride, thus getting him disqualified) at this PRCA-sanctioned rodeo. Events include bareback and saddle bronc riding, a mustang race, calf roping, steer and bull riding, barrel racing, and steer wrestling (bulldogging), the latter an event invented by Bill Pickett during a stint with Buffalo Bill's Wild West Show. For buckaroos under 12, the rodeo means the "Calf Scramble." The arena fills with kids from the audience intent on capturing the ribbon tied around a calf's neck. The winner receives a trophy ribbon. **Stampede Park, Hwys. 14, 16, and 20, Cody, 82414; (307) 587-5155.**

Cody Stampede
4th of July

Fearing the "Old West" would disappear with Buffalo Bill's passing, Clarence Williams, the owner of Red Star Barn, headed up the establishment of the Cody Stampede. Begun in 1919, it showcased western riding and ranching skills. The events, which included a boy's burro race, a ladies' saddle horse race, a wild cow milking contest, an unusual kind of horse race called Roman standing races, and longhorn steer wrestling, are a far cry from modern rodeos. The only event still performed in today's versions is bulldogging. It's kicked off these days with a parade, and followed by foot races, a crafts show, a barn dance, and fireworks. **Stampede Park, Hwys. 14, 16, and 20, Cody, 82414; (307) 587-5155.**

"The Scout."

155

Outdoor Activities

Fishing

Mountain streams abound in the Cody area, exposing anglers to excellent trout fishing in the **North Fork of the Shoshone River,** which runs along the Absaroka (pronounced Ab-SOR-ka) Range. Get details and maps from the **Cody District office of Wyoming Game & Fish, 2820 State Hwy. 120, Cody, 82414; (307) 527-7125. Beck Lake Park and Recreation Area,** owned by the town, is open year-round. In addition to fishing areas, you can enjoy hiking and biking trails and nonmotorized boating on the lake. Wheelchair-

Big Horn Basin Region

Old Trail Town.

accessible fishing pier. No overnight camping. Call the **Cody Parks Department, P.O. Box 2200, Cody, 82414; (307) 527-7511.**

Buffalo Bill Reservoir

Created out of the canyon on the Shoshone River, the reservoir sits between Cedar and Rattlesnake Mountains and offers some fantastic fishing, boating, and windsurfing nestled in indescribable scenery. Six miles west of town, it's right on the way to Yellowstone. Call the **Buffalo Bill State Park** headquarters at **(307) 587-9227, fax (307) 587-4990; (307) 527-6274** for campground information.

River Floating

Whitewater sends a chill down most people's spines—either of fear or excitement. **Shoshone Canyon** and the **North Fork of the Shoshone River** offer everything from a relatively mild version, for those who just want to give running the rapids a first-time try, to a rough ride for the experienced thrill seeker.

Since 1978, **Wyoming River Trips** have specialized in family river trips and those for the "I've never been on whitewater before" crowd. Groups leave periodically throughout the day, starting at 9 A.M. For a whitewater introduction, try a two-hour, six-mile float in Shoshone Canyon, and learn the geology and fur trade era history of men like John Colter

and Jeremiah Johnston while paddling the rapids in this 200-foot red rock canyon. This is a great one for young kids. Or tackle both the upper and lower sections of the canyon on a 13-mile, three-hour excursion. Takeout point is Corbett Stage Stop used by overland stagecoaches during the 1880s and 1890s. You can also make a day of it on the five-hour, 15-mile North Fork gourmet voyage, which includes a great lunch while you soak up the unique beauty of the Shoshone National Forest (part of the Yellowstone Timberland Reserve, which split into the Shoshone and Teton National Forests, the nation's first, established in 1907). This one loads you up on action and fun! Trips run from May 1 to October, depending on weather and water conditions. **233 Yellowstone Avenue., P.O. Box 1541-C, Cody, 82414; (800) 586-6661** or **(307) 587-6661.**

Golf

Play 18 rounds on the **Olive-Glenn Golf and Country Club** PGA Championship course, par 72. Open to the public daily. Green fees. Resident golf professionals provide a full-service pro shop. Practice facilities, lessons, driving range, and putting green, in addition to two tennis courts, indoor swimming pool, jacuzzi, and restaurant. **802 Meadow Lane, Cody, 82414; (307) 587-5551.**

Seeing and Doing

Old Trail Town

Old Trail Town is located on the original townsite. Parts of the onetime road are still discernible in front of the buildings that have been reconstructed on the property, complete with squeaky floorboards, relics of a pioneering way of life that lasted in the Big Horn Basin until well into the twentieth century, and the thrill of walking through history—literally. Bob Edgar and Terry Edgar, Old Trail Town's owners, moved into an old log cabin on the site back in 1967 and fell in love with historic structures. At the time, such buildings were disappearing faster than the archaeological projects Bob worked on for the Buffalo Bill Historical Center. The Edgars' collection currently numbers 26 buildings, ranging in age from 1879 to 1901 with the 1883 Outlaw's Cabin from the Hole-in-the-Wall the most notorious. Among the grave sites in the cemetery lies "Liver Eating" Jeremiah Johnston (1824–1900). Two thousand people attended his reburial at Old Trail Town, including Robert Redford, who portrayed the mountain man in the movie *Jeremiah Johnson*. Another notable site came from the Crow Agency in Montana—the cabin belonging to General George A. Custer's youngest Crow scout, Curley. He survived the Battle of the Little Big Horn and brought word of the defeat. Open daily May through September, this stop shouldn't be missed! The sense of history you'll find here will fill all your senses. **1831 DeMaris Drive, P.O. Box 696, Cody, 82414; (307) 587-5302**.

The Scout

In 1922, the Buffalo Bill Memorial Association commissioned Gertrude Vanderbilt Whitney to sculpt a life-size bronze statue of the showman. Whitney first made a small painted plaster model (currently on loan to the Buffalo Bill Historical Center). The committee that reviewed it for authenticity found fault with a few of its details, such as the shape of Cody's hat. Whitney made the suggested changes, and "The Scout" was dedicated on July 4, 1924—the first milestone that laid the foundation for the start of the Buffalo Bill Historical Center. Located between the Center and West Park Hospital. **720 Sheridan Avenue.**

Colter's Hell

John Colter, a fur trapper and explorer fresh off the Lewis and Clark Expedition, traipsed through present-day Cody back in 1807, carrying 30 pounds of supplies. His estimated 500- to 600-mile trek took him through the heart of what would become Yellowstone National Park and this site on the edge of Cody listed on the National Register of Historic Places. From the

Getting There

Travel to Cody, situated 52 miles from the east entrance to Yellowstone National Park, via **Hwy. 20.** Or if driving from the east, take **Hwy. Alt. 14** through the Big Horn Mountains. Commuter flights into the Yellowstone Regional Airport arrive from Denver, Colorado, and Salt Lake City, Utah, on such carriers as **SkyWest/Delta (800-221-1212 or 307-587-9740)** and **United Express (800-241-6522). Spirit Mountain Aviation** also offers charter and scenic flights from Cody, **3227 Duggleby Drive; (307) 587-6732** or **(307) 587-6932.** A variety of **rental cars** are available at the airport. Bus service to Cody comes from **Powder River Transportation (800-442-3682).**

overlook area you can view the almost extinct geyser region that once spewed odious gases, cauldrons of boiling water, and mud, and thundered as if possessed by angry spirits that people called Colter's "tall tales."

157

Buffalo Bill Dam Visitor Center

In what would prove an overambitious undertaking, the Shoshone Land and Irrigation Company, owned by Cody and his partners, planned to place over 100,000 acres of fertile but arid land under irrigation. But, the canal they had constructed only brought water to approximately 10,000 acres. Eventually Cody turned to friends in the federal government and gained their interest in the work. Reclamation Service engineers investigated, and the "Shoshone Project" was authorized by the secretary of the interior on February 10, 1904. During that year plans were made, and on October 19, 1905, a contract in the amount of $515,750 to build the dam was awarded. Completed in 1910, the dam actually cost $929,658 (a lot of money in those days). The original 325-foot dam was, at the time, the tallest in the world and the first federally developed endeavor under the Reclamation Service, later known as the Bureau of Reclamation. In 1993, the height was raised to 350 feet, adding approximately 250,000 acre feet of water storage capacity to help meet the needs for irrigation and drinking water for much of the Big Horn Basin. Open to the public from May until the end of September, the visitor and interpretive center details the history of the dam site and Bill Cody's contributions. **Hwys. 14, 16, and 20. Mailing address: 1002 Sheridan Avenue, Cody, 82414; (307) 527-6076.**

Museums

Buffalo Bill Historical Center

The center features four world-renowned museums under one roof. As part of the BBHC's commitment to Native American history, the Plains Indian Advisory Committee, representing eight western tribes, helped plan the Plains Indian Museum, one of the center's four permanent museums. Many of its exhibits came from Buffalo Bill's private collection and gifts from Indians who participated in his Wild West Show. The Plains Indian Museum first opened in conjunction with the Buffalo Bill Museum in a log structure during 1927, and its displays depict the everyday life, cultural histories, and artistry of western tribes. Sharps, Colts, Winchesters, and Remingtons take their place in the Cody Firearms Museum in what many consider one of the most impressive collections of rifles and pistols to be found anywhere. The museum, dedicated during 1991, chronicles the development of weaponry from the sixteenth century to the present. Original sculptures, prints, and paintings, such as the landscapes of Albert Bierstadt and Thomas Moran, documentary works by Alfred Jacob Miller and George Catlin, and legendary classics of Charles M. Russell and Frederick Remington, as well as contemporary illustrations by Harry Jackson, portray life in the American West during the nineteenth and twentieth centuries in the Whitney Gallery of Western Art, added in 1959, and the Kriendler Gallery of Contemporary Art, completed in 1995. Finally, the exploits of the scout, hunter, showman, and promoter of all things western

leap out of history through the private and public memorabilia of the man himself in the Buffalo Bill Museum. Open year-round; hours and days vary with the seasons. **720 Sheridan Avenue, P.O. Box 1000, Cody, 82414; (307) 587-4771, ext. 4064; fax (307) 578-4076. Website: www.TrueWest.com/BBHC.**

Scenic Drives

Wapiti Valley

Wapiti (pronounced WHA-pa-tee) means "white rump," an Indian term for the North American elk, and your chances of spotting this magnificent member of the deer family rank pretty high driving through this valley on **Hwys. 14, 16,** and **20** from Cody to the East Entrance of Yellowstone National Park. Depending on the season and time of day, you might also catch a glimpse of bighorn sheep, mule deer, and grizzly bears, and get caught in a traffic jam with a herd of buffalo. Besides the wildlife, you will "ooh" and "aah" over strange rock formations, such as the Chinese Wall, the Holy City, and Sleeping Giant. No wonder President Teddy Roosevelt pronounced this road "the most scenic fifty-two miles in the U.S." Approximately halfway to the park entrance, you'll see the Wapiti Ranger Station, the oldest in the nation, built during 1903. Open year-round. Call the **Forest Service Wapiti District (307-527-6921).**

Chief Joseph Highway

Take Hwy. 120 north out of Cody and turn left onto **Hwy. 296** after 16 miles. The state finished paving this road in 1996. This drive traces the route taken by the Nez Perce Nation, led by Chiefs Joseph, Looking Glass, and Lean Elk, in a desperate bid for freedom, back in 1877 when the U.S. Army hunted them down for refusing to be forced onto a reservation. Chief Joseph planned to take his people to safety in Canada. Forty miles short of the border, however, the army captured them. After traversing Dead Indian Pass, the road winds down into the flats, crossing the historic Two Dot Ranch, and streams past the craggy steeps of Sunlight Basin. A short side trip on the gravel road up Sunlight Creek takes you into some of the finest winter elk range in the West. The Sunlight Ranger Station carries the latest trail information, as well as reports on bear activity. Back on Hwy. 296, you'll cross the Sunlight Creek Bridge, the highest in the state. The Cathedral Cliffs and the 1,200-foot gorge on the Clarks Fork of the Yellowstone River, as well as the area's history, makes this one of the most touchingly beautiful scenic byways in Wyoming. This route terminates at Hwy. 212. Going right will take you over Beartooth Pass (see below) and left leads to Cooke City, Montana, another entrance to Yellowstone National Park. Closed in winter.

South Fork

One and a half miles west of the Buffalo Bill Historical Center, **Hwy. 291** splits off to the left of Hwys. 14, 16, and 20 (known locally as Yellowstone Avenue or Yellowstone Highway). The pavement ends close to the Buffalo Bill Reservoir. This drive winds through the valley of the South Fork of the Shoshone River past working ranches, including Buffalo Bill's beloved TE Ranch, where many dignitaries stayed, and guest ranches that are located in the shadow of the Absaroka Range's Washakie Wilderness. Erosion of this volcanic range created unusual formations like Castle Rock. You'll also pass the Valley Ranch School, established in 1922 to provide a top-notch education to the sons of the families who ran the area's ranches. The dirt road dead-ends approximately 30 miles from town at some privately held horse corrals. This is a favorite trailhead for horsepackers into the Shoshone National Forest.

Beartooth Pass

Traveler and commentator Charles Kuralt called this the Beartooth Highway and ranked it "the number one scenic highway in the United States." Follow the Chief Joseph Hwy. 296 north to the junction with **Hwy. 212.** Turn right. Expect to see snow even in the height of summer and some of the most spectacular vistas in the Rocky Mountains at elevations up to 10,947 feet. Although this is not a route to haul a trailer over, Beartooth Lake, a few

miles along the road, does offer parking space for trailers. Thrill to a view of the distinctive Pilot and Index Peaks, the rock fortress called Beartooth Butte, Rock Creek Canyon, and the Bear's Tooth, from which the range and pass get their names. This route delivers you to Red Lodge, Montana. Closed in winter.

Where to Stay

Accommodations

The Irma—$$$–$$$$

Named after one of Buffalo Bill's daughters, the Irma opened in 1902 with a grand party and a guest list that read like a who's who of the turn of the century. Boston newspaperman Charles Wayland Towne, who would eventually run the hotel and later the *Cody Enterprise*, described how "resolute waddies [dudes] in chaps and spurs paired off with buxom waitresses wearing long, dark skirts and high-collared shirtwaists, the popular Gibson Girl getup of the day." Over 500 people attended the grand opening. Today you can stay in one of the Irma's historic rooms (carefully modernized to include a bathroom without destroying the original character) or in the contemporary hotel rooms next to the native sandstone portion of the Irma that is listed on the National Register of Historic Places. Open year-round. **1192 Sheridan Avenue, Cody, 82414; (800) 745-IRMA or (307) 587-4221.**

159

The historic Irma Hotel.

Shoshone Lodge—$$$–$$$$

Stay in cabins located just four miles from Yellowstone's east entrance. The lodge, which invites nightly or weekly stays, offers a variety of horsepacking adventures into the park—from an hour's ride to all day to extended wilderness trips. Or take a horseback ride and dine out amid the scenic Absaroka Mountains. **349 Yellowstone Hwy., P.O. Box 790, Cody, 82414; (307) 587-4044, fax (307) 587-2681. Website: www.westwyoming.com/shoshone.**

Wind Chimes Cottage B&B—$$$–$$$$

Built in 1923, the house originally belonged to a banker named Stott. Three upstairs bedrooms—the Victorian Lace room; Granny's Attic, with a claw tub; and the Garden room, with wicker furniture and antiques. Handmade quilts grace beds in each of the rooms. In the backyard, try the Jungle Bungalow, decorated with palm trees, bamboo, and even a thatched roof. Plenty of room for the whole family. Not handicapped accessible. The works for breakfast, including homemade biscuits, waffles, and Boy Scout hashbrowns (a specialty of the house). Patio in backyard. No pets. **1501 Beck Avenue, Cody, 82414; (800) 241-5310 or (307) 527-5310.**

The Lockhart B&B Inn and Motel—$$$

Once the home of journalist and novelist Caroline Lockhart, Boston's first woman newspaper reporter. She interviewed Buffalo Bill, and perhaps that influenced her move to Cody. In 1919, she became the owner and editor of the *Cody Enterprise*, still going to press today. Later she sold the paper and turned to ranching. Many of her novels were thinly veiled accounts of the region's residents. The inn, which overlooks the Shoshone River, reflects the early 1900s with the exception that the rooms have private baths. A complete breakfast is served in the dining room just off the parlor. The inn will make reservations for you for things to do or for dining out while you're in the area. Airport transportation. No pets. **109 West Yellowstone Avenue, Cody, 82414; (307) 587-6074, fax (307) 587-8644. E-mail: cbaldwin@wyoming.com.**

Parson's Pillow B&B—$$$

So named because this was once a church, built in 1902. Lee and Elly Larabee fell in love with this historical building and saw a way to restore and preserve it by converting it into the B&B, which they opened in 1991. Original pictures of the church hang on the stairway. The four bedrooms with private baths are all upstairs and are not handicapped accessible. Laundry facilities available. A complete, sit-down breakfast at 7:30 A.M. Turn-of-the-century decor. Lots of antique furnishings are not childproof. Only two people per room allowed. No pets. **1202 14th Street, Cody, 82414; (800) 377-2348 or (307) 587-2382. E-mail: ppbb@trib.com. Website: www.cruising-america.com/parsonspillow.**

Yellowstone Valley Inn—$$–$$$

Cozy rooms clustered in several log buildings in the indescribably beautiful setting of the Wapiti Valley, 20 miles from Cody. Staying here will give you a wonderful taste of Yellowstone's natural backdrop and makes a great alternative to lodging in the park. Some kitchenettes available. On-site dining room serves a great prime rib. Outdoor pool. Handicapped accessible. Pets allowed. **3324 Yellowstone Hwy., Cody, 82414; (307) 587-3961, fax (307) 587-4656.**

Guest Ranches

Castle Rock Ranch—$$$$

In addition to the traditional dude ranch experience, you can try your hand at a llama trek, whitewater rafting, fishing, mountain biking, windsurfing, or climbing. Children's activities will keep them interested. Weekly packages. **412 Road 6NS, Cody, 82414; (307) 587-2076, fax (307) 527-7196.**

Double Diamond X—$$$$

Great family-oriented vacations that give you a real taste of western life. Trail rides, overnight horsepacking trips, jaunts into Yellowstone, fishing, hayrides, and honest-to-goodness cowboy entertainment. Swimming pool. Three mouthwatering, square meals that won't leave you hungry. Weekly stays. **3453 Southfork**

Road, Cody, 82414; (800) 833-RANCH
(7262) or (307) 527-6276. E-mail:
beverly@wave.park.wy.us.

Pashaska Tepee Resort—$$$–$$$$

Pashaska was Buffalo Bill's Crow Indian name
meaning "long hair." Finished in 1901, the
lodge offered the consummate location from
which to repay all the invitations Buffalo Bill's
friends and admirers the world over had show-
ered on him. In conjunction, Pashaska acted
as a launch point for the showman's hunting
trips. Located 30 miles from the nearest
Yellowstone National Park accommodations (a
day's dusty ride in Cody's early days),
Pashaska Tepee also fulfilled Buffalo Bill's secondary goal of catering to tourism. During the
summer, the lodge housed and fed wayfarers
headed into the park, just as it does today.
Located two miles from Yellowstone's east entrance, the lodge accommodates overnight
stays or weekly arrangements year-round.
Dine amid a panoramic view of the Absarokas.
Sign up for trail rides, rent cross-country skis
and glide along 12.5 miles of groomed trails,
or rent a snowmobile and head into the park.
Closed October 31 through December 15 and
March 15 into May, depending on snow conditions. 183-B1 Yellowstone Hwy., Cody,
82414; (800) 628-7791 or (307) 527-
7701.

Camping

In the National Forest

Campgrounds abound in the forest lands
around Cody. Many include access to stream
fishing, horse corrals, and picnic areas.
Wapiti Ranger District, 203 A Yellowstone
Avenue, P.O. Box 1840, Cody, 82414; (307)
527-6921, or the Shoshone National Forest, 808 Meadow Lane, Cody, 82414; (307)
527-6241.

In the State Park

Buffalo Bill State Park, located on what is
locally known as the Yellowstone Hwy., supplies two campgrounds on the north side of the
reservoir and a lodge (by reservation only),
along with numerous picnic areas, play-

*Cowboy entertainers. Photo courtesy of the Wyoming
Division of Tourism.*

grounds, and even a ball field for basketball
and volleyball. Facilities open May 1 and close
September 30, with some limited winter access. Hwys. 14, 16, and 20, Cody, 82414;
(307) 587-9227, fax (307) 587-4990; (307)
527-6274 for campground information.

Private Campgrounds and Cabins

Cody KOA Kampground is located 2.5 miles
east of town on Hwys. 14, 16, and 20. Cabins,
a heated swimming pool, showers, laundry,
store, playground for the kids, picnic area, and
trailer hookups. Open from May 1 to October
1. 5561 Greybull Hwy., Cody, 82414; (307)
587-2369.

Where to Eat

Proud Cut Saloon—$$–$$$$

"Kickass Cowboy Cuisine" with the best steaks
and burgers in town—all Wyoming beef! The
tenderloin takes top honors. Or taste the
Rocky Mountain oysters with cocktail sauce.
Western setting, complete with swinging doors
and stuffed animals. Open year-round for
lunch and dinner from 11 A.M. to 10 P.M. 1227
Sheridan Avenue, Cody, 82414; (307) 527-
6905.

Cassie's Supper Club—$–$$$$

For a unique dining experience, try this local
hangout. The 1922 building began as Cassie

161

Waters's brothel. Under new ownership these days, the place has once again taken on the original decor with lace curtains, red wall hangings, and 80-year-old wall mounts (game animals) bagged in the area. Thirty-eight reproductions by artist Austin Cook of Old West paintings surround the dance floor. There's even nightly entertainment (although not of the original variety) during the summer, provided by the West Band. Or catch one of the blues nights or old-time fiddlers' evenings, or listen to Mark Twain impersonator Danny Smith. Big band music every other Sunday night. The food's good, too. Though visitors from Maine rave about the seafood, the specialty of the house remains hand-cut steaks and prime rib. Open year-round for lunch and dinner from 11 A.M. to 10 P.M. Reservations strongly recommended for dinner. **214 Yellowstone Avenue, Cody, 82414; (307) 527-5500.**

Maxwell's—$$–$$$
The spot for lunch. Lite-side specials and daily lunch specials for the health conscious. Good ribs, trout, and Italian pastas. Open Monday through Saturday for lunch and dinner. Open daily during the summer. Hours are 11 A.M. to

9 P.M. **937 Sheridan Avenue, Cody, 82414; (307) 527-7749.**

The Irma Restaurant—$–$$$
Located downtown in the historic Irma, currently considered one of the West's "grand old hotels," the restaurant's showpiece is its ornate cherry wood bar, a gift to Buffalo Bill from Great Britain's Queen Victoria. Of course, they serve buffalo and a delicious prime rib. A great salad bar. Open year-round for all three meals from 6:30 A.M. to 10 P.M. **1192 Sheridan Avenue, Cody, 82414; (800) 745-IRMA (4762) or (307) 587-4221.**

Services

Visitor Information

Park County Travel Council, P.O. Box 2454, Cody, 82414; (307) 587-2297, fax (307) 527-6228.
Cody Country Visitor Information Center, 836 Sheridan Avenue, Cody, 82414; (307) 587-2297. E-mail: cody@codychamber.org. Website: www.codychamber.org.

Greybull

Both the town and the river received their names from a legendary albino bison that roamed the area near the Greybull River. To the native Indian nations in the region, an albino bison is a sacred animal.

History

Crow Indians hunted the herds of buffalo, elk, deer, and antelope that inhabited the Big Horn Basin and the bighorn sheep that lived on the rocky ledges above the Greybull River long before white men arrived. John Colter (see Cody, above) supposedly was the first to trek through the Crow territory during 1807. Other fur trappers and traders soon followed. By the end of the 1870s, the cattlemen moved huge herds into the area, taking advantage of the good grazing and water. Getting the cattle to market posed a difficult problem until the railroad came through in 1905. With it, the town sprang up.

Because Greybull was primarily an agricultural center, the excitement arrived with the discovery and excavation of more than 20 complete dinosaur skeletons by the Sinclair-American Museum Dinosaur Expedition in 1934. The basin also showed signs of containing all the necessary ingredients for an oil field. In fact, the Sinclair Oil Company coined their famous "Dino-Gasoline" trademark from the association of fossils and fuel found in the basin.

One of the most unusual and little-known aspects of Greybull's history remains the town's semipro baseball team, owned by Midwest Oil, when organized baseball was still in its infancy. Midwest Oil scouted the country and brought in young athletes to Greybull to play ball, giving them pseudo jobs within the refinery. Many families relocated to town because of a son's athletic abilities. Jim Bluejacket, from Oklahoma, was one of the

Devil's Kitchen. Photo courtesy of the Wyoming Division of Tourism.

163

team's finest players. Unfortunately, he was injured, and Midwest Oil traded him to Standard Oil. However, once Bluejacket retired from baseball, he returned to Greybull, as did others. Maybe this explains how such a small community could produce some excellent athletes and professional ballplayers over the years.

Around 100 million years ago (give or take several million), seawater covered the basin. The prevailing winds blew volcanic ash over what would become this portion of Wyoming, eventually creating bentonite clay, the main mining interest in Greybull today. Wyoming currently supplies about 65 percent of the country's bentonite. The petroleum industry uses this slick clay as a "drilling mud." It's also used in the processing of iron ore.

Festivals and Events

Days of '49
mid-June
Held the second weekend in June. Enjoy a rodeo, a demolition derby, a parade, and a dance. Contact **Ronna Collingwood, Spur Road, Greybull, 82426; (307) 765-4609.**

Outdoor Activities

Hiking and Backpacking

You can experience a variety of terrain as you hike in the **Bighorn National Forest.** Trails lead to lakes. Or you can wander along streams, head through grassy parklands, and climb rocky crests. Travel in summer or fall for the best weather conditions in the **Paintrock Ranger District** approximately 38 miles east of Greybull. Access trailheads along **Hwy. 14.** Take **Adelaide Trail** for a great day hike to Adelaide Lake, just over 6 miles one-way. You'll traverse through sagebrush flats and scenic vistas from a beginning elevation of 7,680 feet up to 9,240 feet. The trailhead starts at the Shell Creek Ranger Station on **Forest Road 17.** Open year-round. Contact the forest service for maps and additional information. **Bighorn National Forest, 1969 South Sheridan Avenue, Sheridan, 82801; (307) 672-0751. Website: www.fs.fed.us/-r2/bighorn.**

Skiing

Downhill Skiing
Antelope Butte Ski Area in the Bighorn National Forest means uncrowded slopes and no waiting in lift lines. Groomed slopes, skiing through trees, and snowboarding. Two chairlifts and one surface lift give skiers access to all types of runs—from the beginner "Mickey Mouse" to the two double black diamonds, "Buffalo Jump" and "The Falls." One thousand vertical feet up to an elevation of 9,400 feet from an 8,400-foot base. "Whitetail," the longest, runs for 1.5 miles. Lessons available at the PSIA Ski School, including snowboard lessons. Warm up in the lodge with hot drinks, food, or your favorite brew. Ski and snowboard rentals. Open December through April, Wednesday through Sunday, and holidays. From Greybull, take Hwy. 14 east for 37 miles. **P.O. Box 460, Dayton, 82836; (307) 655-9530, fax (307) 655-9529.**

Cross-Country Skiing
Antelope Butte Ski Area also maintains approximately three miles of groomed cross-country trails that are closed to snowmobiles. The trailhead starts at the parking lot. The lower loop gives beginners a great taste of the Bighorn National Forest, while the upper loop serves intermediate skinny skiers. Map available in the ski lodge. Or contact the **Bighorn National Forest Office, 1969 South Sheridan Avenue, Sheridan, 82801; (307) 672-4096, cellular (307) 652-2363.**

Snowmobiling

Explore 163 miles of marked snowmobile trails at the **Antelope Butte Ski Area.** Snow depths range from 1 to 10 feet at elevations of 7,500 to 10,000 feet. The season lasts from November through early April. Contact the **Bighorn National Forest, 1969 South Sheridan Avenue, Sheridan, 82801; (307) 672-0751.**

Seeing and Doing

Devil's Kitchen
Located five miles northeast of town. Take Hwy. 14 to Road 27. Turn right and stay on it until it dead-ends at Lane 33. Turn right again. It's on the right about two miles down Lane 33. While there are no designated trails through this colorful badlands, it's worth driving out to see. As the turnoff is easy to miss, get a map from the Greybull Chamber of Commerce.

Red Gulch Dinosaur Tracksite
The **Red Gulch Dinosaur Tracksite** is a 40-acre area located out from Shell on the BLM's

Back Country Byway. Approximately 160 million years ago, during the Middle Jurassic Period, dinosaurs roamed parts of the West. Until recently, scientists believed the Big Horn Basin was under the Sundance Sea. This changed with the discovery of hundreds of dinosaur tracks at the Red Gulch site. The tracks are perfectly preserved and became exposed by erosion. At present, scientists are still trying to determine what kinds of animals made the tracks. The BLM asks that visitors refrain from digging, touching, rubbing, or standing on the tracks so they will be preserved for the future. For details and directions, contact the **BLM office in Worland (307) 347-5100.**

Museums

Greybull Museum

Dinosaur and fossil enthusiasts will love this little museum! See one of the largest ammonites ever discovered in North America. It spans five feet in diameter and weighs 960 pounds. When it was alive, it measured seven or eight feet long. In addition, get up close and personal with huge dinosaur bones dating from the Triassic period of roughly 245 million years ago—all found locally. Also view an impressive collection of fossils, such as the cycad trunk, the first known fossil of flower-bearing trees. In the Big Horn Basin, there was a whole forest of them 120 million years ago. More modern memorabilia includes a concertina accordion, army field rations, a salt and pepper shaker collection, and dolls. Open Monday through Saturday from June 1 through Labor Day; Monday through Friday during April, May, September, and October; Monday, Wednesday, and Friday the rest of the year. Call for hours, as they vary depending on volunteers. No charge. **325 Greybull Avenue, Greybull, 82426; (307) 765-2444.**

Museum of Flight and Aerial Firefighting

This museum seeks to preserve an under-recognized area of aviation history—aerial firefighting. Since the 1920s, a variety of aircraft have been utilized to combat forest fires.

Sixteen years after the first flight at Kitty Hawk in 1903, fliers used planes to spot fires and to get word to firefighters on the ground via written notes attached to parachutes. Sometimes the note flew to the ground with carrier pigeons, before radio entered the picture. During the early 1950s, experiments with air tankers began. At first this meant beer kegs filled with water, then sluicing boxes and garden hoses. Today, fire-retardant liquids are dumped from planes and helicopters. See an air tanker, a flying boxcar, a smokejumper, and much more on a self-guided walking tour of the planes. Located at the South Big Horn County Airport. **2441 Hwy. 20, P.O. Box 412, Greybull, 82426; (307) 765-4482.**

Scenic Drives

Big Horn Scenic Byway

Head east from Greybull on Hwy. 14. Pass the Old Stone Schoolhouse and the spectacular red rock bluffs. The road begins to wind into Shell Canyon, and you'll see Fallen City, Steamboat Point, Tongue River Canyon, Granite Pass, Shell Falls, and Copeman's Tomb. The Big Horn Basin typifies Wyoming's landscape. The broad, relatively flat bowl remains dry and windswept. While the surrounding mountains reach as high as 13,000 feet in elevation, their heavily forested slopes remain permanently capped with snow. Hwy. 14 splits at Burgess Junction. Staying on Hwy. 14 takes you into Dayton and Ranchester, where it connects with I-90 into Sheridan (see the Sheridan chapter in the Powder River Region section).

Alternative Hwy. 14 goes to Medicine Wheel (see the Medicine Wheel chapter in the Powder River Region section) and on to Lovell.

Where to Stay

Accommodations

Greybull Motel—$$–$$$

Twelve rooms in western decor, some with refrigerator and microwave. In summer the flowers bloom, creating a lovely sight. Enjoy the covered picnic area. In winter there are electrical hookups for RVs and cars. No kitchenettes. Pets allowed but not horses (no joke). Not handicapped accessible. Open year-round. **300 North 6th Street, Greybull, 82426; (307) 765-2628, fax 765-2933.**

Snowshoe Lodge B&B—$$–$$$

This is more than just a typical B&B. Rates include supper with wine, as well as breakfast. Or you can rent a cabin, sheep wagon, or campsite with no meals. The cabins and sheep wagon come equipped with cookstoves, cooking utensils, and dishes. You provide bed linens and food. They'll board your horses, too, for an additional fee. Snowmobile rentals available in winter. Horseback ride in summer. Located on a gravel road. Nonsmoking establishment. Not handicapped accessible. Open year-round. **Forest Road 17, P.O. Box 215, Shell, 82441; (307) 765-2669 or (307) 765-4661. E-mail: snowshoe@tctwest.net.**

K-Bar—$–$$

Standard motel rooms in western style. Coffee available in the rooms. Cable TV with HBO. Direct dial phones. Pets allowed for an extra fee. Not handicapped accessible. Open year-round. **300 Greybull Avenue, Greybull, 82426; (307) 765-4426, fax (307) 765-9344.**

Guest Ranches

The Hideout—$$$

Six days filled with adventure await you on this working cattle ranch, established in 1906. You'll get a real taste of western life: checking fences, doctoring livestock, herding cows, and participating in a roundup (depending on the time of year). Have fun on a moonlit hayride or mosey along on a trail ride. Encounter cowboy cooking at its best. Open year-round. Three-night minimum stay. **3208 Beaver Creek Road, Greybull, 82426; (800) FLITNER (354-8637) or (307) 765-2080, fax (307) 765-2681. E-mail: hideout@tctwest.net. Website: www.thehideout.com.**

Camping

Private Campgrounds and Cabins

Stay in a camper cabin (log cabins with a place to throw your sleeping bag and a camper stove that doesn't leak and won't blow away). Or pick a tent or trailer site. Cable TV, phone, 32 full hookups, shower, laundry, groceries, picnic tables, grills, water, and propane. Grass on each site. Open year-round. **Greybull KOA Kampground, 333 North 2nd Street, P.O. Box 387, Greybull, 82426; (307) 765-2555.**

Where to Eat

Lisa's—$$–$$$

Open year-round Monday through Saturday, and Sunday in the summer, 11 A.M. to 9 P.M. Enjoy southwestern foods such as the "Charlotta Turkey Enchilada," wonderful pepper steak, and pastas, in a casual atmosphere. Children's menu. Handicapped accessible. **200 Greybull Avenue, Greybull, 82426; (307) 765-4765.**

Services

Visitor Information

Greybull Chamber of Commerce, 333 Greybull Avenue, Greybull, 82426; (307) 765-2100.

Thermopolis

Dating back to prehistoric time, people (and before that, possibly dinosaurs) have traveled to Thermopolis seeking the renowned health-giving properties of the hot springs the Shoshone Nation calls *Bah-gue-wana*, "Smoking Waters." When the Indians ceded the natural phenomenon, located between the Owl Creek and Big Horn Rivers, to the government and the town flourished to the point it needed a post office and a name, Dr. Julius A. Schulke, a German immigrant, suggested a combination of the Latin word *thermo* and the Greek word *polis*, meaning literally "Hot City."

Bah-gue-wana Springs.

History

Traditionally, *Bah-gue-wana* provided a place of peace where Indian nations could come and camp beside the Big Horn River and bathe in the therapeutic hot waters. In 1868, the U.S. government created the Wind River Indian Reservation for the Shoshone (and later forced the Arapaho Nation onto it as well) and *Bah-gue-wana* was included among the lands set aside. Ranchers and homesteaders immediately began moving into the area, settling on property adjoining the reservation, casting acquisitive glances east toward the northeast corner of the reservation.

That same year, Washakie, the peace chief of the Shoshones, and Sharp Nose, an Arapaho chief, headed the list of Native Americans who signed the treaty that gave the U.S. government the 10 square miles of coveted land. In return, the government supplied the two tribes with $60,000 worth of cattle and other food items.

The treaty, however, contained two stipulations set forth by Chief Washakie. A portion of the hot springs must always remain free for anyone to use. Also, a camping spot should be reserved for tribal members to stay for free. During the treaty ratification process, the government carried out Washakie's wishes by ced-

ing a 1-mile tract to the state of Wyoming for the formation of what would become Hot Springs State Park.

Festivals and Events

Gift of the Waters Pageant
early August
Between 60 and 70 Native Americans gather at *Bah-gue-wana* each August to participate in the pageant. They set up tepees and camp near Big Spring in preparation for the reenactment, written and first performed in 1925. The pageant celebrates the landmark transfer with an hour-long display of Shoshone and Arapaho cultures, including the "Song to Smoking Wa-

The Hot Springs State Park raises bison adjacent to the hot springs..

ters," inspired by a dream; the Choke Cherry Dance; prayers; the "Blessing of the Water" by the tribal shaman; and, finally, the "Giving of the Waters." **Hot Springs State Park, 220 Park Street, Thermopolis, 82443; (307) 864-2176.**

Outlaw Trail Ride
mid-August
This is *not* just another outfitted, stick-to-the-trail ride. You supply your own horse and gear and ride a hundred-mile trail in seven days, following the route used by Butch Cassidy, the Sundance Kid, and their famed Wild Bunch between Thermopolis and their Hole-in-the-Wall hideout. Sponsored by nonprofit Outlaw Trail, Inc., the ride began as part of Wyoming's centennial celebration in 1990. The fee covers the grub (which consists of such trail delights as prime rib and rib-eye steaks) cooked up by great outdoor chefs, hay and grain for the horses, trail guides, transportation for your gear, and nightly entertainment. Because this activity occurs only once a year, sign-up is on a first-come, first-served basis. Register early. **Box 1046, Thermopolis, 82443; (307) 864-2287.**

Ranch Days Rodeo
mid-August
This competition offers a glimpse into the origins of true rodeo in the West. The contestants and performers all work on area ranches.

Events such as branding, team penning, roping, and the calf scramble developed from actual ranch chores. Just for fun, ranchers also ride and milk wild cows, and kids try to stay on during the sheep riding. A dance follows the festivities. Call **(800) SUN-N-SPA (786-6778)** or **(307) 864-3192** for details.

Outdoor Activities

Fishing

Public access areas located along the **Wind River** and the **Big Horn River** afford an excellent opportunity to try your hand at some great bank fishing. Some folks brag that the Big Horn River holds 1,300 trout per mile. Part of the Wind River (one of this country's few rivers that actually flow north) runs through the Wind River Indian Reservation and fishing requires a special permit from the tribal government. One-day and reservation fishing licenses may be purchased at **Coast to Coast, 502 Arapaho, Thermopolis, 82443; (307) 864-3672.** Contact the local **Wyoming Game & Fish** office for access points and fishing regulations **(307-864-3834).**

Boysen Reservoir's 19,560 acres of water and 76 miles of shoreline present year-round fishing opportunities for sport and game species such as walleye, crappie, largemouth bass, mountain whitefish, stonecat, bluegill, black bullhead, and several varieties of trout. The ice fishing ranks among the best in the state. The reservoir's first dam was constructed by Asmus Boysen during 1908. Chunks of the original concrete remain at the Lower Wind River Campground adjacent to the canyon tunnels. The dam furnished 710 kilowatts of electricity per hour for the power plant Boysen built. By 1911, the CB&Q Railroad had laid a track that ran through the canyon, but the reservoir kept covering the track with water and had to be removed. A new and relocated dam replaced it in 1951. It currently supplies the power plant with 15,000 kilowatts. Boysen became a state park in 1956. **Boysen Route, Shoshoni, 82649; (307) 876-2796.**

Golf

Tee off for nine holes on top of the hill with an unmatched view of the valley of the Smoking Waters. You'll find everything you need at the pro shop, located next to the airport and the Legion Supper Club. **Airport Hill, Thermopolis, 82443; (307) 864-5294**.

Swimming

The state-run bathhouse at Hot Springs State Park is open year-round and visitors may soak up to 20 minutes at a time free of charge. Two privately operated pools, also open year-round, charge a modest fee for a day's worth of swimming, whirlpools, saunas, and even indoor and outdoor water slides. **Hot Springs State Park Bath House, Thermopolis, 82443; (307) 864-3765. Hot Springs Water Park, Thermopolis, 82443; (307) 864-9250.**

Seeing and Doing

Legend Rock State Petroglyph Site

Located approximately 30 miles northwest of town, these petroglyphs, which consist of 283 pictures carved in 92 panels, are considered by archaeologists to be the work of three different prehistoric cultural groups dating back approximately 5,700 years ago. The area contains public facilities and picnic tables. A word of warning: Part of the road is dirt, and cars may have problems reaching the site during rainy or snowmelt weather. Visiting the site must be arranged through the Hot Springs State Park headquarters. Park officials will supply a map to the location and an access key for the gate. **220 Park Street, Thermopolis, 82443; (307) 864-2176.**

Hot Springs

Bah-gue-wana

Originally an estimated 18 million gallons bubbled forth every day from what the cham-

Getting There

Thermopolis lies along **Hwys. 20 and 789,** 90 miles southeast of Cody. Fly into Cody on **SkyWest/Delta (800-221-1212** or **307-587-9740)** and **United Express (800-241-6522).** Or fly into Riverton on United Express, 60 miles to the south, and rent a car. The Thermopolis airport offers no commercial airline service, taxis, or buses.

ber of commerce proclaims as the "world's largest free-flowing mineral hot springs." Nowadays, the hot springs churn out 3,600,000 gallons daily and maintain a constant temperature of 135 degrees Fahrenheit.

Rain and snowmelt percolate through the rock layers of the Owl Creek Mountains and flow into underground formations to the location of the hot springs. Subterranean volcanic gases and chemicals from the rocks mix with the water, heating it. The water then boils to the surface.

Centuries of mineral deposits along the path the water takes to the Big Horn River have created a series of travertine terraces. Several species of algae, well suited to surviving in the hot water, have stained the terraces with a rainbow of colors. The terraces can be traversed at the Hot Springs State Park.

Hot Springs State Park

The state park maintains a buffalo herd with approximately 20 head on an undeveloped part of the park next to the hot springs. The herd roams free within the pasture boundaries, except during May and June when they are rounded up and confined to the corral area to allow the pastures to rest and rejuvenate. Over the winter the park supplements the free graze in the pastures. The 8:30 A.M. feeding schedule grants visitors a unique chance for up-close viewing of this "Monarch of the Plains." But heed the warning signs and remain in your vehicle. Bison are wild and very dangerous when they feel their space has been invaded. The park also provides the meat for the annual Buffalo Barbecue, held during the Gift of the Waters Pageant and an arts and craft fair.

169

Big Horn Basin Region

Walkways lead through the hot springs to the swinging bridge, a suspension footbridge built across the Big Horn River that provides a great vantage point from which to see the full effect of the Rainbow Terrace. The boat ramp gives river access to anglers and floaters and meets the needs of physically impaired persons. Sheltered and open picnic areas make pleasant spots for meals. **220 Park Street, Thermopolis, 82443; (307) 864-2176.**

Museums

Hot Springs Historical Museum

Open year-round Monday through Saturday from 9 A.M. to 5 P.M., it's well worth the small admission fee. Started in 1979, the museum houses 50-plus displays of regional history. The main attraction, of course, is the Hole-in-the-Wall bar purchased from the saloon where the infamous Wild Bunch gang hung out while here in town. For a bit of more modern history, step into the Depression House, the only one left standing in the area from the Great Depression era. Built in the early 1900s, this refurbished shack is furnished with period pieces, many that came with the house owned by a fortune-teller (rumor has it the seer's predictions often came true). Downstairs you'll find a town with a variety of old shops along the boardwalk and an old log cabin—each stocked with goods originally from the territory. Arrowheads on display came from here as well. Wander through the Middleton School, an old caboose, and a sheepherder's wagon. If you come during the summer months, don't miss the old-time melodrama performed at 7 P.M. Monday through Saturday in the Cultural Center room. There's also a movie room that runs a tape about the district. **700 Broadway, Thermopolis, 82443; (307) 864-5183.**

Wyoming Dinosaur Center

The two-story museum contains fossil remains dug out of over 50 documented fossil sites in the hills around town. Although casts of the skeletons can be purchased by other institutions, the actual bones remain in the museum.

A glass-walled lab lets visitors watch as workers prepare the bones for display. Once they clean away rock and debris, the lab technicians mend broken pieces and begin reassembling them. The fossilized bones are attached to a welded framework the lab techs have constructed. Wherever possible, the workers try to avoid drilling into the actual bone material.

Currently the center hosts 13 full-size, free-standing fossilized dinosaur skeletons, in addition to hundreds of other fossils on display.

The digs began in 1993. Visitors can take a guided shuttle tour to the excavation sites two miles above the museum to witness the extraction of fossilized remains or to participate in a dig-for-a-day adventure, weather permitting.

Crews are extracting an almost complete skeleton of what they originally thought to be a brachiosaur, an herbivore that stood about as tall as a four-story building and weighed approximately 80 tons, but which has been positively identified as an unusually large camarasaurus. They've also discovered a smaller camarasaurus. This dinosaur species lived between 180 million to 130 million years ago during the Jurassic period. Other finds include teeth from the meat-eating allosaurus, remains of a camptosaurus, and a stegosaurus, as well as fossilized footprints. Excavation will continue for many years, with the museum's displays growing accordingly.

Among the center's rare specimens, check out a fossilized dinosaur embryo and a nest of fossilized eggs. The museum also has the only complete fossil skeleton of a triceratops in Wyoming—the official state dinosaur.

The Big Horn Basin Geological Research and Education Foundation offers a lecture series at the center, covering such topics as Jurassic era flora and fauna, the preparation of bones for exhibition, and ongoing discoveries. The museum is open year-round, as are tours to the dig site (when weather permits). The museum shop carries a great selection of books and dinosaur-related materials. Open daily, 8 A.M. to 8 P.M., from May 15 through September 15; 10 A.M. to 5 P.M. the rest of the year. **P.O. Box 868, Thermopolis, 82443; (307)**

864-2997, fax (307) 864-5762. E-mail: Wdinoc@wyodino.org. Website: www.wyo-dino.org.

Nightlife

Safari Club

Nightlife and wildlife mix at the Safari Club, located in the Holiday Inn of the Waters. You can get up close and personal with over 130 big-game mounts—including an impressive native grizzly, cougar, and bighorn sheep, in addition to more exotic animals from around the world. From the upper terrace, you can watch live mule deer on their way down to the river to drink or nibbling on plants. On a cold night, enjoy the two massive fireplaces crackling with warmth from the pine logs. The Safari Club also offers the best selection of beer in town. Open noon to 2 A.M., 2 P.M. to 2 A.M. in winter. **Hot Springs State Park, Thermopolis, 82443; (307) 864-3131.**

Scenic Drives

Wind River Canyon

Wind River Canyon at the edge of town exposes a billion years of history set in stone. Road signs provide a casual geological tour through the canyon. It begins at the turnout area just north of three tunnels blasted out of Precambrian era rock that dates from 4.6 billion to 570 million years ago. White and pink quartz and feldspar slice through dark metamorphic rock farther into the canyon. At the Thermopolis side of the canyon, the spectacular, deep red shales of the Triassic Chugwater (245 million to 208 million years ago) offer an eye-catching welcome to visitors. The canyon is four miles south of Thermopolis on **Hwys. 20** and **789.**

Where to Stay

Quality Inn & Suites, The Plaza Hotel—$$$–$$$$

Not your typical Quality Inn experience. Stay in this recently renovated historic hotel in Hot

Wind River Canyon.

Springs State Park. The Plaza is on the National Historic Register and the new owners have kept the turn-of-the-century feel of the place with log furniture and wood. Thirty-five rooms, 18 of them two-room suites, nine with working (gas) fireplace. Two honeymoon suites with fireplaces in the bedroom. Fresh water outdoor pool, as well as a mineral hot spa outdoors. Free continental breakfast. Open year-round. No smoking. No pets allowed. Two rooms handicapped accessible. Retail store on-site that carries Wyoming-made products, artwork, and log furniture. **Hot Springs State Park, Thermopolis, 82443; (888) 919-9009** or **(307) 864-2939.**

Super 8 Motel—$$$–$$$$

Near the canyon. Enjoy indoor freshwater pools, a jacuzzi, and free continental breakfast. **Hwy. 20 South Lane 5, Thermopolis, 82443; (800) 800-8000** or **(307) 864-5515.**

Holiday Inn of the Waters—$$–$$$

Located in the state park, you are within walking distance of all the park has to offer. The inn also provides a freshwater pool in addition to mineral steam baths, saunas, outdoor jacuzzi, and private soaking tubs with water piped in directly from *Bah-gue-wana* (see above). Or take advantage of massage therapists on staff full-time. A racquetball court and exercise rooms will keep you in shape. The on-site

171

beauty shop offers styling for men as well as women. Special "hot water holidays" available between September 15 and May 15 with advance reservations. Call for details. **Hot Springs State Park, Thermopolis, 82443; (800) HOLIDAY (465-4329) or (307) 864-3131.**

Out West B&B—$$–$$$

Historic Queen Anne–style home built in 1908 with Ashlar stone and leaded stained-glass windows still in use today. The rooms, all on the second floor, carry western themes. Check out the in-house antique and gift shop. Partake of a full breakfast served between 7 A.M. and 9 A.M. Shared bath. No pets. No smoking. **1344 Broadway, Thermopolis, 82443; (307) 864-2700.**

Round Top Mountain Motel—$$

If you're looking for a place that offers a bit of the pioneer spirit, these modern log cabins, some with kitchenettes, have it. Three blocks north of the junction of Hwys. 20 and 120, you're within walking distance of downtown. **412 North 6th Street, Thermopolis, 82443; (800) 584-9126 or (307) 864-3126.**

Guest Ranches

High Island Ranch & Cattle Co.—$$$$

If you've ever dreamed of trailing cows through high mountain pastures, complete with a roundup and branding, then you'll want to experience life on this working cattle ranch. Located 30 miles northwest of Thermopolis on Hwy. 120, you can become part of the action for a week's stay Saturday to Saturday. Repair a fence. Learn doctoring techniques. Fish the crystal-clear Rock Creek for cutthroat trout. Or just supervise things from the front porch. Unlimited horseback riding and cattle drives and branding. Six-night minimum stay. **346 Amoretti, Thermopolis, 82443; (307) 867-2374.**

Camping

In the State Park

Boysen State Park offers daily camping and annual resident camping permits for the 12 campgrounds around the reservoir. Boat ramps, tent camping, and playgrounds are available at some locations. Drinking water, picnic shelters, and trailer sanitary stations are also at hand. Pets must be kept on a leash. You can't beat the view of the lake and the canyon. **Boysen Route, Shoshoni, 82649; (307) 876-2796.**

Private Campgrounds

Country Campin', located five miles north of town along Owl Creek, offers 42 RV hookups, 25 tent sites, tepee rentals, plus showers, a laundry, horse boarding, picnic tables with campfires, and horseshoes and other games. Blue-ribbon trout fishing in the Big Horn River, boat ramp, and nature trails. Open March 1 through November 15. **710 East Sunnyside Lane, Thermopolis, 82443; (307) 864-2416.**

Fountain of Youth RV Park supplies 64 RV sites and four tent sites with a full range of facilities, including a pool with handicapped-accessible ramp, mineral spa, jacuzzi chair, horseshoes, RV storage and supplies, and on-site fishing. A unique feature is the park's two private hot mineral pools, the third largest in the world. Be sure to visit the "liars" tree. March 1 through October 31. **250 North Hwy. 20, P.O. Box 711, Thermopolis, 82443; (307) 864-3265.**

Grandview Trailer Park is located at the south edge of town and accommodates up to 21 full-hookup sites, some with cable. It offers a laundry and showers. Open May 1 through October 15. **122 Hwy. 20 South, Thermopolis, 82443; (307) 864-3463.**

M-K RV Park, right in town, provides 13 hookups and three tent sites, picnic area with outdoor grills, and showers. April 15 through October 15. **720 Shoshoni, Thermopolis, 82443; (307) 864-2778.**

Where to Eat

Legion Supper Club—$$–$$$$

A steak-lover's paradise with a spectacular view of the golf course that overlooks the town. Their filet mignon is the best in the state (which says a lot considering the amount of really good beef available at Wyoming's restaurants). Breakfast buffet on weekends. Closed Monday in winter. Open 11 A.M. to 10 P.M. **Airport Hill, Thermopolis, 82443; (307) 864-3918.**

Pumpernick's—$–$$$

If you love breakfast, then this is the place to eat! Their trout breakfast can't be topped. An outdoor patio adds to your dining enjoyment during the summer months. A nice variety of sandwiches, soups, and dinner menus. Closed Sunday. Open 7 A.M. to 8 P.M. Tuesday through Thursday and 7 A.M. to 9 P.M. Friday and Saturday. Open until 10 P.M. during the summer. **512 Broadway, Thermopolis, 82443; (307) 864-5151.**

The Feedbag—$$

Food with flavor, not the same old thing. They make everything from scratch, and they raise the cattle and lambs on their ranch, grass fed. Big meals that give you your money's worth. Check out the six-egg breakfast with eight ounces of sausage if you're really hungry. Half orders are available as well. Breakfast is served all day, and lamb is served every day. Lunch and dinner menus, too. They'll even split a steak for two people if you want. **1025 Shoshone, Thermopolis; (307) 864-5177.**

Services

Visitor Information

Thermopolis Chamber of Commerce, 700 Broadway, P.O. Box 768, Thermopolis, 82443; (800) SUN-N-SPA (786-6778) or (307) 864-3193, fax (307) 864-3192. E-mail: thercc@trib.com. Website: www.-therm-opolis.com.

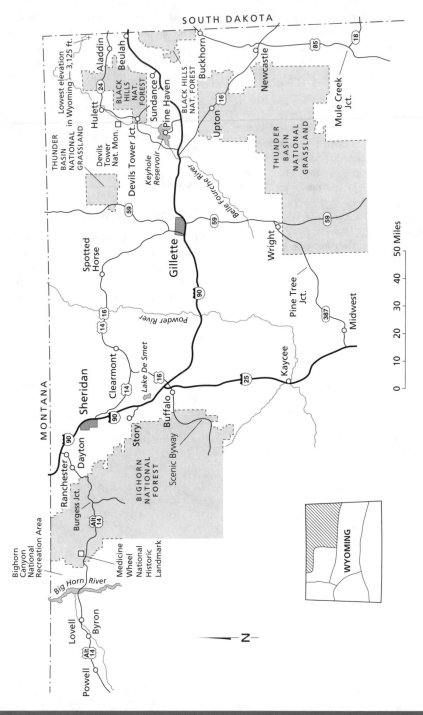

174

Powder River Region

Powder River Region

The Black Hills. Photo courtesy of the Wyoming Division of Tourism.

Buffalo

Buffalo is located in the foothills of the Big Horn Mountains far enough away from the freeway that it appears to be an isolated town more in tune with times past. It is picturesque and serene with Clear Creek flowing right through the heart of this historic town, hardly the place you'd think of as being forged in blood. Be sure to pick up a copy of the historic Main Street walking tour from the chamber of commerce office located at **55 North Main.**

History

Near the present-day site of Buffalo, an ex-army captain, H. E. Palmer, constructed a sod hut and opened a trading post of sorts in 1855. Members of the Cheyenne nation came a week later. They confiscated his goods, returned the sod from where Palmer had taken it, and suggested he relocate his place elsewhere, as the ground he had established his business on was virgin land and belonged to the buffalo. Palmer moved and traded with the Arapaho until the Sioux Wars.

The Powder River region saw many major battles in the Sioux Wars. The first resulted from the Sioux protecting their hunting grounds. John M. Bozeman blazed a trail right through those hunting grounds in 1864, while leading large numbers of miners to gold in Virginia City, Montana. Fort Reno and Fort Phil Kearny were established in 1865 in the Powder River country to safeguard travelers along the Bozeman Trail. In 1866, Captain William J. Fetterman led 80 men out from the fort to guard and escort a wood train. Before reaching the woodcutters, however, he disobeyed orders and took off after some Indians. None of his party survived the battle Fetterman started. The army retaliated, but the Sioux continued to harass wood and hay details from the fort. One such encounter resulted in the Wagon Box Fight of 1867. The Sioux surrounded 32 men behind a corral of wagon boxes. Armed with new repeating rifles, the men held off the Indians, who did not press their advantage of superior numbers.

After the Sioux Wars, sheepherders and cattlemen brought huge herds and flocks into the area while homesteaders moved in to claim land in what became Johnson County. This led to another kind of battle. Seventy-four gunmen, called "Regulators," hired by the powerful Wyoming Stock Growers Association, invaded the county in 1892. They marched toward Buffalo, intent on killing the "rustlers" on their "dead list." The first stop was the KC Ranch, where the Regulators murdered two men. Next, the gunmen hit the TA Ranch.

But word reached town, and the citizens rallied to protect themselves in what would become known as the Johnson County War. They pinned the Regulators down at the ranch. One gunman, however, escaped and sent a message to the governor, asking for reinforcements. The governor and senators of the day were known supporters of the Wyoming Stock Growers Association and passed the message on to President Benjamin Harrison, who ordered troops from Fort McKinney to take the Regulators into custody. The invaders were sent to Cheyenne for trial at the expense of the citizens of Johnson County. A judge finally dismissed the charges, and the Regulators got away scot-free.

Another kind of outlawry took place south of Buffalo in the vicinity of Kaycee. George Leroy Parker, who took the name "Butch Cassidy" from being a butcher in Rock Springs and learning the ropes of cattle rustling from Mike Cassidy, frequented the now famous Hole-in-the-Wall hideout. The region was a perfect getaway from the law. There is only one entrance, which can be defended easily, and on the other side of "the hole" entrance lie about 35 square miles of land suitable for hiding an entire herd of cattle and horses.

Festivals and Events

Bozeman Trail Days
late June
History comes alive in Story during the Bozeman Trail Days at Fort Phil Kearny. Gain an understanding of this historic trail through seminars and tours of the battlefield sites and military and Native American life along the trail—all through living history reenactments. Also see the expanding military presence that led to the Indian Wars (**307-684-7629** in winter, **307-684-7687** in summer).

Sheepherders Rodeo
mid-July
Here is a community-wide event held the first weekend after the 4th of July at the fairgrounds in Kaycee. The two-day event celebrates sheepherders and their dogs. Watch the sheep dog trials. Take part in a real crowd pleaser—the men's and ladies' sheep-hooking contest. It's open to everybody, even if you've never picked up a sheep hook before! In addition, there's sheep roping and a calcutta. Saturday starts off with a parade, then sheering demonstrations. Later there's a free street dance and barbecue. Kids can participate in events such as team sheep penning or sheep riding (**307-738-2522** or **307-738-2444**).

Outdoor Activities

Biking

Mountain Biking

In summer you can bike along the mountain snowmobile trails, as well as in Buffalo. **The Sports Lure** rents bikes and backpacking equipment. They also offer guided fishing trips and lessons. **66 South Main, Buffalo, 82834; (800) 684-7682, (307) 684-7682, fax (307) 684-7165. E-mail: splure@vcn.com. Website: www.sportslure.com.**

The Box Wagon Site.

Fishing

How does 256 fishing lakes sound? That's how many there are in the **Cloud Peak Wilderness** of the Big Horn Mountains. But because they are located in a designated nonmotorized area, you'll have to hike there in order to go fishing. **Buffalo Ranger District** has maps and current information. **1425 Fort Street, Buffalo, 82834; (307) 684-1100.**

One of the state's most popular rainbow trout fisheries is located at **Lake DeSmet** just north of Buffalo. The lake received its name from Father Pierre Jean De Smet. He traveled west with a group of fur trappers in 1840. Fish for Eagle Lake trout that weigh up to 15 pounds. Enjoy boating, swimming, waterskiing, and sailing on the lake as well.

Cast off with **Just Gone Fishing** on one of their one-day guided fishing trips in the Cloud Peak Wilderness and on the Middle Fork of the Powder River. Or just take fly tying or fishing lessons. They have licenses and supplies, too. **777 Fort Street, P.O. Box 655, Buffalo, 82834; (307) 684-2755. E-mail: just-fish@vcn.com.**

Daily fishing trips are also available through **Trails West Outfitters, P.O. Box 111, Buffalo, 82834; (307) 604-5233. E-mail: trailswest@vcn.com. Website: www.wilderwest.com/trailwest/.**

Golf

In 1996 *Golf Digest* ranked the **Buffalo Golf Course** as one of the "Places to Play." The par-71, 18-hole course challenges golfers with running water, deep ravines, and mature trees at the base of the Cloud Peak Wilderness. In addition, you'll find a pro shop, cart and club rentals, and a driving range. **West Hart Street, Buffalo, 82834; (307) 684-5266.**

Hiking and Backpacking

Nearly 200,000 acres of primitive land await you in the **Cloud Peak Wilderness.** It takes about an hour to reach the region from Buffalo. The drive alone is more than worth it, to say nothing of the hiking on over 81 miles of trails.

In town, try the 6.6-mile **Clear Creek Trail** system, a walking path that wanders through Buffalo to the base of the Big Horn Mountains. The trail passes by the Occidental Hotel; a brewery; a mill; the museum; the short-lived Wyoming Railway Company, once nicknamed the "Buffalo, Clearmont & Back, Maybe"; and the Branding Iron Bridge, marked with local cattle-company brands and a brief history of them. A 1.3-mile stretch of the trail in town is paved for handicapped access.

Horseback Riding

Looking for something off the beaten trail? Between June and September **Trails West**

Outfitters will haul in supplies for a drop camp or a guided wilderness horsepacking trip. They also have day trips and hourly trail rides available. Lunch included on the all-day rides. **P.O. Box 111, Buffalo, 82834; (307) 684-5233. E-mail: trailswest@vcn.com. Website: www.wilderwest.com/trailwest/.**

Full-day rides, ride and fishing combinations, drop camp service, and three- or five-day wilderness fishing camp trips with expert guides are available from June through September at **Bear Track Inc., 8885 U.S. Hwy. 16 West, Buffalo, 82834; (307) 684-2528. E-mail: pdube@vcn.com. Website: www.bearktrak.com.**

Skiing

Downhill Skiing

Just over 40 miles west of Buffalo is the **Powder Pass Ski Area.** Eight hundred vertical feet between a base of 8,400 feet and a 9,200-foot summit. Six runs, three for beginners, two intermediate, and one advanced. There's also a wide open bowl at the top and tree skiing for snowboarders. Ski rentals, a ski school, and cafeteria on-site. Open early December to late March on Thursday through Sunday from 9:30 A.M. to 4 P.M. **P.O. Box 457, Buffalo, 82834; (307) 366-2600.**

Cross-Country Skiing

Pole Creek, 22 miles west of Buffalo, and **Willow Park,** 45 miles west of Buffalo, offer groomed cross-country trails. Pole Creek supplies 13 miles and Willow Park 23 miles of loop trails that intersect and provide alternate routes. Pole Creek glides along, crossing over the creek on ice bridges. Willow Park runs along Willow Creek and borders Ten Sleep Creek. It has more challenges, and the snow is generally earlier and more reliable. Much of the time Pole Creek does not get enough snow for skiing until after New Year's Day. Both trails are maintained by the forest service. **Buffalo Ranger District, 1425 Fort Street, Buffalo, 82834; (307) 684-1100.**

The Sports Lure rents downhill and cross-country skis, as well as snowshoes. **66 South**

Main, Buffalo, 82834; (800) 684-7682 or (307) 684-7682, fax (307) 684-7165. E-mail: splure@vcn.com. Website: www.-sportslure.com.

Snowmobiling

Pure powder riding awaits on 130 groomed and 42 ungroomed snowmobile trails in the **Big Horn Mountains.** Gas, food, and some lodging can be found along the trails in the Buffalo Ranger District. **Meadowlark Lake Lodge** rents snowmobiles. **P.O. Box 86, Ten Sleep, 82442; (800) 858-5672 or (307) 366-2424.**

Swimming

Outdoor swimming pools are something of a rarity in Wyoming, unless they are heated from a hot spring. The huge pool in Buffalo is spring-fed from Clear Creek, but it isn't a hot spring. There are slides, a lifeguard on duty, a bathhouse, and a wading pool. The pool is also the centerpiece of the park, which also offers horseshoes, volleyball, tennis, a grassy picnic area, and hundred-year-old cottonwood trees. A block west of Main, the park and the pool are free to the public. **Washington Park, Gillette, 82834; (307) 684-5566.**

Seeing and Doing

Fort Phil Kearny

Located between Buffalo and Sheridan off I-90 (Exit 44), Fort Phil Kearny shows visitors the military's side of the protection of the Bozeman Trail and the fort's role in the Sioux Wars. Wander through the museum and watch the short film about the fort before touring the grounds. You'll get a better overview of the events and significance of the fort. Not much of the actual fort remains today. The museum and visitors center is open daily from May 15 through September 30 from 8 A.M. to 6 P.M., and Wednesday through Sunday during October, November, April, and the rest of May from noon to 4 P.M. They are closed from December

Getting There

Buffalo nestles at the edge of the Big Horn Mountains just off the **intersection of I-25 and I-90 on Hwy. 16.** Buffalo is 33 miles south of Sheridan. The **Johnson County Airport (307-684-9672)** has no commercial flights, but charter service is available. The nearest commercial service is in Sheridan. Public transportation is provided by the **Buffalo Area Transportation Service (307-684-9551).** **Powder River Transportation** offers bus service to Buffalo. Although there is no taxi service in town, everything you need is within walking distance, or you can rent a car locally from **Avis (307-684-5136).** The **chamber of commerce** maintains a list of reliable day-care centers **(800-227-5122 or 307-684-5544).**

179

through March. Tours available by appointment. **P.O. Box 520, Story, 82842; (307) 684-7687 or (307) 684-7629.**

Fetterman Fight Site

On a hill overlooking Hwy. 87, a stone monument stands as silent testament to the Fetterman Fight. While on the way to escort a wood cutting detail on December 21, 1866, Captain William J. Fetterman disobeyed direct orders to not pursue the Indians who had been harassing the wood cutters at Fort Phil Kearny. He and the 80 men under his command chased Crazy Horse and a small group of warriors over Lodge Trail Ridge where over two thousand Sioux, Cheyenne, and Arapaho warriors waited. The soldiers were killed within half an hour. The U.S. Army views it as the second worst defeat at the hands of the Plains Indians. Only the Battle of the Little Big Horn surpassed it.

Wagon Box Fight Site

A dirt road off Hwy. 193 in Story winds through some beautiful farmland and leads to the stone monument of this battle. On August 2, 1867, Indians surrounded 32 men, 4 of them civilians, five miles from Fort Phil Kearny. The group took cover by creating an oval wall from the wagon boxes they were hauling wood in. They managed to hold out until reinforcements arrived from the fort. Only 3 men were killed; indian casualty estimates range from 5 to 60.

Museums

Museum at the Occidental Hotel

This hotel was originally constructed of logs in 1880. The brick building replaced the logs in 1910. In 1998, this old historic hotel received a face-lift under new ownership. In addition, the lobby, saloon (with card and gaming room in back), tea room, and four downstairs rooms were restored and made into a museum. The museum features the Occidental saloon and shows the unique role the frontier hotel played in the West, as well as depicting events of Buffalo's history. The Occidental was one of the sites where Owen Wister wrote his novels. Learn how A. L. Smith won the hotel in a poker game in 1916 and how his wife ran it for 76 years. Antiques, many of them from the original hotel, fill the rooms, so the rooms look just like they did during the hotel's heyday. Historic photos. Open daily June through September from 10 A.M. to 4 P.M. The small fee covers both this museum and the Gatchell (see below). **10 North Main, Buffalo, 82834; (307) 684-0451, fax (307) 684-8858.**

The historic Occidental Hotel.

Jim Gatchell Museum of the West

Housed in the Carnegie building built in 1909. Dioramas tell the story of the Wagon Box Fight, the Johnson County War, and Buffalo in 1880. Lots of artifacts from nearby military forts and battles, including a military weapons collection, homestead and area ranch memorabilia, Native American beadwork and arrowheads, rare frontier photographs, and restored wagons from the 1800s. Open daily, 8 A.M. to 8 P.M., May through October. By appointment only the rest of the year, Monday through Friday between 8 A.M. and 4 P.M. If you're lucky enough to be in Buffalo around mid-July, catch Living History Days at the museum. They emphasize historical events and people of the Powder River region. Live-action displays of quilt making, saddle making, food preserving, horse shoeing, sheepherding, the Basque culture, mountain-man cooking, Lakota culture and dancing, and military weapon demonstrations. Educational tours available for all age groups; call ahead to arrange one. **100 Fort Street, P.O. Box 596, Buffalo, 82834; (307) 684-9331.**

Scenic Drives

Cloud Peak Scenic Byway

Established in 1974, the Cloud Peak Wilderness encompasses 137,000 acres. All of it is in the alpine zone above 8,500 feet—sometime shrouded in clouds. Hwy. 16 west out of Buffalo leaves the foothills covered in pines to cross Powder River Pass, elevation 9,666 feet. The forest gives way to mountain meadows, wide-open vistas, and misty mountains in the background. A new delight meets every curve in the road, which ascends through Precambrian rock approximately three billion years old. On the descent into Tensleep Canyon, the road cuts through sedimentary layers from the Paleozoic, 505 to 286 million years ago. The sheer force of the rock walls guarding this relatively narrow, winding canyon will leave you awestruck. It's the most impressive canyon road in a state full of them. The unusual name of the town of Ten Sleep comes from the fact that it took 10 nights' sleep to travel from Fort Laramie to Yellowstone.

Crazy Woman Canyon

From Buffalo take Hwy. 16 west to Crazy Woman Canyon Road, approximately 26 miles from town. Take the first road on the left. It goes down through the canyon and rejoins Hwy. 196 about 10 miles south of Buffalo. A flood washed out the dirt road in 1997. Now rebuilt, it is still rough and shouldn't be attempted with a trailer in tow, in an RV, or when the weather is bad. Boulders nudge the road in spots and the walls rise with grandeur—the natural beauty of the canyon will take your breath away.

Two local folktales tell in very differing ways how the canyon came by its name. One is that a white woman named Madeline Kindsley ran away from her wealthy Boston family to marry a poor man named Ben Brown. They tied the knot on a wagon train headed West. The couple settled in the foothills of the Rockies, built a cabin, and had a child. Indians attacked one evening, killing everybody but Madeline. Soldiers found her in 1878, wandering the canyon, completely crazy. They attempted to take her back to Fort Laramie, but she died on the trail.

In the other version, it was an Indian woman who went crazy after her whole village was slaughtered. She lived in the canyon until her death.

Where to Stay

Accommodations

Canyon Motel—$$–$$$

West of Buffalo at the base of the foothills, the motel offers standard facilities. Kitchenettes available. Coffee in the rooms. Some have small refrigerators. There's a wide circular drive and one-level parking just five feet from your car to your room door. Handicapped accessible. Pets okay. Open year-round. Large open picnic area, surrounded by trees. **997 Fort Street, Route 16 West, P.O. Box 56,** **Buffalo, 82834; (800) 231-0742 or (307) 684-2957.**

Historic Mansion House Inn—$$–$$$

Enjoy western comfort in a Victorian setting. Seven rooms with private baths, or 11 motel-style accommodations plus a hot tub. Located in the historic area on the Cloud Peak scenic byway, the inn offers a uniquely-Buffalo lodging experience, which you'll understand once you get there. Children welcome. No pets. Open year-round. Continental breakfast. **313 North Main, Buffalo, 82834; (888) 455-9202 or (307) 684-2218.**

Meadowlark Lake Resort—$$–$$$

Looking for a place to get away from it all? Located on the Cloud Peak Scenic Byway about halfway between Buffalo and Ten Sleep, this resort is located in an idyllic spot. Stay in one of the rustic cabins with no plumbing or at the resort. There are a shower and bathroom in the main house. If you are looking for more home comforts, there are motel units and kitchenette cabins. All are available for rent year-round. Fish the 300-acre lake or a dozen or so creeks in the vicinity. Great ice fishing in winter. Fishing boats, paddle boats, and snowmobiles are available for rent at the resort, as well as fishing supplies and licenses; registrations for snowmobiles, too. In summer, hike nearby trails. In winter, connect with the 26 miles of groomed cross-country ski trails at Willow Park. Restaurant and lounge on-site. Not handicapped accessible. Pets okay in some units. **P.O. Box 86, Ten Sleep, 82442; (800) 858-5672 or (307) 366-2424.**

The Pines Lodge—$$–$$$

A great location within the Bighorn National Forest 14 miles west of Buffalo on Hwy. 16. Cabins from the luxurious, with a living room and stone fireplace, to the rustic, with a shower house nearby. Pets for an extra charge. Rent by the night or the week. Fishing on the premises in Clear Creek. Horse rides also available by the hour, half day, or full day from June through September. Restaurant and lounge on-site. Three-day minimum stay between Memorial Day and Labor Day for the bigger cabins. Not handicapped accessible.

181

Open May 1 to October 30. **Box 100; Buffalo, 82834; (307) 684-5204, (307) 351-1010, or (307) 684-5204.**

Story Pines Motel—$$–$$$

Stay close to all the historical battle sites. The Story Pines offers six rooms in town within walking distance of stores and the entrance to the Penrose Trail, which leads up into the Big Horns for snowmobilers or hikers. Or relax in the hot tub, enjoy toasting marshmallows over the fire pit in the delightful picnic area on-site, or just drink in the quiet and comforts. Small pets okay. Not handicapped accessible. Coin operated laundry also located on-site. Open year-round. **46 North Piney Road, P.O. Box 545, Story, 82842; (307) 683-2120, fax, (307) 683-2351.** Call before sending a fax. **E-mail: story@cyberhighway.net. Website: www.cyberhighway.net/~fryers.**

182 Guest Ranches

Paradise Guest Ranch—$$$$

Experience the Big Horns at an altitude of 7,600 feet on this ranch that was homesteaded in the late 1890s. Ride the high meadows. Eat a chuckwagon meal. Soak up breathtaking scenery during a Sunday-to-Sunday minimum stay. Rates include three meals a day, lodging, and ranch activities. Customized fishing excursions or horsepacking trips available. Children under six not allowed to participate in the horse riding program. No pets allowed. Open late May through mid-September. Adults only after Labor Day. No by-the-hour rides or dinners available, as they are for guests only. Handicapped accessible. Extensive children's program, where they are led on pony rides and learn to make western crafts. **P.O. Box 790, Buffalo, 82834; (307) 684-7876, fax (307) 684-9054. Website: www.paradise-ranch.com.**

Willow Creek Ranch at the Hole-in-the-Wall LLC—$$$$

Experience the outlaw life where it actually took place on this 50,000-head working sheep and cattle ranch. Located 25 miles from the interstate "at the edge of the world," Willow Creek Ranch was the site of Sioux trails; an old army road; a buffalo jump; the Fort Houck post office; and a horse-changing station for the stage line—besides being where the famed Hole-in-the-Wall hideout lies. You'll ride out to the Hole and camp out where Butch Cassidy did. Explore the stage station's foundations, and that of other outbuildings and the stockade. Look for the petroglyphs in caves where soldiers also carved their names. Spot old tepee rings. Stay in the remodeled log bunkhouse built in 1890. All meals included in the rates, as well as rides and ranch activities. They encourage a six-night stay, but they will tailor a program for two or three nights. There is also a primitive pioneer cabin you can stay in that will give you the feel of a homesteader's life. It's located seven miles from the ranch and uses propane for light, heat, and the stove. It comes with an outhouse, too. Park your horse in the corral. No pets allowed. They don't encourage bringing small children to the ranch. **P.O. Box 10 Kaycee, 82639; (307) 738-2294, fax (307) 738-2264. E-mail: vieh@trib.com. Website: www.willow-creekranch.com**

Klondike Guest Ranch—$$$–$$$$

Nestled 10 miles south of Buffalo in the Big Horn foothills, ranch life comes alive here. This working cattle ranch has been in the family for four generations, since 1912. Unlike some ranches that take guests, this one caters to individual people and their schedules, not the ranch's. Set on a historical location where the Indian Wars ended and just five miles cross-country from the TA Ranch, the site of the Johnson County War. Ride, fish, watch the ranch hands at work, or join in on cattle drives, caring for cows and calves, haying, and irrigating fields. Overnight pack trips, jeep rides, barbecues, and campfire socials round out the western experience. Three-day minimum or by the week. No age limits on children riding. Can accommodate two parties at a time (up to 10 people in three guest cabins). Pets okay. Open from June 1 through early September. Handicapped accessible. Family oriented. **386 Crazy Woman Canyon Road, Buffalo, 82834; (307) 684-2390, fax (307) 684-**

0386. E-mail: rtass@wyoming.com.
Website: www.klondikeranch.com.

Gardner's Muddy Creek Angus Ranch—$$$

Secluded at the base of the mountains, the ranch offers fishing at two reservoirs, one private with blue-ribbon trout fishing. This is a great peace-and-quiet getaway. Hike, fish, mountain bike, snowmobile, cross-country ski, or participate in daily ranch activities. They can arrange horseback rides, too. Cabins with kitchen and bath facilities. One cabin sleeps six. The other is more rustic. Campsites by the creek. Tent sites. Pets okay. Open year-round. Minimum stay of two days. **482 Muddy Creek Road, Buffalo, 82834; (800) 584-5281** or **(307) 684-7797. E-mail: dgardner@wyoming.com.**

Camping

In the National Forests

Primitive camping abounds in the **Cloud Peak Wilderness.** Or you can stay at one of ten campgrounds along Hwy. 16. These forest campgrounds feature tent and trailer sites, restrooms, and drinking water. They are open from mid-May to mid-September; then expect reduced service (no water) or closure, depending on the elevation. Check with the **Buffalo Ranger District** about restrictions and current changes in campground information. **1425 Fort Street, Buffalo, 82834; (307) 684-1100, reservation center (800) 280-2267.**

Private Campgrounds and Cabins

What makes this campground so unique is 200 huge shade trees. Established in 1963, the owners of the **Indian Campground** designed the space to include the planting of all those cottonwood trees, now 60 to 80 feet tall. Rent one of their rustic cabins with full-size beds and bunk beds. They come with no plumbing, but they do have electricity. Dive into a 30- by 50-foot heated pool. Full RV hookups, hot showers, restrooms, a 24-hour laundry, and grocery store on-site. Conveniently located for people who don't want to cook: They can walk

to several restaurants. There's a park across the street with a carousel and miniature golf. A family-oriented place with easy, close access to I-25. Pets are welcome, and are treated like kids here. The main restroom facilities are handicapped accessible. Seasonal, weekly, and nightly rates. They honor a host of travel club discounts. Group rates as well. Great western hospitality! **660 East Hart, Buffalo, 82834; (307) 684-9601.**

Located four miles from downtown, **Big Horn Mountains Campground** accommodates RVs with pull-through spaces and full hookups. There are also tent sites, a heated swimming pool, restrooms, clean showers, a 24-hour laundry, rec room, dump station, and convenience store. Get the seventh night free! Open year-round. Monthly rates available. Group camping area. Family rates. Not handicapped accessible. Pets okay. **8935 Hwy. 16 West #108, Buffalo, 82834; (307) 684-2307.**

Deer Park has two separate sections, one for overnight campers and families and an adults-only location for seasonal campers staying by the month or throughout the summer. The park offers a heated pool, a whirlpool, a private one-mile walking path, showers, 24-hour laundry, and large lots. Enjoy the ice-cream socials in the summer every night from Memorial Day through Labor Day. The RV park is open the first of May until mid-October. Not handicapped accessible. Pets welcome. There's even a 20-acre field for owners to run with their pets. **146 U.S. 16 East, P.O. Box 568, Buffalo, 82834; (800) 222-9960 reservations, (307) 684-5722. E-mail: information@deerparkrv.com. Website: www.deerparkrv.com.**

Rent rustic cabins with shared bathhouses from **South Fork Inn.** Pets okay on a leash. Picnic area. Fishing pond for kids. Horseback and trail rides May through October. Full-service restaurant on-site. Excellent fishing nearby. Open year-round. Not handicapped accessible. **Hwy. 16 West, P.O. Box 96, Buffalo, 82834; (307) 267-2609.**

Lake Stop at Lake De Smet accommodates RVs with full hookups, tent campground, heated pool, grocery and tackle shop, rental cabins, shower, laundry, as well as fishing or ski-boat rentals or jet skis. Pets okay. Volleyball net and basketball hoop. Exit 51 of I-90. **9 Lake De Smet, P.O. Box 578, Buffalo, 82834; (307) 684-9051.**

Wagonbox Restaurant, Campground & Cabins has a bit of everything. Good meals, summer dining on a patio with quite a view of the area, comfy cabins, a historic lodge, streams to fish in on-site, full hookup campground, rec room, laundry, showers, and volleyball. They can arrange horseback rides and pack trips. Pets okay for extra fee. Cabins and restaurant open year-round. Spring, summer, and fall on the campground. Handicapped accessible. **P.O. Box 248, Story, 82842; (307) 683-2444, fax (307) 683-2443.**

Where to Eat

Tom's Main Street Diner—$–$$$

Real buttermilk and whole-wheat pancakes. Excellent "power muffins" loaded with wheat bran, molasses, honey, raisins, nuts, and sunflower seeds. "Killer Koffee" for those Wyoming winters. Daily breakfast specials such as buttermilk biscuits with gravy and two eggs. Try a full-pound double-decker burger with fries for lunch. Open year-round (except from Christmas until February), Monday through Saturday from 5:30 A.M. to 2 P.M., Sunday from 8 A.M. to 1 P.M. Closed Tuesday. Handicapped accessible. **41 North Main Street, Buffalo, 82834; (307) 684-7444.**

Waldorf A'Story—$–$$$

The atmosphere of this place alone should put it on your list of things to do on the way to see the Wagon Box Fight site. It's a combination general store and deli with an old-time feel and tasty sandwiches. Hearty breakfasts, and dandy ribs for dinner. The soups are homemade. The menu varies from day to day. And then there's the "Mother of All Salads" with everything but the kitchen sink! Open 7:30 A.M. to 9 P.M. during the summer months, and 7:30 A.M. to 7:30 P.M. the rest of the year. Handicapped accessible. **19 North Piney Road, P.O. Box 190, Story, 82842; (888) 683-2400 or (307) 683-2400.**

Sagewood Gifts and Cafe—$–$$

Hearty soups, specialty sandwiches, and homemade desserts. Treat yourself to a "Midnight Ranger," roast beef covered with Buffalo's famous Johnny Midnight black peppercorn sauce. Vegetarian sandwiches. Dessert lovers can't miss with the ultimate brownie. Handicapped accessible into the restaurant. Senior discount. Open 9 A.M. for coffee and cinnamon rolls, and from 11 A.M. to 3 P.M. for lunch, Monday through Saturday. **15 North Main Street, Buffalo, 82834; (307) 684-7670.**

Services

Visitor Information

Buffalo Chamber of Commerce, 55 North Main, Buffalo, (800) 227-5122 or **(307) 684-5544. E-mail: nadgross@wyoming.com. Website: www.buffalo.wyoming.com.**

Devils Tower

The volcanic butte known today as Devils Tower rises 1,267 feet above the Belle Fourche River in northeastern Wyoming. From a base diameter of approximately 800 feet, the tower reaches 600 feet into the air, with a summit elevation of 5,117 feet. The top is relatively flat and supports its own mini-ecosystem.

Over the past few years, controversy has surrounded Devils Tower, the country's first national monument. Countless generations of Native Americans have held the site sacred, conducting religious ceremonies at the base of the tower. Once the whites settled in the area, American Indian religions were actively suppressed by the U.S. government, forcing the Indians to practice their religions in secret until the American Indian Religious Freedom Act was passed in 1978. The resurgence of traditional cultures and the freedom to conduct ceremonies openly has been viewed by many non-Natives as a recent phenomenon and has led to conflicts between Indians and climbers. (See Climbing, below.)

Early maps of the region referred to the butte by an Indian name, *Mato Tipila*, or "Grizzly Bear's Lodge." Then in 1875, Colonel Richard I. Dodge, on a survey mission for the U.S. Army, erroneously called the butte Devils Tower. Supposedly this came from an Indian name of "Bad God's Tower." However, none of the Indian nations historically and geographically tied to the region had such a designation for the tower. Most referred to the butte as "Bear's Lodge," although the Lakota also called it "Mythic-owl Mountain" and "Ghost Mountain," and the Kiowa sacred narrative refers to it as "Tree Rock." Unfortunately, Dodge's name stuck. American Indians feel the name is inappropriate and disrespectful of their cultures and would like to see the monument's name changed back to its original designation.

Devils Tower.

History

Seventy million years ago an ancient sea covered the area. The tower, made up of phonolite porphyry, a hard igneous rock with large crystals of white feldspar, formed out of molten magma that hardened either at the surface or just beneath it about fifty-four million years ago. Erosion of the surrounding sediments of sandstone, shale, gypsum, and siltstone then exposed the tower.

Northern Plains Indian nations who inhabited the region long before whites moved in all have sacred origin narratives for the butte. One of the most well-known stories belongs to the Kiowas. Seven young girls from a Kiowa village were playing some distance from the village when some bears began to chase them. The girls ran toward their village, but the bears were too fast. The girls leaped onto a rock about three feet high and prayed for the rock to take pity on them and save them. The rock began to grow, pushing itself up, higher and higher out of the bears' reach. When they jumped up trying to get the girls, their claws dug into the rock, leaving scratch marks the length of the rock and breaking the bears' claws. The rock continued skyward until the girls became seven stars in the sky, generally known as the Pleiades.

The earliest mention of the tower possibly came in 1857 from Lieutenant G. K. Warren, a member of the Hayden Expedition. He reported looking at the "Bear's Lodge" through a spyglass; however, it is unclear whether he was talking about the tower or the mountains that also went by that name on early maps. Colonel Dodge's description, done while on the U.S. Geological Survey in 1876, remains the first positive written account.

White settlers came to the area within a decade of this government survey. Although the Treaty of 1868 guaranteed the Black Hills region, including the tower and the Bearlodge Mountains, to the Indians, Lieutenant Colonel George A. Custer violated the treaty in 1874 when he led an expedition into the region. His reports of gold in the mountains led to an invasion of miners and other settlers, which led to the Indian Wars.

Concern arose when white settlers to the area sought to exploit the tower for speculative purposes. In 1892, Wyoming Senator Francis E. Warren requested that the tower and the surrounding lands be set aside, and the Land Office set up a temporary forest reserve, encompassing 60.5 square miles. This was reduced to 18.75 square miles a few months later and taken off reserved status altogether in 1898. Warren's bill that same year to make the site a national park was tabled. Then in 1906, after the passage of the Antiquities Act, Wyoming residents pushed for and got President Theodore Roosevelt to proclaim Devils Tower the first national monument.

Outdoor Activities

Climbing

Climbers come to Devils Tower from all over the world. They consider the tower a premier crack-climbing area. The butte's climbing history dates back to 1893, when a couple of local ranchers named Willard Ripley and William Rogers organized the construction of a stake ladder up on the tower. The continuously vertical crack in which native oak, ash, and willow pegs were placed is on the southeast side of the tower. The 350-foot ladder was built up to the current "meadows" area. That left only 175 feet to scramble up to reach the summit, which Ripley did prior to the inaugural climb by Rogers on July 4, 1893. The pair's advertisement of the climb drew 3,000 people who ate, drank, and bought pieces of the American flag Rogers placed on the summit, netting the pair approximately $300 for the one-day event.

Technical climbing of the tower started in 1937 when Fritz Wiessner, Lawrence Coveney, and William P. House made the first ascent using modern rock-climbing techniques. Fifty-one routes were established on the tower between 1937 and 1973. During the 1980s, 117 new routes were established. Currently there are approximately 220 named routes used by over 6,000 climbers annually.

In 1993, the National Park Service began work on a climbing management plan for the tower with the main goal to protect the park's resources. A secondary goal was to balance the recreation (climbing) with the cultural and environmental resources. The plan, in place for the 1995 season, treated the tower for the first time as both a natural and a cultural resource. The plan stipulated no new climbing bolts (which were damaging the rock), raptor protection (climbing has been found to have a disruptive effect on nesting raptors), increased resource monitoring, and a cross-cultural educational program (promoting awareness of

American Indian traditions and culture associated with the sacredness of the site). As part of this, the plan called for a voluntary closure to climbing during the month of June out of respect for American Indians who hold religious ceremonies at the site throughout the month. They view the act of climbing the tower during this time as disrespectful. The ceremonies, which include the Sun Dance, are not open to the public. In June 1995, 193 climbers scaled the fluted sides of the tower, compared with 1,293 in June 1994. All climbers must register with a ranger before beginning a climb.

Fishing

Keyhole Reservoir, about 30 miles southwest of Devils Tower, offers excellent fishing, especially crappie and ice fishing in winter. A full-service marina provides gas on the water, a campground with electricity only (no drinking water), and a six-room motel that's a real getaway from everything, as there are no phones or TV. You can also rent small fishing boats. No pets allowed. Handicapped accessible. Open April 1 until October 1. **Keyhole Marina & Motel, 215 McKean Road, Moorcroft, 82721; (307) 756-9529.**

(For more area fishing details, see the Sundance chapter in this section.)

Hiking and Backpacking

Eight miles of trails in the area include the popular **Tower Trail,** a paved 1.25-mile trail that encircles the tower. An interpretive program along the trail offers thumbnail sketches of the history and the significance of aspects of the butte and the environment. In addition to some excellent photo opportunities of the tower and the surrounding landscape, you might—if lucky—see nesting prairie falcons and golden eagles. The trail is handicapped accessible.

Red Beds Trail makes a sweeping three-mile loop of the area, taking in scenic vistas through the pine forest. **Southside Trail,** a short half-mile excursion, wanders around the amazing prairie dog town near the entrance of the monument.

Getting There

Devils Tower monument is located 27 miles northwest of Sundance on **Hwy. 14.** The nearest airport is in Gillette. It has commercial air service through **United Express Airlines (800-241-6522)** and charter service available from **Flightline Aviation Services, Inc., 2000 Airport Road #2D, Gillette, 82716; (307) 686-7000, fax (307) 686-5770.** Rental cars are available at the airport.

Where to Stay

Accommodations

Cozy Motel—$$–$$$
Twenty-three units, 18 of them open in winter. Pets okay. Not handicapped accessible. Located 33 miles from Devils Tower. **219 West Converse Street, Moorcroft, 82721; (307) 756-3486.**

Hulett Motel—$$–$$$
Sleep in standard motel facilities located next to the Belle Fourche River. Open April through November. No pets allowed. Not handicapped accessible. Clean. Great location. **202 Main Street, P.O. Box 489, Hulett, 82720; (307) 467-5220. E-mail: hulettm@trib.com.**

Guest Ranches

Tumbling T Guest Ranch—$$$–$$$$
This 4,000-acre ranch is located on Mona Road about 12 miles northeast of town. Take guided horseback rides (one and a half to two hours minimum) or ATV rides, go fossil digging, look for arrowheads, or practice target shooting. Fish in the ponds or the trout creeks on-site. Enjoy three meals a day prepared by a trained chef. Open year-round, except for the month of November. No minimum stay. Handicapped accessible. Pets okay at this family oriented place. The ranch runs as a B&B or a guest ranch for the works. **P.O. Box 279, Hulett, 82720; (307) 467-5625.**

Camping

In the National Parks, Monuments, and Recreation Areas

Devils Tower has 50 sites nestled along an oxbow bend in the Belle Fourche River that accommodates RVs up to 35 feet and tents. Drinking water, restrooms, handicapped campsites. No hookups, showers, or dump station. Open mid-spring through fall, depending on the weather. **P.O. Box 10, Devils Tower, 82714; (307) 467-5283.**

Private Campgrounds and Cabins

Devils Tower KOA offers 17 full hookup sites, 28 with water and electricity, and unlimited tenting. Or stay in one of seven cabins. There's a heated pool, horseback rides, a cafe, game room, shower houses, restrooms, and laundry. Handicapped accessible. Pets okay. The movie *Close Encounters of the Third Kind* was filmed on the campground location. The KOA shows the film nightly. **Hwy. 110, Devils Tower Junction, 82714; (307) 467-5395. E-mail: dtkoa@trib.com. Website: www.dcomp.-com/hulett/koa.**

Where to Eat

Donna's Diner—$–$$$

Their hamburgers can't be beat. Kids' menu. Senior discounts and senior meals. Handicapped accessible. Breakfast served until noon. Open daily 5 A.M. to 10 P.M. in winter, until 10:30 P.M. in summer. Closed on Thanksgiving and Christmas Day. **203 Converse Street, Moorcroft, 82721; (307) 756-3422.**

Services

Visitor Information

Devils Tower is open year-round. The visitors center, three miles from the entrance gate, is open daily March through October from 9 A.M. to 4 P.M. and Memorial Day through Labor Day from 8 A.M. to 7:45 P.M. It costs $8 per vehicle to gain entrance to the monument and $3 for walk-ins. **Devils Tower National Monument, P.O. Box 10, Devils Tower, 82714; (307) 467-5283, fax (307) 467-5350.**

Gillette

Known for its cleaner-burning, low-sulfur coal, Gillette, at first glance, appears to have little to offer tourists. Take another look. Much of what is truly Wyoming can be found in this city on the High Plains. The unusual rock formations near town dubbed "haystacks" were created by beds of burned coal and clay capping each individual haystack, protecting it from erosion.

History

Founded in 1891, Gillette gets its name from Edward Gillette, an engineer for the Chicago, Burlington & Quincy Railroad. Soon ranchers brought huge herds of sheep and cattle to town to be shipped east via the railroad. As many as 40,000 head of sheep and 12,000 cattle at a time waited in the stockyards for shipment. The town, however, didn't start to boom until the discovery of oil during the 1950s and the rising need for environmentally friendly coal. Some experts believe coal deposits in this one county alone can supply U.S. fuel needs for the next 200 years.

Festivals and Events

Festival in the Park
early August
Craft lovers will find this festival a delight. All sorts of Wyoming crafts from willow furniture to Native American beadwork are available at the bazaars. Food, music, and outdoor fun. Contact the visitors bureau for details **(800-544-6136)**.

Outdoor Activities

Biking

Touring
Bike paths crisscross the city. Biking is a great way to take in the city parks, especially **Sage**

Oil wells near Tea Pot Dome.

Bluffs Park and **McManamen Park.** Contact the visitors bureau for all the details **(800-544-6136)**.

Fishing

Dalbey Memorial Park and Fishing Lake provides a fun getaway right in town. Stocked with trout for good fishing. **Hwy. 59 and Edwards Road.**

Golf

Try the 18-hole public **Bell Nob Golf Course, 4600 Overdale, (307) 686-7069,** or 9 holes at the **Gillette Golf Club, 1800 Country Club Road, (307) 682-4774.**

Cordero Coal Mine. Photo courtesy of the Wyoming Division of Tourism.

Hiking and Backpacking

McManamen Park was designed to create a natural habitat for water fowl. Walk the self-guided nature trail and learn about the ecosystem around Burlington Lake, a water source for the railroad during the steam engine days and the cattle that the trains carried to market. Be sure to look for the living snow fence of trees. Viewing blinds are available for closer, unobtrusive observation. **West Warlow Drive.**

Skiing

Cross-country skiing is available at the **Cam-Plex Park.** Glide along one-mile groomed trail that loops through the trees and nursery area. There is also a sledding hill. The Campbell County Community Parks & Recreation Center has the details **(307-682-7406).**

Swimming

Swim free at the **Gillette Water Park.** Enjoy the whale fountain, wall sprays, shooting geysers, deep-well diving board, and double tube slide. There's a sand play area and wading pool with a shipwreck slide for the kids. Open Mon-

day through Saturday from 10 A.M. until 8 P.M. and Sunday from 1 P.M. to 5 P.M. **Gillette Avenue and 10th, Gillette, 82718; (307) 682-1962.**

Seeing and Doing

Coal Mine Tours

Gillette produces more coal than any other area in the nation. The coal burns clean because of a low sulfur content. Turn-of-the-century homesteaders in the area discovered coal deposits close to the surface and used it to heat their homes. The Wyodak mine became the first to surface mine in Wyoming. About 40 million years ago, the region was a freshwater swamp in an ancient delta. Huge peat deposits formed over an approximately 110,000-year period, then were buried by sand and shale. The peat eventually compressed into a subbituminous seam of coal.

You can tour the **Eagle Butte Mine** Monday through Friday during the summer at either 9 A.M. or 11 A.M. See the mine. Look into the pit. Learn about strip mining. The tour is free and well worth the time. Not handicapped accessible. The tour lasts about an hour and leaves from the **Gillette Convention & Visitors Bureau, 314 South Gillette Avenue, Gillette, 82716; (800) 544-6136 or (307) 686-0040.**

Durham Buffalo Ranch

Among the nation's largest working buffalo ranches, it encompasses 55,000 acres. Tours available by appointment for bus groups only. Guides will take you into the middle of the herd, and you'll get to see the handling facility. Open summer only. Fee charged. **7835 Hwy. 59 South, Gillette, 82718; (307) 939-1271.**

High Plains Energy Technology Center

Wander around the huge machines and equipment used in building Wyoming's industries. The tires on the truck used to haul coal are an incredible 12 feet in height. Imagine, 60-bias ply! Climb aboard the truck and get a bird's-eye view of the area. Various other rigs, oil pumps, a derrick, and much more. Located outside at the Cam-Plex. **1635 Reata Drive, Gillette, 82718; (307) 682-0552, fax (307) 682-8418. E-mail: camplex@ccg.co.campbell.-wy.us. Website: ccg.co.campbell.wy.us/camplex/index.html.**

Einstein Adventurarium Science Center

Kids will love this one-of-a-kind all-hands-on place. They can operate the big electromagnetic crane or see the huge collision balls in action or spin on the momentum machine. One room is devoted to shadows! Kids can try to crawl through a huge spiderweb without ringing the bells and waking the spider. See live animals native or unique to Wyoming, as well as hedgehogs, salamanders, frogs, birds, doves, box turtles, ferrets, tarantulas, and chinchillas. Experience life in the bubble room. Open during the school year from late August until the first week of June, 8 A.M. to 5 P.M. Group tours available during the summer by appointment only. **525 West Lakeway Road, Gillette, 82834; (307) 686-3821. Website: www.rwilliams@ccsd.k12.wy.us.**

Museums

Rockpile Museum

This free museum offers a peek into the development of Campbell County—from displays of the Ute and Sioux Nations to coal mining and cowboy memorabilia. See the Burlington caboose used until 1978. Explore the one-room schoolhouse built in the 1920s. There are guns, sheep wagons, a horse-drawn hearse from 1900, and a large wooden windmill. Kids will love the interactive audiovisuals throughout the museum. Wyoming art, historical photos, and, of course, rocks! The museum gets its name from the natural rock formation at the edge of the parking lot. Also check out the doughnut rock outside with a hole in its middle where a tree grew. Open every Monday through Saturday, June through August, from 9 A.M. to 8 P.M., Sunday from 12:30 P.M. to 6:30 P.M. The

Getting There

Gillette is an oasis in the High Plains, between the Wyoming Black Hills and the Big Horn Mountains, 61 miles west of Sundance at the crossroads of I-90 East/West, Hwys. 14 and 16 and Hwy. 59 North/South, Hwy. 50 South, Hwy. 387 West, and Hwy. 450 East. Air service is provided by **United Express Airlines (800-241-6522).** Charter service available from **Flightline Aviation Services, Inc., 2000 Airport Road #2D, Gillette, 82716; (307) 686-7000, fax (307) 686-5770. Rental cars** available at the airport. Bus service is available through **Powder River Transportation (800-442-3682** or **307-682-0960). Gillette Bus Depot, 1700 East Hwys. 14 and 16, (307) 682-1888.** Taxi services are available through **Gillette Taxi (307-686-4090)** and **Lord Calvin Limousine Service (307-682-8265).**

191

rest of the year, hours are Monday through Saturday from 9 A.M. to 5 P.M. **900 West 2nd Street/Hwy. 14-16 West; (307) 682-5723. E-mail: rockpile@vcn.com.**

Wright Museum

Explore early homesteading, farming, ranching, and the coal mining industry through the displays. Learn why Ted Marquiss brought buffalo to the region in 1922. Open June through August, Monday through Friday, from 10 A.M. to 5 P.M., and Saturday from 10 A.M. to 3 P.M. Located in **Wright, 82716; (307) 464-1222.**

Scenic Drives

Thunder Basin National Grassland

Spread out over five counties in northeastern Wyoming, the grassland encompasses 572,211 acres. It provides many unique opportunities for recreation—hiking in a semiarid climate at elevations of 3,600–5,200 feet, wildlife watching, and fishing. Though camping is allowed, there are no developed camp-grounds, and parts of the grassland inter-mingle with private property. Bring your own water, as there is none available for drinking. Also, keep in mind that the wind blows quite strong across the grassland, and thunder-storms are frequent in summer. Contact the **Douglas Ranger District, 2250 East Richards Street, Douglas, 82633; (307) 358-4690.**

Where to Stay

Accommodations

Deer Park B&B—$$$-$$$$
Located in a Victorian-era-furnished ranch house, this B&B offers nonsmoking rooms, private baths, and a complete formal breakfast amid antique furnishings. Adults only. Pets okay. Handicapped accessible. Open May through September. Reservations required. On-site Cobweb Shoppe antique store. **2660 Bishop Road, P.O. Box 1089, Gillette, 82732; (307) 682-9832.**

Camping

Private Campgrounds
Green Tree's Crazy Woman Campground is open year-round (shower house closed in win-ter) with over 100 spaces. Some have full hook-ups; many are located in the shade. Tent sites, picnic area, game room, playground, volleyball and tetherball, horseshoes, and laundry facili-ties. Enjoy the pool, tanning beds, and a spa. Pets okay. Partly handicapped accessible. Pro-pane for sale at the store. **1001 West 2nd, Gillette, 82716; (307) 682-3665. E-mail: crazywoman@newwaveis.com.**

High Plains Campground
Located off I-90 (Exit 129), the campground is open all year. Sixty-four hookups, tent area, picnic tables at every site, fire pits, a store, and laundry facilities. Handicapped acces-sible. Gas and propane available. Pets okay on leash. **1600 South Garner Lake Road South, Gillette, 82718; (307) 687-7339.**

Where to Eat

Prime Rib Restaurant & Steak House—$$$-$$$$
A beautifully decorated, upscale dining experi-ence awaits you at this restaurant. It has the feel of a luxurious wine cellar, and they do of-fer an award-winning selection of wines. For lunch try the tampico taco salad. Dinner spe-cials. Don't miss the mile-high mud pie for dessert! Children's menu. Open Monday through Friday from 11 A.M. to 10 P.M., and Saturday and Sunday from 4 P.M. to 11 P.M. Handicapped accessible. **1205 South Dou-glas Hwy., Gillette, 82716; (307) 682-2944.**

The Goings Restaurant—$$-$$$$
Choose fine dining or casually upscale dining. They serve a good steak and a freshly made dessert. Delicious cheesecakes. Weekly spe-cials. Handicapped accessible. Senior dis-counts. Kids' menu. Open Monday through Fri-day from 11 A.M. to 10 P.M., Saturday from 4 P.M. to 10 P.M., and Sunday, for brunch only, from 10 A.M. to 2 P.M. **113 South Gillette Avenue, Gillette, 82716; (307) 682-6805.**

Hong Kong Restaurant—$$-$$$$
Lunch specials. Carryout. Try their great chicken, beef, and shrimp dish, Chow San Shen, served with vegetables and a mushroom sauce. Handicapped accessible. American foods also. Open daily 11 A.M. to 9:30 P.M. **1612 West 2nd Street, Gillette, 82716; (307) 682-5829.**

Bailey's Bar & Grill—$$-$$$
This historic site started as a cafe. Then the building was torn down and the town's original post office was constructed between 1924 and 1935. When the new post office went up in 1978, it became City Hall. In 1984, the build-ing came full circle with the opening of the bar and grill. Great old-timey atmosphere remains from the use of the original wood and brass fixtures. Dandy choice of sandwiches and sal-ads. Try the seafood linguini for dinner. Kids' menu. Open 8 A.M. until 10 P.M., Monday through Saturday. **301 South Gillette Av-enue, Gillette, 82716; (307) 686-7678.**

Humphrey's Bar & Grill—$$–$$$

A TV-and-beer-lover's paradise. Forty sets. Fifty beers on tap. A hundred bottled beers available. On the grill, they specialize in Cajun foods. Tasty crawdads. Senior discounts. Open daily 11 A.M. to 10 P.M. Handicapped accessible. **408 West Juniper, Gillette, 82716; (307) 682-0100.**

Packards Grill—$$–$$$

Traditional breakfast foods. Homemade soups are great for lunch. Barbecue ribs or fish makes a tasty dinner in this restaurant with its casual, comfortable atmosphere. Or try one of their dinner specials. Handicapped accessible. Nonsmoking. Kids' menu. Senior discounts. Check out the Terry Redlin and Michael Atkinson prints on the walls. Open Monday through Saturday from 6 A.M. to 9 P.M., and Sunday from 7 A.M. to 3 P.M. **408 South Douglas Hwy., Gillette, 82716; (307) 686-5149.**

Services

Visitor Information

Gillette Convention and Visitors Bureau, Exit 126 on **I-90** in the Flying J Travel Plaza, **1800 South Douglas Hwy., Gillette, 82718, (800) 544-6136** or **(307) 686-0040. E-mail: gillettecvb@wyoming.com.**

Campbell County Chamber of Commerce, 314 South Gillette Avenue, Gillette, 82716; (307) 682-3673, fax (307) 682-0538. E-mail: ccchamber@vcn.com.

Wright Area Chamber of Commerce, Latigo Hills Mall, P.O. Box 430, Wright, 82732; (307) 464-1312.

Medicine Wheel

The Medicine Wheel is located on a ridge that forms a peak of Medicine Mountain. Its elevation is 9,642 feet. A circular alignment of rocks, 75 feet in diameter, has 28 radial rows of stones extending from a central cairn. Six smaller cairns are placed at intervals around the rim. A well-used trail, paralleling the current forest service access road leading to the wheel, shows that people have traveled this path to the wheel for centuries.

History

Speculation abounds about the origin and meaning of the Medicine Wheel. In reality, few facts are known. Early white travelers in the area reported the Medicine Wheel's existence in the 1880s. Archaeological excavations in 1902 and 1958 turned up few findings. In the later study, only the topmost layer of soil produced artifacts. Twelve pottery shards were unearthed, some tools, and nine different types of beads. The excavation of the central cairn revealed that the Indians had made a two-foot-deep pit in the bedrock by removing slabs of limestone. Fragments of rotted wood were found about 15 inches down, and a piece of wood recovered from the walls of the west cairn provided a tree-ring date of 1760.

Astronomers have also studied the Medicine Wheel. Because there are 28 days in a lunar month, two of the cairns were placed on a north-south line, acting as horizon markers for sunrise and sunset. One cairn that was placed at the end of a spoke by itself outside the rim created a line with the central hub, pointing to the exact spot of the summer solstice sunrise.

In 1915, the Department of the Interior made a proposal to the Secretary of Agriculture that the Medicine Wheel site become a national monument. Nothing was done until the end of 1941, when the Secretary of the Interior approved a study of the Medicine Wheel by the National Park Service, but the study was postponed by World War II. Finally, in 1957, the government established the monument.

The site is sacred to many Indian nations. It is a place of vision quests, prayers, peace, and inspiration. Many Native Americans tie prayer bundles to the fence that surrounds the Medicine Wheel. The fence replaced a huge stone wall built by the forest service in 1935 to protect it from disturbance. The road built to the site in 1958 was closed to vehicular traffic in 1993.

Outdoor Activities

Snowmobiling

The **Burgess Junction** portion of the Big Horn Mountains offers 163 miles of groomed and 40 miles of ungroomed trails at elevations ranging from 8,000 to 9,600 feet. The best snow falls between December and April. Limited food, fuel, and lodging along the trail. **Paint Rock Trail** is recommended for experienced riders only, as there are 75 miles between gas stations. Check with the **Bighorn National Forest** office for maps and trail conditions, **1969 South Sheridan Avenue, Sheridan, 82801; (307) 672-0751. Website: mailroom/r2_bighorn@fs.fed.us.**

Snowmobile rentals available from **Bear Lodge Resort, Route 14A, P.O. Box 159, Dayton, 82836; (307) 655-2444.**

Seeing and Doing

Pryor Mountain Wild Horse Range

The 38,000-acre Pryor Mountain Wild Horse Range (PMWHR) is accessed along Hwy. 37 and is adjacent to the Bighorn Canyon National Recreation Area, 13 miles north of Lovell. PMWHR was created in 1968 by order of then Secretary of the Interior Stewart L.

Udall. This designation was the first of its kind in the United States. Elevations within the range vary from 3,640 to 8,000 feet and contain deep, steep-walled canyons, isolated grassy plateaus, and foothill slopes. The population ranges between 193 and 208 horses, a bit more than the range can support, which is why they occasionally have roundups and place the horses up for adoption. What's really unique about these animals is that they have been identified as a rare wild strain of the Spanish Colonial horse, a breed that no longer exists in Spain. The PMWHR horses stand about 14 hands high and weigh between 700 and 800 pounds, smaller than many other breeds. They have narrow but deep chests, long and angulated shoulders, and sloping croups with relatively low-set tails.

The best way to see the herds while you drive along Hwy. 37 (open year-round) is to get out of your car and scan the horizon back and forth. Binoculars are a big help. You might encounter bighorn sheep in summer, especially ewes and lambs. Be sure to stop at the Devil Canyon Overlook. The canyon is 50 miles long.

If you have four-wheel drive and desire a good loop drive, go up Burnt Timber Ridge Road and down Sykes Ridge Road. It takes about six hours total. Hike out to the end of the ridge for a nice view while you eat lunch. These dirt roads are open from June through October, depending on weather.

The visitors center is open daily, except for Thanksgiving, Christmas, and New Year's Day, from 9 A.M. to 5 P.M. Closed for lunch from noon to 1 P.M. in winter. The north-side visitors center (in Montana) is closed from mid-September to mid-May. **Bighorn Canyon National Recreation Area Visitor Center, 20 Hwy. 14A East, Lovell, 82431; (307) 548-2251.**

Scenic Drives

Bighorn Canyon

The Big Horn River cut through the Big Horn and Pryor Mountains, creating this spectacular canyon. Layers of rock rise up to 2,000 feet above the river, depicting over 500 million years of geologic history. The 71-mile-long Big

Medicine Wheel.

195

Horn Lake was created from the Yellowtail dam project near Fort Smith, Montana. Plenty of fishing, camping, hiking, boating, wildlife viewing, and scenic enjoyment. The visitors center is open daily, except for Thanksgiving, Christmas, and New Year's Day, from 9 A.M. to 5 P.M. Closed for lunch from noon to 1 P.M. in winter. **Bighorn Canyon National Recreation Area Visitor Center, 20 Hwy. 14A East, P.O. Box 487, Lovell, 82431; (307) 548-2251.**

Where to Stay

Accommodations

Bear Lodge Resort—$$$–$$$$
In addition to the motel, there are rustic cabins with wood-burning stoves and electricity,

Powder River Region

but no water; RV sites with water and electricity; and tent sites. Cafe and lounge on-site. Hot tub. A stocked trout pond for kids 12 and under. Open year-round. **Route 14A, P.O. Box 159, Dayton, 82836; (307) 655-2444.**

Arrowhead Lodge—$$–$$$
Stay on top of the Big Horn Mountains. In addition to the motel, there are cabins and RV spaces available. Jacuzzi. A stocked fishing pond, as well as the South Fork of the Tongue River only 100 yards from the lodge. Restaurant, lounge, gas, deli, and grocery store on-site. Pets okay in the cabins. Handicapped accessible. Best snowmobiling in the mountains right from your room door. Hiking not far from the wilderness area. Open year-round. Five-day minimum stay in October. Located on U.S. Hwy. 14, mile marker 60. **P.O. Box 390, Dayton, 82836; (307) 655-2388 or (307) 672-4111.**

Cattlemen Motel—$$–$$$
Free coffee in the lobby. Mini-refrigerators and microwaves for an additional fee. Pets allowed for an extra fee. Not handicapped accessible. Open year-round. True western hospitality. Located in the heart of town. Close to the post office and restaurants. **470 Montana Avenue, Lovell, 82431; (307) 548-2296.**

Park Motel—$$–$$$
Clean and comfortable rooms, friendly service, and location convenient to shopping. Newly remodeled kitchenettes, with refrigerators and microwaves in some rooms. Rooms on ground level with parking in front of door. Smoking and nonsmoking rooms available. Open year-round. Not handicapped accessible. Small pets allowed. **737 East 2nd Street, Powell, 82435; (800) 506-7378 (REST) or (307) 754-2233.**

Camping

In the National Forests
North Tongue Campground offers dandy trout fishing. The North Fork of the Tongue River allows only catch-and-release fishing

using artificial flies and lures. **Bald Mountain, Porcupine,** and **Five Springs Campgrounds** feature hookups for RVs and potable water. **Bighorn National Forest, 1969 South Sheridan Avenue, Sheridan, 82801; (307) 672-0751.**

In the National Parks, Monuments, and Recreation Areas
The campground at **Horseshoe Bend** in **Bighorn Canyon National Recreation Area** offers primitive camping with no electricity or drinking water. However, there are a snack bar, picnic area, and marina on site. There is a Bighorn Canyon Visitor Center just outside Lovell on Hwy. 14A. **Bighorn Canyon National Recreation Area Visitor Center, 20 Hwy. 14A East, Lovell, 82431; (307) 548-2251.**

Private Campgrounds and Cabins
Although there are no hookups, the **Lovell Camper Park** has a shower, drinking water, restrooms, and dump station, all free. **East 2nd and Quebec, Lovell, 82431; (307) 548-6551.**

Where to Eat

Big Horn Restaurant—$$–$$$$
Prime rib and seafood are their specialties. Enjoy the large salad bar. Open daily for breakfast, lunch, and dinner 6 A.M. to 8:30 P.M. during the week and until 9:30 P.M. on weekends. Kids' menu and senior discounts. Not handicapped accessible. **605 East Main Street, Lovell, 82431; (307) 548-6811.**

Services

Visitor Information

The Medicine Wheel site is open Memorial Day weekend through Labor Day, depending on snow. The visitors center opens daily any-

where from mid-June to July 1, again depending on snow, through Labor Day, from 7 A.M. to
7 P.M. Call first if you plan on visiting the site in
June.

**Medicine Wheel Ranger District, Bighorn
National Forest, P.O. Box 367, Lovell,
82431; (307) 548-6541.**

**Powell Valley Chamber of Commerce, 111
South Day Street, P.O. Box 814, Powell,
82435; (307) 754-3494.**

**Lovell Area Chamber of Commerce, 287
East Main Street, P.O. Box 295, Lovell,
82431; (307) 548-7552.**

Getting There

The Medicine Wheel is located between
Sheridan and Lovell on a forest service
road **(FDR 12) just off Hwy. 14A.**
There is a 1.5-mile walk from the
parking area to the Medicine Wheel.
(Only handicapped visitors are allowed
to drive to the site.) The nearest airport
to the Medicine Wheel is in Cody, 45
miles west, or Billings, Montana, 90
miles north. Fly into Cody on **SkyWest/
Delta (800-221-1212** or **307-587-
9740)** and **United Express (800-241-
6522** or **307-527-6443). Spirit
Mountain Aviation** also offers charter
and scenic flights from Cody. **3227
Duggleby Drive; (307) 587-6732** or
(307) 587-6932. A variety of **rental
cars** are available at the airport.

Sheridan

Sheridan's history has been connected to horses—more so than any other Wyoming town. Polo, a game not normally associated with the pioneering and cowboying West, has been played in Sheridan since the 1890s. The Eaton Ranch, established in 1904, drives the ranch's horse herd through town each year between summer and winter pastures. It's quite a treat to watch, if you happen to be lucky enough to be in town when the herd and wranglers ride through! In addition, the Kings have been making saddles here for generations. And, according to Calamity Jane, she earned that nickname when she was scouting for U.S. Army Captain Henry Egan in the area that is now Sheridan. Indians shot Egan. Jane galloped to his side, catching him before he fell from his horse. She lifted the captain onto her horse in front of her and got him back to the post. When he recovered, Egan said, "I name you Calamity Jane, the heroine of the plains."

History

A trapper named Jim Mason came to what is now Sheridan in 1878 and constructed a cabin. Three years later Harry Mandel moved into Mason's one-room cabin. Mandel ambitiously turned it into a post office and store and named this small community after himself.

In 1882, John D. Loucks drew a plat for a town on the back of a sheet of wrapping paper. In honor of Loucks's commander, General Philip H. Sheridan, Loucks called his town "Sheridan." Most of the town's lots from the original 40-acre plat were occupied by the time the town was incorporated in 1884. By 1890, Sheridan boasted a population of 281. At the turn of the century, with the railroad in operation and the opening of coal mines in the vicinity, 1,559 people called Sheridan home. This grew to 4,937 by 1907, firmly establishing Sheridan as a permanent, thriving community.

Festivals and Events

Rodeo Week
mid-July

Things get started with the Boot Kick-Off and Barbecue. PRCA rodeo events include steer roping, bull riding, and bronc riding, plus the World Champion Indian Relay Race. There are a carnival, chuckwagon breakfast, kids' events such as the duck race, a chili cook-off, a street fair, a golf tournament, an Indian dance show, a calcutta, a steeplechase, and polo games. Be sure to visit the Northern Plains Indian camp. For all the details contact the **Sheridan-WYO Rodeo. P.O. Box 742, Sheridan, 82801; (307) 672-2485** for information, **(307) 672-9084** for tickets. **Website: sheridanwyo.com/tourism/wyorodeo.**

Outdoor Activities

Biking

Mountain Biking

Trails in the **Big Horn Mountains** challenge bikers at every skill level. Pedal along logging roads, over plateaus, or along steep slopes. The **forest service** office has maps and information. **1969 South Sheridan Avenue, Sheridan, 82801; (307) 672-0751.**

Fishing

Streams and lakes in the **Big Horn Mountains** teem with brook, brown, cutthroat, golden, and rainbow trout. Blue sparkling water and a fishery await at **Sibley Lake**, elevation 7,900 feet, along with handicapped access to fishing, a campground, and a walking trail around the lake. One of the best ways to experience this lake is in a canoe with a fishing rod. Fishing also abounds along the banks of the **South Fork of the Tongue River** and in **Tongue River Canyon.**

Wyoming Game & Fish runs a visitors center in town. Displays on habitat and Wyoming's wildlife give an excellent overview of the state's outdoor resources. In addition, they carry great information on fishing and state regulations, and the center sells licenses. Check out the brochures on birds and small animals such as ferrets, birds that winter in Wyoming, and viewing routes in the Big Horns. Videos about wildlife are also available. Open weekdays from 8 A.M. to 5 P.M. at **700 Valley View Drive, P.O. Box 6249; Sheridan, 82801; (307) 672-7418.**

Try your hand at fly-fishing in the Big Horns with **Paul Wallop Mountain Fly Fishing** between mid-June and the end of September. Half- or full-day guided trips. Beginning and advanced courses. Equipment rentals. Lodging can be arranged through the Canyon Ranch. Special things for kids to do. **52 Canyon Ranch Road, P.O. Box 11, Big Horn, 82833; (307) 674-6239.**

Golf

Ranked among the top five courses in Wyoming by *Golf Digest*, the **Kendrick Golf Course** offers 18 holes at par 72. Driving range. Rental carts and clubs. Open to the public daily from April 1 to October 15, daylight to dark. **P.O. Box 848, Sheridan, 82801; (307) 674-8148.**

Hiking and Backpacking

The **Bighorn National Forest** contains over 1,143 miles of trails. The district ranger's office carries maps and trail information and can help you decide on the best routes. **1969 South Sheridan Avenue, Sheridan, 82801; (307) 672-0751.**

Horseback Riding

For a different twist on western horseback riding, check out the polo games played every Sunday afternoon from May to September at the **Big Horn Equestrian Center**. Sheridan has one of the oldest polo clubs in the nation. Free admission, unless a special fundraising event is under way for something such as the animal shelter. **P.O. Box 6413, Sheridan,**

Downtown Sheridan.

199

82801; (307) 674-4812. E-mail: nxbar@-cyberhighway.net.

Nelson Outfitters on Hwy. 331 (known as Big Goose Road) provides half- and full-day trail rides on a 10,000-acre ranch for adults and children age eight and older. **900 Big Goose, Sheridan, 82801; (307) 672-6996. E-mail: noutfit@huntwyoming.com.**

Skiing

Cross-Country Skiing

Fifteen miles of well-marked, groomed trails head through the wilderness near **Sibley Lake** in the Big Horns. Elevations range from 7,700 to 8,400 feet. Six loop trails available from long and easy **Dead Horse Park Trail** to the challenging climbs of **Flume Trail**. For a map and details contact the **Bighorn National Forest, 1969 South Sheridan Avenue, Sheridan, WY 82801; (307) 672-0751.**

Seeing and Doing

Historic Sheridan Inn

Built in 1893, the inn represented the establishment of modern culture in the still "wild and woolly" West. It ranked as the finest hotel between Chicago and San Francisco and had the first bathtubs and electric lights in northeast Wyoming. Famed showman Buffalo Bill Cody ran the inn from 1894 to 1896 and watched cowboys trying out for his show from the inn's wide veranda. The Buffalo Bill Bar, made of oak and mahogany, was special ordered from England and was hauled to Sheridan by ox team from Gillette. Rooms cost a dollar a day then. The plush dining room charged a costly quarter for breakfast and 50 cents for lunch or dinner. Guided tours of the third-floor hotel rooms tell of the history, famous guests, and Miss Kate, a seamstress who lived at the inn from 1908 until her death in 1965. She requested that her ashes be placed behind the wall of her room. Her ghost is said to reside in the room to this day. The tour also includes the museum with lots of regional history, the saloon, the ladies' parlor, and the dining room. Open during the summer. Call for hours. **5th and Broadway, P.O. Box 6003, Sheridan, 82801; (307) 674-5440.**

The historic Sheridan Inn.

200

Trail End Historic Site

This was originally the home of John Benjamin Kendrick. Construction began in 1908 and was completed in 1913. The Kendrick family only lived in the house a short time before he became Wyoming's governor in 1914 and later a U.S. senator. Trail End became a summer home and the focal point of Kendrick's collections. The house alone is worth touring. Based on a Flemish design, the mahogany walls and polished hardwood floors, Gothic-style library with stained-glass windows and built-in bookcases with doors of leaded glass, and the elegance of the dining room will leave you awestruck. Then there is the garden. Open June through August daily from 9 A.M. to 6 P.M., and September to mid-December and April through May daily 1 P.M. to 4 P.M. Special hours on Memorial Day and Labor Day weekends (Saturday through Monday), 10 A.M. to 5 P.M. No fee, but donations are welcome. **400 Clarendon Avenue, Sheridan, 82801; (307) 674-4589, fax (307) 672-1720. E-mail: cgeorg@missc.state.wy.us. Website: wave.sheridan.wy.us/~trailend/index.**

WYO Theater

Live performances all year long at the oldest operating vaudeville theater in Wyoming. Built in 1923, the WYO hosts musical performances, the ballet, and children's theater productions in this renovated, art-deco building. **42 North Main, P.O. Box 528, Sheridan, 82801; (307) 672-9083** for information, **(307) 672-9084** for tickets.

Connor Battle State Park

Brigadier General Patrick E. Connor's force of 125 cavalry soldiers and 90 Pawnee scouts attacked an Arapaho village on this site along the Tongue River in 1865. Warriors led by Chief Black Bear fought the army off long enough for Arapaho families to disperse into the surrounding countryside. Troops destroyed the village while Connor led the chase after the Indians. They counterattacked, forcing Connor back down the Tongue River. The army used howitzers to keep the Arapahos at bay while the soldiers retreated. Connor's attack on the village, however, caused the Arapahos to combine forces with the Cheyenne and Sioux and to participate in the Fetterman Fight. A plaque about the Connor Battlefield is in **Ranchester City Park,** 18 miles from Sheridan.

Wyoming Bird Farm

Wyoming Game & Fish has raised ring-necked pheasants since 1937. The farm rears approximately 12,000 pheasants every year that are released around the state. Open to the public from May through September. The best time to see the hatchlings is in early May, June for chicks, and full-color grown birds in September. Learn about the program and its history at the visitors center. It also displays historic pictures of the farm and other wildlife information. In addition to the ring-necked pheasants, the farm raises a wide variety of exotic pheasants—golden, melanistic mutant, turkey, white, and buff—to give people a taste of the 90 species and subspecies of pheasants and their diverse habitats found around the world. Group tours with slide programs by appointment only. No handicapped-accessible paths, but there is access into the building where you can see the pheasants. **326 Bird Farm Road, Sheridan, 82801; (307) 674-7701.**

Historic Downtown Sheridan

Buildings dating from the late nineteenth and early twentieth centuries line Sheridan's Main Street Historic District. Constructed of brick and stone, few of the district's buildings have undergone major exterior alterations. Since the town's earliest times, Main Street has always been the central business district and remains so today. Walking down Main Street is like strolling back in time to Sheridan's turn-of-the-century boom days.

Museums

Bradford Brinton Memorial Historic Ranch

Located on the Quarter A Circle Ranch built in 1892, the Bradford Brinton Memorial Historic

Getting There

Situated in the northeast part of the state on **I-90,** Sheridan is 35 miles north of Buffalo. Commercial passenger flights are available at the **Sheridan County Airport (307-674-4222)** through **United Express (800-241-6522).** There is no bus service to or in Sheridan. Rent a car from **Avis (800-331-1212** or **307-672-2226)** or from **Enterprise (800-325-8007** or **307-672-6910).** Taxi service is available through **Sheridan Transportation (307-674-6814).** The **Sheridan Chamber of Commerce (307-672-2485)** maintains a current list of day-care centers.

Ranch contains an incredible archive of United States history. Brinton purchased the ranch in 1923 and used it as a vacation home and focal point for collecting rare books and manuscripts. In addition to the first edition of Samuel Johnson's life story, there are 141 volumes by Robert Louis Stevenson, William Penn documents, and the complete works of Abraham Lincoln, including letters. In addition, there are 600 works of art, such as Charles M. Russell bronzes and watercolors and 250 Indian artifacts in the Fine Arts Gallery, all displayed in the original house. Rotation displays and art shows. Open May 15 through Labor Day from 9:30 A.M. to 5 P.M. The Saturday after Labor Day the ranch reopens until September 30. Closed then until December 1. Then the gallery reopens only through December 15, noon until 6 P.M. on weekends only. Tours by appointment during the week. Handicapped accessible. **239 Brinton Road, P.O. Box 460, Big Horn, 82833; (307) 672-3173, fax (307) 672-3258. E-mail: qca@cyberhighway.com.**

King's Saddle Museum

This is one of the most uniquely western and Wyomingish museums you'll ever find. Don King started making saddles in 1946. His beautifully hand-tooled saddles are displayed

King Saddle Museum.

at the National Cowboy Hall of Fame and the PRCA Rodeo Hall of Fame. Over the years, he began acquiring saddles that showed the changing trends and styles of saddles. In 1989, he put them on exhibit for the public. The collection includes a seventeenth-century Japanese saddle with a brass stirrup found in a tomb in a cave during World War II, an Argentine saddle named "pato" because of the duck shape of the cantel, a territory side saddle used from 1884 to 1897, and the saddle King's grandfather used while trailing cattle from Texas to Wyoming during 1876. Also on display are Brazilian stirrups that are round and flat, curly chaps, cowboy and Indian memorabilia, and leather-working tools. The museum is free and is located behind the saddle and rope shops. Open 8 A.M. to 5 P.M. Monday through Saturday. **184 North Main, Sheridan, 82801; (800) 443-8919** or **(307) 672-2702** or **2755, fax (307) 672-5235.**

Scenic Drives

(See the Medicine Wheel chapter in this section and the Greybull chapter in the Big Horn Basin section for scenic drives leading to Sheridan on Hwys. 14 and 14A. Also see the Buffalo chapter in this section for historic fort and battle locations around Story, Wyoming, approximately halfway between Buffalo and Sheridan.)

Where to Stay

Accommodations

Mill Inn—$$$–$$$$
Nice rooms, large. Queen-size beds, TV, new bathrooms. Continental breakfast for the sweet tooth. Western look in the lobby. Friendly staff. Clean rooms. **2161 Coffeen Avenue, Sheridan, 82801; (307) 672-6401.**

Sheridan Holiday Inn Atrium Hotel and Conference Center—$$$–$$$$
A cut above the usual chain accommodations. Rooms overlook the atrium with a beautiful waterfall. Indoor heated pool and hot tub. Fully equipped exercise room. Restaurant, lounge, and all the comforts of home. Friendly staff. Handicapped accessible. **1809 Sugarland Drive, Sheridan, 82801; (800) HOLIDAY (465-4329)** for reservations or **(307) 672-8931.**

Spahn's Big Horn Mountain B&B—$$$–$$$$
Mountainside cabins overlooking the Sheridan valley await you at this B&B, located nine miles southwest of Big Horn. A great get-away-from-it-all type of place with one million acres of national forest bordering the B&B. You can see 100 miles from here. Three bedrooms in the main lodge come with private baths. Showers in the two cabins. Cookouts and wildlife tours can be arranged. No TV in the rooms. Children welcome. Three-night minimum stay in the cabins during the summer. Full country-style breakfast with homemade biscuits and pancakes. Gracious services in a comfortable, social atmosphere. Open year-round. **P.O. Box 579, Big Horn, 82833; (307) 674-8150.** E-mail: **spahnbb@wave.sheridan.wy.us.** Website: **www.wave.sheridan.wy.us/-~spahnbb.**

Old Croff House B&B—$$$
Located in downtown Sheridan, just four blocks from uptown. Relax in one of three rooms, one of which is a suite with a sitting room. All have shared bathrooms. Built in

1917, the house is not very fancy, but it is very comfortable. The continental breakfast contains plenty of fresh-baked goods, fruit, cereals, and homemade jams. Candles on the table. Fresh flowers in rooms filled with light from large windows. Children welcome. Not handicapped accessible. No minimum stay. No pets. Open June through September. **508 West Works, Sheridan, 82801; (307) 672-0898.**

Ranch Willow B&B—$$$
Originally a ranch house built in 1901, the B&B is located on 550 acres. Enjoy organically grown breakfast foods, farm fresh eggs, and homemade bread. Rooms with private or semi-private baths. Indoor arena and horse facility for people traveling with their horses. Horse boarding available. Beautiful cottonwood trees surround you. Not handicapped accessible. No pets. Nonsmoking. Children over 12 welcome. Original Bozeman Trail went through the property. They've even found a few cannonballs where a skirmish took place and a wagon tipped over. **501 U.S. Hwy. 14, Sheridan, 82801; (800) 354-2830 or (307) 674-1510, fax (307) 674-1502. Website: www.away-west.com/ACCOMS/RWBANDB/index.**

Guest House Motel—$$–$$$
Standard accommodations with all the rooms on ground level. Not handicapped accessible. Pets okay for an extra fee. Open year-round. Coffee and refrigerators in rooms. Laundry facilities. Next door to The Golden Steer Restaurant. **2007 North Main, Sheridan, 82801; (307) 674-7496, fax (307) 674-7687. E-mail: guesthse@wavecom.net.**

Guest Ranches
Spear-O-Wigwam—$$$$
Thirty miles southwest of Sheridan, this ranch built in the 1920s and 1930s is located in the Big Horn Mountains close to the Cloud Peak Wilderness. Hemingway stayed here in 1928 while finishing *A Farewell to Arms*. Three-night minimum stay. Located within the national forest. Horseback ride through the national forest; fish in the ranch's stocked ponds or in one of several creeks or lakes nearby.

Open mid-June through mid-September. Pets okay with advance notice, and they must be on a leash at all times. Partially handicapped accessible. **P.O. Box 1081, Sheridan, 82801; (888) 818-DUDE (3833) or (307) 674-4496 in summer, (307) 655-3217 in winter. Website: www.guestranchs.com/spear-o-wigwam.**

Camping
In the National Forests
Campgrounds in the Big Horns offer everything from primitive to comfortable campsites. In addition to those around **Sibley Lake**, enjoy the facilities at **Prune Creek, Owen Creek, Tie Flume,** or **Cabin Creek.** The Bighorn National Forest office has all the details **(307-672-0751).**

Private Campgrounds and Cabins
Sheridan RV Park offers full and partial hookups, showers, laundry, shady sites, creek access. Open April through September. Closed in winter. **807 Avoca Avenue, Sheridan, 82801; (307) 674-0722.**

Lazy R Campground, just 15 minutes northwest of Sheridan in Ranchester, has 22 full hookups. Tent sites. Pull-throughs. Telephone hookups. Pets okay. Handicapped accessible. Showers. Walking distance from restaurants, the bank, and the post office. **P.O. Box 286, Ranchester, 82839; (307) 655-9284.**

Where to Eat
Historic Sheridan Inn—$$–$$$$
Located in the historic inn (see above). Elegant dining. Good food. Try the specialty of the house: prime rib. They also make all their breads in-house. Open daily from 9 A.M. to 9 P.M., Memorial Day to Labor Day. A Sunday brunch is served from 11 A.M. to 3 P.M. In winter, open Monday through Saturday for lunch 10 A.M. to 3 P.M., Friday and Saturday for dinner from 5:30 P.M. to 9 P.M., as well as for the Sunday brunch. **5th and Broadway, Sheridan, 82801; (307) 674-5440.**

The Golden Steer—$$–$$$$

203

Large dining room. Decent meals. Children's and seniors' menus, as well as a light menu. Open from 11 A.M. to 2 P.M. for lunch Monday through Friday, and for dinner nightly from 4 P.M. to 9 P.M. (until 10 P.M. on Friday and Saturday, and until 8:30 P.M. Sunday). Make reservations. **2071 North Main, Sheridan, 82801; (307) 674-9334 or (307) 674-8626.**

Golden China Restaurant—$$–$$$

Reliably good Cantonese and Szechwan food. Open Monday through Saturday from 11 A.M. to 9:15 P.M., and Sunday from 4 P.M. to 8:45 P.M. Luncheon specials Monday through Saturday from 11 A.M. to 2 P.M. Corner of **Brundage Lane** and **Coffee Avenue; Sheridan, 82801; (307) 674-7181.**

Cattleman's Cut Steak House—$$–$$$$

Real western family atmosphere where you can get a delicious cut of prime rib. Also a tasty shrimp trio. Children's and seniors' menus. An all-you-can-eat barbecue buffet from 11 A.M. to 4 P.M. weekdays and all day Sunday. Handicapped accessible. Open 11:30 A.M. to 8:30 P.M. Monday through Thursday, and 11:30 A.M. to 9:30 P.M. Friday and Saturday. Open Sunday from noon until 8 P.M. **927 Coffeen Avenue, Sheridan, 82801; (307) 672-2811.**

Melinda's—$$–$$$

If you remember the good old days when grandma cooked up wonders from scratch, then you'll love Melinda's. Try a cup of her TLC chicken soup and real mashed potatoes or zesty garlic dressing on a Caesar salad. Everything made and baked fresh. And they serve a real good cup of coffee. They grind the beans when they are ready to brew the pot. Warm, cozy, homey feel to the place with tables and chairs that don't match, roses on the tables, hanging lights, and a coffee bar in the window. Kids' menu. Handicapped accessible. Open for breakfast at 7 A.M.; lunch from 11 A.M. to 3 P.M. Dinner on Friday and Saturday from 5 P.M. to 9 P.M. Closed Sunday and Monday. **57 North Main, Sheridan, 82801; (307) 674-9188.**

The Chocolate Tree Restaurant—$$–$$$

Start the day with a great cup of coffee in a cheery cafe. Homemade soups for lunch. Try the "Buffalo Bill" beef burger or a marinated Wyoming strip steak. Vegetarian dishes. And chocolate for dessert, of course. The chocolate chip bundt cake is quite tasty! Open for breakfast at 8 A.M. Lunch from 11 A.M. to 3 P.M. Dinner served Tuesday through Friday from 5 P.M. to 8 P.M. with reservations required. Sunday brunch from 10 A.M. to 2 P.M. Children's sandwich menu. **5 East Alger, Sheridan, 82801; (307) 672-6160.**

Services

Visitor Information

Sheridan Chamber of Commerce, P.O. Box 707, Sheridan, 82801; (307) 672-2485, fax (307) 672-7321.

Sheridan Convention and Visitors Bureau, P.O. Box 7155, Sheridan, 82801; (800) 453-3650. E-mail: chamber@wave.-sheridan.wy.us. Website: www.sheridan-wyo.com.

Sundance

This gorgeous Black Hills community is located just half an hour from either Devils Tower or Keyhole State Park in the heart of some of the state's best swimming, boating, and fishing areas. The town took its name from Sundance Mountain, a sacred site where the Sioux Nation gathered to hunt, collect wild foods, and hold their Sun Dance, one of their most sacred religious ceremonies, until the U.S. government outlawed it.

Sundance, however, is most known for its infamous outlaw. Horse thief Harry Longabaugh spent 18 months in the town's jail before taking on the nickname of "Sundance Kid" and hooking up with Butch Cassidy.

History

During the summer of 1874, the U.S. government broke its treaty with the Sioux Nation by allowing then Lieutenant Colonel George Armstrong Custer to lead a military expedition into what the Native Americans called *Mass Sapa*, the Black Mountains, called the "Black Hills" by the whites. The troops' discovery of gold spelled the end for the Indians' control over lands they held sacred and the beginning of the bloody Indian Wars.

By 1877, cattlemen were moving huge herds into the region. Albert Hoge established a trading post at the foot of Sundance Mountain in 1879. Before long, his post became a major gathering place for area farmers and ranchers. By 1882, Sundance had a post office, a grocery store, a couple of restaurants, and the inevitable saloon. Incorporated in 1887, Sundance boasted a population of over 200. Railroad and coal mining really made the region boom.

Fire watchtower.

205

Outdoor Activities

Biking

Mountain Biking

The **Bearlodge Trails** in the **Black Hills National Forest** provide 50 miles of rugged, gorgeous scenery to challenge every level of rider. The trail system is generally open from mid-May through early November. **South Fork Tent Trail** and **Edge Trail** present the most formidable rides. This trail system is strictly nonmotorized. So enjoy! Mountain bikers gather here in June to participate in the Bearlodge Fat Tire Challenge, which uses the Bearlodge Trails as the main portion of the course. See the **Bearlodge Ranger District** for maps and trail information. **121 South 21st Street, P.O. Box 680, Sundance, 82729; (307) 283-1361.**

Fishing

The reservoir at **Keyhole State Park** is an angler's delight with about 14,720 acres of fishing opportunities. Located approximately 40 miles east of town on I-90 (Exit 165), the park gets its name from the "keyhole" livestock brand used by two brothers named McKean who established a ranch in the vicinity. The park claims that some of the biggest fish caught in Wyoming have come out of Keyhole. Regardless of whether or not you believe them, you will find great walleye, northern pike, catfish, smallmouth bass, and crappie fishing. Winter ice fishing. Also sailing, canoeing, waterskiing, and bird watching of approximately 225 species. **353 McKean Road, Moorcroft, 82721; (307) 756-3596.**

Cook Lake in the Bearlodge district of the Black Hills National Forest is not only a great lake to fish in and camp by, it also has a nice hiking trail and is incredibly beautiful. (See the Warren Peak Scenic Drive, below.) Contact the forest service for fishing, camping, and general information about the lake. **Bearlodge Ranger District, 121 South 21st Street, P.O. Box 680, Sundance, 82729; (307) 283-1361.**

Golf

Sundance Country Club (307-283-1191) offers a nine-hole course with watered greens and fairways. Open Monday through Friday. Wednesday afternoon is men's day, and Thursday afternoon is ladies' day.

Hiking and Backpacking

Summer along the **Sundance** and **Carson Draw Trails** provides fun hiking through heavy timbered forest land and canyons or along ridges. Leaving from the **Sundance Trailhead**, the first mile is difficult, then the trail branches off to either backtrack on the moder-

ate **Whitetail Trail** or on to several other moderate trails. Access the **Carson Draw Trail** system at the Reuter Campground for six miles of moderate hiking through pine, aspen, and oaks that is definitely off the beaten path. There is water at the trailheads. Take plenty with you. For an easier hike, try the **Cook Lake Trail,** a gentle one-mile circle of the lake. It's great for bird watching. The trailhead starts at the Cook Lake Recreation Area. Maps, regulations, and trail conditions are available through the **Bearlodge Ranger District, 121 South 21st Street, P.O. Box 680, Sundance, 82729; (307) 283-1361.**

In 1998, the forest service opened an additional 50 miles of trails in the **Wyoming Black Hills** between Sundance and Devils Tower National Monument. Hike, mountain bike, or travel on horseback through the Bearlodge Mountains' scenic ridges and rugged canyons on this system from spring through fall. Excellent wildlife viewing. This is an incredibly secluded region that offers great primitive recreational opportunities. Some camping areas available along the trail. Get the details from the **Bearlodge Ranger District, 121 South 21st Street, P.O. Box 680, Sundance, WY 82729; (307) 283-1361.**

Horseback Riding

Hawken Ranch Vacations offers five-hour trail rides along the new trail system in Wyoming's Black Hills (see Hiking, above, for details). **P.O. Box 863, Sundance, WY 82729; (800) 544-4309** or **(307) 756-9319.**

Skiing

Cross-Country Skiing

The **Carson Draw Cross-Country Ski Area** supplies six miles of trails groomed weekly. Trails range from easy to difficult while you glide through untamed beauty. Get maps and details from the **Bearlodge Ranger District, 121 South 21st Street, P.O. Box 680, Sundance, 82729; (307) 283-1361.**

Snowmobiling

Rev up for 62 miles of groomed trails in the Black Hills National Forest between Sundance and Hulett. Limited food, fuel, and lodging, so come prepared. Trails groomed weekly between December 15 and March 30, when snow permits. Contact the **Bearlodge Ranger District** for maps and trail information. **121 South 21st Street, P.O. Box 680, Sundance, 82729; (307) 283-1361.**

Snowmobiling is also permitted on the reservoir at **Keyhole State Park**. (See Fishing, above.)

Swimming

Sundance City Park provides lighted tennis courts and volleyball/basketball/horseshoe courts, all free. Swim in the heated pool or wander the scenic hiking trail.

Seeing and Doing

Vore Buffalo Jump

Five miles west of the point where Hwy. 14 intersects the Wyoming-South Dakota state line is the Vore Buffalo Jump Site, with I-90 to the immediate south. The wide stretch of flat area surrounding the actual jump site is crossed by the highway and freeway and once was the approach to the pit. Over the course of 350 years, Native Americans trapped and killed approximately 20,000 bison in this natural trap site approximately 100 feet wide at the base of the sinkhole or pit and about 25 feet deep.

At the time of the Vore Buffalo Jump and other jump traps, the horse had not yet become available for hunting the huge plains animal. People on foot drove a small herd of buffalo over the edge of the sinkhole, thus providing food and hides for clothing and shelter.

In the summer of 1971, archaeologist Dr. George Frison, supervising a crew of workers from the University of Wyoming, began investigating the jump site. They dug exploratory trenches. Excavations revealed that the Indians butchered the carcasses at the jump site. A huge storehouse of buffalo bones and arti-

Getting There

Located at the northwest edge of the Wyoming Black Hills, Sundance is just off **I-90** and just 61 miles east of Gillette. **Gillette** offers the nearest **airport** and **rental car** service to Sundance.

facts that provided a wealth of knowledge about this centuries-old method of food procurement were also found. Accessed via **I-90 Aladdin Exit #199,** then drive three miles on **Hwy. 14.**

Aladdin General Store

Built in 1896, the store originally opened as a saloon. Since then, it has become a one-stop place for just about everything, including a post office, antiques shop, cafe, and motel. If you're taking the scenic route along Hwys. 111 and 24 to Devils Tower, it's worth stopping by. Open in summer Monday through Saturday from 8 A.M. to 7 P.M. and Sunday from 9 A.M. to 6 P.M.; open in winter Monday through Saturday from 8 A.M. to 6 P.M. and Sunday from 10 A.M. to 5 P.M. **Aladdin, 82710; (307) 896-2226.**

Museums

Crook County Museum & Art Gallery

Located in the lower level of the courthouse, this is a dandy little free museum. Where else will you find a book with a bullet hole in it on display? A copy of *Pioneers of Crook County*, published in 1981, took the bullet when an angry driver shot the mail truck because the mail carrier had failed to dim the headlights. Of course, articles, photos, and memorabilia about the Sundance Kid abound. The museum also has an excellent interpretive diorama of the Vore Buffalo Jump. Seeing it before going to the jump location will put the prehistoric site into perspective. Open between June and the end of August, Monday through Friday from 8 A.M. to 8 P.M. Off-season hours: 8 A.M. to 5 P.M., Monday through Friday. Closed January and February. **309 Cleveland, Sundance, 82729; (307) 283-3666.**

Scenic Drives

Grand Canyon

Head east out of Sundance on I-90 to the Moskee Road Exit 191. The pavement ends about eight miles down the road, becoming County Road 141 and turning into Forest Road 863 around a bend. The road winds and climbs up through what the locals call the "Grand Canyon." The rock formations and colors are quite beautiful, as is the thickly forested land. You'll pass a natural bridge and travel along Sand Creek with some good fishing spots. Not long before the dirt road rejoins the interstate is the Wyoming Fish Hatchery and Visitor Center next to the historic Ranch A. It began as a $900,000 cabin belonging to Chicago millionaire Moe Annenberg and is now an exclusive, private club.

For the most part, it is a decent, comfortably wide gravel road, although it has some water holes you have to negotiate around, and it gets a bit rough in spots. Not recommended for cars low to the ground.

Warren Peak

Go west out of Sundance on Hwy. 14, two miles beyond the junction with I-90. Turn right onto paved Forest Road 838. It becomes a dirt road after about six miles at the Warren Peak Lookout. For the ambitious, climb the fire lookout tower and visit with the ranger on duty in summer. On a clear day, the horizon leads into South Dakota, a great deal of the northern corner of Wyoming, and some say into Montana as well. From there, the road winds through the forest, along streams, and through the heart of the Bearlodge Mountains. The road makes a wide arc into Forest Road 843. This leads to the Cook Lake junction. A side trip down Forest Road 842 to the lake adds extra touches to the wilderness experience. The lake has a tranquillity about it. Back at the junction, turn left, following Forest Road 843 out of the forest at Hwy. 111. Turn right. This portion is scenic in a different way with red rocks and green grassy knolls. At the next junction, take either Hwy. 14 or I-90 west back to Sundance.

Where to Stay

Accommodations

Bear Lodge Motel—$$–$$$

Western lodge atmosphere, but with all the comforts of home. Cable TV, a jacuzzi, walking distance to the town park. Small pets okay. Open year-round. No kitchenette; however, some rooms have small refrigerators. Not handicapped accessible. **218 Cleveland, Sundance, 82729; (800) 341-8000** reservations only, **(307) 283-1611**.

Best Western Inn at Sundance—$$–$$$

Newly built, the Best Western Inn at Sundance offers in beautiful luxury from the oak-trimmed lobby to 44 comfy, oversized rooms. Heated pool. Free continental breakfast, local calls, expanded cable TV with HBO and the Disney Channel. Pets okay with a refundable deposit. Handicapped accessible. Open year-round. **2700 East Clevland, P.O. Box 927, Sundance, 82729; (800) 238-0965** for reservations, **(307) 283-2800**.

The Bunkhouse B&B—$$–$$$

Located 20 miles northeast of Sundance, The Bunkhouse has a cozy, homey atmosphere. Antique furniture. Ranch-style breakfast. Other meals possible for an additional fee and advance arrangements. Or the kitchen is available for cooking your own lunch and dinner. Children welcome. Three bedrooms with shared bathroom. No pets. No minimum stay. Not handicapped accessible. Open year-round. **#189 Hwy. 111, Aladdin, 82710; (307) 283-3542**.

Guest Ranches

Hawken Guest Ranch—$$$–$$$$

Stay in the oldest established guest ranch in Wyoming's Black Hills. Rustic cabins. The ranch also arranges 90-minute steak rides with eight-oz sirloin and all the trimmings, and two-day, two-night-minimum pack trips near the *Dances with Wolves* film site's winter camp location. Hiking on the ranch. Get the hands to tell you about the spots where you might find dinosaur bones. Hourly trail rides available for nonguests. No pets. The ranch is 13 miles west of Sundance on I-90 (Exit 172). **416 Inyan Kara Road, P.O. Box 863, Sundance, 82729; (800) 544-4309. E-mail: hawken@vcn.com.**

Camping

In the National Forests
The **Black Hills National Forest** maintains summer campgrounds with garbage pickup, drinking water, and toilets for tents and RVs at the **Cook Lake Recreational Area, Reuter Campground**, and **Sundance Campground** and **trailhead. Bearlodge Campground** offers reduced service, garbage pickup, and toilets. **Bearlodge Ranger District, Hwy. 121, South 21st Street, P.O. Box 680, Sundance, 82729; (307) 283-1361.**

In Wyoming State Parks and Recreation Areas
Keyhole State Park provides a variety of tent and self-contained RV camping sites around the reservoir with drinking water, group picnic shelters, playgrounds, restrooms, and a trailer sanitary station. **353 McKean Road, Moorcroft, 82721; (307) 756-3596.**

Private Campgrounds and Cabins
One mile east of Sundance on Hwy. 14, the **Mountain View Campground** offers full and partial hookups, tent sites, tepee rentals, cable TV, a heated pool with a slide and diving board, rec room, laundry, picnic area, groceries, and a playground. Pets okay. Open April 1 to November 1. **North Government Valley Road, P.O. Box 903, Sundance, 82729; (307) 283-2270.**

Where to Eat

Aro Family Restaurant—$$–$$$$
Decent food. Good prime rib on the weekend. Or try a buffalo steak. Open daily in summer 5:30 A.M. to 10 P.M., and the rest of the year 6 A.M. to 9 P.M. Handicapped accessible. **205 Cleveland, Sundance, 82729; (307) 283-2000.**

Flo's Place—$–$$$
Good eating at a great price. Ice cream, pizza from scratch, fast food, sandwiches, dinners.

Look for their daily specials. Fresh homemade doughnuts and buns. Open daily in summer 8 A.M. to 10 P.M., in spring and fall 8 A.M. to 9 P.M., and in winter 8 A.M. to 8 P.M. Handicapped accessible. Delivery within town. **226 South Highway 585, P.O. Box 946, Sundance, 82729; (307) 283-2205.**

Higbee's Cafe—$–$$$
Try the "Devils Tower": sausage or ham and an egg served on a large biscuit smothered with sausage gravy. It will keep you going all day. Local artist Sarah Rogers's stylized paintings hang on the walls. Themes range from Indian designs to funny and intriguing bears and crows. Breakfast served anytime. Handicapped accessible. Kids' menu. Convenient downtown location. Open at 5:30 A.M. until lunch ends at 2 P.M., Monday through Friday, longer if folks keep coming in. Great food, fine art, and erratic hours. **101 North 3rd, Sundance, 82729; (307) 283-2165.**

Log Cabin Cafe—$–$$$
Reliable meals. Home-style cooking. Orders cut in half for kids or seniors. Try the chicken-fried steak with homemade gravy. Pies also homemade. Open seven days a week. Summer hours: 5:30 A.M. to 9 P.M. Winter hours: 5:30 A.M. to 8 P.M. Not handicapped accessible. **1620 East Cleveland, P.O. Box 471, Sundance, 82729; (307) 283-3393.**

Country Cottage and Yogurt Garden—$–$$
Soft-serve frozen yogurt, 12 flavors of ice cream, sundaes, and snowcones. Kids' menu and senior discounts. Open Monday through Saturday from 8 A.M. to 5 P.M. Handicapped accessible. **423 Cleveland Street, Sundance, 82729; (307) 283-2450.**

Services

Visitor Information

Sundance Area Chamber of Commerce, 309 Cleveland, P.O. Box 1004, Sundance, 82729; (800) 477-9340 or (307) 283-1000. Website: www.dcomp.com/sundance.

209

Index

Index

The Wyoming Guide

Notes

Photo by Jeff Corney.

About the Author

A Wyoming resident, Sierra Adare is a Visiting Fellow with the American Indian Program at Cornell University. In addition to teaching and lecturing on writing and marketing techniques, history, and travel, Adare is a regular contributor to *Wild West Magazine, WREN* magazine, and *News from Indian Country*. Adare's travel, outdoor, how-to, American Indian, history, and cooking articles have appeared in both regional and national publications. The award-winning author of eight books, she has also contributed to five others.

While writing *The Wyoming Guide*, Adare traveled the state, experiencing uniquely Wyoming events and outdoor activities, exploring new places, and revisiting old favorites. "It was a fantastic excuse to drive Wyoming's back roads, soak up the incredible scenery, wander the wilderness and the desert, take part in a wide range of fun things, and learn even more about my home state."

From her home at the base of the Wind River Range, Adare enjoys skiing, skydiving, and sailing, in addition to hiking, horsepacking and horseback riding, goatpacking, canoeing, ballooning, and car camping.

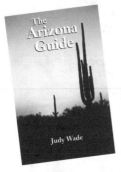

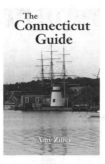
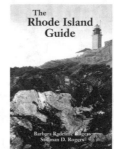